lonely planet

KU-876-098

Budapest

"All you've got to do is decide to go
and the hardest part is over.

So go!"

TONY WHEELER, COFOUNDER – LONELY PLANET

THIS EDITION WRITTEN AND RESEARCHED BY

Steve Fallon

Contents

Plan Your Trip   **4**

Explore Budapest   **44**

Understand Budapest   **169**

Survival Guide   **199**

Budapest Maps   **228**

(left) **Great Synagogue (p114)**

(above) **Gerbeaud cafe (p87)**

(right) **Széchenyi Baths (p142)**

Welcome to Budapest

Straddling the Danube River, with the Buda Hills to the west and the Great Plain to the east, Budapest is a gem of a city.

The Hand of Man

Budapest's beauty is not all God-given; man has played a role in shaping this pretty face too. Architecturally, Budapest is a treasure, with enough baroque, neoclassical, Eclectic and art nouveau (Secessionist) buildings to satisfy anyone's appetite. Overall, though, Budapest has a fin-de-siècle feel to it, for it was then, during the capital's 'golden age', that most of what you see today was built. Nearly every building has some interesting or unusual detail, from art nouveau glazed tiles and neoclassical bas-reliefs to bullet holes and shrapnel scorings left over from WWII and the 1956 Uprising that still cry out in silent fury.

The Past Is Near

They say the past is another country, but it's always been just around the corner in Budapest. Witness those scars from WWII and 1956. There are sad reminders like the poignant *Shoes on the Danube* memorial, but ones, too, of hope and reconciliation – like the 'sword' of the former secret police building on Andrássy út now beaten into the 'ploughshare' that is the House of Terror, with both sides of the story told. And there's joy as much-loved concert halls get built and renovated, metro lines extended and busy streets pedestrianised.

Eat, Drink & Be Magyar

There is a lot more to Hungarian food than goulash and it remains one of the most sophisticated styles of cooking in Europe. Magyars even go so far as to say there are three essential world cuisines: French, Chinese and their own. That may be a bit of an exaggeration, but Budapest's reputation as a food capital dates largely from the late 19th and first half of the 20th centuries and, despite a fallow period during the days of Communism, is once again commanding attention. So, too, are its world-renowned wines – from Villány's big-bodied reds and Somló's flinty whites to honey-gold Tokaj.

In the Soak

Budapest is blessed with an abundance of hot springs – some 123 thermal and more than 400 mineral springs, in fact, from 14 different sources. As a result, 'taking the waters' has been a Budapest experience since the time of the Romans. The choice of bathhouses is generous – you can choose among Turkish-era, art nouveau and modern establishments. Some people come seeking a cure for whatever ails them, but the majority are there for fun and relaxation – though we still maintain it's the world's best cure for what Hungarians call a *macskajaj* ('cat's wail', or hangover).

Why I Love Budapest

By Steve Fallon, Author

I love Budapest for all the right reasons – architecture (especially art nouveau), romance (particularly the views from the bridges) and sticky apricot jam (only on toast) – and some of the wrong ones, too (killer *pálinka*, rickety trolleybuses, and checking bodies out in the Turkish baths). When I first came to Budapest (by chance, as it happened), I was bowled over by an often sad but confident city whose history seemed too complex to comprehend, by a beautiful and expressive language that I considered impenetrable, and by a people I thought I'd never know. I stayed on to learn more about all three.

For more about our author, see p256.

Above: Basilica of St Stephen (p95)

Budapest's
Top 10

JEAN-PIERRE LESCOURRET / LONELY PLANET IMAGES ©

Royal Palace (p50)

1 Bombed and rebuilt at least half a dozen times since King Béla IV established a royal residence here in the mid-13th century, the Royal Palace has been home to kings and queens, occupiers like the Turks in the 16th and 17th centuries, and nondomiciled rulers like the Habsburg royalty. Today the Royal Palace contains important museums, the national library and an abundance of statues and monuments. It is the focal point of Castle Hill and the city's single most visited sight.

◉ *Castle Hill*

Thermal Baths (p26)

2 Budapest sits on a crazy quilt of more than 100 thermal springs, and 'taking the waters' is very much a part of everyday life. Some baths date from Turkish times, others are art nouveau marvels and still others are soulless modern establishments that boast all the accoutrements. Which one you choose is a matter of taste and what exactly you're looking for – be it fun, a hangover cure or relief for something more serious.

◉ *Thermal Baths & Pools*

JEAN-PIERRE LESCOURRET / LONELY PLANET IMAGES ©

The Danube & Its Bridges

3 Budapest's 'dustless highway' is ever present, serving (still) as an important means of communication and neatly dividing the city into Buda and Pest. The Danube bridges (all eight of them, not counting train bridges), both landmarks and delightful vantage points over the river, are the stitches that have bound Buda and Pest together since well before the two were linked politically in 1873. The four bridges in the centre stand head and shoulders above the rest: Margaret Bridge (p107), Széchenyi Chain Bridge (p54), Elizabeth Bridge (p67) and Liberty Bridge (p67).

◉ *Margaret Island, Castle Hill, Gellért Hill*

Andrássy út & Heroes' Square *(p117 & p141)*

4 Andrássy út, an uberelegant leafy boulevard stretching 2.5km, links Deák Ferenc tér to the south with City Park in the north and contains so much to see, do and enjoy that it has been given a place on Unesco's World Heritage List. Along the way are museums, cafes and architectural marvels, but perhaps its most important sight comes at the end. Heroes' Square, the entrance to the park, is the nation's monument to its earliest ancestors and a memorial to its war dead.

◉ *Andrássy út, City Park*

Parliament *(p93)*

5 If the Royal Palace atop Castle Hill is the focal point on the Buda side, Parliament is the centrepiece along the Danube in Pest. Stretching for some 268m along the river and counting a superlative number of rooms (690), courtyards (10) and gates (27), it is Hungary's largest building. Parliament is the seat of the unicameral National Assembly, but parts of it, including the awesome Domed Hall, which contains the Crown of St Stephen, can be visited by guided tour.

◉ *Lipótváros*

Basilica of St Stephen *(p95)*

6 Budapest's largest and most important Christian house of worship (1905) is a gem of neoclassical architecture that took more than half a century to complete (largely due to the setback when its dome came crashing down in a storm). The dome can now be scaled and there is a rich treasury of ecclesiastical objects. But the main reason for coming is to view (and perhaps venerate) Hungary's most sacred object: the holy right hand of King St Stephen.

◉ *Lipótváros*

Great Synagogue *(p114)*

7 The largest Jewish house of worship in Europe, the Moorish-style Great Synagogue is one of Budapest's most eye-catching buildings. Built in 1859 for 3000 Neolog (strict conservative) faithful, the copper-domed structure is next to the Hungarian Jewish Museum and the haunting Holocaust Memorial Room. In the courtyard stands the Holocaust Memorial, a 'tree of life' designed by Imre Varga whose leaves bear the family names of some of the victims.

◉ *Erzsébetváros*

8

Memento Park *(p68)*

8 The park containing statues and other memorials from the communist period can only be described as a cemetery of socialist mistakes, or a well-manicured trash heap of history. In southern Buda, it's home to about four dozen statues, busts and plaques of Lenin, Marx and Béla Kun. Ogle the socialist realist 'art' and try to imagine that some of the monstrosities were still being erected in the late 1980s and in place until the early 1990s.

👁 *South Buda*

Buda Hills *(p74)*

9 They may be short on sights – though Béla Bartók's house, where he spent his final year in Hungary, opens to the public – but the Buda Hills are a very welcome respite from the hot, dusty city in summer. Perhaps their biggest draws are their unusual forms of transport: a narrow-gauge cog railway dating from the late 19th century will get you up into the hills, a train run by children takes you across them and a chairlift will get you back down to terra firma.

◉ *Buda Hills*

Kerepesi Cemetery *(p130)*

10 What is also called the National Graveyard, Budapest's equivalent of London's Highgate Cemetery or Paris' Père Lachaise Cemetery is a pleasant, almost parklike place to walk on a sunny day, with its shady paths, well-tended lawns and monumental tombstones and mausoleums. As well as being the final resting place for such national heroes as Lajos Kossuth, Ferenc Deák and Lajos Batthyány, Kerepesi also contains the graves of many of those who died in the 1956 Uprising.

◉ *Józsefváros*

What's New

Garden Clubs

Kertek – outdoor 'garden clubs' that generally operate from April or May to September – open and close with the speed of summer lightning. Recently, however, along VII Kazinczy utca, another three *kertek* – Mika Tivadar Kert, Kőleves Kert and Ellátó Kert – have joined that old stalwart Szimpla Kert to create what should be known as Garden Club Central. And contrary to what many people will tell you, not all *kertek* are created equal. (p122)

Rácz Baths

Cross your fingers and hope to soak... By the time you read this the wonderful Turkish-era Rácz Baths will almost certainly be open and operational after a long spell closed. (p30)

Gozsdu udvar

This 220m-long passage dating back to 1901, and now fully renovated, has opened to great fanfare. While it links Király utca (No 13) with Dob utca (No 16), it still appears to be waiting for tenants in the way of restaurants and shops, and the few now there look rather forlorn. (p116)

István Zelnik Southeast Asian Gold Museum

As if two weren't enough... This rather flash new museum joins two other Asian museums on (or just off) Andrássy út. (p118)

Music History Museum

This museum set around a lovely courtyard where concerts are sometimes held has reopened to very low-key fanfare on Castle Hill. (p56)

Bródy House

A new type of accommodation – retro boutique/club/gallery – that just opened north of the Hungarian National Museum has all Budapest a-buzzin'. (p165)

Földes Józsi Konyhája

Budapest continues to look over its shoulder when it comes to food, and new *étkezdék* (canteens serving simple Hungarian dishes) like this continue to open. (p80)

Hadik Kávéház

Retro-style coffee houses are also all the rage and this one – with the wonderful Szatyor Bár attached – joins the nearby and perennially popular Café Ponyvaregény in south Buda. (p69)

Váci 1

Central Pest's flashiest shopping centre has opened on Váci utca in the sumptuous Bank Palace that housed the Budapest Stock Exchange until 2007. (p84)

For more recommendations and reviews, see **lonelyplanet.com/budapest**

Need to Know

Currency
Forint (Ft), though some hotels quote in euros (€)

Language
Hungarian

Visas
Generally not required for stays of up to 90 days; not necessary at all for EU citizens.

Money
ATMs are everywhere, including the airport and train and bus stations. Visa, MasterCard and American Express widely accepted.

Mobile Phones
Mobile phones are ubiquitous in Budapest. Three different telecom companies – Telenor, T-Mobile and Vodafone – operate three networks.

Time
Central European Time (GMT/ UTC plus one hour)

Tourist Information
Tourinform (MV Sütő utca 2; ⊙8am-8pm; Ⓜ M1/2/3 Deák Ferenc tér) is the main tourist office; there are smaller branches across the city.

Your Daily Budget
The following are average costs per day.

Budget under €50
➡ Dorm bed €9–€20
➡ Meal at self-service restaurant €7.50
➡ Three-day transport pass €14.50

Midrange €50–€100
➡ Single/double private room from €22/26
➡ Two-course meal with drink €11–€24
➡ Cocktail from €4

Top end over €100
➡ Dinner for two with wine at good restaurant from €48
➡ Two-/three-course set lunch at gourmet restaurant from €13/16
➡ All-inclusive ticket at Museum of Fine Arts adult/ child €13/6.50
➡ Cover charge at a popular club €6.50–€13

Advance Planning
Two months before Book your accommodation if you will be travelling in the high season and want to stay somewhere special. Take a look at the 'what's on' and English-language media websites (p40).

A month before Book top-end restaurants now. It's also the time to reserve seats for a big-ticket concert, musical or dance performance.

A week before Make sure your bookings are in order and you have all booking references.

Useful Websites
➡ **Budapest Sun Online** (www.budapestsun.com) Popular English online weekly, with local news, interviews and features.

➡ **Caboodle** (www.caboodle .hu) Hungary's best English-language portal with daily news, features and events.

➡ **Xpat Loop** (www.xpatloop .com) What the foreign community in Budapest is thinking and talking about.

➡ **Budapest Tourism** (www .budapestinfo.hu) One of the better overall websites.

➡ **Lonely Planet** (www.lonely planet.com/budapest) Includes extensive information on Budapest.

WHEN TO GO

Spring is glorious in Budapest. Summer is festival season. Autumn is beautiful, particularly in the Buda Hills. In winter, some attractions curtail hours.

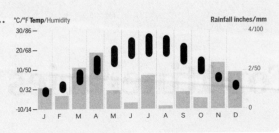

Arriving in Budapest

Ferenc Liszt International Airport Minibuses, buses and trains to central Budapest run from 4am to midnight (365Ft to 2990Ft); taxis cost from 4800Ft.

Keleti, Nyugati and Déli train stations All three are on metro lines of the same name and night buses call when the metro is closed.

Népliget and Puskás Ferenc Stadion bus stations Both are on the M3 metro line and are served by trams 1 and 1A.

For much more on **arrival**, see p200.

Getting Around

Travel passes valid for one day to one month are valid on all trams, buses, trolleybuses, HÉV (within city limits) and metro lines.

➡ **Metro** The quickest but least scenic way to get around. Runs 4am to about 11.15pm.

➡ **Bus** Extensive network of regular buses from around 4.15am to between 9pm and 11.30pm; from 11.30pm to just after 4am a network of 35 night buses kicks in.

➡ **Tram** Faster and more pleasant for sightseeing than buses – a network of 30 lines.

➡ **Trolleybus** Mostly useful to and around City Park in Pest.

For much more on **getting around**, see p202.

Sleeping

Hostels in Budapest range from university residences to very stylish modern affairs; the latter usually offer single and double rooms. **Private rooms** can be good value but make sure they are centrally located. **Hotels** range from very basic former workers' hostels with shared bathroom to five-star luxury accommodation with rooftop pool.

Useful Websites

➡ **Tourinform** (www.tourinform.hu) Wide range of options from official website.

➡ **Discover Budapest** (www.discoverbudapest.com) Tour company that also books accommodation.

➡ **Mellow Mood** (www.mellowmood.hu) Chain with a big variety of options.

➡ **Best Hotel Service** (www.besthotelservice.hu) Good for budget accommodation.

➡ **Hip Homes Hungary** (www.hiphomeshungary.com) Fabulous short-term apartments.

For much more on **sleeping**, see p156.

Top Itineraries

Day One

Castle Hill (p48)

 Spend your first morning in Budapest on Castle Hill, taking in the views from the **Royal Palace** and establishing the lie of the land. There are museums aplenty up here, but don't be greedy: you only have time for one. We recommend either the **Hungarian National Gallery** for fine art or the **Budapest History Museum** to learn more about the city's long and tortuous past.

> ✖️ **Lunch** Do what locals do: have a quick bite at Fortuna Önkiszolgáló (p59).

Víziváros (p48)

In the afternoon ride the **Sikló** (funicular) down to **Clark Ádám tér** and, depending on the day of the week and your sex, make your way up Fő utca to the **Király Baths** for a relaxing soak.

> ✖️ **Dinner** Superb Csalogány 26 (p59) is around the corner from the baths.

Víziváros (p48)

 Depending on your mood, check to see what's on in the way of *táncház* (folk music and dance) at the **Budavár Cultural Centre** or, if you're more into putting your own feet to work and it's a weekend night, head for Déli train station and the retro-style club **DPU Chachacha**.

Day Two

Óbuda (p71)

On your second day have a look at what the west side of the Danube used to be like by following the **Óbuda neighbourhood walk** and learning how Buda, Óbuda and Pest all came together. Again, the choice of museums and attractions is legion, but the **Vasarely Museum** and its hallucinogenic works never fail to please and the newly installed **Hungarian Museum of Trade & Tourism** is a delight. Alternatively, **Aquincum** is just a short HÉV ride away.

> ✖️ **Lunch** The fish soup at Új Sípos Halászkert (p79) goes down a treat.

Óbuda (p71)

In the afternoon head south for **Margaret Bridge**. Just up the hill to the west is **Gül Baba's Tomb**, the only Muslim place of pilgrimage in northern Europe. Spend the rest of the afternoon pampering yourself at the **Lukács Baths**.

> ✖️ **Dinner** Földes Józsi Konyhája (p80) serves homestyle Hungarian.

Margaret Island (p105)

 Cross over Margaret Bridge to Margaret Island and **Holdudvar**, an excellent place to both cool down and kick up your heels. It's open till the wee hours so there's no hurry.

Day Three

Andrássy út (p112)

 On your third day, cross the river and see Pest at its very finest by following the **Andrássy út neighbourhood walk**, which will take you past unmissable sights such as the **House of Terror** and **Heroes' Square**, architectural gems like the **Hungarian State Opera House** and **New Theatre**, and wonderful cafes including **Művész Kávéház** and **Alexandra Book Café**.

> **Lunch** Baraka (p122) has an excellent-value gourmet set lunch.

City Park (p138)

 Over lunch decide whether you want an afternoon of culture or leisure (or both). Heroes' Square is flanked by the **Museum of Fine Arts** and **Palace of Art**, both with excellent exhibitions, and City Park harbours the **Budapest Zoo**, the **Budapest Amusement Park** and the wonderful **Széchenyi Baths**.

> **Dinner** Robinson (p145) by the lake is a wonderful choice.

City Park (p138)

You might have drinks in the park at the retro-style **Pántlika** or boogie the night (and most of the morning) away at the open-air **Dürer Kert**. But if there happens to be a **Cinetrip** at Széchenyi Baths scheduled for that evening, beg, borrow or steal a ticket to get in.

Day Four

Lipótváros (p91)

 On day four it's time to see a few of Budapest's big-ticket attractions. In the morning concentrate on the two icons of Hungarian nationhood and the places that house them: the Crown of St Stephen in the **Parliament** and the saint-king's mortal remains in the **Basilica of St Stephen**. Moving from one to the other cut through **Szabadság tér** and have a glance at the last remaining Soviet memorial in the city.

> **Lunch** Kádár (p121) is an excellent choice for Hungarian soul food.

Erzsébetváros (p112)

In the afternoon concentrate on the Jewish Quarter – what some people still call the Ghetto here. The easiest way to see the most important sights is to follow the **Erzsébetváros and the Jewish Quarter neighbourhood walk**, but make sure you leave ample time to have a good look inside the **Great Synagogue** and the **Hungarian Jewish Museum** and have a slice of something sweet at the **Fröhlich Cukrászda** kosher cake shop.

> **Dinner** The Spinoza Café (p120) is a convivial place for an evening meal.

Erzsébetváros (p112)

There might be *klezmer* (traditional Jewish music) on at the **Spinoza Café**, then move on to the wealth of *kertek* ('garden clubs') within easy striking distance along Kazinczy utca: **Mika Tivadar Kert**, **Kőleves Kert**, **Ellátó Kert** or, the granddaddy of them all, **Szimpla Kert**.

If You Like...

Classical Music

Ferenc Liszt Music Academy
The interior of Budapest's most important classical-music venue; is worth a look even if you're not attending a performance. (p115)

Palace of Arts The two concert halls at this palatial arts centre by the Danube have near-perfect acoustics. (p135)

Matthias Church Organ recitals are best heard in the city's many churches, including this one atop Castle Hill. (p54)

Franz Liszt Memorial Museum
Situated in the Old Music Academy; the great composer lived here until his death in 1886; concerts too. (p118)

Béla Bartók Memorial House
This renovated and enlarged house in the Buda Hills is where Bartók resided until emigrating to the US in 1940. (p78)

Liszt Ferenc Zeneműbolt An excellent classical-music shop; it has CDs and vinyl as well as sheet music. (p126)

Art Nouveau

Royal Postal Savings Bank This extravaganza of floral mosaics, folk motifs and ceramic figures is Budapest's best Secessionist building. (p96)

Bedő House A stunning art nouveau apartment block now contains a museum dedicated to Hungarian Secessionist applied arts. (p96)

Museum of Applied Arts
Purpose-built in 1896, the museum is faced and roofed

Former Royal Postal Savings Bank (p96)

in Zsolnay ceramic tiles, with 'Mogul-style' turrets, domes and ornamental figures. (p132)

Párizsi udvar This arcade in the Belváros built in 1909 contains many influences, including elements of Ödön Lechner's own eclectic style. (p84)

City Park Art Nouveau Buildings Two of the most extravagant art nouveau (Secessionist) buildings are near the park: the National Institute for the Blind and Ödön Lechner's Institute of Geology. (p144)

Jewish Heritage

Synagogues There are three synagogues in what some still call the Ghetto of Erzsébetváros and all can be visited: the Great Synagogue (p114), the Orthodox Synagogue (p117) and the Rumbach Sebestyén utca Synagogue (p117).

Ghetto Wall A 30m fragment of the original ghetto wall can now be seen at the back of a courtyard at VI Király utca 15. (p116)

Spinoza Café If you want to hear live *klezmer* (traditional Jewish music), this is the place to go on a Friday evening. (p120)

Carmel Pince Budapest's most stylish kosher restaurant serves all the old-time favourites in the heart of the Jewish Quarter. (p120)

Fröhlich Cukrászda This time-warp kosher cake shop and cafe makes and sells old Jewish sweets like *flódni* (three-layer cake with apple, walnut and poppy-seed fillings). (p123)

Traditional Coffee Houses

New York Café The city's most extravagant cafe dates from 1894; it has been turned into an opulent hang-out for the haves of Pest. (p123)

Művész Kávéház Still homey and down-to-earth after all these years (1898!), the 'Artist Coffeehouse' is the best cafe for people-watching. (p124)

Gerbeaud Budapest's most fashionable cafe is also its most expensive, but you get what you pay for and the cakes here are sublime. (p87)

Ruszwurm Cukrászda The city's oldest cafe (1827) and also its tiniest is a positive delight – if you can manage to get inside the door. (p61)

Centrál Kávéház The *grande dame* of a traditional cafes dating back to 1887 has reclaimed her title as the place to sit and look intellectual in Pest. (p87)

Folk Culture

Ethnography Museum The sprawling museum opposite Parliament is the best place in Budapest to see and appreciate work by the finest folk artists in Hungary. (p96)

Hungarian Open-Air Ethnological Museum Many of the objects on view in the Ethnography Museum are in use at this huge outdoor museum in Szentendre, an easy day trip from Budapest. (p149)

Táncház One of the best ways to appreciate living folk traditions, hear the music and watch the dancing is at a traditional 'dance house' held regularly at venues around town. (p39)

For more top Budapest spots, see
➡ Thermal Baths & Pools (p26)
➡ Eating (p31)
➡ Drinking & Nightlife (p36)
➡ Entertainment (p39)
➡ Shopping (p42)

PLAN YOUR TRIP IF YOU LIKE...

Folkart Kézművésház Everything Magyar is available at this shop, from embroidered waistcoats and tablecloths to painted eggs and plates. (p90)

Holló Atelier Among the finest folk-craft shops in town, Holló makes and sells traditional items with a contemporary look. (p90)

Communist Heritage

Memento Park Nothing beats this historical trash heap in south Buda for remembering the bad old days. (p68)

Pántlika This time-warp cafe in City Park is housed in a Communist-era kiosk dating back to the 1970s. (p145)

Museum of Military History This sword-rattling place has a facsimile of the electrified fence that once separated Hungary from Austria. (p54)

Bambi Presszó Bambi still has all the hallmarks of the socialist past, including linoleum on the floor and Naugahyde on the seats. (p61)

Kerepesi Cemetery The good and not-so-great buried here include János Kádár; this is also the site of the monumental Workers' Movement Pantheon for party honchos. (p130)

Month by Month

January

Budapest is still festive after the Christmas holidays and she looks lovely in her winter gown, with bright blue skies, a light dusting of snow on church spires, perhaps ice floes in the Danube and ice skating in City Park.

☆ New Year's Day Concert

This annual event (www. hungariakoncert.hu), usually held in the Duna Palota (p102), ushers in the new year.

February

By now winter has hung on a bit too long and the days are cold, short and bleak. Some museums and tourist attractions sharply curtail their hours or close altogether.

✿ International Circus Festival

This biennial event (www .maciva.hu) has been held under the big top of the Great Capital Circus (p145) in early February every other year since 1996.

March

An excellent month to visit. With the start of the city's red-letter event – the annual Budapest Spring Festival – both music and spring are in the air.

☆ Budapest Opera Ball

This prestigious annual event (www.operabal.com) is held at the Hungarian State Opera House (p117), usually on the first Saturday in March.

✿ Budapest Spring Festival

The capital's largest and most important cultural event (www.festivalcity.hu) has more 200 events taking place over two weeks in late March and early April at dozens of venues across the city.

✿ Budapest Fringe Festival

This three-day festival (www.budapestfringe.com) of alternative theatre, music and dance at venues on Nagymező utca and elsewhere is a kind of sideshow to the ongoing Budapest Spring Festival.

April

Full spring is just glorious in Budapest – it looks and feels like the season in e.e. cummings' poem 'in Just-' – 'when the world is puddle-wonderful'.

✿ National Dance House Festival

Hungary's biggest *táncház* (www.tanchaztalalkozo.hu/ eng) is held over two days in early April at the Palace of Arts (p135) and other venues across town.

June

Late spring is wonderful, but the month of June can be pretty wet, especially early in the month. Beware the start of the holiday crowds.

✷ Danube Folklore Carnival

A pan-Hungarian international 10-day carnival (www.dunart.hu) of folk and world music and modern dance is held from mid-June in Vörösmarty tér and on Margaret Island.

✷ Ferencváros Festival

Local groups perform music and dance in the streets of Budapest's district IX (www.kultucca.hu) from mid-June to early July.

✷ Budapest Farewell Festival

Citywide 'Budapesti Búcsú' (Budapest Farewell) of concerts, folklore performances, street theatre and a carnival mark the departure of Soviet troops from Hungarian soil on 19 June 1991.

◉ Museum Night

Two dozen museums across town mark the summer solstice by reopening their doors at 6pm and not closing them till the wee hours, sometimes as late as 2am (www.museum.hu/events).

August

Once called the 'cucumber-growing month' because that was about the only thing happening, August is now festival month.

☆ Formula 1 Hungarian Grand Prix

Hungary's premier sporting event (www.hungaroring .hu) is held in early August at the Hungaroring (p146) in Mogyoród, 24km northeast of Budapest.

✷ Sziget Music Festival

Now one of the biggest and most popular music festivals (www.sziget.hu) in Europe, the 'Island' festival is held in mid-August on Budapest's Óbuda (Hajógyári) Island.

✷ Crafts Days

Prominent craftspeople from around Hungary set up kiosks and hold workshops (www.nesz.hu) in the Castle District over a three-day period in mid-August, and folk dancers and musicians perform.

✷ Jewish Summer Festival

This 10-day festival (www .jewishfestival.hu) starting at the end of August showcases Jewish culture through music and theatre performances, exhibitions, gastronomy and films, with many events taking place at Pest's Great Synagogue (p114).

September

September brings summer to a close and the crowds back from Lake Balaton and Croatia. It's a good time to visit as there's still a lot going on, wine is starting to flow and peak season (and its high prices) has ended.

✷ Budapest International Wine Festival

Hungary's foremost winemakers introduce their vintages to festival-goers (www.aborfesztival.hu) in mid-September in the Castle District.

October

Though the days are getting shorter and everyone is back into their routines, autumn is beautiful, particularly in the Buda Hills.

🏃 Budapest International Marathon

Eastern Europe's most celebrated foot race (www .budapestmarathon.com) goes along the Danube and across its bridges in early October.

✷ Budapest Autumn Festival

Cultural events (www.fest ivalcity.hu) are held at venues throughout the city for 10 days in mid-October.

December

The build-up to Christmas intensifies as December wears on, and the arrival of festive stands in Vörösmarty tér selling holiday items and gifts is a welcome sight.

☆ New Year Gala & Ball

The annual calendar's most coveted ticket is this gala concert and ball (www.opera.hu) held at the Hungarian State Opera House (p117) on 31 December.

With Kids

Budapest abounds in places that will delight children, and there is always a special child's entry rate (and often a family one) to paying attractions. Visits to many areas of the city can be designed around a rest stop or picnic at, say, City Park or on Margaret Island.

Puppet theatre

Come Rain or Shine

Raining cats and dogs? Our select committee of three young Budapesters – Brigitte (8), Viola (6) and Adam Téglássy (3) – chose the Palace of Wonders (p58), the Széchenyi Baths (p142) and the Hungarian Natural History Museum (p130) as their favourite wet-weather venues.

Too hot to trot (or do much else)? They tell us to head for the Margaret Island playground (Map p248), the Palatinus Strand (p108) or the cool underground corridors of the Buda Castle Labyrinth (p55).

Hands-On Learning

The Hungarian Natural History Museum (p130) has a lot of hands-on activities, including a sandpit where younger kids can dig up authentic-looking bones and a special room for stroking exotics like tiger fur and elephant tusks. The Palace of Wonders (p58) was custom-made for this sort of learning, and the Transportation Museum (p143) also has a lot of show-and-tell explanations from enthusiastic attendants. The granddaddy of museums for kids, though, is the Hungarian Railway History Park (p108), with vintage locomotives to clamber about, and carriages and trains to 'drive' via a high-tech simulator.

Culture

Not many museums here or anywhere are suitable for the very young, but the Museum of Fine Arts (p140) has an excellent program in which kids are allowed to handle original Egyptian artefacts and works of art. The Hungarian Agricultural Museum (p143) has all kinds of stuffed animals (for real) and mock-ups of traditional ways of life like hunting and fishing. The Vasarely Museum (p75) might be adult-themed but the wacky art, which seems to move about the canvas of its own accord, will surprise and please kids of all ages.

NEED TO KNOW

➡ An ever-growing number of hotels in Budapest offer babysitting services. While most can oblige on short notice, try to book at least six hours in advance.

➡ Most car-rental firms have children's safety seats for hire at a nominal cost, but they must be booked in advance.

➡ Highchairs and cots (cribs) are standard in many restaurants and hotels but numbers are limited; request them on booking.

➡ The choice of baby food, formulas, milk, disposable nappies (diapers) and the like is great, but the opening hours of stores may be different from what you're used to. Don't get caught out at the weekend.

Thermal Baths & Pools

Both the Széchenyi Baths (p142) and Gellért Baths (p66) are huge and have an abundance of indoor and outdoor pools. Gellért's outdoor pool has a wave machine, Széchenyi's has a whirlpool. Palatinus Strand (p108) and Dagály (p107) have vast lawns for lounging and playing around on a summer's day.

Aquaworld (p108), a new favourite with kids of all ages, is a bit far out of the city but easily reached by public transport. Some of the slides reach five storeys in height (kids have to be 140cm tall to use these), and there's a drop-in day-care room allowing parents to hit the attached spa.

Live Entertainment

The Great Capital Circus (p145), Europe's only permanent big top, is often booked out by school groups at matinees, but there's almost always seats in the evening. Most kids will be transfixed by the marionette and other shows at the Budapest Puppet Theatre (p125).

Táncház (p192), whether they participate or just watch, is always a hit with kids. Most of the children's ones have instructors, with folk musicians playing the tunes. The best are the children's programs at the Budavár Cultural Centre (p61) and the Municipal Cultural House (p70).

Public Transport

Kids love transport and the city's many unusual forms of conveyance will delight. The Cog and Children's Railways (p74)

in the Buda Hills and the Sikló (p49) funicular climbing up to Castle Hill are particular favourites. But even the mainstays of getting around town – the trams, trolleybuses and little M1 metro that are so commonplace to young Budapesters – will be a lot of fun for kids who rarely (if ever) board such forms of public transport.

Playgrounds

Great playgrounds include ones on XIII Margaret Island (Map p248), about 50m northeast of the fountain at the southern end; on III Óbuda (Hajógyári) Island (Map p234), about 200m along the main road (take the HÉV to the island's footbridge); and in XIII Szent István Park (Map p248). Smaller playgrounds are at V Hild tér (Map p244), VII Hunyadi tér (Map p250) and VII Almássy tér (Map p250).

Eating

Most restaurants won't have a set children's menu but will split the adult portion. The few that do exist, like the 1600Ft one at Robinson (p145), usually offer good value. Budapest's traditional cafes and *cukrászdák* (cake shops) will satisfy a sweet tooth of any size, but for a really special occasion treat the little rascals to the all-you-can-eat dessert bar at the **Budapest Marriott Hotel** (☎737 7377; www.marriott.com; Apáczai Csere János utca 4). Just 2100Ft gets you as many cakes as they can manage.

Like a Local

It's not difficult to live like a local in Budapest. The natives are friendly, the food is excellent (and never too strange) and the wine even better. And there are lots of things here that everyone everywhere likes: hot mineral baths, sweet cakes and diamonds-and-rust flea markets.

Nagycsarnok (Great Market; p136)

Eating

Learn to like meat. Hungarians are big carnivores and 'meat-stuffed meat' is an actual dish here. For stick-to-the-ribs fare on the hoof try Belvárosi Disznótoros (p86), a butcher-cum-caterer who satisfies the ravenous daily. Still all the rage are retro-style *étkezdék*, diner-like eateries that serve traditional Hungarian favourites and comfort food like *főzelék* (vegetables fried or boiled and then mixed into a roux with milk). The most local of these are Kádár (p121) in Erzsébetváros and Erdélyi-Magyar Étkezde (p121), which serves both Hungarian and Transylvania specialities. The best fish soup is at the Horgásztanya Vendéglő (p59).

Drinking

Budapesters love their wine and take it seriously, but in summer spritzers of red or white wine and mineral water are consumed in large quantities. Knowing the hierarchy and the art of mixing a spritzer to taste is important and will definitely win you the badge of 'honorary local'. A *kisfröccs* (small spritzer) is 10cL wine and the same amount of mineral water; a *nagyfröccs* (big spritzer) doubles the quantity of wine. A *hosszúlépés* (long step) is 10cL of wine and 20cL of water, while a *házmester* (janitor) trebles the amount of wine. Any bar in town will serve you these but don't expect one at a *borozó*, a traditional 'wine bar' (usually a dive) where rotgut wine is ladled out by metal ladle.

For advice on stronger libations such as *pálinka* (fruit brandy) and Unicum (a bitter aperitif nicknamed the 'Hungarian national accelerator'), see p36. For the best traditional cafes, see p37.

Choosing Wine

Budapest-based wine critic and writer Péter Balikó says that when choosing a Hungarian wine, you should look for the words *minőségi bor* (quality wine) or *különleges minőséű bor* (premium quality wine), Hungary's version of the French quality regulation *appellation contrôlée*.

On a wine label the first word of the name indicates where the wine comes from, while the second word is the grape variety (eg Villányi Kékfrankos) or the type or brand of wine (eg Tokaji Aszú, Szekszárdi Bikavér). Other important words that you'll see include: *édes* (sweet), *fehér* (white), *félédes* (semisweet), *félszáraz* (semidry or medium), *pezsgő* (sparkling), *száraz* (dry) and *vörös* (red). Following are Péter's five top local wines:

Laposa Badacsonyi Olaszrizling Among the best dry white wines for everyday drinking in Hungary, this is a straw-blonde Welschriesling high in acid that has a tart aftertaste and is reminiscent of burnt almonds.

Szepsy Tokaji Furmint With a flavour recalling apples, dry Furmint has the potential to become the best white wine in Hungary; Szepsy's version could pass for a top-notch white Burgundy.

Ráspi Soproni Kékfrankos This increasingly popular red wine is known as Blaufränkisch in neighbouring Austria; its full flavour belies its light colour.

Gere Villányi Syrah Hungary's 'newly discovered' variety of grape is making quite a splash; this one is full-bodied, rustic and simple.

Szepsy Tokaji Aszú (six puttonyos) Hungary's sweetest 'noble rot' wine is from the acknowledged leader of Tokaj vintners.

Entertaining

No self-respecting Budapester ever clubs indoors in the warm summer months; that's what *kertek* – outdoor garden clubs (p36) – are for.

As for entertainment of a more, well, serious nature, while the Ferenc Liszt Music Academy (p125) and Palace of Arts (p135) are incomparable for their acoustics and talent, many Budapesters prefer to hear music in smaller, more intimate venues such as the Óbuda Society (p81) or organ recitals in one of the city's many fine churches such as St Michael's Inner Town Church (p39).

If you really want to see Budapest down and dirty on the playing field, attend a Ferencváros Torna Club (FTC) match at Flórián Albert Stadium (p136).

Shopping

Budapest is reclaiming its title as design capital of Central Europe and no one knows that better than Judit Maróthy, whose company Underguide (www.underguide.com) specialises in lifestyle and shopping tours of the city. Her first bit of advice is to schedule your visit during WAMP (www.wamp.hu), a monthly fair usually held in either V Erzsébet tér (Map p238) in Pest or the Millennium Hall in II Millennium Park (p58) in Buda, where emerging Hungarian designers showcase their work. Check the website for details; it's a super-cool event and very popular with locals.

Away from WAMP, where would Underguide shop if looking for locally designed and – a bonus – highly sustainable goods and fashion that you just won't see anyplace else? Here are some top choices: Printa (p126), Romani Design (p126), M Lamp (p126), PannonArts Design Galéria (p104) and Mono Fashion (p89).

Marketing

The Nagycsarnok (p136) is a great place to shop, but don't expect to see peasant women fresh in from the countryside selling snowdrops in spring or homemade tomato juice in summer. For that sort of thing head for the Rákóczi tér Market (p128) – but never on a Sunday (or a Monday for that matter) – or even the covered Lehel Market (p109) in Újlipótváros.

Locals never go to the Ecseri Piac (p137), Continental Europe's largest flea market, during the week but head out as early as they can make it on Saturday to see what treasures are coming in from the countryside or being flogged by amateurs.

Weekending

Budapesters, especially those living in Pest, love a day out in the fresh air to escape their relatively cramped quarters and the pollution, and nothing is more sacred than the *kirándulás* (outing), which can be a day of hiking in the Buda Hills (p78) or a lazy afternoon swimming and sunning at Lake Balaton (p153).

© TRAVELPIXS / ALAMY ©

Taking the waters at Gellért Baths

Thermal Baths & Pools

Budapest lies on the geological fault separating the Buda Hills from the pancake-flat Great Plain, and more than 30,000 cu metres of warm to scalding (21°C to 76°C) mineral water gush forth daily from more than 100 thermal springs. As a result, the city is a major spa centre and 'taking the waters' at one of the city's many spas or combination spa-swimming pool complexes is a real Budapest experience.

zéchenyi Baths

NEED TO KNOW

Opening Hours

Opening times and whether men, women and/or everyone is welcome depend on the day of the week. See individual listings in the neighbourhood chapters.

Costs

Admission charges start at 2800Ft; in theory this allows you to stay for two hours on weekdays and 1½ hours at weekends, though this rule is not always enforced.

Useful Websites

Budapest Spas and Hot Springs (www.budapestgyogyfurdoi.hu) Excellent source of information.

Points to Ponder

➡ Please note that some baths become gay venues on male-only days, particularly the Király Baths. Not much actually goes on except for some intensive cruising, but those not into it may feel uncomfortable.

➡ Though some of the baths look a little rough around the edges, they are clean and the water is changed regularly. However, you might consider taking along a pair of plastic sandals or flip-flops.

➡ Flip-flops are also useful at some of the pools (eg Palatinus Strand) where the abundant concrete reaches scorching point in hot weather.

History of a Spa City

Remains of two sets of baths found at Aquincum (p73) – both for the public and the garrisons – indicate that the Romans took advantage of Budapest's thermal waters almost two millennia ago. But it wasn't until the Turkish occupation of the 16th and 17th centuries that bathing became an integral part of Budapest life. In the late 18th century, Habsburg Empress Maria Theresa ordered that Budapest's mineral waters be 'analysed and recorded in a list at the expense of the Treasury'. By the 1930s Budapest had become a fashionable spa resort.

As a result, the choice of bathhouses today is legion. Some date from Turkish times, others are art nouveau marvels, and still others are spick-and-span modern establishments. And with Hungarians such keen swimmers, it's not surprising that Budapest boasts dozens of pools. They're always excellent places to get in a few laps (if indoor), cool off on a hot summer's day (if outdoor) or watch all the posers strut their stuff.

Healing Waters

Of course, not everyone goes to the baths for fun and relaxation. The warm, mineral-rich waters are also meant to relieve a number of specific complaints, ranging from arthritis and pains in the joints and muscles, to poor blood circulation and post-traumatic stress. And they are a miracle cure (and we can vouch for this) for that most unpleasant affliction: the dreaded hangover.

What's Inside

The layout of most of Budapest's baths – both old and new – follows a similar pattern: a series of indoor thermal pools, where temperatures range from warm to hot, with steam rooms, saunas, ice-cold plunge pools and rooms for massage. Some have outdoor pools with fountains, sprays and whirlpools.

Most baths offer a full range of serious medical treatments plus more indulgent services such as massage (2500/4000Ft for 15/30 minutes), reflexology (3500Ft for 15 minutes) and pedicure (5500Ft). Specify what you want when buying your ticket.

Depending on the time and day, baths can be for men or women only. There are

Thermal Baths & Pools

Dagály
Huge kid-friendly
swimming complex
(p107)

Palatinus Strand
Largest swimming
complex in town (p108)

*Margaret Island
(Margit-sziget)*

Alfréd Hajós
Where the Olympic
teams train (p108)

Széchenyi Baths
Very hot water in a
wedding-cake building
(p142)

Lukács Baths
For serious
spa fans (p76)

Király Baths
Ancient and
very Turkish
(p58)

*Heroes' Square
(Hősök tere)*

Danube River

*Castle Hill
(Várhegy)*

Rudas Baths
The most famous of
the Turkish baths
(p66)

Citadella

Gellért Baths
Like bathing in a
cathedral (p66)

usually mixed days and some baths – the Széchenyi Baths (p142), for example – are always for men and women together. On single-sex days or in same-sex sections, men are usually handed drawstring loincloths and women apron-like garments to don, though the use of bathing suits is on the increase even on single-sex days. You must wear a bathing suit on mixed-sex days; these are available for hire (1000Ft) if you don't have your own. Many pools require the use of a bathing cap, so bring your own or wear the disposable one provided or sold for a nominal fee. Most pools also rent towels (1000Ft).

Getting In & Out

The procedure for getting out of your street clothes and into the water requires some explanation. All baths and pools have cabins or lockers. In most of the baths nowadays you are given an electronic bracelet that directs you to, and then opens, your locker or cabin. Others – the Gellért Baths (p66) springs to mind – still employ the old, more personal method. Find a free locker or cabin yourself, and after getting changed in (or beside) it, seek out an attendant, who will lock it for you and hand you a numbered tag to tie on your costume or 'apron'. Please note: in order to prevent theft should you lose or misplace the tag, the number is not the same as the one on the locker, so commit the locker number to memory.

Choosing a Bathing Experience

Which bath you decide to visit is really a matter of choice, but certainly consider one of our three favourites:

Rudas Baths (p66) These renovated baths are the most Turkish of all in Budapest,

Above: Outdoor pool at Gellért Baths

Right: Men playing chess at Széchenyi thermal baths

built in 1566, with an octagonal pool, domed cupola with coloured glass and massive columns. They're mostly men-only during the week, but turn into a real zoo on mixed weekend nights.

Gellért Baths (p66) Soaking in the art nouveau Gellért Baths, open to both men and women in separate sections, has been likened to taking a bath in a cathedral. The indoor swimming pools are the most beautiful in the city.

Széchenyi Baths (p142) The gigantic 'wedding-cake' building in City Park houses the Széchenyi Baths, which are unusual for three reasons: their immensity (a dozen thermal baths and five swimming pools); the bright, clean atmosphere; and the high temperature of the water (up to 38°C).

Other baths also have their special features. The waters of the Lukács Baths (p76) are meant to cure just about everything from spinal deformation and vertebral dislocation to calcium deficiency. The four pools at Király Baths (p58), while begging for a renovation, are Turkish and date back to the late 16th century. The facilities at the Danubius Health Spa

Detail of water fountain in thermal pool at Gellért Baths

RETURN OF THE RÁCZ BATHS

Budapest's spa aficionados went into meltdown when the **Rácz Baths** (Map p236; ☎266 0606; www.raczhotel. com; I Hadnagy utca 8-10; ▣18; ▣178, 178A) closed for renovations in 2002; its 19th-century neoclassical exterior designed by Miklós Ybl in a lovely Tabán park hid an authentic 16th-century Turkish delight. Now we hear the rebuild is coming to a close and the spa complex and attached 67-room hotel (total bill: €33 million) should be open by the time you read this.

Margitsziget (p107) on Margaret Island are soulless but modern and the choice of special treatments (lymph drainage, anyone?) is enviable.

As for pools, well, again it depends on what you have in mind. If you're serious about doing laps and keeping fit, visit the pools at Alfréd Hajós (p108) on Margaret Island or Császár-Komjádi (p78) in Óbuda. If you're just after a day of sunbathing, with the occasional dip, consider the Palatinus Strand (p108) on Margaret Island or the Dagály (p107) complex north of Újlipótváros.

Hungarian sausages

 # Eating

The dining scene in Budapest has undergone a sea change in recent years. Hungarian food has 'lightened up', offering the same wonderfully earthy and spicy tastes but in less calorific dishes. A number of vegetarian (or partially meatless) restaurants have opened up, and the choice of eateries with cuisines other than Magyar is greater than ever before.

Restaurant Revolution

You could almost call it a restaurant revolution. Stodgy main dishes have been brought up to date and jocularly christened *kortárs magyar konyha* (modern Hungarian cuisine). And more and more restaurants have a greater selection of 'real' vegetarian dishes – not just fried cheese and stuffed mushroom caps. Many midrange and top-end eateries are concentrating on wine serious wine – as never before, and they are excellent places to try some of Hungary's superb vintages. It won't be long before you discover some of Hungarian cuisine's 'matches made in heaven': sweet Tokaji Aszú with goose liver; ruby-red Kékfrankos with

pörkölt (goulash); bone-dry white Furmint with fish.

Hungarian Specialities
BREAD, DUMPLINGS & NOODLES

Hungarians say they 'eat bread with bread', and leftover *kenyér* (bread) has been used to thicken soups and stews since the reign of 15th-century King Matthias; *kifli* (crescent-shaped rolls) on the other hand gained popularity during the Turkish occupation. Uniquely Magyar are the flour-based *galuska* (dumplings) and *tarhonya* (barley-shaped egg pasta) served with *pörkölt* and *paprikás*.

NEED TO KNOW

Price Ranges
In our Eating reviews the following price indicators represent the cost of a two-course meal with drink for one person.

€	under 3000Ft
€€	3000Ft to 6500Ft
€€€	over 6500Ft

Opening Hours
➡ Most restaurants are open from 10am or 11am to 11pm or midnight.

➡ Arrive by 9pm or 10pm (at the latest) to ensure being seated and served.

Reservations
It is advisable to book tables at midrange to top-end restaurants any time but especially at the weekend.

Tipping
For the curious way people tip at restaurants in Budapest, see p208.

Menu Decoder
For translations of key menu items, see the boxed text, opposite.

Etiquette
➡ People in Budapest tend to meet their friends and entertain outside their homes at cafes and restaurants.

➡ If you are invited to a local person's home, bring a bunch of flowers or a bottle of good local wine.

➡ Hungarians don't clink glasses when drinking beer – wine is fine – because that's how the Habsburgs celebrated the defeat of Lajos Kossuth in the 1848–49 War of Independence.

SOUPS
A Hungarian meal starts with *leves* (soup). This is usually something relatively light like *gombaleves* (mushroom soup) or *húsgombócleves* (tiny liver dumplings in bouillon). More substantial soups are *gulyásleves* (a thick beef soup cooked with onions, cubed potatoes and paprika) and *bableves* (a thick bean soup usually made with meat). Another favourite is *halászlé* (fisherman's soup), a rich soup of fish stock, poached carp or catfish, tomatoes, green peppers and paprika.

MEAT & STEWS
People here eat an astonishing amount of meat. Pork, beef, veal and poultry are the meats most commonly consumed, and they can be breaded and fried, baked, simmered in *lecsó* (a tasty mix of peppers, tomatoes and onions) or turned into some paprika-flavoured creation.

The most popular dish prepared with paprika is the thick beef soup, *gulyás* (or *gulyásleves*), usually eaten as a main course. *Pörkölt* ('stew'), is closer to what foreigners call 'goulash'; the addition of sour cream, a reduction in paprika and the use of white meat such as chicken makes the dish *paprikás*.

Goose legs and livers and turkey breasts though not much else of either bird make an appearance on most menus. Lamb and mutton are rarely seen.

FISH
Freshwater fish, such as the indigenous *fogas* (great pike-perch) and the younger, smaller and more prized *süllő* from Lake Balaton, and *ponty* (carp) from the nation's rivers and streams, is plentiful but often overcooked by Western standards.

VEGETABLE DISHES
Fresh salad is often called *vitamin saláta* and is generally available when lettuce is in season; almost everything else is *savanyúság*, 'sours' that can be anything from mildly sour-sweet cucumbers, pickled peppers and very acidic sauerkraut. Such things actually go very well with heavy meat dishes.

The traditional way of preparing *zöldség* (vegetables) is in *főzelék*, Hungary's unique 'twice-cooked' vegetable dish. To make it, peas, green beans, lentils, marrow or cabbage are fried or boiled and then mixed into a roux with milk. This dish is sometimes topped with a few slices of meat and enjoyed at lunch.

In regular restaurants, vegetarians can usually order any number of types of *főzelék* as well as *gombafejek rántva* (fried mushroom caps) and pasta and noodle dishes with cheese, such as *túrós csusza* and *sztrapacska*. Other vegetarian dishes include *gombaleves* (mushroom soup), *gyümölcsleves* (fruit soup) in season, *rántott sajt* (fried cheese) and *sajtos kenyér* (sliced bread with soft cheese). *Bableves* (bean soup) usually – but not always – contains meat. *Palacsinta*

MENU DECODER

Menus are often translated into German and English, with mixed degrees of success. The following is a sample menu as it would appear in many restaurants in Budapest. It's far from complete, but it gives a good idea of what to expect. The main categories on a menu include those listed here; készételek are ready-made dishes that are kept warm or just heated up, while frissensültek are made to order and thus take longer. Other words you might encounter are halételek or halak (fish dishes), szárnyasok (poultry dishes) and sajtok (cheeses).

Előételek (Appetisers)

Hortobágyi palacsinta Meat-filled pancakes with paprika sauce

libamájpástétom Goose-liver pâté

rántott gombafejek Breaded and fried mushroom caps

Levesek (Soups)

csontleves Consommé/bouillon (usually beef)

Jókai bableves Bean soup with meat

meggyleves Cold sour-cherry soup (served in summer)

tyúkhúsleves Chicken soup with carrot, kohlrabi, parsley and celery root

Saláták (Salads)

cékla saláta Pickled beetroot salad

ecetes almapaprika Pickled small round peppers

paradicsom saláta Tomato salad

uborka saláta Lightly pickled-cucumber salad

vegyes saláta Mixed salad (sometimes of pickles)

Köretek (Side Dishes)

rizi-bizi Rice with peas

sült hasábburgonya Chips (French fries)

Készételek (Ready-Made Dishes)

csirke paprikás Chicken cooked with sour cream and paprika

(marha)pörkölt (Beef) stew (many types)

töltött káposzta Stuffed cabbage

töltött paprika Stuffed peppers

Frissensültek (Dishes Made to Order)

Bécsiszelet Wiener schnitzel

Brassói aprópecsenye Braised pork 'Braşov-style'

cigánypecsenye Roast pork 'Gypsy-style'

csülök Smoked pork knuckle

hagymás rostélyos Beef sirloin fried with onions

rántott hátszínszelet Breaded and fried rump steak

rántott pulykamell Breaded and fried turkey breast

sertésborda Pork chop

sült csirkecomb Roast chicken thigh

sült libacomb Roast goose leg

Édességek (Desserts)

Dobos orta Multilayered 'Dobos' chocolate and cream cake with caramelised brown sugar top

Gundel palacsinta 'Gundel' flambéed pancake with chocolate and nuts

rétes Strudel

Somlói galuska 'Somló-style' sponge cake with chocolate and whipped cream

---

(pancakes) may be savoury and made with *sajt* (cheese) or *gomba* (mushrooms), or sweet and prepared with *dió* (nuts) or *mák* (poppy seeds).

Ethnic Food

A wide choice of ethnic food – from Middle Eastern and Greek to Indian and Chinese has become the norm in Budapest. As elsewhere, imported cuisines can often be 'localised' – that spicy Chinese dish may taste more of paprika than Szechuan peppercorn – but local people are becoming more demanding as they travel more widely. The fast food of choice in the capital is no longer cheap-and-cheerful *lángos* (deep-fried dough with various toppings, usually cheese and sour cream), but kebabs and felafel.

Markets

Budapest counts about 20 large food markets, most of them in Pest. The vast majority are closed on Sunday, and

PAPRIKA: HUNGARY'S RED GOLD

Paprika, the *piros arany* ('red gold') so essential in Hungarian cuisine, is cultivated primarily around the cities of Szeged and Kalocsa on Hungary's Great Plain. About 10,000 tonnes of the spice are produced annually, 55% of which is exported. Hungarians each consume about 500g of the red stuff – richer in Vitamin C than citrus fruits – every year. Not only is paprika used when preparing dishes but it also appears on restaurant tables as a condiment beside the salt and pepper shakers.

There are many types of fresh or dried paprika available in Budapest markets and shops, including the rose, apple and royal varieties. But as a ground spice it is most commonly sold as *csípős* ('hot') or *erős* ('strong') paprika and *édes* ('sweet') paprika.

Monday is always very quiet, with only a few stalls staffed. The Nagycsarnok (p136) is a good introduction but can get crowded with tourists in season. Instead, check out the Rákóczi tér market (p128) or the covered market at Lehel tér (p109) in Újlipótváros. Fresh food at markets is sold by weight or by piece *(darab)*. When ordering by weight, you specify by kilos or *deka* (decagrams; 50dg is equal to 500g, or a little more than 1lb).

Patisseries & Cake Shops

Hungarians love sweets, and desserts taken at *ebéd* (lunch) or *vacsora* (dinner or supper) include *Somlói galuska* (sponge cake with chocolate and whipped cream) and *Gundel palacsinta* (flambéed pancake with chocolate and nuts). More complicated pastries, such as *Dobos torta* (a layered chocolate and cream cake with a caramelised brown sugar top) and the wonderful *rétes* (strudel), filled with poppy seeds, cherry preserves or *túró* (curd or cottage cheese), are usually consumed mid-afternoon in one of Budapest's ubiquitous *cukrászdák* (cake shops). These can either be the traditional variety or the new modern-style cafes; for the best of both, see p38.

Eating by Neigbourhood

➡ **Castle District** (p58) It's relatively expensive and touristy on Castle Hill, but more serious (mostly Hungarian) restaurants have recently arrived on the scene.

➡ **Óbuda & Buda Hills** (p78) Some historical eateries in Óbuda date so far back they appear in literary works; the Buda Hills are known for outdoor restaurants and barbecues.

➡ **Belváros** (p85) The choice is good but prices not always right in what is expense-account territory; head north or south for better deals.

➡ **Parliament & Around** (p97) Some fine eateries catering to all budgets around the basilica and Central European University.

➡ **Erzsébetváros & the Jewish Quarter** (p120) This area has the largest choice of cuisine – from South Slav and Jewish/kosher to French and Nepalese.

➡ **City Park & Beyond** (p144) Splurge territory be it at fancy Gundel or lakeside Robinson.

Lonely Planet's Top Choices

Múzeum (p132) Still going strong a quarter into its second century, this old-world place combines excellent service and top-notch cooking.

Klassz (p122) Unusual for a wine restaurant, both the vintages *and* the food are top-class.

Csalogány 26 (p59) Odd location in Buda but some say this is the best eatery in Budapest.

Tigris (p98) Wine and goose liver (and other bits of the cantankerous bird) figure predominately here.

Kisbuda Gyöngye (p79) Fin-de-siècle atmosphere in an antiques-cluttered Óbuda eatery.

Rosenstein (p133) Upmarket Jewish (but not kosher) and Hungarian cuisine near the Keleti train station.

Best by Budget

€
Vapiano (p86)
Kisharang (p98)
Fruccola (p99)
Ring (p122)
Pozsonyi Kisvendéglő (p109)

€€
Gerlóczy (p86)
Vár: a Speiz (p58)
Kőleves (p120)
Építész Pince (p132)
Café Kör (p98)

€€€
Baraka (p122)
Café Pierrot (p58)
Nobu (p87)
Babel Delikát (p87)

Best by Cuisine

Asian
Seoul House (p59)
Fuji Japán (p81)
Parázs Presszó (p100)
Koreai-Kinai Étterem (p100)
Kilenc Sárkány (p145)

Fish & Seafood
Philippe le Belge (p109)
Horgásztanya Vendéglő (p59)
Új Sípos Halászkert (p79)
Mosselen (p110)

Hungarian (Traditional)
Kádár (p121)
Toldi Konyhája (p60)
Fülemüle (p133)
Kéhli (p79)
Kárpátia (p86)

Hungarian (Modern)
Mák (p98)
21 Magyar Vendéglő (p58)
Tabáni Terasz (p68)
Onyx (p87)

Italian
Marcello (p69)
Trattoria Toscana (p86)
Bottega della Famiglia (p87)
Tom-George Italiano (p98)
Gastronomia Pomo d'Oro (p99)

Sub-Continental
Salaam Bombay (p98)
Bangla Büfé (p121)
Mughal Shahi (p81)
Kashmir (p98)
Pándzsáb Tandoori (p109)

Vegetarian
Éden (p60)
Napfényes (p120)
Govinda (p99)
Napos Oldal (p100)
Falafel Faloda (p121)

Best for Garden Seating
Hemingway (p69)
Robinson (p145)
Náncsi Néni (p80)
Rozmaring (p79)
Flamingo (p120)

Best for Breakfast
New York Café (p123)
Déryné Bisztró (p59)
Centrál Kávéház (p87)
Pastrami (p79)

Best for Good-Value Lunch
RumBach 7 (p121)
Mini Bistro (p59)
Carne di Hall (p60)
Tranzit Art Café (p69)
Café Alibi (p86)

Drinking & Nightlife

Budapest is loaded with cafes, pubs and bars, and there are enough to satisfy every taste. And for popular seasonal outdoor venues, there are the wonderful (and uniquely Budapest) 'garden clubs' and 'ruin bars'. Wine bars, where some pretty serious tasting goes on along with the quaffing, are something new and the club scene is, well, the stuff of legend.

Nightlife Hot Spots

Pest has all sorts of strips dedicated to nightlife – from the ultratouristed V Duna korzó (Map p238) along the Danube, with pricey watering holes commanding fine views of Buda Castle, to leafy VI Andrássy út (Map p250), just the place to watch Budapest high society sashay by. But the two main areas are trendy VI Liszt Ferenc tér (Map p250), where you'll have to fight a duel to the death for a spot under the plane trees, and IX Ráday utca (Map p242), a more subdued pedestrianised street in Józsefváros full of pubs and bars, restaurants and modern cafes. Up-and-coming is car-free V Szent István tér (Map p244) behind the Basilica of St Stephen. On the Buda side, concentrated nightlife areas are few and far between, but include somewhat subdued Castle Hill and the rather dispersed II Széll Kálmán tér (Map p230).

Pubs & Bars

Drinking establishments in Budapest run the gamut from Irish-themed 'pubs' and all-night hostel boozers, where the sole purpose is to drink till you drop, to much more refined wine and cocktail bars.

If you want to sample the local brew (Hungary produces a number of its own beers, including Dreher, Kőbányai and Arany Ászok) head for a *söröző*, a 'pub' with draught beer *(csapolt sör)* served in a *pohár* (0.3L) or *korsó* (0.4L or 0.5L).

Hungary also makes some excellent wines, many unknown outside its borders. The most distinctive reds come from Villány

and Szekszárd in Southern Transdanubia and the best dry whites are produced around Lake Balaton and in Somló. The red Bikavér (Bull's Blood) from Eger and the honey-sweet white Tokaj wines are much better known abroad, however.

A *borozó* is a traditional establishment (usually a dive) serving wine; a *pince* (or *bor pince*) is the same thing but in a cellar. Modern wine bars are the new black. Many serve wine by the *deci* (decilitre, 0.1L) so you can sample a wide range of vintages. And, just in case, they usually serve light dishes (cheese, sliced meats, salads etc) as blotter.

Garden Clubs & Ruin Bars

During the long and often very hot summers, so-called *kertek* (literally 'gardens', but in Budapest any outdoor spot that has been converted into an entertainment zone) empty out even the most popular indoor bars and clubs. These venues, including courtyards and *romkocsmák* (ruin bars) that rise phoenix-like from abandoned buildings, can change from year to year and a definitive list is usually not available until spring. Check the **Ruin Bars** (www.romkocsmak.hu) website for updates. In this book we call these venues 'garden clubs' for lack of a better name in English.

The atmosphere varies from place to place. Some are just outdoor bars with canned music, while others – usually in more remote neighbourhoods (eg on Margaret Island or near City Park) – have live music and dancing and can get quite raucous. Some of them have bars serving *pálinka*, a strong brandy or eau-de-vie distilled from a variety of fruits (most commonly from apricots or plums) that kicks like a mule. These are also good place to try Unicum, a bitter aperitif that has been around since 1790 but has been reclaimed by young Magyars in recent years as the new Jägermeister.

Clubs

Budapest offers a club scene unmatched elsewhere in the region and there's everything on offer from underground (in every sense) venues where DJs spin quality retro and indie to enormous meat markets attracting the posh along with porno stars. Like everywhere, clubs in Budapest don't really get off the ground until well after Cinderella's coach has turned into a pumpkin – or later. Not all clubs and music bars in Budapest levy a cover charge, but those that do will for between 1500Ft and 3500Ft at the door. The trendier (and trashier) places usually let women in free.

Cafes & Teahouses

Cafe life has a long and colourful history in Budapest. The Turks introduced coffee to the Hungarians (who first called it 'black soup') in the early 16th century, and the coffee house was an essential part of the social scene here long before it had even made an appearance in Vienna or Paris. In the final decades of the Austro-Hungarian empire, Budapest counted some 600 cafes.

A *kávéház* is literally a 'coffee house' (ie cafe). An *eszpresszó*, along with being a type of coffee, is essentially a coffee house too (also called *presszó*), but it usually also sells alcoholic drinks and light snacks. A *cukrászda* serves cakes, pastries and ice cream as well as hot and cold drinks. In all these places the drink of choice is *kávé* (coffee) – as a single black (*fekete*) or double (*dupla*). *Tejes kávé* (coffee with frothed milk) is closer to a cappuccino.

Old-style cafes, some of which date back as much as a century and a half, abound in Budapest and some of them are classic examples of their type, with ornate fin-de-siècle decor and sometimes service as antiquated as the surrounds. They were once the centre of social life and in them

NEED TO KNOW

Opening Hours

➡ Cafes: 8am or 9am to anywhere from 6pm to 1am

➡ Bars: 11am to midnight Sunday to Thursday, to 1am or 2am Friday and Saturday

➡ Clubs: anywhere from 8pm to 11pm to 3am to dawn

Print & Online Resources

➡ Useful freebies include *Budapest Funzine* (www.funzine.hu) and *PestiEst* (www.est.hu, in Hungarian).

➡ The *Budapest Times* (www.budapest-times.hu) includes a '14-Day Guide' to entertainment each week.

Costs

➡ *Korsó* (0.5L) of Dreher beer in pub or cafe: 400Ft to 750Ft

➡ Cheap/good bottle of wine (75cL) in supermarket: 700/2500Ft

➡ Cup of coffee in cafe: 250Ft to 550Ft

➡ Glass of wine: from 550Ft

➡ Cocktail: from 1000Ft

➡ Club cover charge (if any): 1500Ft to 3500Ft

Tipping

For tipping conventions in Budapest, see p208.

alliances were formed and momentous events planned and plotted (see p194). Generally, these cafes are frequented by older folk and tourists; places like the Ruszwurm Cukrászda on Castle Hill and Gerbeaud in Belváros can get swamped in season. Younger Budapesters prefer the new breed of coffee house, done up in glass and chrome and serving as much skinny decaf as cappuccino.

Teahouses have become very trendy in Budapest in recent years and they're often quite stylish places. In general, black or 'English' is not so popular (and never served with milk), though you'll always be able to choose from a wide range of herbal teas and fruit tisanes.

Lonely Planet's Top Choices

Gödör (p88) Very central entertainment venue – it used to be a bus station – that has something for everyone: cafe by day and club by night, with everything from folk and world but especially rock and pop.

Action Bár (p88) Head to this men-only bar with nightly shows when you are seriously OFB (out for business).

Café Ponyvaregény (p69) One of the first 'retro cafes' in Budapest, the 'Pulp Fiction' is still cock of the walk.

Ruszwurm Cukrászda (p61) Dating back to the early 19th century, this is the oldest traditional cafe in town.

Bambi Presszó (p61) Bambi hasn't changed a bit in almost half a century, which seems to please just about everyone.

Kiadó Kocsma (p102) A nice alternative to the 'Tér' just across the road, the 'For Sale' is a chilled spot for a pint.

Best Wine & Cocktail Bars

Dobló (p123)

Oscar American Bar (p61)

Szatyor Bár (p69)

Calgary Antik Bár (p81)

Paris Texas (p135)

Best Bars & Pubs

Vittula (p123)

Cökxpôn (p135)

Pántlika (p145)

Caledonia (p102)

Lánchíd Söröző (p61)

Best Clubs

DPU Chachacha (p61)

Anker Klub (p124)

Cinetrip (p145)

A38 Hajó (p69)

Corvintető (p135)

Best Traditional Cafes

Művész Kávéház (p124)

Gerbeaud (p87)

Alexandra Book Café (p124)

Hadik Kávéház (p69)

Best Modern Cafes & Teahouses

Café Csiga (p134)

1000 Tea (p87)

Csendes (p87)

Mozaik (p123)

Két Szerecsen (p125)

Best Garden Clubs & Ruin Bars

Instant (p101)

Holdudvar (p110)

Grandió (p123)

Szimpla Kert (p124)

Romkert (p69)

Best Gay & Lesbian Venues

Le Café M Bar (p100)

Café Eklektika (p102)

Adonis (p135)

CoXx Men's Bar (p123)

Entertainment

For a city its size, Budapest has a huge choice of things to do and places to go after dark – from opera and folk dancing to live jazz and films screened in palatial cinemas that go by the name of 'film palaces'. It's usually not difficult getting tickets or getting in; the hard part is deciding what to do and where to go.

Music

CLASSICAL & OPERA

Apart from the city's main concert halls, including the Ferenc Liszt Music Academy (p115), the Palace of Arts (p135) and the Hungarian State Opera House (p117), many museums and other venues feature chamber music. They include, in Pest, the Old Music Academy, where the Franz Liszt Memorial Museum (p118) is housed; **Magyar Rádió Marble Hall** (Magyar Rádió Márványterme; Map p242; ☎328 7878; VIII Pollack Mihály tér 8; ☒47, 49); and the Hungarian Academy of Sciences (p96). 'Second-tier' venues in Buda include the Budapest History Museum (p52), the Millennium Theatre (p58), the Music History Museum (p56) and the Béla Bartók Memorial House (p78).

Organ recitals are best heard in the city's churches, including Matthias Church (p54) and the Church of St Anne (p56) in Buda, and the Basilica of St Stephen (p95), the Inner Town Parish Church (p85) and **St Michael's Inner Town Church** (Belvárosi Szent Mihály Templom; Map p238; V Váci utca 47/b; Ⓜ M3 Ferenciek tere) in Pest.

ROCK, POP & JAZZ

A number of bars and pubs feature live pop or rock music throughout the week. Top venues include Old Man's Music Pub (p125) and Roham (p136). For jazz, nothing beats the Budapest Jazz Club (p136), though Columbus (p88), on a boat moored in the Danube, is a more interesting venue.

FOLK & TRADITIONAL

Authentic *táncház* (literally 'dance house', but really folk-music workshops) are held at various locations throughout the week, but less frequently in summer. Times and venues often change; consult the publications on p40 and expect to pay 500Ft to 1000Ft. Useful, too, are the websites of the **Dance House Guild** (www.tanchaz.hu, in Hungarian) and **Folkrádió** (www.folkradio.hu). The former also lists bands playing other types of traditional music such as *klezmer* (Jewish folk music); two of the best are the **Budapest Klezmer Band** (www.budapestklezmer.hu) and the **Sabbathsong Klezmer Band** (www.sabbathsong.hu). Hear the latter at the Spinoza Café (p120).

Dance

CLASSICAL & MODERN

The **Hungarian National Ballet** (www.opera.hu) is based at the Hungarian State Opera House (p117), though it occasionally performs at the National Dance Theatre (p62) in the Castle District. The premier venue for modern dance is the MU Színház (p70).

FOLK

Two of Hungary's best-known folk-dance troupes, the Hungarian State Folk Ensemble (Magyar Állami Népi Együttes) and the Rajkó Folk Ensemble (Rajkó Népi Együttes), perform on selected evenings from May to October. For bookings and more information, contact **Hungária Koncert** (☎317 1377, 317 2754; www.ticket.info.hu).

Theatre & Film

It's unlikely you'll brave a play in the Hungarian language, but the József Katona Theatre (p88) is the place to go if you do. The nearby Merlin Theatre (p88) is home to Budapest's only English-language theatre company, Scallabouche.

NEED TO KNOW

Print & Online Resources

➡ The *Budapest Times* (www. budapesttimes.hu) includes a '14-Day Guide' to entertainment each week.

➡ Useful freebies for popular listings include *Budapest Funzine* (www.funzine. hu) and *PestiEst* (www.est.hu, in Hungarian).

➡ The monthly freebie *Koncert Kalendárium* (www.koncertkalendarium. hu) has more serious offerings: classical concerts, opera, dance and the like.

Buying Tickets

You can book almost anything online at www.jegymester.hu, www.showtime-budapest.hu and www.kulturinfo.hu, or try the most useful booking agencies in town:

Ticket Express (Map p250; ☑06-30 303 0999; www.tex.hu; VI Andrássy út 18; ⏰10am-6.30pm Mon-Fri, to 3pm Sat; Ⓜ M1 Opera) Largest ticket-office network in the city.

Ticket Pro (Map p250; ☑555 5155; www. ticketpro.hu; VII Károly körút 9; ⏰10am-6pm Mon-Fri, to 2pm Sat; Ⓜ M1/2/3 Deák Ferenc tér) Smaller, more personable agency, with tickets to plays and shows, concerts and sporting events.

Rózsavölgyi és Társa (Map p238; ☑318 3500; www.lira.hu, in Hungarian; V Szervita tér 5; ⏰10am-7pm Mon-Fri, to 5pm Sat; Ⓜ M1/2/3 Deák Ferenc tér) In the music shop of that name (p90) and good for classical concerts and the like.

A couple of dozen cinemas in Budapest screen English-language films with Hungarian subtitles. Consult the listings in the freebie *Budapest Funzine* (www .funzine.hu) or *PestiEst* (www.est.hu, in Hungarian) to find out where and when these showings are on.

Be aware though that many foreign films are also dubbed into Hungarian, usually indicated in listings with the words *magyarul beszélő* or simply 'mb'. Films that have been given Hungarian subtitles (*feliratos),* rather than being dubbed, will retain their original soundtrack.

Spectator Sport

The most popular spectator sports are football and water polo, although motor racing (especially during the Formula 1 Hungarian Grand Prix; p146) and horse racing – both trotting and flat racing – at Kincsem Park (p146) also have their fans.

The best source of information on sport is the mass-circulation daily **Nemzeti Sport** (National Sport; www.nem zetisport.hu, in Hungarian).

FOOTBALL

Once on top of the heap of European football – the national team's victory over England both at Wembley (6-3) in 1953 and at home (7-1) the following year are still talked about as if the winning goals were scored yesterday – Hungary has failed to qualify for any major tournament since 1986 (though they were semi-finalists at the 2008 European Under-19 Championship). The national team plays at Ferenc Puskás Stadium (p146).

There are five premier league football teams in Budapest out of a total of 16 nationwide, including Újpest, which plays at far-flung **Ferenc Szusza Stadium** (IV Megyeri út 13; ☐96, 196), seating 13,500 fans; and MTK, based at **Nándor Hidegkúti Stadium** (VIII Salgótarjáni utca 12-14; ☐1, 1A), accommodating 12,700 spectators. But no club has dominated Budapest football over the years like Ferencváros Torna Club (FTC), who play at Flórián Albert Stadium (p136) in Pest.For match schedules pick up a copy *Nemzeti Sport* or check the **Hungarian Football** (www.hungarian football.com) website.

WATER POLO

Hungary has dominated the European Championships in water polo a dozen times since 1926 and taken nine gold medals at Olympic Games, so it's worthwhile catching a professional or amateur game of this exciting seven-a-side sport. The **Hungarian Water Polo Association** (MVLSZ; www.waterpolo.hu, in Hungarian) is based at the Alfréd Hajós (p108) swimming complex on Margaret Island.

Lonely Planet's Top Choices

Ferenc Liszt Music Academy (p115) Budapest's premier venue for classical concerts (though closed for renovations at the time of writing) – not just a place to go to hear music but an opportunity to ogle the wonderful decorative Zsolnay porcelain and frescoes as well.

Palace of Arts (p135) The city's newest cultural venue with two concert halls and near-perfect acoustics.

Hungarian State Opera House (p117) Small but perfectly formed home to both the state opera company and the Hungarian National Ballet.

Trafó House of Contemporary Arts (p136) A mixture of music, theatre and especially the cream of the crop of dance in southern Pest.

Budapest Operetta (p103) Campy fun for the whole family on Nagymező utca, Budapest's Broadway or West End.

Uránia National Cinema (p136) Art-deco/neo-Moorish extravaganza – a palatial place to see a film.

Best for Film

Kino (p110)

Művész Art Mozi (p103)

Örökmozgó (p125)

Puskin Art Mozi (p88)

Best for Jazz & Blues

Budapest Jazz Club (p136)

Jedermann (p136)

Columbus (p88)

Nothin' but the Blues (p136)

Best for Live Music

Spinoza Café (p120)

Old Man's Music Pub (p125)

Roham (p136)

Ladó Café (p125)

Szikra Cool House Tour (p102)

Best for Sport

Flórián Albert Stadium (p136)

Hungaroring (p146)

Kincsem Park (p146)

Alfréd Hajós (p108)

Best for Dance

National Dance Theatre (p62)

MU Színház (p70)

Aranytíz Cultural Centre (p103)

Municipal Cultural House (p70)

Budavár Cultural Centre (p61)

Best for Theatre

József Katona Theatre (p88)

Merlin Theatre (p88)

National Theatre (p136)

Budapest Puppet Theatre (p125)

PLAN YOUR TRIP ENTERTAINMENT

Shopping

Budapest is a fantastic city for shopping, whether you're in the market for traditional folk craft with a twist, cutting-edge designer goods, the latest in flash headgear or honey-sweet dessert wine. Traditional markets stand side by side with mammoth shopping malls, and old-style umbrella makers can still be found next to avant-garde fashion boutiques.

Specialities & Souvenirs

Traditional items with a Hungarian stamp – now called Hungarica – include folk embroidery and ceramics, pottery, wall hangings, painted wooden toys and boxes, dolls, all types of basketry, and porcelain (especially from Herend and Zsolnay). Feather or goose-down pillows and duvets (comforters) are of exceptionally high quality and are second only to the Siberian variety.

Foodstuffs that are expensive or difficult to buy elsewhere – goose liver (both fresh and potted), dried mushrooms, jam (especially the apricot variety), prepared meats like Pick salami, the many types of paprika – make nice gifts (as long as you're allowed to take them home). Some of Hungary's 'boutique' wines also make excellent gifts; a bottle of six-*puttonyos* (the sweetest) Tokaji Aszú dessert wine always goes down a treat. Fruit brandy (*pálinka*) is a stronger option.

Books and CDs are affordable, and there's an excellent selection, especially of folk and classical music.

Markets & Malls

Some people consider a visit to one of Budapest's flea markets – famous Ecseri Piac (p137) or the smaller City Park one (p146) – a highlight, not just as a place to indulge their consumer vices but as the consummate Budapest experience.

In the mid-1990s Budapest began to go mall crazy, and at last count the city had more than 20, both in the centre of town and on the fringes. However, 'mall' may not properly describe what the Hungarians call *bevásárló és szorakoztató központ* (shopping and amusement centres); here you'll find everything from designer salons, traditional shops and dry cleaners to food courts, casinos, cinemas and nightclubs. It's a place to spend the entire day, much as you would just about anywhere in the globalised world of the 3rd millennium. Don't bother, we say.

Shopping Streets

Some streets or areas in Budapest specialise in certain goods or products. For example, antique shops line V Falk Miksa utca (Map p244) in Pest and, to a lesser extent, II Frankel Leó út (Map p234) in Buda. Along V Múzeum körút (Map p238) in Pest you'll find a string of antiquarian and secondhand bookshops. Central (and very high-rent) V Váci utca (Map p238) is chock-a-block with both top-end boutiques and tourist schlock both north and south of Szabadsajtó utca. VI Király utca (Map p250) is turning into a centre for high-end designed goods and fashion.

Lonely Planet's Top Choices

BÁV (p103) Check out any branch of this pawn and secondhand shop chain if you can't make it to the flea markets.

Herend Village Pottery (p62) Big, bold and colourful platters make a lovely change from traditional Herend porcelain.

Billerbeck (p126) The place to buy an all-goose-down duvet (comforter) or set of pillows.

Magma (p90) Excellent choice for 'Made in Hungary' gifts and furnishings, from glassware and porcelain to toys and textiles.

Mézes Kuckó (p111) Still the very best place in town for nut-and-honey cookies.

Bomo Art (p90) The finest paper and paper goods are sold here, including leather-bound notebooks, photo albums and address books.

Best for Hungarica

Holló Atelier (p90)

Herend (p104)

Intuita (p90)

Folkart Kézművésház (p90)

Best for Food & Drink

Nagycsarnok (p136)

Bortársaság (p62)

Cadeau (p90)

Magyar Pálinka Ház (p137)

T Nagy Tamás (p90)

Best for Fashion & Clothing

Romani Design (p126)

Valeria Fazekas (p89)

Retrock (p89)

Vass Shoes (p89)

Katti Zoób (p104)

Best for Books

Bestsellers (p103)

Szőnyi Antikváriuma (p103)

Írók Boltja (p126)

Massolit (p125)

Book Station (p111)

NEED TO KNOW

Opening Hours

Shops are generally open from 9am or 10am to 6pm Monday to Friday and from 9am or 10am to 1pm on Saturday. Some stay open late (usually 8pm) on Thursday.

VAT/Sales Tax

If you're not an EU resident you can get a refund on the ÁFA (VAT or sales tax) you've paid, provided you've spent more than 50,000Ft in any one shop and take the goods out of the country (and the EU) within 90 days; see p209 for details.

Buying Antiques

Any item over 100 years old requires a permit from the Ministry of Culture for export; this involves a visit to a museum expert, photos of the piece and a Hungarian National Bank form with proof-of-purchase receipts. Companies that will take care of all this for you and ship the piece(s) include **Move One** (☑266 0181; www.moveoneinc. com). Be aware that most art shippers won't take a job for under US$500, so if the piece is small enough and not really valuable, consider taking it in your suitcase.

Explore Budapest

BUDAPEST
TOP SIGHTS

Neighbourhoods at a Glance

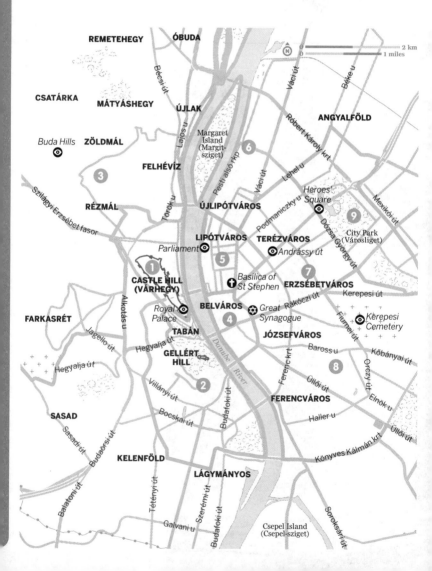

REMETEHEGY ÓBUDA

CSATÁRKA MÁTYÁSHEGY ÚJLAK

Buda Hills ZÖLDMÁL

FELHÉVÍZ

RÉZMÁL

Bécsi út

Lajos u

Margaret Island (Margit-sziget)

Pesti alsó rkp

Török u

Szilágyi Erzsébet fasor

ÚJLIPÓTVÁROS

Váci út

Lehel u

Podmaniczky u

Váci út

Robert Károly krt

ANGYALFÖLD

Béke u

Heroes Square

City Park (Városliget)

Mexikói út

Dózsa György út

LIPÓTVÁROS TERÉZVÁROS

Parliament Andrássy út

CASTLE HILL (VÁRHEGY)

Basilica of St Stephen ERZSÉBETVÁROS

Kerepesi út

FARKASRÉT

Alkotás u

Royal Palace BELVÁROS Great Synagogue

Rákóczi út

Kerepesi Cemetery

Fiumei út

TABÁN JÓZSEFVÁROS

Jagello út

Hegyalja út

GELLÉRT HILL

Baross u

Kőbányai út

Hegyalja út

Villányi út

Ferenc krt

Üllői út

Orczy út

Elnök u

FERENCVÁROS

SASAD

Bocskai út

Budafoki út

Haller u

Üllői út

Sasadi út

Budaörsi út

KELENFÖLD

Könyves Kálmán krt

LÁGYMÁNYOS

Balatoni út

Tétényi út

Szerémi út

Budafoki út

Galvani u

Csepel Island (Csepel-sziget)

Soroksári út

2 km
1 miles

① Castle District p48

The Castle District encompasses Castle Hill (Várhegy) – nerve centre of Budapest's history and packed with many of the capital's most important museums and other attractions – and ground-level Víziváros (Watertown). What the latter lacks in sights it makes up for in excellent restaurants, many of them around newly renamed Széll Kálmán tér, major transport hub and centre of urban Buda.

② Gellért Hill & Tabán p63

Standing atop Gellért Hill and proclaiming freedom throughout the city is the Liberty Monument, Budapest's most visible statue. She looks down on the Tabán, a leafy neighbourhood originally settled by the Serbs which later turned into Budapest's version of Montmartre in Paris, and a great many students; Budapest University of Technology and Economics (BME) is here.

③ Óbuda & Buda Hills p71

Óbuda is the oldest part of Buda and still retains a lost-in-the-past village feel; here you'll find excellent museums, the remains of the Roman settlement of Aquincum and some legendary eateries. The Buda Hills are a breath of fresh air and offer forms of transport that will delight kids of all ages.

④ Belváros p82

The 'Inner Town' is just that – the centre of Pest's universe, especially when it comes to tourism. This is where you'll find Váci utca, with its luxury shops, restaurants and bars, and Vörösmarty tér, home to the city's most celebrated *cukrászda* (cake shop) and one of its just two Michelin-starred restaurants. Deák Ferenc tér, where all three metro lines converge, is here too.

⑤ Parliament & Around p91

Just north of the Inner Town is Lipótváros (Leopold Town), with the landmark Parliament building facing the Danube to the west and the equally iconic Basilica of St Stephen to the east. In this book we've included part of the district called Terézváros (Teresa Town), named in

honour of Empress Maria Theresa, as well. If Budapest has a single centre for nightlife, the district's Nagymező utca is it.

⑥ Margaret Island & Northern Pest p105

Lovely Margaret Island is neither Buda nor Pest but its shaded walkways, large swimming complexes, thermal spa and gardens offer refuge to the denizens of both sides of the river. Northern Pest in this section means Újlipótváros (New Leopold Town). It's a neighbourhood vaguely reminiscent of New York's Upper West Side, with tree-lined streets, antique shops, boutiques and lovely cafes.

⑦ Erzsébetváros & the Jewish Quarter p112

There's no doubt you'll be spending the bulk of your time in this area, which takes in 'Elizabeth Town' and most of Terézváros, including well- and high-heeled Andrássy út, the long, dramatic and *très chic* boulevard that slices through Terézváros. Here you'll find a high percentage of the accommodation listed in the Sleeping chapter, restaurants serving everything from Chinese to Serbian, and Pest's hottest and coolest nightspots.

⑧ Southern Pest p127

The districts of Józsefváros (Joseph Town) and Ferencváros (Francis, or Franz, Town) – no prizes for guessing which Habsburg emperor these were named after – are traditionally working class and full of students. They're very colourful areas and it's a lot of fun wandering the backstreets, poking your nose into courtyards and small shops.

⑨ City Park & Beyond p138

The 'green lung' at the northern end of momentous Andrássy út, City Park is the largest park in Budapest but a lot more than just a pretty face. Its main entrance, Heroes' Square, is ringed by important museums and historically significant monuments. The streets on the fringes of the park are paradise for fans of art nouveau and Secessionist architecture.

Castle District

CASTLE HILL | VÍZIVÁROS

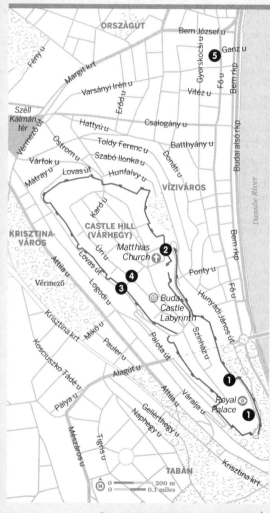

Neighbourhood Top Five

1 Comprehending Budapest's long and at times convoluted story by visiting the **Budapest History Museum** (p52) and then viewing many of the events captured forever by some of the nation's greatest artists at the **Hungarian National Gallery** (p50).

2 Enjoying views of the Danube, Gellért Hill and Pest from the iconic **Fishermen's Bastion** (p54).

3 Reliving the WWII siege of Budapest by descending into the **Hospital in the Rock** (p55) deep below Buda Castle.

4 Savouring a *Dobos torta* (a layered chocolate-and-cream cake with a caramelised brown-sugar top) at the famous **Ruszwurm Cukrászda** (p61).

5 Soaking the travel-weary blues away at the **Király Baths** (p58), another legacy of the Turkish occupation.

For more detail of this area, see Map p230 ➡

Explore: Castle District

Castle Hill (Várhegy), also called the Castle Quarter (Várnegyed), is a 1km-long limestone plateau towering 170m above the Danube. The premier sight in the capital, and Unesco World Heritage listed, it contains Budapest's most important medieval monuments and museums.

The walled area consists of two distinct parts: the Old Town to the north, where commoners lived in the Middle Ages (the present-day owners of the coveted burgher houses are anything but 'common'); and the Royal Palace, the original site of the castle built in the 13th century, now housing important sights, to the south.

There are many ways to reach Castle Hill but the most fun is to board the **Sikló** (Map p230; one-way adult/child 840/520Ft; return 1450/940Ft; ⊙7.30am-10pm, closed 1st & 3rd Mon of each month), a funicular railway built in 1870 that ascends from Clark Ádám tér at the western end of Chain Bridge to Szent György tér near the Royal Palace.

Víziváros (Watertown) is the narrow area between the Danube and Castle Hill that widens as it approaches Óbuda to the north and Rózsadomb (Rose Hill) to the northwest, spreading as far west as Széll Kálmán tér, one of Buda's most important transport hubs. In the Middle Ages those involved in trades, crafts and fishing lived here. Many of the district's churches were used as mosques under the Turks, and they built baths here, including the Király Baths (p58).

Local Life

➡ **Eating** Locals working on Castle Hill avoid the tourists by eating at the Fortuna Önkiszolgáló (p59).

➡ **Sleeping** Sleep on Castle Hill at bargain-basement prices by checking into the Hotel Kulturinnov (p159) at the former Finance Ministry.

➡ **Entertainment** Try to catch something – anything – at the elegantly renovated Jenő Hubay Music Hall (p62); most Budapesters have never even heard of it.

Getting There & Away

➡ **Bus** I Clark Ádám tér for bus 16 to I Dísz tér on Castle Hill or V Deák Ferenc tér in Pest; I Fő utca for bus 86 to Óbuda and south Buda.

➡ **Funicular** I Clark Ádám tér for Sikló to I Szent György tér on Castle Hill.

➡ **HÉV** Batthyány tér.

➡ **Metro** M2 Batthyány tér and Széll Kálmán tér.

➡ **Tram** II Vidra utca for No 17 to Óbuda; I Batthyány tér for No 19 to I Szent Gellért tér and south Buda; Nos 4 and 6 to Pest (Big Ring Rd).

Lonely Planet's Top Tip

A real 'insider's' way to get to and from Castle Hill is from I Dózsa tér (bus 16 from Pest), where you'll find a **lift** (100Ft; ⊙6am-7pm Mon, to 9pm Tue-Sat, 9am-6.30pm Sun) that will whisk you up to the Lion Court and National Széchenyi Library. Glass cases in the hallway where the lift starts and ends are filled with archaeological finds from the Royal Palace.

 CASTLE DISTRICT

 Best Places to Eat

➡ Csalogány 26 (p59)
➡ Vár: a Speiz (p58)
➡ Déryné Bisztró (p59)
➡ Horgásztanya Vendéglő (p59)
➡ Antigiana Gelati (p60)

For reviews, see p58 ➡

Best Places to Drink

➡ Ruszwurm Cukrászda (p61)
➡ Oscar American Bar (p61)
➡ Bambi Presszó (p61)
➡ DPU Chachacha (p61)

For reviews, see p61 ➡

Best Places to Shop

➡ Mester Porta (p62)
➡ Bortársaság (p62)
➡ Herend Village Pottery (p62)

For reviews, see p62 ➡

TOP SIGHTS
ROYAL PALACE

The enormous Royal Palace (Királyi Palota) complex on Castle Hill has been razed and rebuilt at least six times over the past seven centuries. Béla IV established a royal residence here in the mid-13th century and subsequent kings added on to it. The palace was levelled in the battle to rout the Turks in 1686; the Habsburgs rebuilt it, but spent very little time here. Today the Royal Palace contains two important museums, the national library and an abundance of statues and monuments.

There are two entrances to the Royal Palace. The first is via the **Habsburg Steps**, southeast of Szent György tér and through an ornamental gateway dating from 1903. The other way in is via **Corvinus Gate**, with its big black raven symbolising King Matthias Corvinus, southwest of the square. Either is good for the museums.

Hungarian National Gallery

The **Hungarian National Gallery** (Map p230; Magyar Nemzeti Galéria; www.mng.hu; Royal Palace, Wings A–D; adult/child 1500/1000Ft; ⊙10am-6pm Tue-Sun) is an overwhelming collection spread across four floors that traces Hungarian art from the 11th century to the present day. The largest collections include medieval and Renaissance stonework, Gothic wooden sculptures and panel paintings, late-Gothic winged altars and late-Renaissance and baroque art. The museum also has an important collection of Hungarian paintings and sculpture from the 19th and 20th centuries.

The museum was formed in 1957 from a collection started in the mid-19th century that was previously exhibited at the Museum of Fine Arts (p140) and the Hungarian National Museum (p129), and moved to this site in 1975. The permanent collection is, for the most part, exhibited in Wings B to D, with Wing A reserved for temporary exhibits. The

DON'T MISS...

➡ Late-Gothic altarpieces

➡ Csontváry's *Solitary Cedar*

➡ Rippl-Rónai's *Father and Uncle Piacsek Drinking Red Wine*

➡ Gothic statues and heads

➡ Renaissance door frame

PRACTICALITIES

➡ Map p230

➡ 🚌16, 16A, 116

➡ 🚋Sikló (funicular)

lapidarium with medieval and Renaissance stone carvings may be closed for renovations.

Gothic Works

The winged altarpieces in the so-called **Great Throne Room** on the 1st floor of Wing D date from the 15th and early 16th centuries and form one of the greatest collection of late-Gothic painting in the world. *The Visitation* (1506) by Master MS is both lyrical and intimate, but keep an eye open for the monumental Annunciation Altarpiece (1515–20) and the intense, almost Renaissance face of John the Baptist in the triptych (1490) named in his honour.

Renaissance & Baroque Works

The finest 18th-century baroque painters in Hungary were actually Austrians, including Franz Anton Maulbertsch (1724–96; *Death of Joseph*) and his contemporary Stephan (István) Dorfmeister (1725–97; *Christ on the Cross*). Other greats of the period (with more of a Magyar pedigree) include Jakob Bogdány (1660–1724), whose *Two Macaws, a Cockatoo and a Jay, with Fruit* is a veritable Garden of Eden; and Ádám Mányoki (1673–1757), court painter to Ferenc Rákóczi II. You'll find their works in the galleries adjoining the Great Throne Room.

19th-Century Works

Move into Wing C for examples of the saccharine Romantic Nationalist school of heroic paintings, whose most prolific exponents were Bertalan Székely (1835–1910; *Women of Eger*) and Gyula Benczúr (1844–1920; *Recapture of Buda Castle, The Baptism of Vajk*). This style of painting gave way to the realism of Mihály Munkácsy (1844–1900), the so-called painter of the *puszta* (Dusty Road, or Great Plain) and of intense religious subjects *(Golgotha, Christ before Pilate),* and László Paál (1846–79; *Forest at Fontainebleau*). In the late 19th century European developments in art began to influence Hungarian painting; Pál Szinyei Merse (1845–1920), who rates his own gallery in Wing B, is the country's foremost Impressionist painter *(Picnic in May, The Skylark).*

20th-Century Works

The greatest painters working in the late 19th and early 20th centuries were Tivadar Kosztka Csontváry (1853–1919), who has been compared to Van Gogh, and József Rippl-Rónai (1861–1927), the key exponent of Secessionist painting in Hungary. Among the latter's greatest works (Wing C, 2nd floor) are *Father and Uncle Piacsek Drinking Red Wine* and *Woman with Bird Cage.* Don't overlook the harrowing depictions of war and the dispossessed

TIVADAR KOSZTKA CSONTVÁRY

Many critics consider Tivadar Kosztka Csontváry – a symbolist artist whose tragic life is sometimes compared with that of his contemporary, Vincent van Gogh – to be Hungary's greatest painter. He certainly is the most uncommon. Csontváry produced his major works in just half a dozen years starting in 1903 when he was 50. His efforts met with praise at his first exhibition in 1907 in Paris, but critics panned his work at a showing in Budapest the following year. This lack of understanding and recognition by his peers pushed what was already an unstable, obsessive personality into insanity, and he died penniless in Budapest just after WWI.

Though Tivadar Kosztka Csontváry belonged to no specific school of art per se, elements of post-Impressionism and expressionism can be seen in such works as *Trees at Jajce Illuminated by Lightning* (1903; Wing C, 2nd floor) and *Ruins of the Greek Theatre at Taormina* (1905; Wing C, 2nd floor), and in his most famous work, *Solitary Cedar* (1907; Wing C, 1st floor).

CASTLE DISTRICT ROYAL PALACE

HUNGARIAN NATIONAL GALLERY

2nd Floor

Father & Uncle Piacsek Drinking Red Wine by Rippl-Rónai

20th-Century Painting & Sculpture (to 1945)

WWI Paintings by Mednyánszky

Procession by Aba-Novák

1st Floor

19th-Century Painting & Sculpture

Solitary Cedar by Csontváry

Great Throne Room (Gothic Altarpieces)

National Romantic School (Székely & Benczúr)

Pál Szinyei Merse Room

Works by Munkácsy & Paál

Renaissance & Baroque Paintings

Ground Floor

Wing C

Wing D

Wing A

Temporary Exhibitions

Wing B

Lapidarium (Medieval & Renaissance Stone Carvings)

by the WWI artist László Mednyánszky (1852–1919; *In Serbia, Soldiers Resting*) and the colourful, upbeat paintings of carnivals and celebrations by Vilmos Aba-Novák (1894–1941; *Procession, The Fair at Csíkszereda*).

Budapest History Museum

The **Budapest History Museum** (Budapesti Történeti Múzeum; Map p230; www.btm.hu; Royal Palace, Wing E; adult/child 1400/700Ft; ☉10am-6pm Tue-Sun Mar-Oct, to 4pm Tue-Sun Nov-Feb) looks at the 2000 years of the city, over four floors. Restored palace rooms dating from the 15th century can be entered from the basement, where there are three vaulted halls, one with a magnificent Renaissance door frame in red marble bearing the seal of Queen Beatrice and tiles with a raven and a ring (the seal of her husband King Matthias Corvinus), leading to the Gothic and Renaissance Halls, the Royal Cellar and the 14th-century Tower Chapel dedicated to King St Stephen.

On the ground floor, exhibits showcase Budapest during the Middle Ages, with dozens of important Gothic statues, heads and fragments of courtiers, squires and saints discovered during excavations in 1974. There are also artefacts recently recovered from a well dating back to Turkish times, most notably a 14th-century tapestry of the Hungarian coat-of-arms with the fleur-de-lis of the House of Anjou. The exhibit on the 1st floor – *Budapest in Modern Times* – traces the city's history from the expulsion of the Turks in 1686 to the present. On the 2nd floor the exhibits reach way back – Budapest from prehistoric times to the arrival of the Avars in the late 6th century.

Statue outside front of the Royal Palace on Castle Hill

STATUES AROUND THE ROYAL PALACE

To the east of the Habsburg Steps entrance is a bronze statue from 1905 of the **Turul** (Map p230), a hawk-like totemic bird that had supposedly impregnated Emese, the grandmother of Árpád. To the southeast, just in front of Wing C, stands a statue of **Eugene of Savoy** (Map p230), the Habsburg prince who wiped out the last Turkish army in Hungary at the Battle of Zenta in 1697. Designed by József Róna 200 years later, it is considered to be the finest equestrian statue in Budapest. In the middle of the square on the other side of Wing C of the Royal Palace is a statue of a **Hortobágyi csikós** (Map p230), a Hungarian cowboy in full regalia breaking a mighty *bábolna* steed. The sculpture won international recognition for its creator, György Vastagh, at the Paris World Exhibitions of 1900 and 1901.

National Széchenyi Library

The **National Széchenyi Library** (Országos Széchenyi Könyvtár; Map p230; www.oszk.hu; Royal Palace, Wing F; ☺10am-9pm, stacks to 7pm Tue-Sat) contains codices and manuscripts, a large collection of foreign newspapers and a copy of everything published in Hungary or the Hungarian language. It was founded by Count Ferenc Széchenyi (1754–1820) – father of István Széchenyi (p177) – who endowed it with 15,000 books and 2000 manuscripts. This library allows **members** (annual adult/student 6500/3500Ft, 6 months 3500/2000Ft, daily per person 1200Ft) to do research, peruse the general stacks and read the large collection of foreign newspapers and magazines.

Matthias Fountain

Facing the Royal Palace's large northwestern courtyard is the **Matthias Fountain** (Mátyás kút; Map p230), a Romantic-style fountain that portrays the young king Matthias Corvinus in hunting garb. To his right below is Szép Ilona (Beautiful Helen), the protagonist in a Romantic ballad by the poet Mihály Vörösmarty. The rather smug-looking fellow with the shiny foot below to the left is Galeotto Marzio, an Italian chronicler at Matthias' court. The middle one of the king's three dogs was blown up during the war; canine-loving Hungarians (and most of them are) quickly had an exact copy made.

Poor Ilona, the girl featured prominently in the Matthias Fountain, apparently fell in love with the dashing 'hunter' — who was in reality King Matthias — and, upon learning his true identity and feeling unworthy, died of a broken heart.

 SIGHTS

⊙ Castle Hill

ROYAL PALACE PALACE

See p50.

SZÉCHENYI CHAIN BRIDGE BRIDGE

Map p230 This twin-towered span is the city's oldest and arguably most beautiful bridge. It is named in honour of its initiator, István Széchenyi (p177), but was built by a Scotsman named Adam Clark. When it opened in 1849, Széchenyi Chain Bridge (Széchenyi lánchíd) was unique for two reasons: it was the first permanent dry link between Buda and Pest; and the aristocracy, previously exempt from all taxation, had to pay the toll.

FISHERMEN'S BASTION ARCHITECTURE

Map p230 (Halászbástya; adult/child 500/250Ft; ⊙9am-7pm; 📮16, 16A, 116) The bastion is a neo-Gothic masquerade that most visitors (and many Hungarians) believe to be much older. But who cares? It looks medieval and offers among the best views in Budapest. Built as a viewing platform in 1905 by Frigyes Schulek, the architect behind Mathias Church, the bastion's name was taken from the medieval guild of fishermen responsible for defending this stretch of the castle wall. The seven gleaming white turrets represent the Magyar tribes that entered the Carpathian Basin in the late 9th century. In front of the bastion is an ornate equestrian monument to St Stephen by sculptor Alajos Stróbl.

MUSEUM OF MILITARY HISTORY MUSEUM

Map p230 (Hadtörténeti Múzeum; www.hm-him .hu, in Hungarian; I Tóth Árpád sétány 40; adult/ child 800/400Ft; ⊙10am-6pm Tue-Sun Apr-Sep, to 4pm Tue-Sun Oct-Mar; 📮16, 16A, 116) Loaded with weaponry dating from before the Turkish conquest, the Museum of Military History also does a good job with uniforms, medals, flags and battle-themed fine art. Exhibits focus particularly on the 1848–49 War of Independence and the Hungarian Royal Army under the command of Admiral Miklós Horthy (1918–43). Outside in the back courtyard is a mock-up of

---

TOP SIGHTS
MATTHIAS CHURCH

Parts of Castle Hill's landmark church date back some 500 years, notably the carvings above the southern entrance (Mary Portal). But basically the Matthias Church (Mátyás-templom) – named because King Matthias Corvinus married Beatrice here in 1474 – is a neo-Gothic creation designed by architect Frigyes Schulek in 1896.

The church has a delicate spire and colourful tiled roof, which a massive US$20-million restoration has restored to its 19th-century glory. The interior houses remarkable stained-glass windows, frescoes and glistening wall decorations by the Romantic painters Károly Lotz and Bertalan Székely. Organ concerts take place in the church on certain evenings (usually Friday and Saturday at 8pm), continuing a tradition dating from 1867 when Franz Liszt's *Hungarian Coronation Mass* was first played here for the coronation of Franz Joseph and Elizabeth.

Steps to the right of the main altar inside the church lead to the crypt. The **Matthias Church Collection of Ecclesiastical Art** (Mátyás-templom Egyházművészeti Gyűteménye), included in the church admission fee and keeping the same hours, contains ornate monstrances, reliquaries and chalices plus replicas of the Crown of St Stephen and other items of the coronation regalia.

DON'T MISS...

➡ Zsolnay-tiled roof
➡ Mary Portal
➡ Reproduced medieval rose window

PRACTICALITIES

➡ Map p230
➡ ☑355 5657
➡ www.matyas -templom.hu
➡ I Szentháromság tér 2
➡ adult/child 990/650Ft
➡ ⊙9am-5pm Mon-Fri, 9am-1pm Sat, 1-5pm Sun
➡ 📮16, 16A, 116

TOP SIGHTS
CASTLE HILL CAVES

Below Castle Hill is a 28km-long network of caves formed by thermal springs that contain a couple of attractions. The caves were used for military purposes during the Turkish occupation, as air-raid shelters during WWII, and as a secret military installation during the Cold War.

The **Buda Castle Labyrinth** (Budavári Labirintus; Map p230; www.labirintusbudapest.hu; I Úri utca 9; adult/child 2000/600Ft; ☉10am-7pm; 🚌16, 16A, 116) is a 1200m-long cave system 16m under the Castle District, looking at how the caves have been used since prehistoric times in five separate labyrinths encompassing 10 halls and galleries. It's good fun and a relief from the heat on a hot summer's day (it's always 20°C down here), but it can get scary if you lose your way. You can enter at any time throughout the night with a daytime ticket. There's a second entrance at Lovas út 4/a.

Far more instructive is the **Hospital in the Rock** (Sziklakórház; Map p230; www.hospitalintherock.com; I Lovas út 4/c; adult/child 3000/1500Ft; ☉10am-8pm Tue-Sun; 🚌16, 16A, 116), used extensively during WWII and again during the 1956 Uprising. It contains original medical equipment and 100 wax figures. The guided hour-long tour includes a walk through a Cold War nuclear bunker.

DON'T MISS...
→ Prehistoric labyrinth
→ Ápád vaults
→ WWII hospital
→ Cold War nuclear bunker

PRACTICALITIES
→ Map p230
→ 🚌16, 16A, 116

the electrified fence that once separated Hungary from Austria. Around the corner, along Anjou Bastion (Anjou bástya), with displays detailing the development of the cannon, lies the stone turban-topped grave of Abdurrahman, the last Turkish governor of Budapest, who was killed here in 1686 at the age of 70, on the day Buda was liberated. The tablet reads, 'He was a heroic foe. May he rest in peace.'

MARY MAGDALENE TOWER RUINS
Map p230 (Magdolna-torony; I Kapisztrán tér; 🚌16, 16A, 116) The big steeple on the south side of Kapisztrán tér, opposite the Military History Museum and visible for kilometres to the west of Castle Hill, is the reconstructed spire of an 18th-century church. The church, once reserved for Hungarian speakers in this district (German speakers worshipped at Matthias Church), was used as a mosque during the Turkish occupation and was destroyed in a 1944 air raid.

GOLDEN EAGLE PHARMACY MUSEUM MUSEUM
Map p230 (Arany Sas Patika; www.semmelweis .museum.hu; I Tárnok utca 18; adult/child 500/250Ft; ☉10.30am-6pm Tue-Sun Mar-Oct,

to 4pm Tue-Sun Nov-Feb; 🚌16, 16A, 116) Just north of Dísz tér on the site of Budapest's first pharmacy (1681), this branch of the Semmelweis Museum of Medical History (p66) contains an unusual mixture of displays, including a mock-up of an alchemist's laboratory with dried bats and tiny crocodiles in jars, and a small 'spice rack' used by 17th-century travellers for their daily fixes of curative herbs.

HOUSE OF HUNGARIAN WINES WINE CELLAR
Map p230 (Magyar Borok Háza; www.magyar borokhaza.com, in Hungarian; I Szentháromság tér 6; tastings 3/6 wines from 3000/4000Ft; ☉noon-8pm; 🚌16, 16A, 116) This wine centre next door to the Castle Hill branch of Tourinform (p210) offers a crash course in Hungarian viticulture with hundreds of wines from Hungary's five main regions and 22 districts to try. Be careful though; 'crash' may soon become the operative word. Do what the pros do and *try* not to swallow.

ROYAL WINE HOUSE & WINE CELLAR MUSEUM WINE CELLAR, MUSEUM
Map p230 (Királyi Borház és Pincemúzeum; www .kiralyiborok.com; I Szent György tér, Nyugati

sétány; adult/child 1300/800Ft; ☉noon-8pm; 🚇16, 16A, 116) Housed in what once were the royal cellars below Szent György tér dating back to the 13th century, this 1400-sq-metre attraction offers a more commercial approach to Hungarian wine. Tastings cost 1920/2550/3830Ft for three/four/six wines. You can also elect to try various types of Hungarian champagne and *pálinka* (fruit brandy). There's a large shop here.

MEDIEVAL JEWISH PRAYER HOUSE
SYNAGOGUE

Map p230 (Középkori Zsidó Imaház; www.btm.hu; ❙ Táncsics Mihály utca 26; adult/child 600/350Ft; ☉10am-5pm Tue-Sun May-Oct; 🚇16, 16A, 116) With sections dating from the late 14th century, this tiny ancient house of worship contains documents and items linked to the Jewish community of Buda, as well as Gothic stone carvings and tombstones.

MUSIC HISTORY MUSEUM
MUSEUM

Map p230 (Zenetörténeti Múzeum; www.zti.hu; ❙ Táncsics Mihály utca 7; adult/child 600/250Ft; ☉10am-4pm Tue-Sun; 🚇16, 16A, 116) Housed in an 18th-century palace with a lovely courtyard, this wonderful little museum, which has reopened after a protracted refurbishment, traces the development of music and musical instruments in Hungary from the 18th century till today in five exhibition rooms. There are rooms devoted to the work of Béla Bartók, Franz Liszt and Joseph Haydn, with lots of instruments and original scores and manuscripts.

TELEPHONY MUSEUM
MUSEUM

Map p230 (Telefónia Múzeum; www.postamuzeum .hu; ❙ Úri utca 49 & Országház utca 30; adult/child 750/375Ft; ☉10am-4pm Tue-Sun; 🚇16, 16A, 116) This museum, set within a lovely backstreet garden, documents the history of the telephone in Hungary since 1881, when the world's first switchboard – a Rotary 7A1, still working and the centrepiece of the exhibition – was set up in Budapest. Other exhibits pay tribute to Tivadar Puskás, a Hungarian associate of Thomas Edison, and cover the latter's fleeting visit to Budapest in 1891. Enter from Országház utca 30 on Saturday and Sunday.

☉ Víziváros

CLARK ÁDÁM TÉR
SQUARE

Map p230 (🚇16, 86) Víziváros begins at 'Adam Clark Sq', named after the 19th-century Scottish engineer who supervised the building of the Széchenyi Chain Bridge, which leads from the square, and who designed the all-important tunnel *(alagút)* under Castle Hill, which took just eight months to carve out of the limestone in 1853. What looks like an elongated concrete doughnut hidden in the bushes to the south is the **0km stone**. All Hungarian roads to and from the capital are measured from this spot.

FŐ UTCA
STREET

Map p230 (🚇86) Fő utca is the arrow-straight 'main street' running from Clark Ádám tér through Víziváros; not surprisingly, it dates from Roman times. At the former **Capuchin church** (❙ Fő utca 30-32), used as a mosque during the Turkish occupation, you can see the remains of an Islamic-style ogee-arched door and window on the southern side. Around the corner there's the seal of King Matthias Corvinus – a raven with a ring in its beak – and a little square called Corvin tér with the delightful **Lajos Fountain** (Lajos kútja) dating from 1904. The Eclectic building on the north side at No 8 is the **Buda Concert Hall** (p62). To the north the **Iron Stump** (Vastuskó; cnr ❙ Vám utca & Iskola utca) is an odd-looking tree trunk into which itinerant artisans and merchants would drive a nail to mark their visit in medieval times.

BATTHYÁNY TÉR
SQUARE

Map p230 (Ⓜ M2 Batthyány tér) Some 500m to the north is Batthyány tér, the centre of Víziváros and the best place to take pictures of the photogenic Parliament building across the Danube. In the centre of this rather shabby square is the entrance to both the M2 metro and the HÉV suburban line to Szentendre. On the southern side is the 18th-century baroque **Church of St Anne** (Szent Ana templom; ❙ Batthyány tér 7), with one of the most eye-catching interiors of any baroque church in Budapest, including a magnificent late-18th-century pulpit and organ.

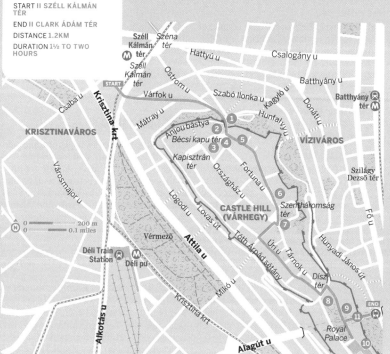

Neighbourhood Walk
Castle Hill

➡️ Walk up Várfok utca from Széll Kálmán tér to ① **Vienna Gate** (Bécsi kapu), the medieval entrance to the Old Town. The large building to the west with the superbly coloured majolica-tiled roof contains the ② **National Archives** (Országos Levéltár; 1920). To the west of Béci kapu tér (Vienna Gate Sq – a weekend market in the Middle Ages) there's an attractive group of ③ **burgher houses**.

Narrow ④ **Táncsics Mihály utca** is full of little houses painted in lively hues and adorned with statues. In many courtyard entrances you'll see *sedilia* – 13th-century stone niches perhaps used as merchant stalls.

Further along the road to the southeast at Táncsics Mihály utca 9 is the ⑤ **Lajos Kossuth prison** where the leader of the 1848–49 War of Independence was imprisoned from 1837 to 1840.

The controversial ⑥ **Hilton Budapest**, incorporating parts of a Middle-Ages Dominican church and a baroque Jesuit college, is further south.

Southeast, in the centre of ⑦ **I Szentháromság tér** there's a statue of the Holy Trinity (Szentháromság szobor), another one of the 'plague pillars' erected by grateful (and healthy) Buda citizens in the early 18th century.

Walking along Úri utca south to Dísz tér you'll come face to face with the bombed-out ⑧ **former Ministry of Defence**, a casualty of WWII, and NATO's supposed nuclear target for Budapest during the Cold War. Further south on the left is the restored ⑨ **Sándor Palace** (Sándor palota), now housing the offices of the President of the Republic.

Just south of the upper Sikló funicular station are the ⑩ **Habsburg Steps**, a 1903 ornamental gateway leading to the Royal Palace. The nearby ⑪ **Sikló** (funicular) descends to I Clark Ádám tér.

NAGY IMRE TÉR   SQUARE

Map p230 (**M**M2 Batthyány tér) A couple of streets to the northwest is Nagy Imre tér, with the former **Military Court of Justice** (II Fő utca 70-78) on the northern side. Imre Nagy and others were tried and sentenced to death here in 1958 for their role in the 1956 Uprising (p183). It was also the site of the notorious **Fő utca prison**, where many other victims of the Communist regime were incarcerated and tortured.

FOUNDRY MUSEUM   MUSEUM

Map p230 (Öntödei Múzeum; www.omm.hu, in Hungarian; II Bem József utca 20; adult/child 500/250Ft; ⊙9am-5pm Tue-Sun; 🚊4, 6; 🚋86) This museum – a lot more interesting than it sounds – is housed in the Ganz Machine Works foundry that was in use until the 1960s, and the massive ladles and cranes still stand, anxiously awaiting employment. Alas, time has frozen them all. The exhibits also include cast-iron stoves, bells and street furniture. Have a look at the church a short distance to the east across pedestrianised Ganz utca: it's the Greek Catholic **Chapel of St Florian** (Szent Flórián kápolna; II Fő utca 88), built in 1760 and dedicated to the patron saint of fire-fighters.

MILLENNIUM PARK   PARK

Map p230 (Millenáris Park; www.millenaris.hu; II Kis Rókus utca 16-20; ⊙6am-1am; **M**M2 Széll Kálmán tér; 🚊4, 6) Millennium Park is an attractive landscaped complex behind the huge Mammut shopping mall complex, comprising fountains, ponds, little bridges, a theatre, a gallery and, for kids, the wonderful **Palace of Wonders** (Csodák Palotája; www.csodapalota.hu; II Kis Rókus utca 16-20, Bldg D; adult/child 1400/1100Ft; ⊙9am-5pm Mon-Fri, 10am-6pm Sat & Sun). It's an interactive playhouse for children of all ages with 'smart' toys and puzzles, most of which have a scientific bent. **Millennium Theatre**, where events take place, is also here. You can also enter the park from Fény utca 20-22 and Lövőház utca 37.

KIRÁLY BATHS   THERMAL BATHS

Map p230 (Király Gyógyfürdő; 🕿202 3688; www .budapestgyogyfurdoi.hu; II Fő utca 84; admission 2200Ft; ⊙men 9am-8pm Tue & Thu-Sat, women 7am-6pm Mon & Wed, mixed 9am-8pm Sun; 🚋86) The four pools here, with water temperatures of between 26°C and 40°C, are genuine Turkish baths erected in 1570 and have a wonderful skylit central dome (though the place is begging for a renovation). Be advised that during the time of research there was some discussion that the Király Baths would have mixed admission every day of opening; check the website and pack a swimsuit.

✖ EATING

The Castle District is a picturesque and romantic neighbourhood in which to break bread, but many – though not all – of the restaurants up here are touristy and overpriced. A better idea is to take the Sikló funicular down to Víziváros and choose from the recommended eateries on or just off I Fő utca.

✖ Castle Hill

TOP CHOICE VÁR: A SPEIZ   HUNGARIAN, INTERNATIONAL €€

Map p230 (🕿488 7416; www.varaspeiz.hu; I Hess András tér 6; mains 2400-4600Ft; ⊙noon-1am; 🚋16, 16A, 116) This romantic bistro just opposite the Hilton Budapest is a very welcome addition to the Castle Hill dining experience. Vár: a Speiz takes its food very seriously indeed and the five-course tasting menu is memorable.

RIVALDA   INTERNATIONAL €€

Map p230 (🕿489 0236; www.rivalda.net; I Színház utca 5-9; mains 3100-5800Ft; 🚋16, 16A, 116) An international cafe-restaurant in a former convent next to the National Dance Theatre, Rivalda has a thespian theme, delightful garden courtyard and excellent service. The menu changes frequently, and the wine list is among the best. There's a four-course set menu for 13,000/9800Ft with/without wine.

CAFÉ PIERROT   INTERNATIONAL €€€

Map p230 (🕿375 6971; www.pierrot.hu; I Fortuna utca 14; mains 3980-6440Ft; 🚋16, 16A, 116) This very stylish and long-established cafe-cum-bar-cum-restaurant is one of the very few places to be recommended on Castle Hill. The decor is, well, clownish, and there's live piano music nightly and garden seating in the warmer months.

21 MAGYAR VENDÉGLŐ   HUNGARIAN €€

Map p230 (🕿202 2113; www.21restaurant.hu; I Fortuna utca 21; mains 3600-4900Ft; 🚋16, 16A,

116) This new place with a less-than-inspiring name (at least you get the address and the cuisine in one go) has some wonderfully innovative modern takes on traditional Hungarian. Super old/new decor, friendly service and they bottle their very own wine.

FORTUNA ÖNKISZOLGÁLÓ HUNGARIAN €

Map p230 (Fortune Self-Service Restaurant; I Fortuna utca 4; mains 650-980Ft; ⊘11.30am-2.30pm Mon-Fri; ⊞16, 16A, 116) You'll find cheap and quick weekday lunches in a place you'd least expect it – on Castle Hill – at this very basic but clean and cheerful self-service restaurant. Reach it via the stairs on the left side as you enter the Fortuna Passage (and note the *sedile* – medieval stone niche – to the right as you enter).

VÖRÖS ÖRDÖG HUNGARIAN €€

Map p230 (vorosordogbt@freemail.hu; I Országház utca 20; mains 2300-3900Ft; ⊘11am-10pm; ⊞16, 116) The 'Red Devil' is a relatively inexpensive eatery on Castle Hill with a cellar, a delightful courtyard and traditional Hungarian dishes like sautéed goose liver and *pörkölt* (what you might call goulash). There's also a cafe and a set menu for two people for 3500Ft.

✘ Víziváros

TOP CHOICE CSALOGÁNY 26 INTERNATIONAL €€

Map p230 (☑201 7892; www.csalogany26.hu; I Csalogány utca 26; mains 3600-4000Ft; ⊘noon-3pm & 7pm-midnight Tue-Sat; ⋈M2 Batthyány tér; ⊞39) Judged by Hungary's most respected food guide to be the best restaurant in town, this intimate restaurant with the unimaginative name and decor turns its imagination to its superb food. Try the suckling *mangalica* (a kind of pork) with Savoy cabbage (4000Ft) or the braised kid with polenta (2200Ft). A three-course set lunch is a budget-pleasing 2500Ft; four-/eight-course tasting menus are 8000/12,000Ft.

DÉRYNÉ BISZTRÓ HUNGARIAN, BISTRO €€

Map p230 (☑225 1407; www.cafederyne.hu, in Hungarian; I Krisztina tér 3; mains 1850-4950Ft; ⊘7.30am-midnight Sun-Wed, to 1am Thu-Sat; ⊞16, 105, 178; ⊞18) What was until not too long ago a very untouristed traditional cafe near the entrance to the Alagút (the tunnel running under Castle Hill) has metamorphosed into a beautiful bistro with

excellent breakfast (1850Ft to 2390Ft) and more substantial meals throughout the day. Great horseshoe-shaped bar and music; lovely terrace; open kitchen.

HORGÁSZTANYA VENDÉGLŐ FISH €€

Map p230 (www.horgasztanyavendeglo.hu; II Fő utca 20; mains 2190-2850Ft; ⊞86) A classic fish restaurant by the Danube where soup is served in bowls, pots or kettles, and your carp, catfish or trout might be prepared Baja-, Tisza- or more spicy Szeged-style.

SEOUL HOUSE KOREAN €€

Map p230 (I Fő utca 8; dishes 2500-5500Ft; ⊘noon-3pm & 6-11pm Mon-Sat; ⊞86) This place serves pretty authentic Korean food, from barbecue grills (from 3500Ft) and *bibimbap* (rice served in a sizzling pot topped with thinly sliced beef and cooked with preserved vegetables, then bound with a raw egg and flavoured with chilli-laced soy paste; 2700Ft) to *kimchi* (pickled spicy cabbage) dishes. Not the most atmospheric place in town and service can be less than welcoming but, well, that's part of the experience.

MEZZO MUSIC RESTAURANT HUNGARIAN €€

Map p230 (☑356 3565; www.mezzorestaurant.hu; XII Maros utca 28; mains 3100-4800Ft; ⋈M2 Széll Kálmán tér; ⊞128) A glamorous bistro between Széll Kálmán tér and Déli train station, Mezzo has upmarket Hungarian dishes and nightly jazz (7.30pm) on the menu. The decor, varying shades of brown with the slightest of Asia touches, is restful.

KACSA HUNGARIAN €€

Map p230 (www.kacsavendeglo.hu; II Fő utca 75; mains 3800-5100Ft; ⊞86) The 'Duck' is the place to go, well, 'quackers', though you need not restrict yourself to the eight dishes with a bill (4400Ft to 5100Ft); they do a couple things prepared from Hungarian grey-horned cattle, for example. It's a fairly elegant place dating back 100 years, with art on the walls and piano and violin music in the evening, so dress appropriately. Fresh ingredients but somewhat stuffy service and pricey wines.

MINI BISTRO INTERNATIONAL, BISTRO €€

Map p230 (☑225 3794; www.theminibar.hu; I Krisztina tér 3; mains 3150-4950Ft; ⊘noon-1am Mon-Wed, to 2.30am Thu-Sat; ⊞16, 105, 178; ⊞18) Little sister to Déryné Bisztró (p59) and just next door, Mini has learned a thing or three from her older sibling and is pulling in the punters with rocking interior design, nightly live music and an international menu prepared by an American chef. Set lunch is just 990Ft.

TOLDI KONYHÁJA HUNGARIAN €

Map p230 (I Batthyány utca 14; mains 980-1590Ft; ⊗11am-4pm Mon-Fri; 🍴; MM2 Batthyány tér; 🚊39) This little eatery west of Fő utca is the place to come if you're in search of Hungarian comfort food at lunchtime on weekdays. Unusually for this kind of place, 'Toldi's Kitchen' has on offer about a half-dozen *real* vegetarian dishes (1100Ft to 1290Ft) to choose from.

CARNE DI HALL STEAKHOUSE €€

Map p230 (📞201 8137; carnedihall@gmail.com; I Bem rakpart 20; mains 2250-4100Ft; MM2 Batthyány tér; 🚊39) Not just steaks but very meaty indeed in a nation of ubercarnivores, Carne di Hall also dabbles in venison and goose liver. It's in a cellar with outside seating facing the Danube. A two-/three-course lunch is 990/1290Ft.

NAGYI PALACSINTÁZÓJA HUNGARIAN €

Map p230 (I Hattyú utca 16; pancakes 130-640Ft, set menus 760-950Ft; ⊗24hr; MM2 Széll Kálmán tér) 'Granny's Palacsinta Place' serves Hungarian pancakes – both savoury and sweet – round the clock and is always packed. There are other branches with the same prices and hours, including one on **Batthyány tér** (Map p230; I Batthyány tér 5; MM2 Batthyány tér).

PATER MARCUS BELGIAN €€

Map p230 (www.patermarcus.hu, in Hungarian; I Apor Péter utca 1; mains 1150-2590Ft; 🚊86) Located 50m from Chain Bridge, this basement pub-restaurant done up like a monastery is short on monks but heavy on mussels and fries. Try one of the seven flavoured Belgian beers on offer; there's another 140 brews available by the bottle.

SZENT JUPÁT HUNGARIAN €€

Map p230 (www.stjupat.hu; II Dékán utca 3; mains 1790-3400Ft; 🍴; MM2 Széll Kálmán tér) It's not as cheap as it once was and no longer burns the midnight oil to the wee hours, but

Szent Jupát is still a solid choice for hearty Hungarian fare – consider splitting a dish with a friend. There's a trio of vegetarian choices as well. Set lunch is 990Ft. It's opposite the Fény utca market; enter from II Retek utca 16.

MONGOLIAN BARBECUE ASIAN, BUFFET €€

Map p230 (www.mongolianbbq.hu; XII Márvány utca 19/a; buffet before/after 5pm & weekends 3490/4990Ft; ⊗noon-5pm & 6pm-midnight; 🚊105; 🚌61) Just south of Széll Kálmán tér, this is one of those all-you-can-eat Asian-ish places where you choose the raw ingredients and legions of cooks stir-fry it for you. The difference here is that as much beer, wine and sangria you can sink is included in the price. During summer there's also seating in an attractive, tree-filled courtyard.

ÉDEN VEGETARIAN €

Map p230 (www.edenetterem.hu; I Iskola utca 31; mains 590-890Ft; ⊗8am-9pm Mon-Thu, to 6pm Fri, 11am-9pm Sun, closed Sat; 🍴; 🚌86) Located in an early-19th-century townhouse just below Castle Hill, this self-service place offers stodgy but healthy vegetarian platters and ragouts without a single no-no (fat, preservatives, MSG, white sugar etc). Seating is in the main dining room on the ground floor or, in warmer months, in the atrium courtyard or terrace.

DURAN SANDWICHES €

Map p230 (www.duran.hu; II Retek utca 18; sandwiches 170-300Ft; ⊗8am-6pm Mon-Fri, to 1pm Sat; MM2 Széll Kálmán tér) Just behind the Mammut shopping mall in Buda, this place offers an alternative to the fast-food places in the mall.

ANTIGIANA GELATI ICE CREAM €

Map p230 (XII Csaba utca 8; per scoop 330Ft; ⊗10.30am-7pm Tue-Fri, to 7.30pm Sat & Sun; MM2 Széll Kálmán tér; 🚊128) We're told by readers that this place sells the best shop-made ice cream and sorbet in Buda, and with flavours like fig, pomegranate and gorgonzola-walnut, they're also the most unusual.

🍷 DRINKING & NIGHTLIFE

🍸 Castle Hill

TOP CHOICE RUSZWURM CUKRÁSZDA CAFE
Map p230 (www.ruszwurm.hu; I Szentháromság utca 7; ⊙10am-7pm; 🚌16, 16A, 116) This diminutive cafe dating from 1827 is the perfect place for coffee and cakes (350Ft to 550Ft) in the Castle District, though it can get pretty crowded. Indeed, in high season it's almost always impossible to get a seat.

WALTZER CAFÉ CAFE
Map p230 (www.waltzercafe.hu, in Hungarian; I Táncsics Mihály utca 12; ⊙10.30am-6.30pm Tue-Sun; 🚌16, 16A, 116) This sweet and friendly little cafe just opposite the Music History Museum (p56) is a great spot for a bit of R&R while sightseeing. The choice of South American, African and Asian coffees is enviable.

OSCAR AMERICAN BAR COCKTAIL BAR
Map p230 (www.oscarbar.hu, in Hungarian; I Ostrom utca 14; ⊙5pm-2am Mon-Thu, to 4am Fri & Sat; Ⓜ︎M2 Széll Kálmán tér) The decor is cinema inspired (film memorabilia on the wood-panelled walls, leather directors chairs) and the beautiful crowd often act like they're on camera. Not to worry, the potent cocktails – from daiquiris and cosmopolitans to mojitos – go down a treat. There's music most nights.

🍸 Víziváros

LÁNCHÍD SÖRÖZŐ BAR
Map p230 (www.lanchidsorozo.hu; I Fő utca 4; 🚌86; 🚋19) The 'Chain Bridge Pub', at the southern end of Fő utca, has a wonderful retro Magyar feel to it, with old movie posters and advertisements on the walls and red-checked cloths on the tables. Friendly service.

TOP CHOICE BAMBI PRESSZÓ CAFE
Map p230 (II Frankel Leó út 2-4; ⊙7am-10pm; 🚌86) The words 'Bambi' and 'modern' do not make comfortable bedfellows; nothing about this place (named after a Communist-era soft drink) has changed since the 1960s. And that's just the way the crowd here likes it. Surly, set-it-down-with-a-crash service

completes the distorted picture. Outside seating in the warmer months.

ANGELIKA KÁVÉHÁZ CAFE
Map p230 (www.angelikacafe.hu; I Batthyány tér 7; ⊙9am-midnight Mon-Sat, to 11pm Sun; Ⓜ︎M2 Batthyány tér) Attached to an 18th-century church, Angelika is a charming cafe with a raised terrace. The more substantial dishes are just so-so; come here for the cakes (420Ft to 450Ft) and the views across the square to the Danube and Parliament.

AUGUSZT CUKRÁSZDA CAFE
Map p230 (www.augusztcukraszda.hu, in Hungarian; II Fény utca 8; ⊙10am-6pm Tue-Fri, from 11am Sat; Ⓜ︎M2 Széll Kálmán tér) Tucked away behind the Fény utca market and Mammut shopping mall complex, this is the original Auguszt (there are newer branches) and only sells its own shop-made cakes (200Ft to 500Ft), pastries and biscuits. There's seating on the 1st floor.

CHAMPS SPORT BAR BAR
Map p230 (www.champsbuda.hu; II Erőd utca 22; 🚌4, 6) Established by a group of Olympic medallists (a swimmer, runner, pentathlete, kayaker and motor racer), Champs is the place for sports fans and the vicarious, with 15 LCD screens. There's a wide choice of low-fat 'fitness meals' along with the less healthy favourites of armchair athletes.

DPU CHACHACHA CLUB
Map p230 (www.dpu.hu; I Krisztina körút 37; ⊙10pm-6am Fri & Sat; Ⓜ︎M2 Déli pályaudvar) Housed in the former self-service cafeteria in Déli train station, this retro-style club hosts house DJs at the weekend.

☆ ENTERTAINMENT

BUDAVÁR CULTURAL CENTRE CONCERT VENUE, DANCE
Map p230 (Budavári Művelődési Háza; 📞201 0324; www.bem6.hu, in Hungarian; Bem rakpart 6; 🚌86) This cultural centre just below Buda Castle has frequent programs for both children and adults, including the excellent Sebő Klub Táncház the first Sunday afternoon of every month.

MARCZIBÁNYI TÉR CULTURAL CENTRE CONCERT VENUE, DANCE
Map p230 (Marczibányi téri Művelődési Központ; 📞212 2820; www.marczi.hu, in Hungarian; II Marczibányi tér 5/a; 🚌4, 6) This venue has

Hungarian, Moldavian and Slovakian dance and music every Thursday at 8pm and *táncház* (folk music and dance) every second Sunday from 2pm.

BUDA CONCERT HALL   CONCERT VENUE, DANCE

Map p230 (Budai Vigadó; ☏225 6049; http://regi .hagyomanyokhaza.hu; I Corvin tér 8; ☒86; ☒19) The 30 artistes of the Hungarian State Folk Ensemble (Magyar Állami Népi Együttes) perform at this venue at 8pm on Tuesday and Thursday from May to early October, with occasional performances at other times during the rest of the year.

NATIONAL DANCE THEATRE   DANCE

Map p230 (Nemzeti Táncszínház; ☏201 4407, box office 375 8649; www.nemzetitancszinhaz.hu, in Hungarian; I Színház utca 1-3; tickets 650-4500Ft; ☒16, 16A, 116) The National Dance Theatre on Castle Hill hosts at some point every troupe in the city, including the national ballet company and the **Budapest Dance Theatre** (www.budapestdancetheatre.hu), one of the most exciting contemporary troupes in the city.

JENŐ HUBAY MUSIC HALL   CONCERT VENUE, THEATRE

Map p230 (☏457 8080; www.hubayzeneterem .hu; I Bem rakpart 11; tickets 2800Ft; ☒86; ☒19) The recently renovated 19th-century music hall attached to the Hotel Victoria (p159) now serves as a small concert venue and theatre. It's a wonderfully intimate place to hear a concert as there are only 70 seats.

SHOPPING

Castle Hill

HAND-MADE BAZAR   HANDICRAFTS

Map p230 (www.schmici.hu; Fortuna köz off Hess András tér 4; ◷10am-6pm; ☒16, 16A, 116) This attractive little shop conveniently located on Castle Hill sells Hungarica and quality Hungarian handicrafts.

HEREND   PORCELAIN, GLASSWARE

Map p230 (www.herend.com; I Szentháromság utca 5; ◷10am-6pm Mon-Fri, to 4pm Sat & Sun; ☒16, 16A, 116) For both contemporary and traditional fine porcelain, there is no other place to go but Herend, Hungary's answer to Wedgwood. Among the most popular motifs produced by the company is the Victoria pattern of butterflies and wildflowers designed for the lemon-lipped British queen during the mid-19th century. Closes at 2pm on weekends from November to March.

Víziváros

MESTER PORTA   MUSIC

Map p230 (www.etnofon.hu; I Corvin tér 7; ◷10am-6pm Mon-Fri; ☒86) This wonderful shop on the east side of Corvin tér has CDs and DVDs of Hungarian and other folk music as well as musical instruments, scores and books.

BORTÁRSASÁG   WINE

Map p230 (www.bortarsasag.hu; I Batthyány utca 59; ◷10am-7pm Mon-Fri, to 6pm Sat; ⓂM2 Széll Kálmán tér) Once known as the Budapest Wine Society, this place has a half-dozen retail outlets with an exceptional selection of Hungarian wines. No one, but no one, knows Hungarian wines like these guys do.

TOP CHOICE/HEREND VILLAGE POTTERY   PORCELAIN, HOMEWARES

Map p230 (www.herendimajolika.hu; II Bem rak-part 37; ◷9am-5pm Tue-Fri, 9am-noon Sat; ⓂM2 Batthyány tér) An alternative to delicate Herend porcelain is the hard-wearing Herend pottery and dishes sold here, decorated with bold fruit patterns. You can also enter this shop from II Fő utca 61.

SPORTHORGÁSZ   FISHING EQUIPMENT

Map p230 (Sport Angler; www.sport-horgasz.hu, in Hungarian; II Bem József utca 8; ◷9am-5pm Mon-Fri, 9am-1pm Sat; ☒86; ☒4, 6) This is the place to come for rods, reels, flies and anything else it takes to get you out fishing.

Gellért Hill & Tabán

Neighbourhood Top Five

1 Taking in incomparable views of Castle Hill, the Danube and Pest from **Liberty Monument** (p65), then moving on to any of those three to look back at Miss Liberty herself, proclaiming freedom throughout the city.

2 Soaking in the art nouveau **Gellért Baths** (p66), which has been likened to taking a bath in a cathedral.

3 Being moved by the **former Swedish Embassy** (p67) from where Raoul Wallenberg and others rescued thousands of Hungarian Jews.

4 Reliving the not-so-distant past by visiting **Memento Park** (p68), a 'cemetery' of Communist monuments.

5 Learning more about Hungary's unsung hero, Dr Ignác Semmelweis, at the **Semmelweis Museum of Medical History** (p66).

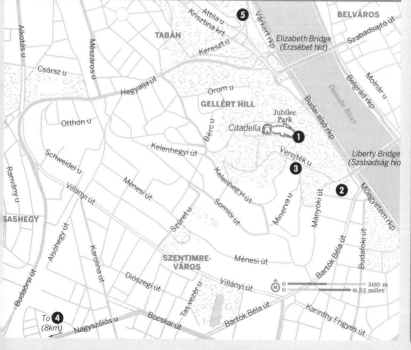

For more detail of this area, see Map p 236 ➡

Lonely Planet's Top Tip

A couple of thermal spas in this district make good use of the hot springs gushing from deep below, including the Gellért Baths (p66) and the Rudas Baths (p66). If you don't like getting wet or you don't have the time, do what locals do and try a 'drinking cure' by visiting the **Pump Room** (Ivócsarnok; ⊙11am-6pm Mon, Wed & Fri, 7am-2pm Tue & Thu), which is just below the western end of Elizabeth Bridge. A half-litre/litre of the hot, smelly water, which is meant to cure whatever ails you, is just 60/30Ft.

Best Places to Eat

⇒ Tabáni Terasz (p68)
⇒ Hemingway (p69)
⇒ Marcello (p69)

For reviews, see p67 ⇒

Best Places to Drink

⇒ Hadik Kávéház(p69)
⇒ Café Ponyvaregény (p69)
⇒ Kisrabló Pub (p69)

For reviews, see p69 ⇒

Best Places to Relax

⇒ Gellért Baths (p66)
⇒ Rudas Baths (p66)
⇒ Tranzit Art Café (p69)

For reviews, see p66 ⇒

Explore: Gellért Hill & Tabán

Gellért Hill (Gellért-hegy) is a 235m-high rocky hill southeast of Castle Hill. Crowned with a fortress of sorts and the Liberty Monument, it is Budapest's unofficial symbol. You can't beat the views of the Royal Palace or the Danube and its fine bridges from Gellért Hill, and Jubilee Park on the south side is an ideal spot for a picnic.

The Tabán, the leafy area between Gellért and Castle Hills, and stretching northwest towards Déli train station, is associated with the Serbs, who settled here after fleeing from the Turks in the early 18th century. Plaques on I Döbrentei utca mark the water level of the Danube during two devastating floods in 1775 and 1838 that hit the area particularly hard.

The Tabán later became known for its restaurants and wine gardens – a kind of Montmartre for Budapest. Most of these burned to the ground at the turn of the 20th century. All that remains is a lovely little renovated building with a fountain designed by Miklós Ybl in 1878, known as the **Castle Garden Palace** (Várkert Palota; I Ybl Miklós tér 9), which was once a pump house for Castle Hill and is now a conference/events venue; try the door to see if it's open. The steps and archways across the road are all that is left of the Castle Bazaar (Várbazár) pleasure park.

Local Life

⇒ **Views** If you walk west for a few minutes along Citadella sétány north of the Citadella (p65) itself, you'll come to a lookout with the best vantage point in Budapest.

⇒ **Táncház** For the best *táncház* (traditional Hungarian music and dance) in town head for the Municipal Cultural House (p70).

⇒ **Architecture** Not just a great place to soak away your cares and aches, the Rudas Baths (p66) boasts some of the best Turkish architecture in Hungary.

Getting There & Away

⇒ **Bus** XI Szent Gellért tér can be reached from V Ferenciek tere in Pest on bus 7, and from points in Óbuda or south Buda on bus 86. Bus 27 runs almost to the top of Gellért Hill from XI Móricz Zsigmond körtér.

⇒ **Tram** XI Szent Gellért tér is linked to Déli station by tram 18, and to I Batthyány tér by tram 19. Trams 47 and 49 cross over to Pest and follow the Little Ring Rd from the same place. Trams 18 and 47 run south along Fehérvári út – useful for several folk-music venues mentioned in this chapter.

CITADELLA & LIBERTY MONUMENT

The Citadella atop Gellért Hill is a fortress that never saw a battle. Built by the Habsburgs after the 1848–49 War of Independence to defend the city from further insurrection, by the time it was ready in 1851 the political climate had changed and the Citadella had become obsolete.

Today the Citadella contains some big guns and dusty displays in the central courtyard, and the hokey **1944 Bunker Waxworks** (1944 Bunkér Panoptikum) inside a bunker used during WWII, and a hotel-cum-hostel (p160). Take a look from the outside.

Just east of the Citadella is the **Liberty Monument** (Szabadság-szobor), the lovely lady with a palm frond in her outstretched arms, proclaiming freedom throughout the city from atop Gellért Hill. Standing 14m high, she was erected in 1947 in tribute to the Soviet soldiers who died liberating Budapest in 1945. But the victims' names (previously in Cyrillic letters on the plinth) and the statues of the Soviet soldiers were removed in 1992 and sent to what is now called Memento Park (p68). In fact, the monument had been designed by the politically 'flexible' sculptor Zsigmond Kisfaludi Strobl (1884–1975) much earlier for the ultraright government of Admiral Miklós Horthy. After the war, when pro-Communist monuments were in short supply, Kisfaludi Strobl passed it off as a memorial to the Soviets.

To reach Gellért Hill from Pest, cross Elizabeth Bridge and take the stairs leading up behind the St Gellért Monument or cross Liberty Bridge and follow Verejték utca (Perspiration St) through the park starting at the Cave Chapel. Bus 27 runs almost to the top of the hill from Móricz Zsigmond körtér.

DON'T MISS...

➡ Liberty Monument

➡ Citadella (from outside)

➡ The views from both

PRACTICALITIES

➡ Map p236

➡ www.citadella.hu

➡ XIII Gellért-hegy

➡ Waxworks: admission 1200Ft

➡ ⊘9am-8pm May-Sep, to 5pm Oct-Apr

➡ 🚌27

 **SIGHTS**

CITADELLA & LIBERTY MONUMENT FORTRESS, MONUMENT

See p65.

RUDAS BATHS THERMAL BATHS, POOLS

Map p236 (Rudas Gyógyfürdő; ☑356 1010; www
.budapestgyogyfurdoi.hu; Döbrentei tér 9;
admission 2800Ft; ⊘men 6am-8pm Mon & Wed-
Fri, women 6am-8pm Tue, mixed 9pm-4am Fri,
6am-8pm & 10pm-4am Sat, 6am-8pm Sun; ⊡18,
19; ⊡7, 86) Built in 1566, these recently
renovated baths are the most Turkish of
all in Budapest, with an octagonal pool,
domed cupola with coloured glass and
massive columns. It's a real zoo on mixed
weekend nights, when bathing costumes
are compulsory. You can enter the renovated
swimming pool (admission with locker/cabin
1600/2000Ft; ⊘6am-6pm Mon-Fri, to 5pm Sat &
Sun) at the Rudas Baths separately without
using the thermal bath facilities if you're
more interested in swimming than soaking.

CAVE CHAPEL CHURCH

Map p236 (Sziklakápolna; adult/child 500/400Ft;
XI Szent Gellért rakpart 1; ⊘10am-7pm; ⊡47, 49)
This chapel is on a small hill directly north
of the landmark art nouveau Danubius
Hotel Gellért (p159). The chapel was built
into a cave in 1926 and was the seat of the
Pauline order in Hungary until 1951 when
the priests were arrested and imprisoned
by the Communists, and the cave sealed off.
It was reopened and reconsecrated in 1992.
Behind the chapel there is a monastery,
with neo-Gothic turrets that are visible
from Liberty Bridge. There's a five-minute
introductory film and audioguide too. Mass
is said most days at 4.30pm.

SEMMELWEIS MUSEUM OF MEDICAL HISTORY MUSEUM

Map p236 (Semmelweis Orvostörténeti Múzeum;
www.semmelweis.museum.hu; I Apród utca 1-3;
adult/child 700/350Ft; ⊘10.30am-6pm Tue-Sun
mid-Mar-Oct, to 4pm Tue-Sun Nov-mid-Mar; ⊡19)
This museum traces the history of medicine
from Greco-Roman times through medical
tools, instruments and photographs; yet
another antique pharmacy also makes an
appearance. Ignác Semmelweis (1818–65),
the 'saviour of mothers', who discovered the
cause of puerperal (childbirth) fever, was
born in this house and much is made of his
life and works.

◉ **TOP SIGHTS**
GELLÉRT BATHS

Soaking in thermal waters of the art nouveau Gellért
Baths (Gellért Gyógyfürdő), open to men and women
in separate sections Monday to Saturday but mixed on
Sundays (bathing suit required), has been likened to
bathing in a cathedral. The eight thermal pools range in
temperature from 26°C to 38°C, and the water – high in
calcium, magnesium and hydrogen carbonate – is good
for joint pains, arthritis and blood circulation.

In most other baths nowadays you are given an
electronic bracelet which directs you to and then opens
your locker or cabin. At the time of research the Gellért
was still doing it the old way, meaning you find a free
locker or cabin yourself. After getting changed in (or
beside) it, call the attendant, who will lock it for you
and hand you a numbered tag. Note: In order to prevent
theft should you lose or misplace the tag, the number
is not the same as the one on the locker, so commit the
locker number to memory.

The swimming pools at the Gellért are always
mixed. The indoor ones, open year-round, are the most
beautiful in Budapest; the outdoor one (open May to
September) has a wave machine and nicely landscaped
gardens.

DON'T MISS...

➡ Art nouveau mosa-
ics and statues
➡ Glass-domed main
swimming pool
➡ Wave machine

PRACTICALITIES

➡ Map p236
➡ ☑466 6166
➡ www.budapest
gyogyfurdoi.hu
➡ XI Kelenhegyi út
2-4
➡ locker before/after
5pm 3800/2800Ft,
cabin 4100/3000Ft
➡ ⊘6am-8pm
➡ ⊡18, 19, 47, 49
➡ ⊡7, 86

RAOUL WALLENBERG, HERO FOR ALL TIMES

The **former Swedish Embassy** (Map p236; Minerva utca 3a/b; ◪27) on Gellért Hill bears a plaque attesting to the heroism of Raoul Wallenberg, a Swedish diplomat and businessman who, together with colleagues Carl-Ivan Danielsson (1880–1963) and Per Anger (1913–2002), rescued as many as 35,000 Hungarian Jews during WWII.

Wallenberg began working in 1936 for a trading firm whose owner was a Hungarian Jew. In July 1944 the Swedish Foreign Ministry, at the request of Jewish and refugee organisations in the US, sent the 32-year-old Swede on a rescue mission to Budapest as an attaché to the embassy there. By that time almost half a million Jews in Hungary had been sent to Nazi death camps in Germany and Poland.

Wallenberg immediately began issuing Swedish safe-conduct passes (called 'Wallenberg passports') from the Swedish embassy here. He also set up a series of 'safe houses' flying the flag of Sweden and other neutral countries where Jews could seek asylum. He even followed German 'death marches' and deportation trains, distributing food and clothing and actually pulling some 500 people off the cars along the way.

When the Soviet army entered Budapest in January 1945, Wallenberg went to report to the authorities, but in the wartime confusion was arrested for espionage and sent to Moscow. In the early 1950s, responding to reports that Wallenberg had been seen alive in a labour camp, the Soviet Union announced that he had in fact died of a heart attack in 1947. Several reports over the next two decades suggested Wallenberg was still alive, but none was ever confirmed. Many believe Wallenberg was executed by the Soviets, who suspected him of spying for the USA.

Wallenberg was made an honorary citizen of the city of Budapest in 2003.

ELIZABETH BRIDGE   BRIDGE

Map p236 A gleaming white (though rather generic-looking) suspension bridge dating from 1964, Elizabeth Bridge (Erzsébet híd) enjoys a special place in the hearts of many Budapesters as it was the first newly designed bridge to reopen after WWII (the original span, erected in 1903, was too badly damaged to rebuild). Boasting a higher arch than the other Danube bridges, it offers dramatic views of both Castle and Gellért Hills and, of course, the more attractive bridges to the north and south.

LIBERTY BRIDGE   BRIDGE

Map p236 Opened for the millenary exhibition in 1896, Liberty Bridge (Szabadság híd) has a fin-de-siècle cantilevered span. Each post of the bridge, which was originally named after Habsburg Emperor Franz Joseph, is topped by a mythical *turul* bird ready to take flight. It was rebuilt in the same style in 1946.

ST GELLÉRT MONUMENT   MONUMENT

Map p236 (Szent Gellért emlékmű; XI Szent Gellért-hegy) Looking down on Elizabeth Bridge from Gellért Hill is a large and quite theatrical monument to St Gellért, an Italian missionary invited to Hungary by King Stephen to convert the natives. The monument marks the spot where pagan Magyars, resisting the new faith, hurled the bishop to his death in a spiked barrel in 1046.

QUEEN ELIZABETH STATUE   STATUE

Map p236 (Erzsébet királyné szobor; I Döbrentei tér) To the northwest of Elizabeth Bridge is s statue of Elizabeth, Habsburg empress and Hungarian queen. Consort to Franz Joseph, 'Sissi' was much-loved by the Magyars because, among other things, she learned to speak Hungarian. She was assassinated by an Italian anarchist in Geneva in 1898. Brute.

✖ EATING

Second only to eating atop Castle Hill is dining below looking up. The Tabán, an area once known for its jolly outdoor cafes and wine gardens – a kind of Montmartre as in Paris – still has some wonderful places

WORTH A DETOUR

SOUTH BUDA SIGHTS

Memento Park

Home to almost four dozen statues, busts and plaques of Lenin, Marx, Béla Kun and 'heroic' workers that have ended up on trash heaps in other former socialist countries, **Memento Park** (www.mementopark.hu; XXII Balatoni út 16-18; adult/child 1500/1000Ft; ☉10am-dusk; ☐150 from XI Kosztolány Dezsö tér in south Buda), 10km southwest of the city centre, is truly a mind-blowing place to visit. Ogle the socialist realism and try to imagine that at least four of these monstrous relics were erected as recently as the late 1980s; a few of them, including the Béla Kun memorial of our 'hero' in a crowd by fence-sitting sculptor Imre Varga (p75) were still in place when this author moved to Budapest in early 1992. Other attractions here are the replicated remains of Stalin's boots (all that was left after a crowd pulled the enormous statue down from its plinth on XIV Dózsa György út during the 1956 Uprising); and an exhibition centre in an old barracks with displays on the events of 1956, the changes since 1989, and a documentary film with rare footage of secret agents collecting information on 'subversives'.

To reach this socialist Disneyland, take tram 19 from I Batthyány tér in Buda, tram 47 or 49 from V Deák Ferenc tér in Pest, or bus 7 from V Ferenciek tere in Pest to XI Kosztolány Dezsö tér in south Buda, then board city bus 150 (25 minutes, every 20 to 30 minutes) for the park. A much easier – though more expensive – way to go is via the direct **park bus** (adult/child return incl park admission 4500/3500Ft), which departs from in front of the Le Meridien Budapest Hotel (Map p238) on V Deák Ferenc tér at 11am year-round, with an extra departure at 3pm in from July to August.

Tropicarium

The vast and enlarged aquarium complex called **Tropicarium** (www.tropicarium.hu; XXII Nagytétényi út 37-45; adult/child 2300/1600Ft; ☉10am-8pm; ☐33, 33E from XI Móricz Zsigmond körtér in south Buda) at the Campona shopping mall in south Buda is apparently the largest in Central Europe. The place prides itself on its local specimens – 'fish species of the Hungarian fauna' – though there's an 11m-long shark aquarium containing all manner of the carnivorous beasties. Feeding time at the zoo is between 3pm and 4pm on Thursday.

Nagytétény Castle Museum

Housed in a baroque mansion in deepest south Buda, the **Nagytétény Castle Museum** (Nagytétényi Kastélymúzeum; www.nagytetenyi.hu; XXII Kastélypark utca 9-11; adult/child 600/300Ft; ☉10am-6pm Tue-Sun; ☐33 from XI Móricz Zsigmond körtér in south Buda), a branch of the Museum of Applied Arts (p132), traces the development of European furniture – from the Gothic to Biedermeier styles (approximately 1450 to 1850) – with some 300 items on display in more than two dozen rooms.

in which to eat and drink, as does the area south of Gellért Hill.

ARANYSZARVAS   HUNGARIAN €€

Map p236 (☎375 6451; www.aranyszarvas.hu; I Szarvas tér 1; mains 2550-5150Ft; ☐86) Set in an 18th-century inn literally down the steps from the southern end of Castle Hill, the 'Golden Stag' serves up some very meaty and unusual dishes (like kohlrabi soup with hare kidney, and duck breast with bok choy). The covered outside terrace is a delight in summer and the views upward fantastical.

TABÁNI TERASZ   HUNGARIAN €€

Map p236 (☎201 1086; www.tabaniterasz.hu; I Apród utca 10; mains 2500-4600Ft; ☐86) This delightful restaurant below Castle Hill set in a 250-year-old inn has two lovely terraces, with a courtyard outside and a main dining room and candlelit cellar within. The menu takes a somewhat modern look at Hungarian cuisine, with less caloric dishes, and an excellent wine selection. Set lunch is good value at 1200Ft.

MARCELLO
ITALIAN €

Map p236 (XI Bartók Béla út 40; pizzas 900-1100Ft, mains 2080-2400Ft; ⊘Mon-Sat; 47, 49) A perennial favourite with students from the nearby university since it opened two decades ago, this father-and-son-owned operation just down the road from XI Gellért tér offers reliable Italian fare at affordable prices. The pizzas are good value as is the salad bar, and the lasagne (1250Ft) is legendary in these parts.

DAIKICHI
JAPANESE €€

Map p236 (I Mészáros utca 64; mains 2200-3600Ft, set menus 2600-4200Ft; ⊘noon-3pm & 5-10pm Tue-Sat, noon-9pm Sun; 8, 112, 178) Everyone's favourite little Japanese eatery on the Buda side, this minuscule restaurant (with additional seating below) serves up decent soba noodles and seafood and pork dishes.

TOP CHOICE HEMINGWAY
ITALIAN, HUNGARIAN €€

Map p236 (381 0522; www.hemingway-etterem.hu; XI Kosztolányi Dezső tér 2; mains 2590-2990Ft; ⊘noon-midnight Mon, to 5pm Sun; 7; 19, 49) This very stylish Italian-Hungarian hybrid, in a fabulous location in small park overlooking Feneketlen-tó (Bottomless Lake) in south Buda, has a varied and ever-changing menu and a wonderful terrace. There's pizza and pasta (1290Ft to 2490Ft) should you want something easy, and Sunday brunch (3990Ft) is a crowd-puller.

🍷 DRINKING & NIGHTLIFE

TRANZIT ART CAFÉ
CAFE

Map p236 (www.tranzitcafe.com; XI Kosztolányi Dezső tér 7; ⊘9am-11pm Mon-Fri, 10am-10pm Sat & Sun; 7; 19, 49) As chilled a place to drink, nosh and relax as you'll find in south Buda, the Tranzit found its home in a small disused bus station, put art on the walls and filled the leafy courtyard with hammocks and comfy sofas. There's breakfast and sandwiches available, and two-course lunches (including a veggie one) for 1200Ft.

TOP CHOICE HADIK KÁVÉHÁZ & SZATYOR BÁR
CAFE, BAR

Map p236 (www.hadikkavehaz.com, www.szatyor bar.blog.hu, in Hungarian; XIII Bartók Béla út 36; ⊘Hadik 9am-11pm, Szatyor noon-1am Mon-Fri, 2pm-1am Sat & Sun; 18, 19, 47, 49) This dynamic duo sharing the same building and separated by just a door has brought history back to Bartók Béla út. The Hadik is a revived olde-worlde cafe that pulled in the punters for almost four decades before being shut down in 1949. The Szatyor – 'Carrier Bag'– is the funkier of the twins, with cocktails, trash art on the walls and a Lada driven by the poet Endre Ady. Cool or what?

TOP CHOICE CAFÉ PONYVAREGÉNY
CAFE

Map p236 (www.cafeponyvaregeny.hu; XI Bercsényi utca 5; 18, 19, 47, 49) The 'Pulp Fiction' is quirky little place that has a loyal following despite all the new competition in this part of south Buda. The old books and fringed lampshades are a nice touch, and the coffee is some of the best in town.

SHAMBALA CAFÉ
TEAHOUSE

Map p236 (www.cafeshambala.hu, in Hungarian; XI Villányi út 12; ⊘11am-11pm Mon-Sat, 1-11pm Sun; 7; 19, 49, 61) This well-groomed basement teahouse (ignore what its name says) with a slick modern Asianesque decor has upwards of 50 types of cha on offer, including exotic Chinese white teas, fruit tisanes and Argentine mate. Great sandwiches and shop-made cakes too.

KISRABLÓ PUB
BAR

Map p236 (www.kisrablopub.hu, in Hungarian; XI Zenta utca 3; ⊘11am-2am Mon-Sat; 18, 19, 47, 49) Close to the Budapest University of Technology & Economics (BME), the 'Little Pirate' is, not surprisingly, very popular with students. But don't be misled – it's an attractive and well-run place with decent food available, including cheap two-/three-course set lunches at 790/990Ft.

A38 HAJÓ
CLUB

Map p236 (www.a38.hu, in Hungarian; XI Pázmány Péter sétány 3-11; ⊘11am-4pm, terraces 4pm-4am Tue-Sat; 4, 6) Moored on the Buda side just south of Petőfi Bridge, the 'A38 Ship' is a decommissioned Ukrainian stone hauler from 1968 that has been recycled as a major live-music venue. It's so cool it's hot in summer, and the hold rocks throughout the year.

ROMKERT
CLUB

Map p236 (www.rudasromkert.hu; I Döbrentei tér 9; ⊘11am-5am Apr-Sep; 18, 19) Tucked away behind the Rudas Baths (p66) with Moorish cupolas in sight, the seasonal 'Ruin Garden' attracts a younger crowd with a large dance area and themed nights.

GELLÉRT HILL & TABÁN DRINKING & NIGHTLIFE

ZÖLD PARDON   CLUB
Map p236 (www.zp.hu; XI Goldman György tér 6; ☉11am-5am Apr-Sep; ⊞4, 6) What bills itself as the 'world's longest summer festival' is a rocker's paradise in Buda just south of Petőfi Bridge. The place counts nine bars as well as a *pálinkaház* serving Hungarian fruit brandies.

 ENTERTAINMENT

MUNICIPAL CULTURAL HOUSE   MUSIC, DANCE
off Map p236 (Fővárosi Művelődési Háza; www .fmhnet.hu, in Hungarian; XI Fehérvári út 47; ☉box office noon-7pm Mon, 4-7pm Wed, 2-7pm Thu, 1-6pm Fri, plus 1hr before performance; ⊞18, 41) There's folk music at what is also called the Folklore Theatre (Folklór Színház) every Friday, the first and third Monday and the second and fourth Saturday of each month at 7pm. A children's dance house hosted by the incomparable Muzsikás (p192) runs every Tuesday from 5pm.

FONÓ BUDA MUSIC HOUSE   MUSIC
(Fonó Budai Zeneház; ☎206 5300; www.fono .hu, in Hungarian; XI Sztregova utca 3; ☉box office 9am-5pm Mon-Fri; ⊞18, 41) This place has *táncház* programs several times a week at 8pm, as well as concerts by big-name bands (mostly world music) throughout each month; it's one of the best venues in town for this sort of thing. Consult the website for more details.

MU SZÍNHÁZ   DANCE
Map p236 (☎209 4014; www.mu.hu; XI Kőrösy József utca 17; ☉box office 10am-6pm Mon-Fri; ⊞4) Virtually everyone involved in the Hungarian dance scene got their start in the business at this place in south Buda, where excellent modern-dance performances can still be enjoyed.

Óbuda & Buda Hills

Neighbourhood Top Five

❶ Touring the Buda Hills by three of the most unusual conveyances you're likely to encounter: the **Cog Railway** (p74) up, the unique **Children's Railway** (p74) through the hills, and the **Chairlift** (p74) down.

❷ Walking backwards in time by strolling though Roman-era **Aquincum** (p73).

❸ Exploring the world beneath you by visiting any of the Buda Hills' three caves: **Mátyáshegy** (p78), **Pálvölgy** (p78) or **Szemlőhegy** (p78).

❹ Spacing out viewing the truly mind-blowing works of op art at the **Vasarely Museum** (p75).

❺ Enjoying Bartók's music at the place where it was born: the **Béla Bartók Memorial House** (p78).

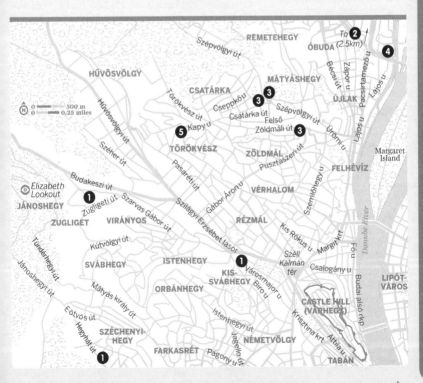

For more detail of this area, see Map p234 and Map p233 ➡

Lonely Planet's Top Tip

You can reach Óbuda and Aquincum by bus, or take tram 17 to Óbuda, but the fastest and easiest way is to hop on to the HÉV suburban train from Batthyány tér or Margit híd in Buda. Remember, though, that passes are valid only as far as the city limits and if you are carrying on north from Aquincum to, say, Szentendre (p147), you must buy an extension after the Békásmegyer stop. Tickets are *always* checked by a conductor on the HÉV.

◉ Best Museums & Galleries

➡ Aquincum Museum (p73)

➡ Vasarely Museum (p75)

➡ Kiscell Museum & Municipal Picture Gallery (p75)

➡ Béla Bartók Memorial House (p78)

For reviews, see p73 ➡

◉ Best for Taking the Plunge

➡ Lukács Baths (p76)

➡ Béke Boat Club (p78)

➡ Császár-Komjádi (p78)

For reviews, see p76 ➡

✕ Best Places to Eat

➡ Kisbuda Gyöngye (p79)

➡ Fuji Japán (p81)

➡ Pastrami (p79)

➡ Náncsi Néni (p80)

➡ Földes Józsi Konyhája (p80)

For reviews, see p78 ➡

Explore: Óbuda & Buda Hills

Ó means 'ancient' in Hungarian – no prizes for guessing that Óbuda is the oldest part of Buda. The Romans established Aquincum, a military garrison and civilian town, north of here at the end of the 1st century AD (p172), and it became the seat of the Roman province Pannonia Inferior in AD 106. When the Magyars arrived, they named it Buda, which became Óbuda when the Royal Palace was built on Castle Hill and turned into the real centre.

Most visitors en route to Szentendre (p147) on the Danube Bend are put off by what they see of Óbuda from the highway or the HÉV suburban train. Prefabricated housing blocks seem to go on forever, and the Árpád Bridge flyover splits the heart of the old district – Flórián tér – in two. But behind all this are some of the most important Roman ruins in Hungary, plus museums and small, quiet neighbourhoods that recall fin-de-siècle Óbuda.

Contiguous with Óbuda to the west is the start of the Buda Hills (Budai-hegység), with 'peaks' exceeding 500m, a comprehensive system of trails and some unusual modes of public transport. The hills are the city's playground – a welcome respite from hot, dusty Pest in summer. But apart from the Béla Bartók Memorial House (p78), there are few sights here per se, though you might want to explore one of the hills' caves (p78).

Local Life

➡ **Sleeping** If you take your swimming seriously, stay at Hotel Császár (p160), where some of the rooms look onto the Olympic-size pools of the Császár-Komjádi.

➡ **Classical Music** One of the finest and most intimate spots to hear a concert is the Óbuda Society (p81).

➡ **Museum** An easy and very colourful introduction to Budapest's social history is the *Contemporary City History Collection* at the Kiscell Museum (p75).

Getting There & Away

➡ **Bus** Bus 86 links Fő utca in Buda with Flórián tér in Óbuda. Buses 34 and 106 go to Aquincum from Óbuda. Bus 291 links the Chairlift's lower terminus on Zugligeti út with Szilágyi Erzsébet fasor.

➡ **Trams** Trams 1 and 1A run along the Outer Ring Rd (eg Róbert Károl körút) from City Park in Pest to Flórián tér in Óbuda. Trams 59 and 61 run from Széll Kálmán tér to the Cog Railway's lower terminus. Tram 17 links II Margit körút with Bécsi út.

➡ **HÉV** Árpád híd stop serves Óbuda; the Aquincum stop is handy for the Roman ruins.

TOP SIGHTS
AQUINCUM

Aquincum, the most complete Roman civilian town in Hungary and now both an open-air and enclosed museum, had paved streets and sumptuous single-storey houses with courtyards, fountains and mosaic floors, as well as sophisticated drainage and heating systems. Not all that is apparent today as you walk among the ruins, but you can see its outlines as well as those of the big public baths, the *macellum* (market), an early Christian church and a temple dedicated to the god Mithra, the chief deity of a religion that once rivalled Christianity (p75).

The purpose-built **Aquincum Museum** (Aquincumi Múzeum), on the southwestern edge of what remains of the Roman civilian settlement, puts the ruins in perspective, with a vast collection of coins and wall paintings. Look out for the replica of a 3rd-century portable organ called a hydra (and the mosaic illustrating how it was played), and the mock-up of a Roman bath. Most of the big sculptures and stone sarcophagi are outside to the left of the old museum building or behind it in the lapidary. Across the road to the northwest, and past the pylons of a Roman aqueduct preserved in the central reservation (median strip) of Szentendrei út, is the **Roman Civilian Amphitheatre** (Római polgári amfiteátrum), about half the size of the amphitheatre reserved for the garrisons (p75). Much is left to the imagination, but you can still see the small cubicles where lions were kept and the 'Gate of Death' to the west through which slain gladiators were carried.

DON'T MISS...

⇒ Aquincum's main thoroughfare
⇒ Colonnaded courtyard
⇒ Public baths
⇒ Hydra (portable organ)
⇒ Civilian amphitheatre

PRACTICALITIES

⇒ Map p234
⇒ www.aquincum.hu
⇒ III Szentendrei út 139
⇒ adult/child summer 1300/650Ft, winter 850/450Ft
⇒ ⊙ruins 9am-6pm Tue-Sun May-Sep, to 5pm Tue-Sun 15-30 Apr & Oct, museum 10am-6pm Tue-Sun May-Sep, to 5pm Tue-Sun 15-30 Apr & Oct
⇒ ℝAquincum
⇒ 🚌34, 106

TOP SIGHTS
TOURING THE BUDA HILLS

Visitors to Budapest head for the hills – the city's 'green lungs' – for a variety of reasons. There's great hiking, a couple of trip-worthy sights, summer homes of well-heeled Budapest families to ogle, and a plethora of unusual forms of transport that everyone from age nine to 90 enjoys riding. If you're planning to ramble, take along a copy of Cartographia's 1:30,000 *A Budai-hegység* map (No 6; 1290Ft) available from bookshops and newsstands throughout the city.

With all the unusual transport options, getting to/from the hills is half the fun. From Széll Kálmán tér metro station on the M2 line in Buda, walk westward along Szilágyi Erzsébet fasor for 10 minutes (or take tram 59 or 61 for two stops) to the circular Hotel Budapest at II Szilágyi Erzsébet fasor 47. Directly opposite is the terminus of the **Cog Railway** (Fogaskerekű vasút; www.bkv.hu; Szilágyi Erzsébet fasor 14-16; admission 1 BKV ticket or 320Ft; ☺5am-11pm), which is actually designated tram 60. Built in 1874, the Cog climbs for 3.7km in 14 minutes twice to four times an hour to Széchenyi-hegy (427m), one of the prettiest residential areas in Buda.

At Széchenyi-hegy, you can stop for a picnic in the attractive park south of the old-time station or board the unique narrow-gauge **Children's Railway** (Gyermekvasút; www .gyermekvasut.hu; adult/child section ticket 500/300Ft, entire line 700/350Ft), two minutes to the south on Hegyhát út. The railway, with eight stops, was built in 1951 by Pioneers (socialist Scouts) and is now staffed entirely by schoolchildren aged 10 to 14 (the engineer excepted). The little train chugs along for 11km, terminating at Hűvösvölgy. Departure times vary widely depending on the day of the week and the season (consult the website), but very roughly they depart once an hour between 9am or 10am and 5pm to 7pm. The line is closed on Monday from September to April.

There are walks fanning out from any of the stops along the Children's Railway line or you can return to Széll Kálmán tér on tram 61 from Hűvösvölgy. A more interesting way down, however, is to get off at János-hegy, the fourth stop and the highest point (527m) in the hills. From atop the 23.5m-tall **Elizabeth Lookout** (Erzsébet kilátó), with 101 steps, you can see the Tatra Mountains in Slovakia on a clear day. It was designed in 1910 by Frigyes Schulek, the same architect who did the neo-Gothic Matthias Church and Fishermen's Bastion (p54) on Castle Hill. About 700m to the east is the **Chairlift** (libegő; www.bkv.hu; adult/child 750/450Ft; ☺9am-7pm Jul & Aug, 9.30am-5pm May, Jun & Sep, 10am-4pm Oct-Apr, closed 2nd & 4th Mon of every month), which will take you down 1040m at 4km/h to Zugligeti út. From here bus 291 will take you to Szilágyi Erzsébet fasor.

DON'T MISS...

➡ Cog Railway
➡ Children's Railway
➡ Elizabeth Lookout
➡ Chairlift

PRACTICALITIES

➡ Map p233

⊙ SIGHTS

⊙ Óbuda

AQUINCUM
RUINS

See p73.

VASARELY MUSEUM
MUSEUM

Map p234 (www.vasarely.hu; III Szentlélek tér 6; adult/child 800/400Ft; ◷10am-5.30pm Tue-Sun; 🚊86) Sharing space in the imposing Zichy Mansion (Zichy kastély) built in 1757, this museum contains the works of Victor Vasarely (or Vásárhelyi Győző as he was known before he emigrated to Paris in 1930), the late 'father of op art'. The works, especially ones such as *Tlinko-F* and *Ibadan-Pos,* are excellent and fun to watch as they 'swell' and 'move' around the canvas. We love *Ganz.*

IMRE VARGA COLLECTION
MUSEUM

Map p234 (Varga Imre Gyűtemény; www.buda pestgaleria.hu; III Laktanya utca 7; adult/child 800/400Ft; ◷10am-6pm Tue-Sun; 🚊86) Part of the Budapest Gallery (p76), this collection includes sculptures, statues, medals and drawings by Varga, who is nearly 90 and one of Hungary's foremost sculptors. Like others before him, notably Zsigmond Kisfaludi Strobl (p65), Varga seems to have sat on both sides of the fence politically for decades – sculpting Béla Kun and Lenin as dextrously as he did St Stephen, Béla Bartók and even Imre Nagy (p68). But his work always remains fresh and is never derivative. Note the fine bust of Winston Churchill (2003) on display near the entrance.

KISCELL MUSEUM
MUSEUM, GALLERY

Map p234 (Kiscelli Múzeum; www.btm.hu; III Kis celli utca 108; adult/child 900/450Ft; ◷10am-6pm Tue-Sun Apr-Oct, to 4pm Tue-Sun Nov-Mar; 🚊17; 🚊160, 165) Housed in an 18th-century monastery – later a barracks, badly damaged in WWII and again in 1956 – this museum contains two excellent sections. In the **Contemporary City History Collection** (Újkori Várostörténeti Gyűjtemény) you'll find a complete 19th-century apothecary moved here from Kálvin tér; a wonderful assembly of ancient signboards advertising shops and other trades; and rooms (both public and private) furnished in Empire, Biedermeier and art nouveau furniture and bric-a-brac. The **Municipal Picture Gallery** (Fővárosi Képtár), with its impressive collection of art works by József Rippl-Rónai, Lajos Tihanyi, István Csók and Béla Czóbel (among others), is upstairs.

FREE ROMAN MILITARY AMPHITHEATRE
RUINS

Map p234 (Római Katonai Amfiteátrum; III Pac sirtamező utca; ◷24hr; 🚇Tímár utca; 🚊86) Built in the 2nd century for the Roman garrisons, this amphitheatre, about 800m south of Flórián tér, could accommodate up to 15,000 spectators and was larger than the Colosseum in Rome. The rest of the

ÓBUDA & BUDA HILLS SIGHTS

MITHRA & THE GREAT SACRIFICE

Mithraism, the worship of the god Mithra, originated in Persia. As Roman rule extended into the West, the religion became extremely popular with traders, imperial slaves and mercenaries of the Roman army, and spread rapidly throughout the Empire in the 1st and 2nd centuries AD. In fact, Mithraism was the principal rival of Christianity until Constantine, a convert to that religion, came to the throne in the 4th century.

Mithraism was a mysterious religion and its devotees (mostly male) were sworn to secrecy. What little is known of Mithra, the god of justice and social contract, has been deduced from reliefs and icons found in temples, like the one found at Aquincum. Most of these portray Mithra wearing a Persian-style cap and tunic and sacrificing a white bull in front of Sol, the sun god. From the bull's blood sprout grain and grapes, and from its semen animals grow. Sol's wife Luna, the moon, begins her cycle and time is born.

Mithraism and Christianity competed strongly because of a striking similarity in many of their rituals. Both religions involved the birth of a deity on winter solstice (around 25 December), shepherds, death and resurrection and a form of baptism. Devotees of Mithraism knelt when they worshipped and a common meal – a 'communion' of bread and water – was a regular feature of the liturgy.

military camp extended north to Flórián tér. Archaeology and classical-history buffs taking bus 86 to Flórián tér should get off at III Nagyszombat utca; HÉV passengers should get off at the Tímár utca stop.

FREE **HERCULES VILLA** RUINS

Map p234 (Herkules Villa; 250 1650; www .btm.hu; III Meggyfa utca 19-21; 86) Hercules Villa, in the middle of a vast housing estate northwest of Fő tér, is the name given to some reconstructed Roman ruins. The name is derived from the astonishing 3rd-century floor mosaics of Hercules' exploits found in what was a Roman villa. Phone in advance; visits are usually by arrangement for groups only, but you might get lucky.

ÓBUDA MUSEUM MUSEUM

Map p234 (Óbudai Múzeum; www.obudaimuzeum .hu; III Fő tér 1; adult/child 800/400Ft; 10am-6pm Tue-Sun; 86) Anchor tenant of the Zichy Mansion, where you'll also find the Vasarely and the Kassák museums, but with its own flashy new entrance on Fő tér, this museum contains a motley assortment of exhibits related to Óbuda's past through three distinct periods: medieval, industrial and present-day. Highlights include a three-room 19th-century farmhouse from Békásmegyer, the output of master cooper Simon Tóbiás, and toys through history.

BUDAPEST GALLERY GALLERY

Map p234 (Budapest Galéria; www.budapest galeria.hu; III Lajos utca 158; adult/child 600/300Ft; 10am-6pm Tue-Sun; 86) Budapest Gallery hosts some interesting avant-garde exhibitions. It also contains a standing exhibition of works by Pál Pátzay (1896–1979), whose sculptures, including *The Serpent Slayer* in Szent István Park (p108), can be seen throughout the city.

FREE **THERMAE MAIORES BATHS MUSEUM** MUSEUM

Map p234 (Thermae Maiores Fürdő Múzeum; www.btm.hu; 10am-6pm Tue-Sun May-Sep, to 5pm Tue-Sun Apr & Oct; 86) Built in the 2nd century AD for the Roman garrisons stationed at Aquincum, these baths featured a gymnastics hall, sweat rooms and hot and cold pools.

HUNGARIAN MUSEUM OF TRADE & TOURISM MUSEUM

Map p234 (Magyar Kereskedelmi és Vendéglát-óipari Múzeum; www.mkvm.hu; Korona tér 1; adult/child 800/400Ft; 11am-7pm Wed-Sun; Tímár utca; 86) Having moved from its original base on Castle Hill to a spot next to the Basilica of St Stephen and now in Óbuda opposite the Óbuda Society concert hall, this peripatetic museum looks at the catering and hospitality trade. Exhibits include restaurant items, tableware, advertising, packaging and original shop signs.

KASSÁK MUSEUM MUSEUM

Map p234 (www.kassakmuzeum.hu; III Fő tér 1; adult/child 500/200Ft; 10am-5pm Wed-Sun; 86) This three-room art gallery contains some real gems of early 20th-century modernist, avant-garde and contemporary art, as well as the complete works of the artist and writer Lajos Kassák (1887–1967). It's the third of three museums in the Zichy Mansion.

FRANKEL LEÓ ÚT STREET

Map p234 (86; 17) At Bem József tér, Fő utca, the busy main drag in Víziváros, becomes Frankel Leó út, a quiet, tree-lined street of antique shops and boutiques. At its southern end is the Lukács Baths (p76), which tends to attract older and quite serious thermal enthusiasts. A short distance north and tucked away in an apartment block is the **Újlak Synagogue** (Map p234; Újlaki zsinagóga; II Frankel Leó út 49 & Árpád fejedelem útja 70), built in 1888 on the site of an older prayer house and still the city's main functioning synagogue on the Buda side.

FREE **GÜL BABA'S TOMB** RELIGIOUS SITE

Map p234 (Gül Baba türbéje; II Türbe tér 1; 10am-6pm Tue-Sun; 4, 6, 17) This reconstructed tomb contains the remains of one Gül Baba, an Ottoman Dervish who took part in the capture of Buda in 1541 and is known in Hungary as the 'Father of Roses'. The tomb and mosque is a pilgrimage place for Muslims, especially from Turkey, and you must remove your shoes before entering. To reach the tomb from Török utca, which runs parallel to Frankel Leó út, walk west up steep, cobbled Gül Baba utca to the set of steps just past the house at No 16. You can also get here from Mecset utca, which runs north from Margit utca.

LUKÁCS BATHS THERMAL BATHS, POOLS

Map p234 (Lukács Gyógyfürdő; 326 1695; www.budapestgyogyfurdoi.hu; II Frankel Leó út 25-29; admission locker/cabin Mon-Fri before 5pm 2600/3000Ft, after 5pm 2000/2400Ft, Sat

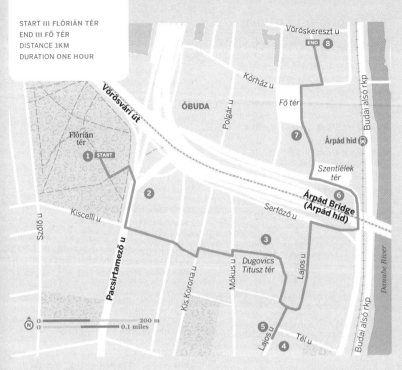

ÓBUDA & BUDA HILLS NEIGHBOURHOOD WALK

Neighbourhood Walk
Óbuda

Begin the tour in ❶ **Flórián tér**, which is split in two by the Árpád Bridge flyover and encircled by mammoth housing blocks. It is not the best introduction to the neighbourhood, but it remains the district's historical centre. Roman objects discovered in the area are on display in the subway below the square and in the adjacent ❷ **Thermae Maiores Baths Museum**. There are more Roman ruins, including a reconstructed temple, in the park above the underpass.

Dominating the eastern side of III Flórián tér is the yellow baroque ❸ **Óbuda Parish Church** at Lajos utca 168. It was built in 1749 and is dedicated to SS Peter and Paul. There's a lovely rococo pulpit inside.

To the southeast of the church, the large neoclassical building at III Lajos utca 163 beside the landmark Corinthia Aquincum Hotel is the ❹ **former Óbuda Synagogue**, built in 1821. For many years it housed Hungarian TV (MTV) sound studios, but is now functioning at least part-time as a *súl* (Jewish prayer house). Opposite the synagogue is the ❺ **Budapest Gallery**, which served as a pub in the 18th century. The area around it was a marketplace in the Middle Ages.

Tiny ❻ **Szentlélek tér** (Holy Spirit Sq), a transport hub east of Flórián tér, contains two of Óbuda's most important museums: the Vasarely and Óbuda. To reach it, walk north on Budai alsó rakpart and under the flyover.

Contiguous to Szentlélek tér is ❼ **Fő tér** (Main Sq), a quiet restored square of baroque houses, public buildings and restaurants. Particularly fine is the century house at No 4, built in the 1780s and showing influences of the Louis XVI style.

A very short distance northeast of Fő tér, you'll see a group of ❽ **outdoor sculptures by Imre Varga**. They portray four rather worried-looking women holding umbrellas in the middle of the street.

ON THE DEEP BLUE DANUBE

The best place for canoeing and kayaking in Budapest is on the Danube in Rómaifürdő. To get there, take the HÉV suburban line to the Rómaifürdő stop and walk east towards the river. Reliable places to rent kayaks and canoes include the following, both about 5km north of the Árpád Bridge:

Béke Boat Club (☎388 9303, 06-30 951 5049; www.romaipart.com; III Nánási út 65; canoe per day for 2/4 people 2400/3000Ft, kayak for 1/2 people 1500/2400Ft; ☺8am-6pm Apr–mid-Oct)

Óbuda Sport Club (ÓSE; ☎240 3353; www.ose.hu; III Rozgonyi Piroska utca 28; canoes & kayaks per day from 2000Ft; ☺8am-6pm May-Sep, 10am-4pm Oct-Apr)

& Sun 2700/3100Ft; ☺6am-8pm; ☒17; ☒86) Housed in a sprawling, 19th-century complex, these baths are popular with keen spa aficionados. The thermal baths (temperatures 24°C to 40°C) are mixed and a bathing suit is required. The use of the three swimming pools is included in the general admission.

CSÁSZÁR-KOMJÁDI — POOLS

Map p234 (☎326 1478; II Árpád fejedelem útja 8; adult/child 1700/1050Ft; ☺6am-7pm; ☒17; ☒86) This swimming complex, which includes three 50m pools, is used by serious swimmers and fitness freaks – so don't come here for fun and games.

CSILLAGHEGY — POOLS

Map p234 (☎250 1533; www.budapestgyogy furdoi.hu; III Pusztakúti út 3; adult before/after 4pm 1600/1200Ft, child 1100Ft; ☺7am-7pm daily May–mid-Sep, 6am-7pm Mon-Fri, 6am-4pm Sat, 6am-noon Sun mid-Sep–Apr; ☒Csillaghegy) The popular Csillaghegy complex 3km north of Óbuda is the oldest open-air bath in Budapest. There are three pools in a 90-hectare terraced park; in winter they are covered by canvas tenting and heated.

⊙ Buda Hills

TOURING THE BUDA HILLS — RAILWAYS, CHAIRLIFT
See p74.

BÉLA BARTÓK MEMORIAL HOUSE — MUSEUM

Map p233 (Bartók Béla Emlékház; www.bartokmu seum.hu; II Csalán út 29; adult/child 1200/600Ft; ☺10am-5pm Tue-Sat; ☒5, 29) North of Szilágyi Erzsébet fasor but still very much in the Buda Hills, this is the house where the great composer resided from 1932 until 1940, when he emigrated to the US. It has been recently renovated and enlarged, including a new floor displaying the old Edison recorder (complete with wax cylinders) that Bartók used to record Hungarian folk music in Transylvania, as well as furniture and other objects he collected. Chamber-music concerts take place here throughout the year; see the website for details.

MÁTYÁSHEGY CAVE — CAVE

off Map p234 (Mátyáshegyi-barlang; www.bar langaszat.hu; Szépvölgyi út; adult/child 4500/3500Ft; ☺tours 4.30pm Mon, Wed & Fri; ☒65 from Kolosy tér in Óbuda) Budapest contains some 200 caves and several can be visited on walk-through guided tours (usually in Hungarian). Most of the hostels also offer adventurous 2½- to three-hour caving excursions to this cave, which is opposite to and links up with Pálvölgy Cave.

PÁLVÖLGY CAVE — CAVE

off Map p234 (Pálvölgyi-barlang; www.dinpi.hu; II Szépvölgyi út 162; adult/child 1150/900Ft; ☺10am-5pm Tue-Sun; ☒65 from Kolosy tér in Óbuda) The second largest in Hungary, this 19km-long cave discovered in 1904 is noted for both its stalactites and its bats. Be advised that the 500m route involves climbing about 120 steps and a ladder, so it may not be suitable for the elderly or young children. The temperature is a constant 8°C so wear a jacket or jumper. Tours lasting 45 minutes depart hourly from 10.15am to 4.15pm.

SZEMLŐHEGY CAVE — CAVE

Map p234 (Szemlőhegyi-barlang; www.dinpi.hu; II Pusztaszeri út 35; adult/child 950/750Ft; ☺10am-4pm Wed-Mon; ☒29 from III Kolosy tér) A beautiful cave with stalactites, stalagmites and weird grapelike formations, Szemlőhegy is about 1km southeast of Pálvölgy Cave. The temperature here is 12°C. The tour lasts 35 to 45 minutes.

EATING

Some of the little neighbourhood eateries of Óbuda are so long established they make cameos in Hungarian literature, while

one of the fine-dining restaurants atop affluent Rózsadomb to the southwest is the best known restaurant in Buda. Few of the restaurants in the Buda Hills are posh, but some are so popular they've become legends in their own lunchtime.

✖ Óbuda

TOP
CHOICE **KISBUDA GYÖNGYE** HUNGARIAN €€€
Map p234 (📞368 6402; www.remiz.hu; III Kenyeres utca 34; mains 2480-4980Ft; ⊙closed Sun; 🚌160, 260; 🚋17) Operating since the 1970s, this traditional yet very elegant Hungarian restaurant has an antique-cluttered dining room and attentive service, and manages to create a fin-de-siècle atmosphere. Try the excellent goose liver speciality plate with a glass of Tokaj (3580Ft), or a much more pedestrian dish like *tanyasi csirke paprikás* (farmhouse chicken paprika; 2980Ft), which still manages to be out of this world.

VADRÓZSA HUNGARIAN, INTERNATIONAL €€€
Map p234 (📞326 5817; www.vadrozsa.hu; II Pentelei Molnár utca 15; mains 4880-7880Ft; ⊙noon-3pm & 7-11pm; 🚌91, 291) Housed in a beautiful neo-Renaissance villa on Rózsadomb (pretty much the top shelf of Budapest), the 'Wild Rose' remains one of the swishest (and most expensive) restaurants in Buda after four decades in operation. It's filled with roses, antiques and soft piano music. You can order from the menu (fish, steaks and game dishes are especially good) or choose from the cart of raw ingredients and specify the style.

PATA NEGRA SPANISH €€
Map p234 (www.patanegra.hu; Frankel Leó út 51; tapas 380-750Ft, plates 850-2200Ft; 🚋17) The 'Black Foot' (it's a special kind of Spanish cured ham, not a podiatric affliction) is a lovely Spanish tapas bar and restaurant and a much needed addition to this desert-district of gastronomy in Buda. The decor is fine, and the floor tiles and ceiling fans help create a mood *à la valenciana*. Good cheese and an excellent wine selection too.

KÉHLI HUNGARIAN €€
Map p234 (📞368 0613; www.kehli.hu; III Mókus utca 22; mains 1990-4790Ft; 🚋Árpád híd; 🚌86) A self-consciously rustic place, Kéhli has some of the best traditional Hungarian food in town. In fact, one of Hungary's best-loved writers, the novelist Gyula Krúdy (1878–1933), who lived in nearby Dugovits Titusz tér, moonlighted as a restaurant

critic and enjoyed Kéhli's *forró velőscsont pirítóssal* (bone marrow on toast; 990Ft) so much that he included it in one of his novels.

PASTRAMI INTERNATIONAL €€
Map p234 (www.pastrami.hu; III Lajos utca 93-99; mains 2200-3900Ft; ⊙8am-11pm; 🚌86) A kind-of/sort-of attempt at a New York-style deli in a loft-like building in Óbuda's Újlak district, this place does indeed serve its namesake in all its many guises, including the celebrated Reuben sandwich. But come here too for breakfast, more extravagant mains, and their out-of-this-word sweet-and-sour Sicilian relish called *caponata*.

SYMBOL ITALIAN, HUNGARIAN €€€
Map p234 (www.symbolbudapest.hu; mains 2980-5980Ft; III Bécsi út 56; 🚋17) Flagship of Óbuda's ambitious Symbol complex of seven bars and restaurants built in and around a late-18th-century townhouse, this eatery serves relatively reasonably priced 'Italian fusion' (meaning they Magyarise the pasta) as well as simpler fare like pizza (980Ft to 2980Ft). Always busy/buzzy.

ÚJ SÍPOS HALÁSZKERT HUNGARIAN €€
Map p234 (New Piper Fisher's Garden; www.ujsipos.hu; III Fő tér 6; mains 1890-3590Ft; 🚌86) This old-style eatery faces (and, in the warmer weather, has outside seating in) Óbuda's most beautiful and historical square. Try the signature *halászlé* (fish soup; 1190Ft to 2490Ft), which comes in various guises. As the restaurant's motto puts it so succinctly: *Halászlében verhetetlen* (You can't beat fish soup). Our feelings exactly.

ROZMARING HUNGARIAN €€
Map p234 (📞367 1301; www.rozmaringkertvendeglo.hu; III Árpád fejedelem útja 125; mains 1350-3950Ft; 🚋Tímár utca) You probably wouldn't want to come all the way up to this part of Óbuda just for the food (average Hungarian at best). But the flower-bedecked, covered terraces at this 'garden restaurant' that look out onto the Danube and the western side of Margaret Island, with the water tower just visible above the trees, are a delight in warm weather and well worth the schlep. Closes at 9pm on Sundays.

LEROY CAFÉ INTERNATIONAL €€€
Map p234 (www.leroycafeobuda.hu; III Bécsi út 63; mains 2450-5350Ft; 🚌86) The international cuisine at this cafe-restaurant is not especially inspired but is of a certain standard –

ÓBUDA & BUDA HILLS EATING

and it's right there in Óbuda just when you've ordered one too many pints of Dreher. They've got a new line of wok dishes (2390Ft to 2990Ft), and pasta (1650Ft to 2250Ft) is always a good bet. The large terrace fills up (and stays that way) very early in the warm weather. Two-course weekday lunches are a big draw at just 1250Ft.

WASABI
JAPANESE €€

Map p234 (www.wasabi.hu; III Szépvölgyi út 15; mains 4490-5990Ft; ☐86) This sushi restaurant with a central conveyor belt has more than 60 items to choose from and the decor is dark, minimalist and very cool.

VAPIANO
ITALIAN €

Map p234 (www.vapiano.hu; II Bécsi út 33-35; mains 1250-1250Ft; ☺8am-11pm Mon-Thu, to midnight Fri, 11am-midnight Sat, to 11pm Sun; ☐Szépvölgyi út) This branch of the popular pizza and pasta bar in Belváros (p86) is a welcome addition to Óbuda's dining scene.

FÖLDES JÓZSI KONYHÁJA
HUNGARIAN, ÉTKEZDE €

Map p234 (www.foldesjozsikonyhaja.hu, in Hungarian; Frankel Leó út 30-34; mains 990-1200Ft; ☺noon-3.30pm Sun & Mon, to 10pm Tue-Sat; ☐4, 6, 17) So Joe Earthy – hey, that's what his name means – leaves his post as chef at the Duna Inter-Con and decides to open this rustic little place in Óbuda just opposite the Lukács Baths. And we can't get enough of his cooking.

MAHARAJA
INDIAN €€

Map p234 (www.maharaja.hu; III Bécsi út 89-91; mains 1400-4600Ft; ☐17) This Óbuda institution was the first Indian restaurant to open in Budapest. It specialises in northern Indian dishes, especially tandoori ones (1400Ft to 4600Ft). It's never been the best subcontinental eatery in town, but it does manage some kick-arse samosas.

DON PEPE
PIZZERIA €

Map p234 (www.donpepe.hu; II Árpád fejedelem útja 8; mains 1390-2280Ft; ☑; ☐17; ☐86) A branch of a chain but a good one nonetheless, Don Pepe ventures further afield than just pizzas with an array of pasta, meat and vegetarian dishes. It's attached to the Császár-Komjádi swimming complex, so is quite convenient if you've taken the plunge.

KOLOSY TÉRI SÜTÖDE
BAKERY €

Map p234 (Mozai; III Szépvölgyi út 5; cakes from 250Ft; ☺5am-8pm Mon-Fri, to 7pm Sat & Sun; ☐86) Many local people say that this purveyor of baked goods, which is also called Mozai, is the best takeaway bakery in the city. We can at least agree that their *mákos rétes* (poppy-seed strudel) is scrumptious.

GASZTRÓ HÚS-HENTESÁRU
HUNGARIAN €

Map p234 (II Margit körút 2; dishes from 200Ft; ☺7am-6pm Mon, 6am-7pm Tue-Fri, 6am-1pm Sat; ☐4, 6) Opposite the first stop of trams 4 and 6 on the west side of Margaret Bridge, this place with the unappetising name of 'Gastro Meat and Butcher Products' is a traditional butcher shop also serving cooked sausages and roast chicken to be eaten in situ.

NAGYI PALACSINTÁZÓJA
HUNGARIAN €

off Map p234 (III Szentendrei út 131; pancakes 130-640Ft, set menus 760-950Ft; ☺24hr; ☐34, 106) This branch of 'Granny's Palacsinta Place', the popular pancake chain, is handy when visiting Aquincum.

TRÓFEA GRILL
INTERNATIONAL, BUFFET €€

Map p234 (www.trofeagrill.hu; I Margit körút 2; lunch/dinner Mon-Thu 3299/4999Ft, lunch & dinner Fri-Sun 4999Ft; ☺noon-midnight Mon-Fri, 11.30am-midnight Sat, 11.30am-8.30pm Sun; ☐4, 6) This Buda branch of the popular all-you-can-eat buffet in Újlipótváros (p109) is just over Margaret Bridge and offers live music nightly.

🍴 Buda Hills

⬆️TOP CHOICE NÁNCSI NÉNI
HUNGARIAN €€

(Auntie Nancy; ☑397 2742; www.nancsineni.hu; II Ördögárok út 80; mains 1670-2980Ft; ☐61 then bus 157) Auntie Náncsi (generic for any loopy old lady in Hungarian) is a perennial favourite with locals and expats alike, and she's very much of sound mind. Housed in a lovely cabin up in Hűvösvölgy, the restaurant specialises in game in autumn and winter. In summer it's the lighter fare – lots of stuff cooked with grapes and morello cherries – and garden seating that attracts.

ARCADE BISTRO
INTERNATIONAL €€

off Map p233 (☑225 1969; www.arcadebistro.hu; XII Kiss János altábornagy utca 38; mains 2790-5450Ft; ☺noon-midnight Mon-Sat, to 4pm Sun; ☐105) This family-run eatery in Buda's well-heeled district XII, southwest of the Déli train station, has superb and very creative international cuisine created by master chef László Fazekas. There's also a much-coveted leafy terrace set between two converging roads, seamless service and a very good wine list.

REMÍZ
HUNGARIAN, INTERNATIONAL **€€**

Map p233 (☎2751396; www.remiz.hu; II Budakeszi út 5; mains 2320-4980Ft; ☎61) Next to a *remíz* (tram depot) in the Buda Hills, this virtual institution remains popular for its reliable food (try the grilled dishes, especially the ribs; 2980Ft to 3580Ft), competitive prices and verdant garden terrace. Portions are huge, and service flawless.

SZÉP ILONA
HUNGARIAN **€€**

Map p233 (☎275 1392; www.szepilonavendeglo.hu, in Hungarian; II Budakeszi út 1-3; mains 1400-3900Ft; ☎noon-11pm; ☎61) This old Buda Hills favourite next to Remíz is the place to come for hearty indigenous fare at very modest prices. The name refers to the 'Beautiful Helen' in the ballad by poet Mihály Vörösmarty: she falls in love with a dashing 'hunter', who turns out to be the young King Matthias Corvinus (see p53).

FUJI JAPÁN
JAPANESE **€€€**

Map p233 (☎325 7111; www.fujirestaurant.hu; II Csatárka út 54; dishes 2200-6600Ft; ☎29) Above Rózsadomb in district II and on the corner of Zöld lomb utca and Zöldkert út, Fuji is a long way to go for sushi and sashimi and hot mains like sukiyaki. But this is the most authentic Japanese game in town, judging from the repeat clientele who nip in regularly for noodles and more. Set weekday lunch is just 1990Ft.

MUGHAL SHAHI
PAKISTANI **€€**

Map p233 (www.pakistani-etterem.hu; XII Városmajor utca 57; mains 1600-2600Ft; ☎128) Authentic (and reasonably priced) Pakistani fare on the way up to the Buda Hills (of all places). Pakistani dishes usually pack more of a punch than their Indian equivalents: hotter, spicier and somewhat more salty.

 DRINKING & NIGHTLIFE

PUSKÁS PANCHO
BAR

Map p234 (www.symbolbudapest.hu; III Bécsi út 56; ☎17) In Óbuda's sprawling Symbol entertainment complex, this popular sports pub is named after Ferenc Puskás (1927–2006), Hungary's greatest football player who emigrated to Spain after the 1956 Uprising and played for Real Madrid. Ferenc in Hungarian and Pancho in Spanish are the same name: Frank.

CALGARY ANTIK BÁR
BAR

Map p234 (II Frankel Leó utca 24; ☎6pm-late; ☎4,6) Teensy bar just over Margaret Bridge hides an Aladdin's Cave, filled to bursting with antiques and a host of loyal regulars who stay up all night, playing cards, drinking and gossiping with owner Viky Szabo, ex-model turned junk shop owner. A real local secret, this one.

DAUBNER CUKRÁSZDA
CAFE

Map p234 (www.daubnercukraszda.hu, in Hungarian; II Szépvölgyi út 50; ☎bakery 9am-7pm daily, cafe 9am-7pm Sat & Sun; ☎65) It may seem quite a journey for your *Sachertorte* (chocolate cake) and you can only stand and nibble here during the week, but Daubner gets rave reviews from locals and expats alike as the best shop for cakes (220Ft to 460ft) in Buda. The entrance to the cafe is on Pusztaszeri út around the corner.

 ENTERTAINMENT

ÓBUDA SOCIETY
CONCERT VENUE

Map p234 (Óbudai Társaskör; ☎250 0288; www.obudaitarsaskor.hu; III Kis Korona utca 7; tickets 2500-3000Ft; ☎Tímár utca; ☎86) This very intimate venue surrounded by appalling Óbuda housing estates takes its music very seriously and hosts recitals and some chamber orchestras.

INTERNATIONAL BUDA STAGE
THEATRE

Map p233 (IBS; ☎391 2525; www.ibsszinpad.hu; II Tárogató út 2-4; tickets free-3000Ft; ☎box office 10am-6pm Mon-Fri; ☎29; ☎61) Further afield on the way to the Buda Hills, the theatre at the International Business School is a relative newcomer and has occasional performances – often comedies – in English as well as folk music and dance specials.

 SHOPPING

BÁV
ANTIQUES

Map p234 (www.bav.hu, in Hungarian; II Frankel Leó utca 13; ☎10am-6pm Mon-Fri, to 2pm Sat; ☎4, 6) This branch of BÁV (p103) is good for jewellery, lamps and fine porcelain.

ÓBUDA & BUDA HILLS DRINKING & NIGHTLIFE

Belváros

Neighbourhood Top Five

1 Strolling up (or down) **Váci utca** (p84), the nerve centre of Budapest tourism, and taking in all that entails: unusual architecture, some fine shops, the odd eatery worth consideration and crowds of people.

2 Savouring a cup of something warm and a slice of something sweet at **Gerbeaud** (p87), Budapest's finest *cukrászda* (cake shop).

3 Taking in a play in English at the **Merlin Theatre** (p88) or – for the brave – in Hungarian at the **József Katona Theatre** (p88).

4 Welcoming in the new day and saying goodbye to the old one at **Gödör** (p88), Budapest's most central club.

5 Browsing through the antiquarian bookshops, such as **Központi Antikvárium** (p88), that line V Múzeum körút.

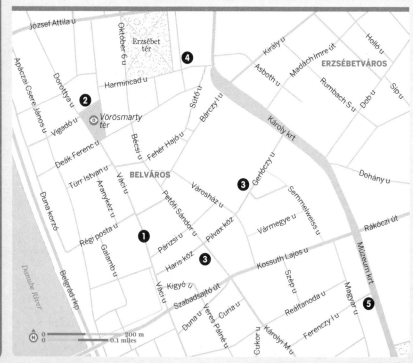

For more detail of this area, see Map p238

Explore: Belváros

Belváros ('Inner Town') is the very heart of Pest and contains the most valuable commercial real estate in the city. The area north of busy Ferenciek tere is full of flashy boutiques and well-frequented bars and restaurants; you'll usually hear more German, Italian, Spanish and English spoken here than Hungarian. The neighbourhood to the south was once rather studenty, quieter and much more local; now much of it is reserved for pedestrians, and there is no shortage of trendy shops and cafes along with the usual souvenir shops and boutiques.

Belváros contains four important 'centres': V Deák Ferenc tér is a busy square in the northeast corner, the only place where all three metro lines (M1/2/3) converge, also accessible by trams 47 and 49; touristy V Vörösmarty tér is on the M1 metro at the northern end of V Váci utca; V Ferenciek tere, on metro M3, divides the Inner Town at Szabad sajtó út; and V Egyetem tér (University Sq) is a five-minute walk south along V Károly Mihály utca from Ferenciek tere and 250m northwest of Kálvin tér on the M3 metro along leafy V Kecskeméti utca.

Local Life

➡ **Eating** A *disznótor* is a 'pig slaughter' in Hungarian, but is also where the animal is turned into sausages and other comestibles. Think 'feast' and that's what you'll find at the very local Belvárosi Disznótoros (p86).

➡ **Shopping** Souvenirs and that hat you've been coveting will be a lot cheaper if you head for lower Váci utca (p84), the bit of Budapest's main shopping street that runs south from Szabad sajtó út to Vámház körút.

➡ **Museum** Visiting a museum devoted to literature when you don't speak the language might sound like a waste of time, but the palace housing the Petőfi Museum of Literature (p85) is well worth a look.

Getting There & Away

➡ **Bus** V Ferenciek tere for 7 or 7E to Buda or points east in Pest; V Egyetem tér for 15 or 115 to IX Boráros tér and northern Pest.

➡ **Ferry** Vigadó tér pier for ferries to III Rómaifürdő and Csillaghegy in Óbuda and Szentendre.

➡ **Metro** M3 Ferenciek tere, M1 Vörösmarty tér, M1/2/3 Deák Ferenc tér.

➡ **Tram** Little Ring Rd (Károly körút and Múzeum körút) for 47 or 49 from V Deák Ferenc tér to Liberty Bridge and points in south Buda; Belgrád rakpart for the 2 to V Szent István körút or south Pest.

Lonely Planet's Top Tip

A lovely way to see the Belváros from a different angle altogether is to hop on one of the BKV passenger ferries (p204) that make some 14 stops along the Danube from IX Boráros tér in Pest to III Pünkösdfürdő in Óbuda. The most convenient stop here is V Vigadó tér. Simply take the ferry over to I Batthyány tér or carry on further afield.

 Best Places to Eat

➡ Bottega della Famiglia (p87)

➡ Kárpátia (p86)

➡ Gerlóczy (p86)

➡ Taverna Dionysos (p86)

For reviews, see p85 ➡

 Best Places to Drink

➡ Gerbeaud (p87)

➡ Csendes (p87)

➡ Columbus (p88)

For reviews, see p87 ➡

Best Places to Shop

➡ Valeria Fazekas (p89)

➡ Holló Atelier (p90)

➡ Magma (p90)

➡ Rododendron (p90)

➡ Múzeum Antikvárium (p88)

For reviews, see p88 ➡

BELVÁROS

TOP SIGHTS
VÁCI UTCA & VÖRÖSMARTY TÉR

The best way to see the 'have' side of Belváros is to walk up pedestrian Váci utca, the capital's premier shopping street, with designer clothes, antique jewellery shops, pubs and some bookshops for browsing. This was the total length of Pest in the Middle Ages. A good place to start is at the Párizsi Udvar (Parisian Court) at V Ferenciek tere 5, built in 1909. Walk through the decorated arcade with its ornately decorated ceiling and out onto tiny Kigyó utca. Váci utca is immediately to the west.

Many of the buildings on Váci utca are worth a closer look, but as it's a narrow street you'll have to crane your neck or walk into one of the side lanes for a better view. **Thonet House** at No 11/a is a masterpiece built by Ödön Lechner (p144) in 1890 and the **Philanthia** flower and gift shop at No 9 has an original (and very rare) art nouveau interior from 1906. The **Polgár Gallery** next door at No 11/b, in a building dating from 1912, contains a stunning stained-glass domed ceiling. To the west, at Régi Posta utca 13, there's a relief of an old postal coach by the ceramist Margit Kovács of Szentendre.

Just off the top of Váci utca in Kristóf tér is the little **Fishergirl Fountain** dating from the 19th century and complete with a ship's wheel that actually turns. On the square is a brick outline of the foundations of the Vác Gate (Váci kapu), part of the old city wall. A short distance to the northwest is the sumptuous **Bank Palace** (Bank Palota) at V Deák utca 5, built in 1915 and once the home of the Budapest Stock Exchange. It has recently been converted into a shopping gallery called **Váci 1** (www.vaci1.hu).

Váci utca empties into **Vörösmarty tér**, a large square of smart shops, galleries, cafes and a smattering of artists who will draw your portrait or caricature. Suitable for framing maybe... In the centre is a **statue of Mihály Vörösmarty**, the 19th-century poet after whom the square is named. It is made of Italian marble and is protected in winter by a bizarre plastic 'iceberg' that kids love sliding on. The first – or last – stop of the little yellow M1 metro line is also in the square, and at the northern end is **Gerbeaud** (p87), Budapest's fanciest and most famous cafe and cake shop.

The **Pesti Vigadó**, the Romantic-style concert hall built in 1865 but badly damaged during WWII, faces the river on Vigadó tér to the west. A pleasant way to return to Ferenciek tere is along the **Duna korzó**, the riverside 'Danube Promenade' between Chain and Elizabeth Bridges that is full of cafes, musicians and handicraft stalls.

DON'T MISS...

➡ Párizsi Udvar
➡ Philanthia
➡ Gerbeaud
➡ Bank Palace
➡ Duna korzó

PRACTICALITIES

➡ Map p238
➡ V Váci utca
➡ Ⓜ M1 Vörösmarty tér, M3 Ferenciek tere
➡ 🚌7
➡ 🚊2

⊙ SIGHTS

**VÁCI UTCA &
VÖRÖSMARTY TÉR**   STREET, SQUARE

See p84.

INNER TOWN PARISH CHURCH   CHURCH

Map p238 (Belvárosi plébániatemplom; V Március 15 tér 2; ⊙9am-7pm; 🚇2) On the eastern side of Március 15 tér, now uncomfortably close to the Elizabeth Bridge flyover, is where a Romanesque church was first built in the 12th century within a Roman fortress. You can still see bits and pieces of the fort, **Contra Aquincum**, protected under plexiglas in the small park to the north. The present church was rebuilt in the 14th century and again in the 18th century, and you can easily spot Gothic, Renaissance, baroque and even Turkish – eg the mihrab (prayer niche) in the eastern wall – elements.

UNDERGROUND RAILWAY MUSEUM   MUSEUM

Map p238 (Földalatti Vasúti Múzeum; www.bkv.hu; 1 BKV ticket or adult/child 320/260Ft; ⊙10am-5pm Tue-Sun; MM1/2/3 Deák Ferenc tér) In the pedestrian subway beneath V Deák Ferenc tér, next to the main ticket window, the Underground Railway Museum traces the history of the capital's three (soon to be four) underground lines and displays plans for the future. Much emphasis is put on the little yellow metro (M1), Continental Europe's first underground railway, which opened for the millenary celebrations in 1896 and was completely renovated for the millecentenary 100 years later. In fact, the museum is housed in a stretch of tunnel and station (called Gizella tér) that once formed part of the M1 line until it was diverted in 1955.

LUTHERAN CHURCH   CHURCH

Map p238 (Evangélikus templom; V Deák Ferenc tér 4; ⊙10am-6pm Tue-Sun; MM1/2/3 Deák Ferenc tér) This very central church on the south side of V Deák Ferenc tér, designed by Mihály Pollack in 1799, is one of the best examples of early neoclassical architecture in the city. In the attached presbytery, which also functioned as a school (attended at one point by the poet Sándor Petőfi), you'll find the **National Lutheran Museum** (Evangélikus Országos Múzeum; www.evangelikusmuzeum.hu; adult/child 500/200Ft; ⊙10am-6pm Tue-Sun), tracing the history of the Reformation in Hungary. Exhibits include a church plate and a copy of Martin Luther's will.

EGYETEM TÉR   SQUARE

Map p238 (MM3 V Ferenciek tere; 🚌15, 115) 'University Sq' takes its name from the branch of the prestigious **Loránd Eötvös Science University** (ELTE; V Egyetem tér 1-3). Attached to the main university building to the west is the lovely baroque 1742 **University Church** (Egyetemi templom; V Papnövelde utca 5-7; ⊙7am-7pm). Over the altar is a copy of the Black Madonna of Częstochowa so revered in Poland. The church is often full of young people praying, no doubt for a miracle on their exams. The building to the north of the square with the multicoloured dome is **University Library** (Egyetemi könyvtár; V Ferenciek tere 10). Southwest of Egyetem tér, at the corner of Szerb utca and Veres Pálné utca, stands the **Serbian Orthodox Church** (Szerb ortodox templom; V Veres Páné utca 19; admission 500Ft; ⊙9.30am-1pm & 2-5pm), built by Serbs fleeing the Turks in the 17th century. The **iconostasis** is worth a look.

PETŐFI MUSEUM OF LITERATURE   MUSEUM

Map p238 (Petőfi Irodalmi Múzeum; www.pim.hu; V Károlyi Mihály utca 16; adult/child 600/300Ft; ⊙10am-6pm Tue-Sun; MM3 Kálvin tér; 🚌15, 115) Just north of Egyetem tér and housed in the sumptuous neoclassical **Károly Palace** (Károlyi Palota), dating from 1840, this museum has rooms devoted to Sándor Petőfi, Endre Ady, Mór Jókai and Attila József. Also here is a centre for contemporary literature, a library, a concert/lecture hall and a terrace restaurant in the courtyard.

✗ EATING

In general, central Pest offers a wider range of restaurants than Buda – especially when it comes to ethnic cuisine. That's not so true in the Belváros, preserve of expense accounts, well-heeled tourists and one of Budapest's two Michelin-starred restaurants.

SPOON   INTERNATIONAL €€

Map p238 (☎411 0933; www.spooncafe.hu; off V Vigadó tér 3; mains 3900-4950Ft; ⊙noon-midnight; ✈; 🚇2) If you like the idea of dining on the high waters but still remaining tethered to the bank (just in case), Spoon is for you. The choice of seating is legion – cafe, lounge, winter garden or breezy terrace – and the cuisine international fusion, with good choices for vegetarians. You can't beat the views of the castle and Chain Bridge.

TOP CHOICE KÁRPÁTIA HUNGARIAN €€€

Map p238 (☎317 3596; www.karpatia.hu; V Ferenciek tere 7-8; mains 3800-7900Ft; ⓂM3 Ferenciek tere) A veritable palace of fin-de-siècle design dating some 135 years that has to be seen to be believed, the 'Carpathia' serves almost modern Hungarian and Transylvanian specialities in both a palatial restaurant in the back and less-expensive *söröző* (brasserie); there is also a lovely covered garden terrace. This is one place to hear authentic *csárdás* (Gypsy-style folk music), played nightly from 6pm to 11pm.

PESTI LAMPÁS HUNGARIAN, INTERNATIONAL €€

Map p238 (☎266 9566; www.pestilampas.hu; V Károlyi Mihály utca 12; mains 1800-4800Ft; ⊗10am-midnight Mon-Fri, noon-2am Sat; ☑; ⓂM3 Ferenciek tere; ☑15, 115) The light leads the way (we're being figurative here) to the 'Pest Lantern', a very welcoming restaurant and coffee house. The place beckons not so much for the food (though it is very good) but for its location in a renovated mansion near ELTE university. It has a wonderful terrace in the palace courtyard open in the warmer months and the menu has lots of options for vegetarians (950Ft to 1800Ft).

TRATTORIA TOSCANA ITALIAN €€

Map p238 (☎327 0045; www.toscana.hu; V Belgrád rakpart 13; mains 1850-4490Ft; ⊗noon-midnight; ☑15, 115; ☑2) Hard by the Danube, this trattoria serves rustic and very authentic Italian and Tuscan food, including *pasta e fagioli* (a hearty soup of beans and pasta) and a wonderful Tuscan farmer's platter of prepared meats. The pizza and pasta dishes are excellent too, as is the antipasto buffet.

FATÁL HUNGARIAN €€

Map p238 (☎266 2607; www.fatalrestaurant .com; V Váci utca 67; mains 2890-3590Ft; ⊗noon-midnight; ☑47, 49) No, this is not what you risk when visiting this place. Fatál might be a tourist trap but it serves massive Hungarian meals on a *fatál* (wooden platter) or in iron cauldrons in three rustic rooms. And follow the rules: bring your appetite and its friends; avoid the noisy backroom; book in advance; and bring cash (no cards).

BANGKOK HOUSE THAI €€

Map p238 (www.thaietterem.hu; V Só utca 3; mains 1790-5390Ft; ⊗noon-11pm; ☑47, 49) Bangkok House is done up in kitsch, Asian-esque decor that recalls takeaway places around the world. The Thai- and Laotian-inspired dishes are fine, though, and service all but seamless. A lunch menu (1500Ft) is available from noon to 4pm.

TAVERNA DIONYSOS GREEK €€

Map p238 (☎318 1222; www.taverna-dionysos .hu; V Belgrád rakpart 16; mains 2590-5320Ft; ⊗noon-midnight; ☑2) All faux Greek columns and a blue-and-white colour scheme, this taverna facing the river packs in diners on its three floors. Expect all the usual Greek favourites – from tzatziki and souvlaki to grilled octopus – and more.

VAPIANO ITALIAN €

Map p238 (www.vapiano.hu; V Bécsi utca 5; mains 1250-1250Ft; ⊗closed Sun; ⓂM1 Vörösmarty tér) A very welcome addition to the Inner Town is this pizza and pasta bar where everything is prepared on-site. You'll be in and out in no time, but the taste will certainly linger. Caters mostly to office workers in the centre; outside seating in warm weather.

CAFÉ ALIBI INTERNATIONAL €€

Map p238 (www.cafealibi.hu; V Egyetem tér 4; salads 1890-2490Ft, mains 2290-2790Ft; ⊗8am-11pm; ⓂM3 Ferenciek tere) We ususally come to this cafe-restaurant with a great terrace in the heart of university land for late breakfast (till noon weekdays, 4pm Saturday and Sunday) with coffee roasted in-house, plus snacks (990Ft to 1890Ft) or an excellent-value set lunch (990Ft).

GERLÓCZY BISTRO €€

Map p238 (☎501 4000; www.gerloczy.hu; V Gerlóczy utca 1; mains 1800-4500Ft, 2-/3-course set lunch 1400/1800Ft; ⊗7am-11pm; ☑47, 49) The expanded terrace of this wonderful retro-style cafe looks out onto one of Pest's most attractive little squares and serves excellent breakfast (600Ft to 2200Ft) and light meals, including a cheese plate sent over from the superb T Nagy Tamás (p90) cheese shop around the corner, as well as full meals. Live music (harp or piano) nightly.

BELVÁROSI DISZNÓTOROS HUNGARIAN €

Map p238 (V Károlyi Mihály utca 17; dishes 350-900Ft; ⊗8.30am-7pm Mon-Fri, to 3pm Sat; ⓂM3 Kálvin tér; ☑15, 115) If your level of hunger could be described as ravenous, visit this butcher-cum-caterer that does every type of Hungarian sausage known to man and woman, and whose name could be loosely translated as 'Inner Town Feast'. Take away or eat standing up at the counters outside.

NOBU
JAPANESE €€€

Map p238 (☎429 4242; www.noburestaunars .com; Kempinski Hotel Corvinus, V Erzsébet tér 7-8; mains 2200-10,800Ft; ☺noon-11.45pm; Ⓜ M1/2/3 Deák Ferenc tér) How chichi is this? Budapest knows it has arrived when it gets a branch of the London glitterati's favourite canteen. As elsewhere, Nobu is minimalist in decor to the point of excess, anonymously efficient in service, and out of this world when it comes to exquisitely prepared and presented sushi and sashimi.

ONYX
HUNGARIAN €€€

Map p238 (☎429 9023; www.onyxrestaurant .hu; V Vörösmarty tér 7-8; mains 6500-7500Ft; ☺noon-2pm & 6.30-11.30pm; Ⓜ M1 Vörösmarty tér) This Michelin-starred eatery adjacent to (and owned by) Gerbeaud (p87) has taken it upon its own lofty shoulders to modernise Hungarian cuisine, and its seven-course 'Hungarian Evolution' tasting menu (19,900Ft) suggests it's well on its way in achieving that goal. Decor is a little too bejewelled for us, though.

BOTTEGA DELLA FAMIGLIA
ITALIAN €€

Map p238 (V Szende Pál utca 5; mains 1800-3500Ft; ☺9am-3pm Mon & Tue, to 9pm Wed-Sat; Ⓜ M1 Vörösmarty tér) This wonderful 'pop-up' restaurant (no one knows it's here despite the central location north of Vörösmarty tér and there's no sign outside) serves some of the best homestyle Italian in town. There's no menu as such; just a list of dishes that the chef has decided to make that day.

BABEL DELIKÁT
FUSION €€€

Map p238 (☎338 2143; www.babeldelicate.hu; V Szarka utca 1; mains 3500-6500Ft; ☺6pm-midnight Tue-Sat; 🚌47, 49) This smart eatery will bowl you over with its ambient lighting and black lacquer surfaces, but stick around for the food – a marriage of Hungarian and Asian tastes that, incongruous as they sound, work very well together.

NAGYI PALACSINTÁZÓJA
HUNGARIAN €

Map p238 (V Petőfi Sándor utca 17-19; pancakes 130-640Ft; set menus 760-950Ft; ☺24hr; Ⓜ M1/2/3 Deák Ferenc tér) The most central branch of 'Granny's Palacsinta Place', Budapest's popular chain selling both savoury and sweet Hungarian-style pancakes.

DRINKING & NIGHTLIFE

🅃🄾🄿 CHOICE GERBEAUD
CAFE

Map p238 (www.gerbeaud.hu; V Vörösmarty tér 7-8; ☺9am-9pm; Ⓜ M1 Vörösmarty tér) Founded on the northern side of Pest's busiest square in 1858, Gerbeaud has been the most fashionable meeting place for the city's elite since 1870. Along with exquisitely prepared cakes and pastries (from 750Ft), it serves continental/full breakfast (1950/2650Ft) and sandwiches. A visit is mandatory.

AZTÉK CHOXOLAT
CAFE

Map p238 (www.choxolat.hu; V Károly körút 22 & V Semmelweis utca 19; ☺7am-7pm Mon-Fri, 9am-2pm Sat; Ⓜ M1/2/3 Deák Ferenc tér) This temple to all things chocolate hidden up a small passage west of the Little Ring Rd has the best hot chocolate (490Ft to 790Ft) in Budapest, as well as excellent pastries and individual chocolates to munch on.

CSENDES
CAFE, BAR

Map p238 (www.kiscsendes.hu; V Ferenczy István utca 5; ☺8am-midnight Mon-Fri, from 10am Sat, from 2pm Sun; Ⓜ M2 Astoria) A quirky cafe just off the Little Ring Rd with 'found objects' decorating the walls and floor space, the 'Quietly' is just that until the regular DJ arrives and cranks up the volume. Loyal crowd.

CENTRÁL KÁVÉHÁZ
CAFE

Map p238 (www.centralkavehaz.hu; V Károlyi Mihály utca 9; ☺8am-midnight; Ⓜ M3 Ferenciek tere) After reopening a few years ago following extensive renovations, this *grande dame* of a traditional cafe dating back to 1887 (see p194) has reclaimed her title as the place to sit and look intellectual in Pest. It serves meals as well as breakfast (230Ft to 980Ft), a set lunch (1200Ft to 1590Ft) and, of course, cakes and pastries (390Ft to 690Ft).

1000 TEA
TEAHOUSE

Map p238 (www.1000tea.hu, in Hungarian; V Váci utca 65; ☺noon-9pm Mon-Thu, to 10pm Fri & Sat; 🚋15, 115) In a small courtyard off lower Váci utca, this is the place if you want to sip a soothing blend made by tea-serious staff and lounge on pillows in a Japanese-style tearoom. You can also sit on the teachests and sip in the courtyard. There's a shop here too.

BÉLVÁROS ENTERTAINMENT

JANIS PUB BAR

Map p238 (www.janispub.hu; V Királyi Pál utca 8; ◷4pm-3am Tue-Sat; Ⓜ M3 Kálvin tér) Close to the university, this popular pub is a shrine to the late, great singer Janis 'Pearl' Joplin, which puts something of a bizarre slant on a place describing itself as a 'traditional Irish pub'. Still it's a good place to stop for a quick one on the way to somewhere else.

[TOP CHOICE] GÖDÖR CLUB, CAFE

Map p238 (www.godorklub.hu; V Erzsébet tér; ◷10am-2am Sun-Wed, to 4am Thu-Sat; Ⓜ M1/2/3 Deák Ferenc tér) The 'Pit' is a city-sponsored cultural centre in the old bays below Erzsébet tér in central Pest where international buses used to drop off and pick up passengers. It's a real mixed bag – cafe by day and club offering everything from folk and world, but specially rock and pop, by night.

MERLIN CLUB

Map p238 (www.merlinbudapest.org; V Gerlóczy utca 4; ◷11pm-5am; Ⓜ M1/2/3 Deák Ferenc tér) This high-ceilinged venue that moonlights as a theatre is one of those something-for-everyone kind of places, with anything from jazz and breakbeat to techno and house. It turns into a bar and club most nights, but the party and the atmosphere very much depend on who's on stage.

[TOP CHOICE] ACTION BÁR GAY

Map p238 (www.action.gay.hu; V Magyar utca 42; ◷9pm-4am; Ⓜ M3 Kálvin tér) Action is where to head if you want just that (though there's a strip show at 12.30am on Friday and at 12.45am on Saturday, which may distract). Take the usual precautions and don't forget to write home.

HABROLÓ GAY

Map p238 (www.habrolo.hu; V Szép utca 1; ◷9am-dawn Mon-Fri, from 7pm Sat & Sun; Ⓜ M3 Ferenciek tere) Welcoming neighbourhood gay bar on 'Beautiful St' (could it be anywhere else, Mary?) is a cafe with a tiny lounge space upstairs and small stage.

☆ ENTERTAINMENT

COLUMBUS JAZZ

Map p238 (www.columbuspub.hu; V Pesti alsó rakpart at Chain Bridge; ◷11am-midnight; 🚋2) On a boat moored on the Danube off the northern end of V Vigadó tér, this club's nightly live music includes jazz, with big-name local and international bands. Music starts at 7.30pm and there are usually two concerts lasting 45 minutes.

PUSKIN ART MOZI CINEMA

Map p238 (www.artmozi.hu; V Kossuth Lajos utca 18; 🚋7) The long-established 'Pushkin Art Cinema' shows a healthy mix of art-house and popular releases.

JÓZSEF KATONA THEATRE THEATRE

Map p238 (Katona József Színház; ☎318 3725; www.katonajozsefszinhaz.hu; V Petőfi Sándor utca 6; tickets 1200-3900Ft; ◷box office 11am-7pm Mon-Fri, from 3pm Sat & Sun; Ⓜ M3 Ferenciek tere) The József Katona Theatre is the best known in Hungary and is a public theatre supported mainly by the city of Budapest. Its studio theatre, Kamra, hosts some of the best troupes in the country.

MERLIN THEATRE THEATRE

Map p238 (☎317 9338; www.merlinszinhaz.hu; V Gerlóczy utca 4; tickets 1000-2500Ft; ◷box office 2-7pm Mon-Fri; Ⓜ M1/2/3 Deák Ferenc tér; 🚋47, 49) This international theatre stages numerous plays in English, often performed by Budapest's resident English-language improvisational company, Scallabouche, and the Madhouse Company.

🛍 SHOPPING

MÚZEUM ANTIKVÁRIUM BOOKS

Map p238 (www.muzeumantikvarium.hu; V Múzeum körút 35; ◷10am-6pm Mon-Fri, to 2pm Sat; Ⓜ M3 Kálvin tér) Just opposite the Hungarian National Museum is this well-stocked bookshop with both used and antique volumes in a Babel of languages, including English. It's our favourite of the – count 'em – nine bookshops on this street.

KÖZPONTI ANTIKVÁRIUM BOOKS

Map p238 (☎317 3514; V Múzeum körút 13-15; ◷10am-6pm Mon-Fri, to 2pm Sat; Ⓜ M2 Astoria) For antique and secondhand books in Hungarian, German and English, try the 'Central Antiquarian'. Established in 1885, it is the largest antique bookshop in Budapest.

BÁV ANTIQUES

Map p238 (www.bav.hu, in Hungarian; V Bécsi utca 1-3; ◷10am-6pm Mon-Fri, to 2pm Sat; Ⓜ M1/2/3 Deák Ferenc tér) This branch of the BÁV (p103) chain is good for knick-knacks, porcelain, glassware, carpets and artwork.

RED BUS BOOKSTORE
BOOKS

Map p238 (www.redbusbudapest.hu; V Semmel-weis utca 14; ☺11am-6pm Mon-Fri, 10am-2pm Sat; MM1/2/3 Deák Ferenc tér) Below the popular hostel (p162) of the same name, the Red Bus has a good selection of secondhand English-language books.

LIBRI STÚDIUM
BOOKS

Map p238 (www.libri.hu; V Váci utca 22; ☺10am-7pm Mon-Fri, 10am-3pm Sat & Sun; MM3 Ferenciek tere) This branch of the large Hungarian bookshop chain stocks lots of English-language books, including novels, guidebooks and maps. Importantly, books on Hungarian subjects and Hungarian novels in translation are available here.

IMMEDIO
BOOKS

Map p238 (V Városház utca 3-5; ☺7am-7pm Mon-Fri, 7am-2pm Sat, 8am-noon Sun; MM3 Ferenciek tere) The best place in Budapest for foreign-language newspapers and magazines is Immedio, which also has a nearby **branch** (☏318 5604; V Váci utca 10; ☺8am-8pm).

ECLECTICK
FASHION, CLOTHING

Map p238 (www.eclectick.hu; V Irányi utca 20; ☺10am-7pm Mon-Fri, noon-5pm Sat; MM3 Ferenciek tere) Just opposite the Centrál Kávéház (p87), local designer Edina Farkas' boutique mostly sells her own innovative creations, but also stocks clothing and accessories by Aquanauta, Balkan Tango, Red Aster and PUCC.

VALERIA FAZEKAS
FASHION, CLOTHING

Map p238 (www.valeriafazekas.com; V Váci utca 50; ☺10am-6pm Mon-Fri, to 4pm Sat; MM3 Ferenciek tere) Are they hats or is it art? We'll say both. Some of the limited headgear in a wide range of colours and fabrics on offer in this small gem of a boutique are out of this world (or at least on their way there). Artist-designer Fazekas also does silk scarves and stylish tops.

BALOGH KESZTYŰ ÜZLET
GLOVES

Map p238 (V Haris köz 2; ☺11am-6pm Mon-Thu, to 5pm Fri, to 1pm Sat; MM3 Ferenciek tere) If he can have a pair of bespoke shoes from Vass Shoes, why can't she have a pair of custom-made gloves lined with cashmere? You'll get them here at the 'Balogh Gloves Shop' – and there's any number of materials to choose from for men too, including shearling-lined leather gloves.

RETROCK
FASHION, CLOTHING

Map p238 (V Ferenczy István utca 28; ☺10.30am-7.30pm Mon-Sat, to 3.30pm Sat; MM3 Ferenciek tere) This ultra-hip establishment has streetwear and accessories mostly from local designers inspired by street art, music and retro fashion. For vintage clothing and bags, go round the corner to **Retrock Deluxe** (Map p238; V Henszlmann Imre utca 1; ☺10.30am-7.30pm Mon-Sat, to 3.30pm Sat; MM3 Kálvin tér).

BYBLOS
FASHION, CLOTHING

Map p238 (www.byblos.hu; V Deák Ferenc utca 17; ☺10am-7pm Mon-Sat, 10am-6pm Sun; MM1/2/3 Deák Ferenc tér) Anchor tenant of the pedestrianised thoroughfare that wants everyone to call it 'Fashion Street', this ultra-elegant establishment has both casual wear and formal attire for men and women from international (mostly Italian) designers.

MONO FASHION
FASHION, CLOTHING

Map p238 (www.monofashion.hu; V Kossuth Lajos utca 20; ☺10am-8pm Mon-Fri, to 6pm Sat; MM2 Astoria) Stocks the work of local clothes designers as well as its own brand NUBU. Great window displays.

MANU-ART
CLOTHING, ACCESSORIES

Map p238 (www.manu-art.hu; V Károly körút 10; ☺10am-6pm Mon-Fri, to 2pm Sat; MM2 Astoria) This small shop is stuffed to the gills with brightly coloured T-shirts, bags and bean-bag chairs produced by local designers. And you can tick the green box – most of the materials used are cotton, hemp and linen.

VASS SHOES
SHOES

Map p238 (www.vass-cipo.hu; V Haris köz 2; ☺10am-6pm Mon-Fri, to 2pm Sat; MM3 Ferenciek tere) A traditional shoemaker that stocks ready-to-wear and cobbles to order, Vass has a reputation that goes back to 1896, and some people travel to Hungary just to have their footwear made here.

LE PARFUM CROISETTE
PERFUME

Map p238 (www.leparfum.hu; V Deák Ferenc utca 16-18; ☺10am-7pm Mon-Fri, to 5pm Sat & Sun; MM1/2/3 Deák Ferenc tér) Hungary's only *parfumeur*, Zsolt Zólyomi, makes scents (and sense too) at his atelier-shop tucked behind Le Meridien Budapest hotel. Zólyomi, who foresees a renaissance in the once great Hungarian perfume industry, holds workshops here too.

TOP CHOICE HOLLÓ ATELIER HANDICRAFTS, GIFTS

Map p238 (http://hollomuhely.blogspot.com; V Vitkovics Mihály utca 12; ☺10am-6pm Mon-Fri, to 2pm Sat; Ⓜ M1/2/3 Deák Ferenc tér) Holló Atelier has attractive folk art with a modern look and remains a personal favourite place to shop for gifts and gewgaws. Everything is handmade on-site.

INTUITA CRAFT, GIFTS

Map p238 (V Váci utca 67; ☺11am-6pm; 🚍15, 115) You're not about to find painted eggs and *pálinka* (fruit brandy) here, but it's chock-a-block with contemporary crafted items such as jewellery, ceramics and notebooks. The **branch** (📞3371248; V Váci utca 61) several doors away keeps the same hours but concentrates on clothing and apparel.

RODODENDRON CRAFT, GIFTS

Map p238 (www.rododendron.hu; V Semmelweis utca 19; ☺10am-7pm Mon-Fri, to 4pm Sat; Ⓜ M2 Astoria) This delightful shop near Astoria presents the work of some 30 local designers, with everything from jewellery and cuddly toys to handbags and shows on offer. Looking for a gadget? You couldn't do better than getting hold of a lomography camera, based on a Soviet camera that takes distinctive, colourful and charmingly blurry photos with – *egad!* – film.

TOP CHOICE MAGMA CRAFT, HOMEWARES

Map p238 (www.magma.hu; V Petőfi Sándor utca 11; ☺10am-7pm Mon-Fri, to 3pm Sat; Ⓜ M3 Ferenciek tere) This showroom in the heart of the Inner Town focuses on Hungarian design and designers exclusively – with everything from glassware, porcelain and toys to textiles and furniture.

TOP CHOICE BOMO ART CRAFT

Map p238 (www.bomoart.hu; V Régi Posta utca 14; ☺10am-6.30pm Mon-Fri, to 2pm Sat; Ⓜ M3 Ferenciek tere) This tiny shop just off Váci utca sells some of the finest paper and paper goods in Budapest, including leather-bound notebooks, photo albums and address books.

FOLKART KÉZMŰVÉSHÁZ HANDICRAFTS, SOUVENIRS

Map p238 (www.folkartkezmuveshaz.hu; V Régi Posta utca 12; ☺10am-6pm Mon-Fri, to 3pm Sat & Sun; Ⓜ M3 Ferenciek tere) This is a large shop where everything Magyar (and all of it made here) is available, from embroidered waistcoats and tablecloths to painted eggs and plates. The staff are helpful.

BABAKLINIKA TOYS

Map p238 (V Múzeum körút 5; ☺9.30am-5.30pm Mon-Fri; Ⓜ M2 Astoria) Just down the road from the Astoria metro station, the 'Doll Clinic' specialises in selling (and repairing) handmade dolls and teddy bears.

CADEAU CHOCOLATE

Map p238 (www.cadeaubonbon.hu; V Veres Pálné utca 8; ☺10am-6pm Mon-Fri, to 2pm Sat; Ⓜ M3 Ferenciek tere) 'Death by chocolate' has arrived in Budapest by way of Gyula, a city in Hungary's southeast where the delectable handmade bonbons sold here are made and served at the celebrated Százéves Cukrászda (Century Cake Shop). Best in Budapest.

SZAMOS MARCIPÁN MARZIPAN

Map p238 (www.szamosmarcipan.hu; V Párizsi utca 3; ☺10am-7pm; Ⓜ M3 Ferenciek tere) 'Many Kinds of Marzipan' sells just that – in every shape and size imaginable. Its ice cream (180Ft per scoop) rates among the best in town – another major draw.

RÓZSAVÖLGYI ÉS TÁRSA MUSIC

Map p238 (www.lira.hu, in Hungarian; V Szervita tér 5; ☺10am-7pm Mon-Fri, to 5pm Sat; Ⓜ M1/2/3 Deák Ferenc tér) A great choice for CDs and tapes of traditional folk and classical music, with a good selection of sheet music.

T NAGY TAMÁS CHEESE, WINE

Map p238 (www.tnagytamas.hu; V Gerlóczy utca 3; ☺9am-6pm Mon-Fri, to 1pm Sat; Ⓜ M1/2/3 Deák Ferenc tér) Budapest's best local cheese shop stocks more than 200 varieties of Hungarian and imported cheeses, as well as wines. In summer ask for the *kecskesajt* (goat's cheese).

PRÉSHÁZ WINE

Map p238 (www.preshaz.hu; V Váci utca 10; ☺10am-7pm Mon-Fri, to 6pm Sat) A central wine dispensary, Présház stocks hundreds of wines from major vintners across Hungary in an 18th-century courtyard cellar. There are bottles open for tasting and the staff are very knowledgeable.

Parliament & Around

LIPÓTVÁROS | TERÉZVÁROS (WEST)

Neighbourhood Top Five

1 Entering the hallowed halls of the **Parliament** (p93), arguably the most iconic of all Budapest's buildings, and making your way to the Crown of St Stephen, symbol of the Hungarian nation for more than 1100 years.

2 Doing the right thing by visiting the **Basilica** of St Stephen (p95) and Hungary's most revered religious relic, the Holy Right (hand) of St Stephen.

3 Carousing in and around Nagymező utca, Budapest's own 'Broadway' and home to a plethora of wild and crazy clubs, including **Instant** (p101).

4 Ogling the sinuous curves and asymmetrical forms of the **Royal Postal Savings Bank** (p96), one of Budapest's many incomparable art nouveau buildings.

5 Eating at one of the little eateries called *étkezde*, such as **Kisharang** (p98), that serve Hungarian soul food.

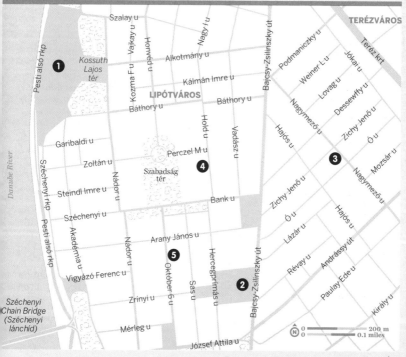

For more detail of this area, see Map p244 ➡

Lonely Planet's Top Tip

One of our favourite places to while away part or all of a Saturday morning is along V Falk Miksa utca (Map p244), which is lined with antique and curio shops. Start at the northern end with BÁV (p103) to get an idea of what your average householder might be getting rid of during spring cleaning and move south on to the various other shops, ending up at the mother of them all: Pintér Antik (p103).

Best Places to Eat

➡ Café Kör (p98)

➡ Mák (p98)

➡ Most! (p99)

➡ Kisharang (p98)

➡ Fruccola (p99)

For reviews, see p97 ➡

Best Places to Drink

➡ Instant (p101)

➡ Club AlterEgo (p101)

➡ Ötkert (p101)

➡ Cake (p101)

➡ Teaház a Vörös Oroszlánhoz (p102)

For reviews, see p100 ➡

Best Places to Shop

➡ BÁV (p103)

➡ Bestsellers (p103)

➡ PannonArts Design Galéria (p104)

➡ Haas & Czjzek (p104)

For reviews, see p103 ➡

PARLIAMENT & AROUND

Explore: Parliament & Around

North of Belváros, the district called Lipótváros (Leopold Town) is full of offices, government ministries, 19th-century apartment blocks and grand squares. Its confines are, in effect, Szent István körút to the north, V József Attila utca to the south, the Danube to the west and, to the east, V Bajcsy-Zsilinszky út, the arrow-straight boulevard that stretches from central Deák Ferenc tér to Nyugati tér, where Nyugati train station is located. It's an easy and fun neighbourhood to explore on foot and its key squares are V Széchenyi István tér (until recently Roosevelt tér) facing the river; V Szabadság tér, with the only Soviet memorial left in the city; and V Kossuth Lajos tér, fronted by Parliament.

Teréz körút carries on from Szent István körút after Nyugati train station, which is on the M3 metro. The neighbourhood on either side of this section of the ring road – district VI – is known as Terézváros (Theresa Town) and was named in honour of Maria Theresa. It extends as far as VI Király utca and the start of VII Erzsébet körút, but in this section we only include everything up to Andrássy út, the long and dramatic boulevard that slices through Terézváros. Places of interest actually on the boulevard can be found in Chapter 22, Erzsébetváros & the Jewish Quarter.

Local Life

➡ **Entertainment** Everyone goes to the Hungarian state Opera House; dare to be different and take in a very glitzy production at the Budapest Operetta (p103).

➡ **Museum** The Ethnography Museum (p96) will take you on a colourful tour of the folk-art heritage and traditions of Hungary without your even leaving Budapest.

➡ **Eating** If you want to try authentic Hungarian sausage and salami but don't feel up to eating at food stalls, head for the Pick Ház (p99) near Parliament.

Getting There & Away

➡ **Bus** V Szabadság tér for 15 or 115 to IX Boráros tér and northern Pest; V Deák Ferenc tér for 16 to Castle Hill and 105 to Buda.

➡ **Metro** M2 Kossuth Lajos tér, M3 Arany János utca and M1/2/3 Deák Ferenc tér.

➡ **Tram** Pesti alsó rakpart for 2 to V Szent István körút or south Pest; V Szent István körút for 4 or 6 to Buda or Big Ring Rd in Pest.

TOP SIGHTS
PARLIAMENT

Hungary's largest building, Parliament (Országház) stretches for some 268m along the left bank of the Danube in Pest from Kossuth Lajor tér. The choice of location was not by chance. As a counterweight to the Royal Palace rising high on Buda Hill on the opposite side of the river, the idea behind its placement was that the nation's future lay with popular democracy and not royal prerogative.

Architecture

Designed by Imre Steindl and completed in 1902, it is thought that the inspiration for this iconic structure was the Houses of Parliament, which had opened in 1860. The building is a blend of many architectural styles (neo-Gothic, neo-Romanesque, neo-Baroque). Sculptures of the great and the good – kings, princes and historical figures – gaze out onto the river from the western facade, while the main door, the so-called **Lion Entrance**, is on the opposite side. Unfortunately, what was spent on the design wasn't matched in the building materials. The ornate structure was surfaced with a porous form of limestone that does not resist pollution very well. Renovations began just two decades after it opened and replacement of the stone blocks will continue for a very long time.

Interior

The interior contains just short of 700 sumptuously decorated rooms, but you'll only get to see a handful on a guided tour of the north wing, including the sweeping **main staircase** leading to the **Domed Hall** where the **Crown of St**

DON'T MISS...

➡ Crown of St Stephen
➡ Domed Hall
➡ Main Staircase
➡ Royal Sceptre
➡ Congress Hall

PRACTICALITIES

➡ Map p244
➡ 441 4904
➡ www.parlament.hu
➡ V Kossuth Lajos tér 1-3, Gate X
➡ adult/child 3400/1700Ft, free for EU citizens
➡ ⊙ticket office 8am-6pm Mon-Fri, to 4pm Sat, to 2pm Sun; English-language tours 10am, noon & 2pm
➡ M2 Kossuth Lajos tér
➡ 2

PARLIAMENT BY NUMBERS

Rooms: 690

Roof: 1.8 hectares

Gates: 27

Courtyards: 10

Staircases: 29

Lifts: 13

Light bulbs: 8730

Clocks: 108

Statues outside/inside: 90/152

Decorative gold: 40kg

You can join a tour in any of eight languages – they depart continuously in Hungarian, but the English-language ones are at 10am, noon and 2pm daily. To avoid disappointment, book ahead (in person). The tour takes about 45 minutes. Note that tours of Parliament are not conducted when the National Assembly is in session.

Stephen, the nation's most important national icon, is on display, along with the ceremonial sword, orb and the oldest object among the coronation regalia: the 10th-century Persian-made **sceptre** with a crystal head depicting a lion. You'll also see one of the **vaulted lobbies**, where political discussions take place; and the **Congress Hall**, where the House of Lords of the one-time bicameral assembly sat until 1944. It is almost identical to the National Assembly Hall, where parliamentary sessions are held.

Crown of St Stephen

Legend tells us that it was Asztrik, the first abbot of the Benedictine monastery at Pannonhalma in western Hungary, who presented a crown to Stephen as a gift from Pope Sylvester II around AD 1000, thus legitimising the new king's rule and assuring his loyalty to Rome over Constantinople. It's a nice story but has nothing to do with the object on display in the Domed Hall. The two-part crown here, with its characteristic bent cross, pendants hanging on either side and enamelled plaques of the Apostles, dates from the 12th century. Regardless of its provenance, the Crown of St Stephen has become the very symbol of the Hungarian nation. The crown has disappeared several times over the centuries – purloined or otherwise – only to later reappear. During the Mongol invasions of the 13th century, the crown was dropped while being transported to a safe house, giving it that slightly skewed look. More recently, in 1945, Hungarian fascists fleeing ahead of the Soviet army took the crown to Austria. Eventually it fell into the hands of the US army, which transferred it to Fort Knox in Kentucky. In January 1978 the crown was returned to Hungary with great ceremony – and relief. Because legal judgments had always been handed down 'in the name of St Stephen's Crown' it was considered a living symbol and thus to have been 'kidnapped'!

Government

Hungary's constitution provides for a parliamentary system of government. The unicameral assembly sits in the National Assembly Hall in the South Wing from February to June and September to December. The 386 members are chosen for four years in a complex, two-round system that balances direct ('first past the post') and proportional representation. Of the total, 176 MPs enter parliament by individual constituency elections, 152 on the basis of 20 district lists and 58 on the basis of national lists. The prime minister is head of government. The president, the head of state, is elected by the house for five years.

TOP SIGHTS
PARLIAMENT

TOP SIGHTS
BASILICA OF ST STEPHEN

The Basilica of St Stephen (Szent István Bazilika) is the most important Catholic church in all of Hungary if for no other reason than it contains the nation's most revered relic: the mummified right hand of the church's patron. The basilica is the Budapest seat of the shared Metropolitan Archdiocese of Esztergom-Budapest.

The neoclassical cathedral was originally designed by József Hild, the man behind Eger Cathedral (p151), and though work began in 1851 it was not completed until 1905. Much of the interruption had to do with 1868 when the dome collapsed during a storm, and the structure had to be demolished and rebuilt from the ground up by Hild's successor, Miklós Ybl (p188).

The facade of the basilica is anchored by two large **bell towers**, one of which contains a bell weighing 9 tonnes, a replacement for one looted by the Germans during WWII. Behind them is the 96m-high dome; statues of the four Evangelists fill its niches. The top of the **dome** (adult/child 500/300Ft; ⊘10am-4.30pm mid-Mar–Apr, to 5.30pm May-Jun & Sep-Oct, to 6pm Jul-Aug) can be reached by lifts and offers one of the best views in the city.

To the right as you enter the basilica is a small **treasury** (kincstár; adult/child 400/300Ft; ⊘9am-5pm Apr-Sep, 10am-4pm Oct-Mar) of ecclesiastical objects.

The basilica is rather dark and gloomy inside, Károly Lotz's golden **mosaics** on the inside of the dome notwithstanding. It is in the form of a Greek cross and can accommodate 8000 worshippers. Noteworthy items include the Gyula Benczúr's painting of St Stephen dedicating Hungary to the Virgin Mary and the statue of the king-saint on the main altar by Alajos Stróbl.

Behind the main altar and to the left is the basilica's major draw card: the **Holy Right Chapel** (Szent Jobb kápolna; ⊘9am-5pm Mon-Sat, from 1pm Sun May-Sep, 10am-4pm Mon-Sat, 1-4.30pm Sun Oct-Apr). It contains the Holy Right (also known as the Holy Dexter), the mummified right hand of St Stephen and an object of great devotion. It was returned to Hungary by Habsburg empress Maria Theresa in 1771 after it was discovered in a monastery in Bosnia. Like the Crown of St Stephen (p94) it was snatched by the bad guys after WWII but was soon, er, handed over to the rightful (ugh) owners.

English-language guided tours of the basilica (2000/1500Ft with/without dome visit) usually depart weekdays at 9.30am, 11am, 2pm and 3.30pm and on Saturday at 9.30am and 11am, but phone or check the website to confirm. Organ concerts are held here at 8pm on Tuesday in summer.

DON'T MISS...

➡ Holy Right
➡ Views from the dome
➡ Treasury
➡ Dome interior mosaics

PRACTICALITIES

➡ Map p244
➡ ☑338 2151
➡ www.bazilika.biz, in Hungarian
➡ V Szent István tér
➡ ⊘7am-7pm
➡ Ⓜ M2 Arany János utca

◉ SIGHTS

◉ Lipótváros

PARLIAMENT　　　　　　　　HISTORIC BUILDING
See p93.

BASILICA OF ST STEPHEN　　　　　　CHURCH
See p95.

ETHNOGRAPHY MUSEUM　　　　　MUSEUM
Map p244 (Néprajzi Múzeum; www.neprajz.hu;
V Kossuth Lajos tér 12; adult/child 1000/500Ft;
⊙10am-6pm Tue-Sun; ⓂM2 Kossuth Lajos tér)
Visitors are offered an easy introduction to
traditional Hungarian life at this sprawling
museum opposite Parliament with
thousands of displays in 13 rooms on the 1st
floor. The mock-ups of peasant houses from
the Őrség and Sárköz regions of Western and
Southern Transdanubia are well done, and
there are some priceless objects collected
from Transdanubia. On the 2nd floor, most
of the excellent temporary exhibitions deal
with other peoples of Europe and further
afield: Africa, Asia, Oceania and the
Americas. The building itself was designed
in 1893 by Alajos Hauszmann to house the
Supreme Court; note the **ceiling fresco** in
the lobby of *Justice* by Károly Lotz.

SZÉCHENYI ISTVÁN TÉR　　　　　SQUARE
Map p244 (🚊16, 105; 🚊2) Named in 1947 after
the long-serving (1933–45) American president, Franklin Delano Roosevelt, Roosevelt
tér has a new designation honouring the
statesmen and developer of Chain Bridge
it faces. The square offers among the best
views of Castle Hill in Pest.

On the southern end of Széchenyi István
tér is a **statue of Ferenc Deák**, the Hungarian minister largely responsible for the
Compromise of 1867, which brought about
the Dual Monarchy of Austria and Hungary
(p179). The statue on the western side is of
an Austrian and a Hungarian child holding
hands in peaceful bliss. The Magyar kid's
hair is tousled and he is naked; the Osztrák
is demurely covered by a bit of the patri-
cian's robe and his hair neatly coifed.

The art nouveau building with the gold
tiles to the east is the **Gresham Palace** (V
Széchenyi István tér 5-6), built by an English
insurance company in 1907. It now houses
the sumptuous Four Seasons Gresham Palace Hotel (p162). The **Hungarian Academy
of Sciences** (Magyar Tudományos Akadémia; V

Széchenyi István tér 9), founded by Count István Széchenyi, is at the northern end of the
square.

BEDŐ HOUSE　　　HISTORIC BUILDING, MUSEUM
Map p244 (Bedő-ház; www.magyarszecessziohaza.hu;
V Honvéd utca 3; adult/child 1500/1000Ft;
⊙10am-5pm Mon-Sat; ⓂM2 Kossuth Lajos tér)
Just around the corner from Kossuth Lajos
tér is this stunning art nouveau apartment
block (1903) designed by Emil Vidor. Now a
shrine to Hungarian Secessionist interiors,
its three floors are crammed with furniture,
porcelain, ironwork, paintings and objets
d'art. The lovely **Art Nouveau Café** (p101) is
on the ground floor.

IMRE NAGY STATUE　　　　　　　STATUE
Map p244 (V Vértanúk tere; ⓂM2 Kossuth Lajos
tér) Southeast of V Kossuth Lajos tér is an
unusual statue of Imre Nagy standing in
the centre of a small footbridge. Nagy was
the reformist Communist prime minister
executed in 1958 for his role in the uprising two years earlier (p183). It was unveiled
with great ceremony in the summer of 1996.

SZABADSÁG TÉR　　　　　　　　SQUARE
Map p244 (🚊15) 'Liberty Sq', one of the largest in Budapest, is a few minutes' walk
northeast of Széchenyi István tér. As you
enter you'll pass a new feature, a delightful
fountain that works on optical sensors and
turns off and on as you approach or back
away from it. In the centre of the square is
a **Soviet army memorial**, the last of its type
still standing in the city.

At the eastern side is the fortresslike **US
Embassy** (V Szabadság tér 12), now cut off
from the square by high metal fencing and
concrete blocks. It was here that Cardinal
József Mindszenty (p97) sought refuge after
the 1956 Uprising and stayed for 15 years
until departing for Vienna in 1971. The
embassy backs onto Hold utca (Moon St),
which, until 1990, was named Rosenberg
házaspár utca (Rosenberg Couple St) after
the American husband and wife Julius and
Ethel Rosenberg who were executed as Soviet spies in the US in 1953.

On the same street to the south you'll
find the sensational former **Royal Postal
Savings Bank** (V Hold utca 4), a Secessionist extravaganza of colourful tiles and folk
motifs built by Ödön Lechner (p144) in
1901. It is now part of the **National Bank of
Hungary** (Magyar Nemzeti Bank; V Szabadság
tér 9) next door, which has terracotta reliefs

CARDINAL MINDSZENTY

Born József Pehm in the village of Csehimindszent near Szombathely in western Hungary in 1892, Mindszenty was politically active from the time of his ordination in 1915. Imprisoned by Communist Béla Kun in 1919 and again by the fascist Arrow Cross in 1944, Mindszenty was made archbishop of Esztergom (and thus primate of Hungary) in 1945, and cardinal in 1946.

In 1948, when he refused to secularise Hungary's Roman Catholic schools under the new Communist regime, Mindszenty was arrested, tortured and sentenced to life imprisonment for treason. Released during the 1956 Uprising, Mindszenty took refuge in the US embassy when the Communists returned to power. He remained there until 1971.

As relations between the Kádár regime and the Holy See began to improve in the late 1960s, the Vatican made several requests for Mindszenty to leave Hungary, which he refused to do. Following the intervention of US president Richard Nixon, Mindszenty left for Vienna, where he continued to criticise the Vatican's relations with Hungary. He retired in 1974 and died in 1975. Mindszenty had vowed not to return to Hungary until the last Russian soldier had left Hungarian soil, so his remains were returned in May 1991, several weeks before that pivotal date.

that illustrate trade and commerce through history: Arab camel traders, African rug merchants, Chinese tea salesmen – and the inevitable solicitor witnessing contracts. The **MNB Visitor Centre** (www.lk.mnb.hu; admission free; ☉9am-4pm Mon-Wed & Fri, to 6pm Thu) contains an interesting exhibition on the history of currency and banking in Hungary, but most people come to gawp at the stunning entrance hall and staircase.

SHOES ON THE DANUBE
MEMORIAL   MONUMENT

Map p244 (V Pesti alsó rakpart; ☐2) Along the banks of the river – halfway between Széchenyi István tér and Parliament – is a monument to Hungarian Jews shot and thrown into the Danube by members of the fascist Arrow Cross Party in 1944 (p180). Entitled *Shoes on the Danube (Cipők a Dunaparton)* by sculptor Gyula Pauer and film director Can Togay, it's a simple affair – 60 pairs of old-style boots and shoes in cast iron, tossed higgledy-piggledy on the bank of the river – but one of the most poignant monuments in Budapest.

☉ Terézváros (West)

NYUGATI TRAIN STATION   HISTORIC BUILDING

Map p244 (Nyugati pályaudvar; VI Teréz körút 55-57; ⓜM3 Nyugati pályaudvar) The large iron-and-glass structure on Nyugati tér (known as Marx tér until the early 1990s) is the 'Western' train station, built in 1877 by the

Paris-based Eiffel Company. In the early 1970s a train actually crashed through the enormous glass screen on the main facade when its brakes failed, coming to rest at the 4 and 6 tram line. The old dining hall on the south side now houses one of the world's most elegant McDonald's.

HOUSE OF HUNGARIAN
PHOTOGRAPHERS   GALLERY

Map p244 (Magyar Fotográfusok Háza; www.maimano.hu; VI Nagymező utca 20; adult/child 1000/500Ft; ☉2-7pm Mon-Fri, 11am-7pm Sat & Sun; ⓜM1 Opera; ☐70, 78) An extraordinary venue in the city's theatre district, with top-class photography exhibitions. It is in Mai Manó Ház, which was built in 1894 as a photo studio and worth a visit in itself. There's a great cafe here too.

✖ EATING

Lipótváros is a happy hunting ground for fine eating, especially around the area of the basilica and the Central European University. Terézváros within the Big Ring Rd is really where you head for after-dark fun and games, especially around Nagymező utca, but there is no shortage of eateries, including a few late-night venues.

✖ Lipótváros

┌TOP┐ MÁK
└CHOICE┘
HUNGARIAN €€

Map p244 (☎06-30 333 6869; wwwmakbistro.hu; V Vigyázó Ferenc utca 4; mains 1900-5200Ft; ◷noon-4pm & 6pm-midnight Tue-Sat; ◨15; ◨2) A wonderful new addition to the Lipótváros eating scene, the 'Poppy' serves inventive new Hungarian dishes from a chalkboard menu that changes daily. Casual surrounds and seamless service with good advice on wine. A three-course lunch from the menu is a budget-enhancing 3500Ft.

CAFÉ KÖR
INTERNATIONAL €€

Map p244 (☎311 0053; www.cafekor.com; V Sas utca 17; mains 1990-4100Ft; ◷10am-10pm Mon-Sat; ◨15, 115) Just behind the Basilica of St Stephen, the 'Circle Café' is a long-standing favourite for lunch or dinner but a great place for a light meal at any time, including breakfast (150Ft to 790Ft), which is served till noon. Service is friendly and helpful.

┌TOP┐ TIGRIS
└CHOICE┘
HUNGARIAN €€

Map p244 (☎317 3715; www.tigrisrestaurant.hu; V Mérleg utca 10; mains 3600-5900Ft; ◷noon-midnight Mon-Sat; ◨15; ◨2) What at first appears as no more than an upbeat modern Hungarian restaurant, with its wooden tables covered in red-checked tablecloths and antique-looking cupboards, is a very serious Michelin-rated restaurant owned by the Gere family of wine fame. Expect faultless service, a sommelier who will take you on a giddy tour of Hungary's major wine regions, and as many variations on goose liver as you can imagine.

KASHMIR
INDIAN €

Map p244 (www.kashmiretterem.hu; V Arany János utca 13; mains 1890-2990Ft; ◷noon-3pm & 6-11pm Tue-Sun; ☎; Ⓜ M3 Arany János utca) Our new favourite subcontinental in Pest, this places serves the cuisine of its namesake, which is always a bit sweeter than ordinary Indian food, as well as a variety of tandoori cooked meats. There's a dozen vegetarian choices and a buffet lunch for 1390Ft.

TOM-GEORGE ITALIANO
ITALIAN €€

Map p244 (☎266 3525; www.tomgeorgeitaliano .hu; V Október 6 utca 8; mains 2900-5600Ft; ◷noon-midnight; ◨15, 115) The restaurant that set a new standard for Budapest a decade ago has changed its spots and gone all Italian. OK, it's uber-trendy and could

be in London or New York, but the service is great, decor *très contemporain* and food the usual T&G standard. Excellent pasta (1790Ft to 2500Ft). Set lunch is 1800Ft.

SALAAM BOMBAY
INDIAN €€

Map p244 (www.salaambombay.hu; V Mérleg utca 6; mains 1890-3990Ft; ◷noon-3pm & 6-11pm; ☎; ◨15; ◨2) If you're hankering for a fix of authentic curry or tandoori in a bright, upbeat environment, look no further than this attractive eatery just east of Széchenyi István tér. Don't believe us? Even staff from the Indian embassy are said to come here regularly. A large choice of vegetarian dishes (950Ft to 1990Ft).

WASABI
JAPANESE €€

Map p244 (www.wasabi.hu; VI Podmaniczky utca 21; mains 4490-5990Ft; Ⓜ M3 Nyugati pályaudvar) Branch of a popular 'conveyor belt' sushi restaurant (p80) in Óbuda.

ELSŐ PESTI RÉTESHÁZ
HUNGARIAN €€

Map p244 (www.reteshaz.com; V Október 6 utca 22; mains 2590-4690Ft; ◷9am-11pm; ◨15, 115) It may be a bit overdone (think Magyar Disneyland, with 'olde worlde' counters, painted plates stuck on the walls and old letters and curios embedded in plexiglas washbasins), but the 'First Strudel House of Pest' is just the place to taste this Hungarian stretched pastry (240Ft to 290Ft) filled with apple, cheese, poppy seeds or sour cherry – with or without a full meal preceding it. Breakfast (1290Ft to 2490Ft) is served till noon.

KISHARANG
HUNGARIAN, ÉTKEZDE €

Map p244 (V Október 6 utca 17; mains 590-2300Ft; ◷11.30am-8pm; ◨15, 115) Centrally located 'Little Bell' is an *étkezde* (canteen serving simple Hungarian dishes) that is on the top of the list with students and staff of the nearby Central European University. The daily specials are something to look forward to and the retro decor is fun. *Főzelék* (380Ft to 520Ft), the traditional Hungarian way of preparing vegetables, is always good here.

CULINARIS
INTERNATIONAL €

Map p244 (www.culinaris.hu; XIII Balassi Bálint utca 7; mains 1590-2900Ft; ◷8am-3pm Mon-Sat, 10am-6pm Sun; ◨2) Is it a restaurant? A cafe? A gourmet food shop? Apparently all three and we love it for its welcoming colours and chaotic selection (Waldorf salad, Moroccan lamb pita, duck quesadilla etc) but not its bankers' hours. Still, the store stays open till the evening so self-catering is an option.

MOMOTARO RAMEN
ASIAN €

Map p244 (www.momotaroramen.com; V Nádor utca 24; noodles & dumplings 500-1700Ft, mains 1600-3400Ft; ☺10.30am-10pm Tue-Sun; 🚇15; 🚌2) A favourite pit stop for noodles – especially the soup variety – and dumplings when *pálinka* (fruit brandy), Unicum and other lubricants have been a-flowin' the night before. Also good for more substantial dishes.

IGUANA
MEXICAN €€

Map p244 (www.iguana.hu; V Zoltán utca 16; mains 1800-4490Ft; ☺11.30am-12.30am; Ⓜ M2 Kossuth Lajos tér; 🚇15) Iguana serves decent enough Mexican food (not a difficult task in this cantina desert), but it's hard to say whether the pull is the enchilada and burrito combination *platos*, the fajitas or the frenetic and boozy 'we-party-every-night' atmosphere. Busy bar.

GASTRONOMIA POMO D'ORO
ITALIAN €

Map p244 (www.gastronomiapomodoro.com; V Arany János utca 9; dishes 1590-2390Ft; ☺9am-10pm Mon-Sat; 🚇15; 🚌2) Next door to a much more extravagant trattoria bearing the same name, this Italian delicatessen/caterer has a little dining area on the 1st floor where you can choose from a small selection of dishes or sample cheese and prepared meats by the 100g measure (400Ft to 1200Ft). Sandwiches are 1090Ft to 1590Ft.

FRUCCOLA
SANDWICHES €

Map p244 (www.fruccola.hu; V Arany János utca 32; breakfast 640-930Ft, sandwiches 400-780Ft; ☺7am-7pm Mon-Fri; Ⓜ M3 Arany János utca; 🚇72, 73) Alive and well and bursting with flavour, Budapest's only 'fast casual restaurant' (so far) pulls in the punters with its excellent baguettes, self-build salads and fresh vegetable and fruit juices.

HUMMUS BAR
MIDDLE EASTERN €

Map p244 (V Október 6 utca 19; dishes 600-1600Ft; ☺noon-11pm; 🍴; 🚇15, 115) If you're looking for an easy vegetarian dish on the, err, hoof, this is the place to go for mashed chickpeas blended with sesame-seed paste, oil and lemon juice. Enjoy it au naturel (we mean the hummus) on pita or in a dish with accompaniments such as mushrooms or felafel. Not all dishes are vegetarian.

GOVINDA
VEGETARIAN €

Map p244 (www.govinda.hu; V Vigyázó Ferenc utca 4; dishes 480-1450Ft; ☺11am-9pm Mon-Fri, from noon Sat & Sun; 🍴; 🚇15; 🚌2) This basement restaurant northeast of the Chain Bridge serves wholesome salads, soups and desserts as well as a daily set menu plate (790Ft to 1450Ft).

ROOSEVELT ÉTTEREM
HUNGARIAN €

Map p244 (www.rooseveltetterem.hu, in Hungarian; cnr Széchenyi István tér & Vigyázó Ferenc utca; mains around 2500Ft; ☺8am-5pm Mon-Fri; 🚇15, 16; 🚌2) This brightly coloured caf that *used* to be on Roosevelt tér is a modern take on a Hungarian *önkiszolgáló* (self-service restaurant) where, along with light meals available throughout the day, main dishes are sold by weight (230Ft per 100g).

PICK HÁZ
HUNGARIAN €

Map p244 (V Kossuth Lajos tér 9; sandwiches & salads from 250Ft, mains 300-650Ft; ☺6am-7pm Mon-Thu, to 6pm Fri; Ⓜ M2 Kossuth Lajos tér) Next to Kossuth Lajos tér metro station, this self-service eatery sits above the famous salami manufacturer's central showroom opposite the Parliament building. It's convenient for lunch if you're visiting Parliament or any of the sights in the area.

SZERÁJ
TURKISH, FAST FOOD €

Map p244 (XIII Szent István körút 13; dishes 450-1400Ft; ☺9am-4am; 🚌4, 6) A very inexpensive self-service Turkish place good for *lahmacun* (Turkish 'pizza'), felafel and kebabs, with up to a dozen varieties on offer. It heaves after midnight so whoever you were cruising with in the pub or on the dance floor probably got here before you did.

DURAN
SANDWICHES €

Map p244 (www.duran.hu; V Október 6 utca 15; sandwiches 170-300Ft; ☺8am-6pm Mon-Fri, to 1pm Sat; 🚇15, 115) This branch of the popular sandwich bar is by the Central European University and crowded with students.

🍴 Terézváros (West)

MOST!
INTERNATIONAL €

Map p244 (www.mostjelen.blogspot.com, in Hungarian; VI Zichy Jenő utca 17; mains 1450-2200Ft; ☺10am-2am Sun & Mon, to 4am Tue-Sat; Ⓜ M3 Arany János utca) The exclamation says it all... From the people who brought you Jelen (p135), Most! – that's 'Now!' to you –

is a restaurant-cafe-bar that wants to be everything to everyone. And it almost succeeds. There is a small bar, a stage and roof terrace, a large indoor dining room with communal tables and a big garden. Food is a mixed bag. They say the burgers are the best in town and there are some Indian dishes too, but we come here for the brunch menu (1690Ft) available from 10.30am to 4pm on Saturday and Sunday.

⭐ TOP CHOICE CAFÉ BOUCHON FRENCH €€

Map p244 (☎353 4094; www.cafebouchon.hu; VI Zichy Jenő utca 33; mains 2390-4980Ft; ☺9am-11pm Mon-Fri, from 10am Sat; ⓂM3 Arany János utca; 🚊70, 78) A little bit pricey for what and where it is but *Ooo la la, c'est si bon*. A family-run *bouchon* (small restaurant) with an art-nouveau-style interior, this place serves provincial French food stirred with a little Hungarian inspiration and the occasional stray (eg osso bucco) making an appearance. Warm welcome.

PARÁZS PRESSZÓ THAI €€

Map p244 (www.parazspresszo.com; VI Szobi utca 4; mains 1450-3850Ft; ☺noon-midnight Mon-Fri, from 1pm Sat & Sun; 🚊4, 6) This *presszó* (coffee shop) serving Thai on the wrong side of the tracks has a loyal following.

KOREAI-KINAI ÉTTEREM KOREAN, CHINESE €

Map p244 (VI Zichy Jenő utca 9; mains 1400-1990Ft; ☺noon-11pm Mon-Fri, to 10pm Sat & Sun; ⓂM3 Arany János utca) The 'Korean-Chinese Restaurant' serves dishes from both great nations but, for the sake of authenticity, veer toward the former. It's tiny and you may have to wait, but it's worth it.

NAPOS OLDAL VEGETARIAN €

Map p244 (www.naposoldal.com; VI Jókai utca 7; dishes 355-460Ft, set meals 910-1300Ft; ☺10am-8pm Mon-Fri, to 2pm Sat; 🖉; ⓂM1 Oktogon; 🚊4, 6) This tiny cafe-restaurant inside a health-food shop on the 'Sunny Side' of the street serves fresh salads, pastries and soups.

MARQUIS DE SALADE INTERNATIONAL €€

Map p244 (www.maquisdesalade.hu; VI Hajós utca 43; mains 2600-4200Ft; ☺11am-midnight; 🖉; ⓂM3 Arany János utca; 🚊72, 73) This basement restaurant is a strange hybrid of a place, with dishes from Russia and Azerbaijan as well as Hungary. There are lots of quality vegetarian choices. And, by the way, it's not just about *salade* (though there are more than two dozen to choose from).

FŐZELÉK FALÓ HUNGARIAN, ÉTKEZDE €

Map p244 (VI Nagymező utca 18; dishes 399-920Ft; ☺9am-9pm Mon-Fri, 10am-9pm Sat, 11am-6pm Sun; ⓂM1 Opera; 🚊70, 78) Some people say that this *étkezde*, which keeps relatively extended hours and is convenient to the bars of Liszt Ferenc tér and the music academy, is the best in town.

GANGA VEGETARIAN €

Mapp244 (www.gangavega.hu; VI Bajcsy-Zsilinszky út 25; dishes 450-500Ft; ☺8am-10pm Mon-Fri, from noon Sat; 🖉; ⓂM3 Arany János utca) It's not exactly a pretty face – an ordinary rectangle of a room with pots simmering somewhere in the back – but it's the real McCoy, with some vegan choices too. A basic set menu starts at 890Ft.

BUTTERFLY ICE CREAM €

Map p244 (VI Teréz körút 20; ☺10am-7pm Mon-Fri, to 2pm Sat; ⓂM1 Oktogon) This place – and not the pastry shop next door – is *the* place in Pest for ice cream (170Ft per scoop), as you'll be able to deduce from the queues.

DRINKING & NIGHTLIFE

🍸 Lipótváros

BECKETTS IRISH BAR BAR

Map p244 (www.becketts.hu; V Alkotmány utca 20; ☺noon-1am Sun-Thu, to 3am Fri & Sat; ⓂM3 Nyugati pályaudvar) Of the capital's ubiquitous 'Irish' pubs, this is arguably the best (and definitely the largest) of the lot.

FEHÉR GYŰRŰ BAR

Map p244 (www.fehergyuru.hu, in Hungarian; V Balassi Bálint utca 27; ☺3pm-midnight Mon-Sat, from 5pm Sun; 🚊2, 4, 6) The 'White Ring' has always been a firm favourite and, frankly, it's never been clear why. Perhaps it's because it is opposite the so-called White House (p108) and it's always fun to play 'spot the MP'.

LE CAFE M BAR GAY

Map p244 (V Nagysándor József utca 3; ☺4pm-2am; ⓂM3 Arany János utca) One of our favourite Budapest neighbourhood gay bars has supercool decor and friendly staff.

TERV ESZPRESSZÓ BAR

Map p244 (V Nádor utca 19; ⊘9am-midnight Mon-Fri, to 11pm Sat, 10am-11pm Sun; MM3 Arany János utca; ⊠15, 115) 'Plan' (as in 'Five-Year') is a retro-style cafe-bar on two levels decorated with photographs of Hungarian athletes, politicians, actors and so on from the 1950s and '60s. Unlike a lot of such places, the theme doesn't get old in a half-hour.

CAKE CAFE

Map p244 (www.thecake.hu; V Október 6 utca 6; ⊘7.30am-7.30pm Mon-Fri, from 10am Sat & Sun; ⊠15) Excellent cafe with contemporary black-and-white decor, outside tables and very artistic (and delicious) cakes (320Ft to 420Ft) and house-made ice cream (170Ft per scoop).

NEGRO CAFÉ BAR BAR, CAFE

Map p244 (www.negrobar.hu V Szent István tér 11; ⊘noon-1am; MM3 Arany János utca) This sleek and very stylish cafe-bar with the non-PC name and stunning views of the basilica attracts a well-heeled crowd dressed to the nines (or did we see 10s there too?) while sipping from an impressive cocktail menu. Sandwiches and light meals are available throughout the day and evening.

FARGER KÁVÉ CAFE

Map p244 (www.farger.hu, in Hungarian; V Zoltán utca 18; ⊘7am-10pm Mon-Fri, 9am-6pm Sat & Sun; MM2 Kossuth Lajos tér) This modern cafe is among the leafiest in Pest thanks to an ingenious 'urban gardening' plan and has first-rate views of Szabadság tér from the window seats and terrace.

CAFÉ MONTMARTRE CAFE, LIVE MUSIC

Map p244 (http://cafemontmartre.wordpress.com; V Zrínyi utca 18; ⊘9am-1am; MM3 Arany János utca; ⊠15, 115) This very unpretentious cafe-cum-art gallery in full splendid view of the Basilica of St Stephen is always fun, especially on the nights when there is live Latino and jazz. The welcome here is always warm.

ART NOUVEAU CAFÉ CAFE

Map p244 (www.magyarszecessziohaza.hu; V Honvéd utca 3; ⊘8am-7pm Mon-Fri, 9am-6pm Sat; MM2 Kossuth Lajos tér) This small but comfortable cafe on the ground floor of delightful Bedő House (see p96) is tailor-made for fans of the Secessionist style. The cakes (290Ft to 420Ft) are pretty average though.

SZALAI CUKRÁSZDA CAFE

Map p244 (V Balassi Bálint utca 7; ⊘9am-7pm Wed-Mon; ⊠2) This humble cake shop in Lipótváros just north of Parliament, dating back to 1917, probably has the best cherry strudel (260Ft to 360Ft) in the capital, though its cream cakes go down a treat too.

MORRISON'S 2 CLUB, LIVE MUSIC

Map p244 (www.morrisons.hu; V Szent István körút 11; ⊘5pm-4am Mon-Sat; ⊠4, 6) Far and away Budapest's biggest party venue, this cavernous cellar club attracts a younger crowd with its four dance floors, the same number of bars (including one in a covered courtyard) and an enormous games room upstairs. Live bands from 9pm to 11pm during the week.

ÖTKERT CLUB

Map p244 (http://otkert.blogspot.com; V Zrínyi utca 4; ⊘4pm-5am; ⊠15, 115) It's not really a 'garden club' though the 'Five Garden' ('five' as in district) does suggest that. This rather chichi champagne bar (glass/bottle from 850/2800Ft) has great drinking and dancing spaces, including a cool central courtyard.

⬤ Terézváros (West)

INSTANT CLUB

Map p244 (www.instant.co.hu; VI Nagymező utca 38; ⊘4pm-3am; MM1 Opera; ⊠70, 78) We still love this 'rubble bar' on Pest's most vibrant nightlife strip and so do all our friends. It has five bars on three levels with underground DJs and dance parties. If you want a taste of things to come and can't wait till lunchtime, head for the ground-floor coffee shop (open the same hours but closed on Monday).

CLUB ALTEREGO GAY

Map p244 (www.alteregoclub.hu; VI Dessewffy utca 33; ⊘10pm-6am Fri & Sat; MM3 Arany János utca; ⊠4, 6) Still Budapest's premier gay club, with the chic-est (think attitude) crowd and the best dance music on offer. If you'd rather be on the receiving end of the entertainment, check out its central sister **Café AlterEgo** (Map p244; V Erzsébet tér 1; ⊘noon-late MM1/2/3 Deák Ferenc tér Opera), with karaoke and drag shows, depending on the night.

SANDOKAN LISBOA SOLINGBAR   CLUB

Map p244 (www.sandokanlisboa.hu; VI Hajós utca 23; ⊗noon-2am Mon-Fri, from 4pm Sat & Sun; Ⓜ M1 Opera; ⎙70, 78) Modelled on stand-up bars in Portugal (that's the 'Lisboa Solingbar' part of the name), this tiny place serves great cocktails and has live DJ sets Wednesday to Saturday. And Sandokan? A fictional pirate who was the subject of a TV series hugely popular in Hungary in the 1970s, we're told.

PÓTKULCS   LIVE MUSIC

Map p244 (www.potkulcs.hu; VI Csengery utca 65/b; ⊗5pm-1.30am Sun-Wed, to 2.30am Thu-Sat; Ⓜ M3 Nyugati pályaudvar) The 'Spare Key' is a fine little drinking venue with a varied menu of live music most evenings and occasionally *táncház* (Hungarian music and dance). The small central courtyard is a wonderful place to chill out in summer.

CAFÉ EKLEKTIKA   GAY

Map p244 (www.eklektika.hu; VI Nagymező utca 30; ⊗8am-midnight Mon-Thu, 9am-1am Fri & Sat, 9am-midnight Sun; Ⓜ M1 Opera; ⎙70, 78) While there are no specifically lesbian bars in Budapest that we know about, Café Eklektika – love the name and the concept – comes the closest and attracts a very mixed, gay-friendly crowd, including some of Budapest's flashiest clitorati.

PICASSO POINT   BAR

Map p244 (www.picassopoint.hu, in Hungarian; VI Hajós utca 31; ⊗noon-1am; Ⓜ M3 Arany János utca) A stalwart of the Budapest entertainment scene, Picasso Point has spruced itself up recently and even (partly) calls itself a gallery. But it's still a laid-back place for a drink, listening to canned (and occasional live) blues and jazz and meeting people.

CALEDONIA   BAR

Map p244 (www.kaledonia.hu; VI Mozsár utca 9; ⊗11am-midnight Sun-Thu, to 1am Fri & Sat; Ⓜ M1 Oktogon; ⎙4, 6) Think anything Scottish and the Caledonia does it – whisky (40-plus types) with or without Irn-Bru, plus smoked salmon, breakfast (with or without haggis), not to mention big-screen sports coverage, a monthly boot sale and so on. It's all good fun and something of an expat magnet.

⎙ KIADÓ KOCSMA   BAR

Map p244 (VI Jókai tér 3; ⊗10am-1am Mon-Fri, from 11am Sat & Sun; Ⓜ M2 Oktogon) The 'Pub for Rent' is a great place for a swift pint

and a quick bite (salads and pasta dishes 1350Ft to 1500Ft) a stone's throw – and light years – away from flashy VI Liszt Ferenc tér. Breakfast is on till 1pm and there's a bargain set lunch for 850Ft.

CAPTAIN COOK PUB   BAR

Map p244 (www.cookpub.hu, in Hungarian; VI Bajcsy-Zsilinszky út 19/a; ⊗10am-1.30am Mon-Sat, from 2pm Sun; Ⓜ M2 Arany János utca) There's not much to say about the Cook except that it enjoys an enviable location diagonally opposite the basilica, the terrace is a delight in the warm weather, there are four beers on tap and the staff are welcoming and friendly. Enough said?

TEAHÁZ A VÖRÖS OROSZLÁNHOZ TEAHOUSE

Map p244 (www.vorosoroszlanteahaz.hu; VI Jókai tér 8; ⊗11am-11pm Mon-Sat, from 10am Sun; Ⓜ M1 Oktogon) This serene place with quite a mouthful of a name (it means 'Teahouse at the Sign of the Red Lion') just north of Liszt Ferenc tér is quite serious about its teas (670Ft to 1130Ft).

BALLETT CIPŐ   CAFE

Map p244 (www.balettcipo.hu; VI Hajós utca 14; ⊗10am-midnight Mon-Fri, from noon Sat; Ⓜ M1 Opera) The pretty little 'Ballet Slipper' in the theatre district – just behind the Hungarian State Opera House – is a delightful place to stop for a rest and refreshment or to have a snack or light meal.

☆ ENTERTAINMENT

DUNA PALOTA   CONCERT VENUE

Map p244 (☎235 5500; www.dunapalota.hu; V Zrínyi utca 5; tickets 3300-6200Ft; ⎙15, 115) The elaborate 'Danube Palace' is diagonally opposite the main Central European University building. It hosts any number of cultural performances, from light-classical music concerts to folk dance by the Rajkó Folk Ensemble, at 7pm throughout the week for the most part from May to October.

SZIKRA COOL HOUSE TOUR   LIVE MUSIC

Map p244 (☎911 0911; www.szikra.eu, in Hungarian; VI Teréz körút 62; ⊗8am-2am Mon-Thu, to 6am Fri, 10am-6am Sat, to 2am Sun; Ⓜ M3 Nyugati pályaudvar) This alternative cultural centre offers everything from live DJs and dance floors to performance art and film screenings in a grand antique theatre. Flashy outside neon will beckon; you may never want to leave with everything on offer here.

MŰVÉSZ ART MOZI CINEMA

Map p244 (www.artmozi.hu; VI Teréz körút 30; M M1 Oktogon; 4, 6) The 'Artist Art Cinema' shows, appropriately enough, artsy and cult films, but not exclusively so.

TOP CHOICE BUDAPEST OPERETTA OPERA

Map p244 (Budapesti Operettszínház; 312 4866; www.operettszinhaz.hu; VI Nagymező utca 17; tickets 1000-5900Ft; box office 10am-7pm Mon-Fri, 1-7pm Sat & Sun; M M1 Opera) This theatre presents operettas, which are always a riot, especially campy ones such as *The Gypsy Princess* by Imre Kálmán or Ferenc Lehár's *The Merry Widow,* with their over-the-top staging and costumes. Think baroque Gilbert and Sullivan. There's an interesting bronze statue of Kálmán outside the main entrance.

ARANYTÍZ CULTURAL CENTRE LIVE MUSIC, DANCE

Map p244 (Aranytíz Művelődési Központ; 354 3400; www.aranytiz.hu, in Hungarian; V Arany János utca 10; box office 2-9pm Mon & Wed, 8am-noon & 4pm-midnight Sat; 15) At this cultural centre in the northern Inner Town, the wonderful Kalamajka Táncház has programs from 7pm on Saturday that run till about midnight. Bring the kids in earlier (about 5pm) for a kiddies' version.

 SHOPPING

TOP CHOICE BÁV ANTIQUES

Map p244 (www.bav.hu, in Hungarian; XIII Szent István körút 3; 10am-6pm Mon-Fri, to 2pm Sat; 4, 6) This chain of pawn and secondhand shops, with a number of branches around town, is a fun place to comb for trinkets and treasures, especially if you don't have time to get to the Ecseri or City Park flea markets. Check out this branch for chinaware, textiles and furniture.

PINTÉR ANTIK ANTIQUES

Map p244 (www.pinterantik.hu; V Falk Miksa utca 10; 10am-6pm Mon-Fri; 2, 4, 6) With a positively enormous antique showroom (some 1500 sq metres) in a series of cellars near the Parliament building, Pintér has everything – from furniture and chandeliers to oil paintings and china – and is the best outfit on Falk Miksa utca for browsing.

DÁRIUS ANTIQUES ANTIQUES

Map p244 (www.dariusantiques.com; V Falk Miksa utca 24-26; 10am-6pm Mon-Sat; 2, 4, 6) This shop handles antique furniture, paintings, glass and porcelain; it's another good option on V Falk Miksa utca and the owner is particularly knowledgeable and helpful.

ANNA ANTIKVITÁS ANTIQUES

Map p244 (www.falkmiksa3d.com; V Falk Miksa utca 18-20; 10am-6pm Mon-Fri, to 1pm Sat; 2, 4, 6) Anna is the place to go if you're in the market for embroidered antique tablecloths and bed linen. They're stacked up all over the shop and of very high quality.

BESTSELLERS BOOKS

Map p244 (www.bestsellers.hu; V Október 6 utca 11; 9am-6.30pm Mon-Fri, 10am-5pm Sat, 10am-4pm Sun; M M1/2/3/Deák Ferenc tér; 15, 115) Probably the best English-language bookshop in town, with fiction, travel guides and lots of Hungarica, as well as a large selection of newspapers and magazines overseen by master bookseller Tony Láng. Helpful staff are at hand to advise and recommend.

SZŐNYI ANTIKVÁRIUMA BOOKS

Map p244 (www.szonyi.hu; V Szent István körút 3; 10am-6pm Mon-Fri, 9am-1pm Sat; 4, 6) This long-established antiquarian bookshop has, in addition to old tomes, an excellent selection of antique prints and maps. Just open the drawers in the chests at the back and have a look.

CEU BOOKSHOP BOOKS

Map p244 (V Zrínyi utca 12; 10am-7pm Mon-Fri, to 2pm Sat; M M1/2/3 Deák Ferenc tér; 15, 115) The bookshop at Budapest's renowned Central European University has an excellent selection of academic and business titles with a regional focus. The literary fiction in translation section is among the best.

CARTOGRAPHIA MAPS

Map p244 (www.cartographia.hu; VI Bajcsy-Zsilinszky út 37; 9am-5pm Mon-Fri; M M3 Arany János utca) This outlet of the national mapmaking company stocks the full range of maps including the best folding ones of Budapest at scales of 1:22,000 (990Ft) and 1:30,000 (750Ft). If you plan to explore the city more thoroughly, its 1:20,000 *Budapest Atlas* (small/large format 2590/3890Ft) is indispensable. There's also a 1:25,000 pocket atlas available for 1690Ft.

TÉRKÉPKIRÁLY
MAPS

Map p244 (www.mapking.hu; VI Bajcsy-Zsilinszky út 21; ⊙8am-8pm Mon-Sat; M M3 Arany János utca) The nearby 'Map King' stocks a wide variety of maps and its staff are particularly helpful and knowledgeable.

KATTI ZOÓB
FASHION

Map p244 (www.kattizoob.hu; V Szent István körút 17; ⊙10am-6pm Mon-Fri; M M3 Nyugati pályaudvar) Modern art-deco-inspired ready-to-wear and bespoke foundation pieces and accessories from Katti Zoób, the doyenne of Hungarian haute couture. She's also worked with Zsolnay porcelain on a new jewellery line.

MANIER
FASHION

Map p244 (www.manier.hu; VI Hajós utca 12; ⊙11am-7pm Mon-Sat; M M1 Opera) Just behind the Opera House, Anikó Németh's new outlet shows her luxury ready-to-wear and designer streetwear to dramatic effect amid a forest of folded-paper trees.

NÁRAY TAMÁS ATELIER
FASHION, CLOTHING

Map p244 (www.naraytamas.hu; VI Hajós utca 17; ⊙11am-7pm Mon-Fri; M M1 Opera) The principal outlet for one of Hungary's most celebrated and controversial designers, Paris-trained Tamás Náray, stocks elegant ready-to-wear fashion for women and accepts tailoring orders. Ball gowns a speciality.

PANNONARTS DESIGN GALÉRIA
JEWELLERY, FOOD

Map p244 (www.pannonarts.hu, in Hungarian; VI Lazár utca 8; ⊙10am-6pm Mon-Fri, to 2pm Sat; M M3 Arany János utca; 🚌73) This showroom exhibits and sells the output of the crème de la crème of Hungarian jewellery designers, many of them award winners. The shop itself is a designer's delight and there are also handbags on display as well as food and wine produced by the monks at the Pannonhalma Monastery in western Hungary.

MALATINSZKY WINE STORE
WINE

Map p244 (www.malatinszky.hu; V József Attila utca 12; ⊙10am-6pm Mon-Fri, to 3pm Sat; M M1/2/3 Deák Ferenc tér) Owned and operated by a one-time sommelier at the Gundel restaurant, this shop has an excellent selection of high-end Hungarian wines. Ask the staff to recommend a bottle.

KIESELBACH GALÉRIA ÉS AUKCIÓSHÁZ
ART

Map p244 (www.kieselbach.hu; V Szent István körút 5; ⊙10am-6pm Mon-Fri, to 1pm Sat; 🚌4, 6) This is without a doubt the best source in the city for serious Hungarian painting and other art, and there are frequent auctions of both local and international works.

NÁDORTEX
HOMEWARES

Map p244 (http://nadortex-kft.m-e-n.hu, in Hungarian; V József nádor tér 12; ⊙10am-5pm Mon-Fri; M M1/2/3 Deák Ferenc tér) Goose-feather or down products such as pillows or duvets (comforters) are of excellent quality in Hungary and a highly recommended purchase. Nádortex, small and monolingual but reliable, has some of the best prices.

HEREND
PORCELAIN, GLASSWARE

Map p244 (www.herend.com; V József nádor tér 11; ⊙10am-6pm Mon-Fri, to 4pm Sat & Sun; M M1 Vörösmarty tér) A central branch of the iconic Hungarian brand (p62).

HAAS & CZJZEK
PORCELAIN, GLASSWARE

Map p244 (www.porcelan.hu; VI Bajcsy-Zsilinszky út 23; ⊙10am-7pm Mon-Fri, to 3pm Sat; M M3 Arany János utca) Just up from Deák Ferenc tér, this chinaware and crystal shop, in situ since 1879, sells Herend and Zsolnay pieces as well as more affordable Hungarian-made Hollóháza and Alföldi porcelain.

AJKA KRISTÁLY
GLASSWARE

Map p244 (www.ajka-crystal.hu; V József Attila utca 7; ⊙10am-6pm Mon-Fri; M M1/2/3 Deák Ferenc tér) Established in 1878, Ajka has Hungarian-made lead crystal pieces and stemware. A lot of it is very old-fashioned and ornate, but there are some more contemporary pieces worth a second look.

JÁTÉKSZEREK ANNO
TOYS

Map p244 (www.jatekanno.hu, in Hungarian; VI Teréz körút 54; ⊙10am-6pm Mon-Fri, 9am-1pm Sat; M M3 Nyugati pályaudvar; 🚌4, 6) The tiny but exceptional 'Anno Playthings' shop sells finely made reproductions of antique wind-up and other old-fashioned toys.

WAVE MUSIC
MUSIC

Map p244 (www.wave.hu; VI Révay köz 1; ⊙11am-7pm Mon-Fri, to 3pm Sat; M M1 Bajcsy-Zsilinszky út) Wave is an excellent outlet for both Hungarian and international indie guitar music, as well as underground dance music.

Margaret Island & Northern Pest

MARGARET ISLAND | ÚJLIPÓTVÁROS

Neighbourhood Top Five

1 Reliving Budapest's medieval past on Margaret Island by strolling from the ruins of the **Franciscan church and monastery** (p107), past the one-time **Dominican convent** (p107) where St Margaret is buried and on to the Romanesque **Premonstratensian Church** (p107).

2 Pampering yourself at the **Danubius Health Spa Margitsziget** (p107), one of the most modern spas in Budapest.

3 Paying homage to the heroic Raoul Wallenberg at his statue in **Szent István Park** (p108).

4 Exploring the length and breadth of Margaret Island on two or four wheels with a **rental bicycle** or **pedal coach** (p106).

5 Getting behind the wheel of one of the big locomotives at the **Hungarian Railway History Park** (p108).

For more detail of this area, see Map p248 ➡

Lonely Planet's Top Tip

The variety of moving conveyances available on Margaret Island knows no bounds. You can hire a bicycle from one of several stands, including **Bio Rent a Bike** (per hour/day 700/2000Ft; ⊗9am-dusk) on the northern end of the athletic stadium as you walk from Margaret Bridge. Nearby is **Electric Car Rental** (minicar for 4 people per half/full hour 2900/4300Ft). **Bringóhintó** (www.bringohinto.hu; pedal coach for 4 people per half/full hour 1980/2980Ft; ⊗8am-dusk) rents out equipment from the refreshment stand near the Japanese Garden in the northern part of the island. There are horse-drawn carriages nearby too.

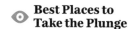

⊙ Best Places to Take the Plunge

➡ Danubius Health Spa Margitsziget (p107)

➡ Aquaworld (p108)

➡ Dagály (p107)

For reviews, see p107 ➡

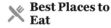

✕ Best Places to Eat

➡ Firkász (p109)

➡ Pozsonyi Kisvendéglő (p109)

➡ Café Panini (p110)

For reviews, see p109 ➡

☐ Best Places to Drink

➡ Holdudvar (p110)

➡ Amélie (p110)

➡ Dunapark (p110)

For reviews, see p110 ➡

Explore: Margaret Island & Northern Pest

Neither Buda nor Pest – though part of district XIII – 2.5km-long Margaret Island (Margit-sziget) in the middle of the Danube was always the domain of one religious order or another until the Turks arrived and turned what was then called the Island of Rabbits into – appropriately enough – a harem, from which all 'infidels' were barred. It's been a public park open to everyone since the mid-19th century.

Margaret Island is not overly endowed with important sights and landmarks. But boasting a couple of large swimming complexes, a thermal spa, gardens and shaded walkways, the island is a lovely place to head on a hot afternoon. Cars are allowed on Margaret Island from Árpád Bridge only as far as the two big hotels at the northern end; the rest is reserved for pedestrians and cyclists.

Szent István körút, the northernmost stretch of the Big Ring Rd (Nagykörút) in Pest, runs in an easterly direction from Margaret bridge to Nyugati tér. The area north of Szent István körút is known as Újlipótváros (New Leopold Town) to distinguish it from Lipótváros (Leopold Town) to the south of the Big Ring Rd. It is a wonderful neighbourhood with tree-lined streets, antique shops, boutiques and a few cafes, and is best seen on foot.

Local Life

➡ **Sport** The Alfréd Hajós (p108) swimming complex is a good spot to catch the water polo league at the weekend.

➡ **Eating** Catering is limited on Margaret Island, so visit Gasztró Hús-Hentesáru (p80) opposite the tram stop (4 or 6) on the Buda side of Margaret Bridge to stock up on edibles.

➡ **Swimming** One of the best places to watch Hungarians at play is the Palatinus Strand (p108) on Margaret Island.

Getting There & Away

➡ **Tram** Both districts served by trams 4 and 6. Tram 2 to XIII Jászai Mari tér from the Inner Town.

➡ **Bus** 26 to cover the length of Margaret Island running between Nyugati train station and Árpád Bridge. Újlipótváros via buses 15 and 115.

➡ **Trolleybus** 75 and 76 excellent for Újlipótváros.

➡ **Metro** The eastern end of Újlipótváros best reached by metro (M3 Nyugati pályaudvar).

◉ SIGHTS

◉ Margaret Island

MARGARET BRIDGE   BRIDGE

Map p248 At the time of writing, Margaret Bridge (Margit híd) had just undergone a massive three-year reconstruction. It introduces the Big Ring Rd to Buda, and is unique in that it doglegs in order to stand at right angles to the Danube at its confluence at the southern tip of Margaret Island. It was originally built by French engineer Ernest Gouin in 1876; the branch leading to the island was added in 1901.

CENTENNIAL MONUMENT   MONUMENT

Map p248 (Centenariumi emlékmű; 🚊4, 6; 🚃26) This monument, in the flower-bedded roundabout 350m north of the tram stop (4 or 6) on Margaret Bridge, was unveiled in 1973 to mark the 100th anniversary of the union of Buda, Pest and Óbuda. During an entirely different era in Budapest, the sculptor filled the strange split cone with all sorts of socialist and nationalist symbols.

WATER TOWER &
OPEN-AIR THEATRE   TOWER

Map p248 (Víztorony; 🚃26) Erected in 1911 in the north-central part of the island, the octagonal water tower rises 66m above the **open-air theatre** (szabadtéri színpad; info@szabadter.hu), which is used for opera, plays and concerts in summer. The tower contains the **Lookout Gallery** (Kilátó Galéria; adult/child 300/200Ft; ⏰11am-7pm May-Oct). Climbing the 153 steps will earn you a stunning 360-degree view of the island, Buda and Pest.

FRANCISCAN CHURCH
& MONASTERY   RUINS

Map p248 (Ferences templom és kolostor; 🚃26) The first of the island's three great ruins is just off the main thoroughfare in almost the exact centre of the island. It's the remains of a Franciscan church and monastery, including a late 13th-century tower and wall. The summer residence built here by Habsburg Archduke Joseph when he inherited the island in 1867 was later converted into a hotel that ran until 1949.

DOMINICAN CONVENT   RUINS

Map p248 (Domonkos kolostor; 🚃26) North-east of the Franciscan complex is all that remains of the 13th-century convent built by Béla IV, where his daughter, St Margaret (1242–71) lived. According to the story, the king promised to commit his daughter to a life of devotion in a nunnery if the Mongols were driven from the land. They were and she was – at nine years of age. St Margaret, only canonised in 1943, commands something of a cult following in Hungary. A red-marble sepulchre cover surrounded by a wrought-iron grille marks her original resting place; a short distance southeast there's also a much-visited brick shrine with ex-votives thanking her for various favours.

PREMONSTRATENSIAN CHURCH   CHURCH

Map p248 (Premontre templom; 🚃26) Some 200m north of the convent ruins is the reconstructed Romanesque Premonstratensian Church dedicated to St Michael and originally dating back to the 12th century. Its 15th-century bell mysteriously appeared one night in 1914 under the roots of a walnut tree knocked over in a storm. It was probably buried by monks during the Turkish invasion.

JAPANESE GARDEN   GARDEN

Map p248 (Japánkert; 🚃26) This attractive garden at the northwestern end of the island has koi, carp and lily pads in its ponds, as well as bamboo groves, Japanese maples, swamp cypresses, a small wooden bridge and a waterfall. Just north on a raised gazebo is the **Musical Fountain** (Zenélőkút), a replica of one in Transylvania. A tape plays chimes and snatches of a folk song on the hour.

DANUBIUS HEALTH SPA
MARGITSZIGET   THERMAL BATHS, POOLS

Map p248 (📞889 4700; www.danubiushotels.com; admission Mon-Fri 4900Ft, Sat & Sun 5900Ft; ⏰6.30am-9.30pm; 🚃26) Among the most modern (but least atmospheric) of all the baths, this modern thermal spa is in the Danubius Thermal Hotel Margitsziget on leafy Margaret Island. The baths are open to men and women in separate sections. A daily ticket includes entry to the swimming pools, sauna and steam room, as well as use of the fitness machines.

DAGÁLY   POOLS

Map p248 (www.spasbudapest.com; XIII Népfürdő utca 36; admission before/after 6pm Mon-Fri 2000/1650Ft, Sat & Sun 2300/2000Ft; ⏰outdoor pools 6am-8pm May-Sep, indoor pools 6am-

WORTH A DETOUR

FUN FOR THE FAMILY

Hungarian Railway History Park

The mostly outdoor **Hungarian Railway History Park** (Magyar Vasúttörténeti Park; www.mavnosztalgia.hu; XIV Tatai út 95; adult/child 1100/400Ft; ⊙10am-6pm Tue-Sun Apr-Oct, to 3pm Tue-Sun Nov-early Dec & mid-Mar–Apr; ⊟30, 30A; ⊟14) contains more than 100 locomotives (many of them still working) and an exhibition on the history of the railroad in Hungary. For kids there's a wonderful array of hands-on activities – mostly involving getting behind the wheel. From late March to October a special train on the Esztergom line leaves Nyugati train station for the park three times a day at 10.20am, 11.20am and 1.20pm.

Aquaworld

The huge water park called **Aquaworld** (www.aqua-world.hu; Íves út 16; 2hr/day Mon-Fri adult 2500/4900Ft, child 1200/1900Ft, Sat & Sun adult 2900/5600Ft, child 1500/2500Ft; ⊙6am-10pm; ⊟30 from Keleti train station) in northern Pest is one of Europe's largest, with an adventure centre covered by a 72m dome, pools with slides and whirlpools, and an array of saunas to keep the whole family gainfully at play. A free shuttle bus departs from in front of the Museum of Fine Arts in Heroes' Square (ⓂM1 Hősök tere) up to eight times a day between 9am and 9pm.

7pm Mon-Fri, 6am-5pm Sat & Sun Oct-Apr; ⓂM3 Árpád híd; ⊟1) This huge complex has a total of 10 pools, including two thermal ones and a whirlpool. The surrounding park offers plenty of grass and shade.

PALATINUS STRAND   POOLS
Map p248 (www.budapestgyogyfurdoi.hu; admission before/after 5pm Mon-Fri 2200/1500Ft, Sat & Sun 2500Ft; ⊙9am-8pm May-Aug; ⊟26) The largest series of pools in the capital, the 'Palatinus Beach' complex on Margaret Island has a total of upwards of a dozen pools (three with thermal water), wave machines, water slides, kids' pools etc.

DANUBIUS HEALTH SPA
HÉLIA   THERMAL BATHS, POOLS
Map p248 (☑889 5800; www.danubiushotels .com; XIII Kárpát utca 62-64; admission before/after 8pm Mon-Fri 4100/2800Ft, Sat & Sun 5200/3200Ft; ⊙7am-10pm; ⓂM3 Dózsa György út; ⊟75) This ultramodern swimming and spa centre in the four-star Danubius Hélia Hotel boasts three pools, a sauna and steam room and an abundance of therapies.

ALFRÉD HAJÓS   POOLS
Map p248 (☑340 4946; adult/child 1700/1050Ft; ⊙outdoor pools 6am-6pm May-Sep, indoor pools 6am-6pm Mon-Fri, 6am-5pm Sat & Sun Oct-Apr; ⊟4, 6) The two indoor and three outdoor pools at the Alfréd Hajós swimming complex make up the National Sports Pool,

where the Olympic swimming and water-polo teams train. You can watch water polo league on the weekends.

⊙ Újlipótváros

JÁSZAI MARI TÉR   SQUARE
Map p248 (⊟2, 4, 6) The gateway to both Margaret Island and Újlipótváros, Jászai Mari tér is split in two by the foot of Margaret Bridge. The modern building south of the square, nicknamed the **White House** (Fehér Ház; V Széchenyi rakpart 19), is the former headquarters of the Central Committee of the Hungarian Socialist Workers' Party. It now contains offices of the members of Hungary's parliament. To the north of the square is an elegant apartment block forming part of the **Palatinus Houses** (Palatinus Házak; XIII Pozsonyi út 2), built in 1912 and facing the Danube. They contain some of the most expensive flats for sale or rent in Budapest.

SZENT ISTVÁN PARK   PARK
Map p248 (XIII Pozsonyi út; ⊟75, 76) Northeast of the Palatinus Houses is 'St Stephen Park', where a **Raoul Wallenberg statue** doing battle with a snake (evil) was erected in 1999. It is titled *Kígyóölő* (Serpent Slayer) and replaces one created by sculptor Pál Pátzay that was mysteriously removed the

night before its unveiling in 1948. Facing the river is a row of Bauhaus apartments. They may not look like much today after decades of bad copies, but they were the bee's knees when they were built in the late 1920s.

COMEDY THEATRE
NOTABLE BUILDING

Map p248 (Vígszínház; www.pestiszinhaz.hu; XIII Szent István körút 14; ⊠4, 6) The attractive little building on Szent István körút roughly halfway between the Danube and Nyugati tér is where comedies (including Shakespearean ones in translation) and musicals are staged. When it was built in 1896, it was criticised for being too far out of town.

LEHEL CHURCH
CHURCH

Map p248 (Lehel templom; XIII Lehel tér; ⓂM3 Lehel tér) If you look north up XIII Váci út north from Nyugati tér you'll catch sight of the twin spires of this 1933 copy of a celebrated 13th-century Romanesque church (now in ruins) at Zsámbék, 33km west of Budapest. Just beyond it is **Lehel Market** (Lehel Csarnok; XIII Lehel tér; ⊙6am-6pm Mon-Fri, to 2pm Sat, to 1pm Sun; ⓂM3 Lehel tér), a great traditional market now housed in a hideous boatlike structure designed by László Rajk, son of the communist minister of the interior executed for 'Titoism' in 1949. They say this building is his revenge.

✕ EATING

There's not a lot of options on Margaret Island unless you like uninspired and pricey hotel fare. The same is not true of Újlipótváros, which captures a tremendous amount of eateries in a relatively small area.

POZSONYI KISVENDÉGLŐ
HUNGARIAN €

Map p248 (XIII Radnóti Miklós utca 38; mains 980-2400Ft; ⊠75, 76) Visit this neighbourhood restaurant on the corner of Pozsonyi út for the ultimate local Budapest experience: gargantuan portions of Hungarian classics, rock-bottom prices and a cast of local characters. There's a bank of tables on the pavement in summer and simple set weekday menus for 750Ft.

FIRKÁSZ
HUNGARIAN €€

Map p248 (✆450 1118; www.firkaszetterem .hu; Tátra utca 18; mains 2190-4690Ft; ⊙noon-3.30pm & 6-10pm; ⊠15, 115) Set up by former journalists, this retro-style restaurant called 'Hack', with lovely old mementos on the walls, great homestyle cooking and a good wine list, has been one of our favourite Hungarian eateries for years.

PÁNDZSÁB TANDOORI
INDIAN €

Map p248 (www.indiaietterem.hupont.hu; XIII Pannónia utca 3; mains 1090-2490Ft; ⊙noon-11pm; ⊿; ⊠15, 115) It may not look like much, but get closer and your olfactories will tell you that this little hole-in-the-wall with seating upstairs serves some of the best home-cooked Indian food in Budapest. The signature tandoori dishes are excellent, and there's also a good choice of vegetarian dishes.

PHILIPPE LE BELGE
SEAFOOD €€€

Map p248 (✆350 0411; www.philippe.hu; XIII Balzac utca 35; mains 4500-8900Ft; ⊙noon-3pm & 6-10pm Tue-Sat; ⊠15, 115) The ultramarine exterior is the cue that this swish establishment takes the sea and its produce very seriously indeed. It's fine dining at a price, but oysters, lobster and any manner of finned creature do not come cheaply in a landlocked country. Come for lunch when a five-course tasting menu is on offer for – wait for it – under 2000Ft.

KISKAKUKK
HUNGARIAN €€

Map p248 (✆450 0829; www.kiskakukk.hu; XIII Pozsonyi utca 12; mains 2190-3690Ft; ⊙noon-midnight; ⊠4, 6; ⊠75, 76) Since the year before WWI broke out this ever-so-traditional Hungarian eatery has been serving up *gulyásleves* (hearty beef soup; 780Ft) and Kaposvár-style stuffed cabbage (2250Ft). It's tried and tested and true.

OKAY ITALIA
ITALIAN €€

Map p248 (www.okayitalia.hu; XIII Szent István körút 20; pizza & pasta 1090-2290Ft, mains 1890-4690Ft; ⊙11am-midnight Mon-Fri, noon-midnight Sat & Sun; ⊠4, 6) Perennially popular eatery originally started by Italians does a full range of dishes, but most people come for the pasta and pizza. The terrace on the Big Ring Rd is a lively place to meet in summer.

TRÓFEA GRILL
INTERNATIONAL, BUFFET €€

Map p248 (www.trofeagrill.hu; XIII Visegrádi utca 50; lunch/dinner Mon-Thu 3199/4499Ft, lunch & dinner Fri-Sun 4999Ft; ⊙noon-midnight Mon-Fri, 11.30am-midnight Sat, 11.30am-8.30pm Sun; ⓂM3 Lehel tér) This is the place to head when you really could eat a horse (which may or may not be on one of the tables). It's an enormous buffet of more than 100 cold and hot dishes over which appreciative diners swarm like bees.

CAFÉ PANINI SANDWICHES €

Map p248 (www.cafepanini.hu; XIII Radnóti Miklós utca 45; sandwiches & salads 750-1550Ft; ⏰8am-10pm Mon-Thu, 8am-11pm Fri, 9am-11pm Sat, 10am-10pm Sun; ⏹75, 76) With an enviable location along the Danube, this upbeat and very casual venue is worth a visit for the tasty views of Margaret Island alone. But come for great *panini* and salads, breakfast (1490Ft to 1990Ft) at any time and a two-course set lunch for 1390Ft.

🍷 DRINKING & NIGHTLIFE

MOSSELEN BAR

Map p248 (www.mosselen.hu; XIII Pannónia utca 14; ⏰noon-midnight; ⏹15, 115) This pleasant 'Belgian beer cafe' in Újlipótváros has a wide selection of almost three dozen Belgian beers, many of them fruit-flavoured ones. Of course, with a name like 'Mussels' it just has to serve those much-loved bivalves (3990Ft to 4390Ft), prepared in several different ways, but at night it's very much a fun bar.

BLUE TOMATO BAR

Map p248 (www.bluetomato.hu; XIII Pannónia utca 5-7; ⏰noon-midnight Sun-Tue, to 2am Wed & Thu, to 4am Fri & Sat; ⏹15, 115) This big boozer is like something straight out of the old TV sitcom *Cheers,* especially the upstairs bar. It's been a popular feature of the district for more than a decade and the food – mostly Med-Hungarian, with mains from 1590Ft to 2990Ft – is more than just the usual bar blotter.

HOLDUDVAR GARDEN CLUB

Map p248 (www.holdudvar.net; XIII Margit-sziget; ⏰10am-5am Apr-Sep; ⏹26) Trying to be all things to all people – restaurant, bar, gallery, open-air cinema and *kert* (outdoor garden club) – is not always advisable, but the 'Moon Court', occupying a huge indoor and outdoor space, does a decent job of juggling all five remits. Still, most come for the pulsating seasonal outdoor club

(no noise worries here!), which rocks to different music styles each night.

AMÉLIE CAFE

Map p248 (XIII Pozsonyi út 28; ⏰8am-11pm Mon-Fri, 10am-10pm Sat & Sun; ⏹75, 76) This movie-themed cafe (remember the 2001 French film and the eponymous do-gooder?) is a popular addition to a neighbourhood that cries out for more of them. The welcome is warm.

DUNAPARK CAFE

Map p248 (XIII Pozsonyi út 38; www.dunapark kavehaz.hu; ⏰8am-midnight Mon-Fri, 10am-midnight Sat, 10am-10pm Sun; ⏹75, 76) Built in 1938 and originally meant to be a cinema, this art-deco place with a lovely upstairs gallery and views of Szent István Park is also a restaurant. But we still think of – and use – it as a *cukrászda;* its cakes (370Ft to 590Ft) are among the best this side of the Danube.

☆ ENTERTAINMENT

KINO CINEMA

Map p248 (www.akino.hu, in Hungarian; XIII Szent István körút 16; ⏹4, 6) Formerly the Szindbád cinema, named after the seminal (and eponymous) 1971 film by director Zoltán Huszárik and based on the novel by Gyula Krúdy, this renovated cinema shows good Hungarian and foreign films with subtitles. Excellent cafe attached.

🛍 SHOPPING

PENDRAGON BOOKS

Map p248 (XIII Pozsonyi út 21-23; ⏰10am-6pm Mon-Fri, to 2pm Sat; ⏹4, 6; ⏹75, 76) This exclusively English-language bookshop, which takes its name from the legend of King Arthur, has an excellent selection of books and guides (including Lonely Planet titles).

MOUNTEX OUTDOOR EQUIPMENT

Map p248 (www.mountex.hu; XIII Váci út 19; ⏰10am-7pm Mon-Fri, to 2pm Sat; Ⓜ M3 Lehel tér) This huge emporium on two levels with branches throughout the city carries all the gear you'll need for camping, hiking, trekking and climbing. In fact, it runs the **Boulder Club climbing wall** (☉8am-10pm Mon-Fri, 10am-8pm Sat & Sun) round the corner should you want to get in a little practice while shopping.

BOOK STATION BOOKS

Map p248 (www.bookstation.hu; XIII Katona József utca 13; ☉10am-7pm Mon-Sat; Ⓜ M3 Nyugati pály-audvar) A relatively new and very key player in the used-books business, Book Station has upwards of 5000 secondhand English-language titles.

⌂TOP CHOICE MÉZES KUCKÓ FOOD

Map p248 (Honey Nook; XIII Jászai Mari tér 4; ☉10am-6pm Mon-Fri, 9am-1pm Sat; ☐4, 6) This hole-in-the-wall is the place to go if you have the urge for something sweet; its nut-and-honey cookies (240Ft per 10dg) are to die for. A colourfully decorated *mézeska-lács* (honey cake; 420Ft to 850Ft) in the shape of a heart makes a lovely gift.

MATYÓ DESIGN FASHION

Map p248 (www.matyodesign.hu; XIII Radnóti Miklós utca 25, 2nd fl; ☉11am-4pm Mon, Tue, Thu & Fri, 3-8pm Wed; ☐2, 4, 6) This is one of those companies that makes you wonder why someone didn't think of it before... Two sisters who grew up in a small village near Mezőkövesd in northern Hungary have taken the Matyó needlework famous in that area (p196) and dragged it into the 21st century. Goodbye voluminous skirts and heavy vests embellished with embroidery; hello jeans, T-shirts and other contemporary apparel as well as baby clothes. Stunning. Ring the bell at No 27 to gain entry.

Erzsébetváros & the Jewish Quarter

ERZSÉBETVÁROS | ANDRÁSSY ÚT | TERÉZVÁROS (EAST)

Neighbourhood Top Five

1 Marvelling at the exotic architecture of the **Great Synagogue** (p114), the largest Jewish house of worship in Europe, and accompanying the Jews on a 2000-year tour of their history in Hungary at the **Hungarian Jewish Museum** (p114).

2 Enjoying a performance at the **Hungarian State Opera House** (p125), the capital's sumptuously appointed temple to classical music.

3 Strolling along **Andrássy út** (p117), the gracious tree-, shop- and sight-lined boulevard that appears on Unesco's World Heritage List.

4 Drinking and/or dancing the night away at any of central Pest's *kertek* (outdoor garden clubs), such as **Szimpla Kert** (p124) or **Ellátó Kert** (p124).

5 Tasting something sweet along with something warm on the terrace of a traditional cafe like the **Művész Kávéház** (p124) on Andrássy út.

For more detail of this area, see Map p250 ➡

Explore: Erzsébetváros & the Jewish Quarter

The Nagy körút – the Big Ring Rd, consisting of Teréz körút and Erzsébet körút in this neighbourhood – slices district VI (Terézváros) and district VII (Erzsébetváros; Elizabeth Town) in half, the latter between two busy squares: Oktogon and Blaha Lujza tér. While Terézváros continues on merrily up to Városliget (Pest's sprawling 'City Park', seemingly just an extension of Andrássy út), Erzsébetváros is quite different on either side of the Big Ring Rd. The eastern side is rather run-down, with little of interest to travellers except the Keleti train station on Baross tér. The western side, bounded by the Little Ring Rd, has always been predominantly Jewish, and this was the ghetto where Jews were forced to live when the Nazis occupied Hungary in 1944.

Andrássy út, listed as a Unesco World Heritage Site, starts a short distance north of Deák Ferenc tér and stretches for 2.5km to the northeast, ending at Heroes' Square (Hősök tere) and City Park. Andrássy út is such a pretty boulevard and there's so much to see, do and enjoy en route that the best way to see it is on foot (p119).

Local Life

→ **Architecture** Don't hesitate to explore the inner courtyards like the Gozsdu Udvar (p116) in Erzsébetváros – if Dublin is celebrated for its doorways and London for its squares, Budapest is known for its lovely *udvarok* (courtyards).

→ **Classical Music** It's hard to imagine a better way to start a Saturday than a classical music performance at the Franz Liszt Memorial Museum (p118).

→ **Museum** The Hungarian Electrical Engineering Museum (p115) is one of the quirkiest museums in town, and its guides as enthusiastic as you'll find anywhere.

Getting There & Away

→ **Metro** Oktogon is on the M1 metro line and Blaha Lujza tér on the M2; also useful are the M2 Astoria & Keleti pályaudvar stations.

→ **Tram** VII Erzsébet körút for No 4 or 6 to Buda or rest of the Big Ring Rd in Pest.

→ **Trolleybus** VII Wesselényi utca & Dohány utca for No 74 to Little Ring Rd or City Park.

Lonely Planet's Top Tip

It may not be immediately apparent, but the M1 metro, also known as the Kis Metró (Little Metro), which runs just below Andrássy út from Deák Ferenc tér as far as the City Park, sticks to its side of the road underground and there is no interchange down below. So if you are heading north, board the trains on the east side of Andrássy út. For points south, it's the west side. Another possible source of confusion on the M1 is that one station is called Vörösmarty tér and another, five stops away, is Vörösmarty utca.

 Best Places to Eat

→ Kádár (p121)
→ Kőleves (p120)
→ Klassz (p122)
→ Ring (p122)
→ Baraka (p122)

For reviews, see p120 →

Best Places to Drink

→ Vittula (p123)
→ Elíató Kert (p124)
→ CoXx Men's Bar (p123)
→ Bar Ladino (p124)
→ Alexandra Book Cafe (p124)

For reviews, see p122 →

Best Places to Shop

→ Romani Design (p126)
→ Printa (p126)
→ Massolit (p125)
→ M Lamp (p126)
→ Billerbeck (p126)

For reviews, see p125 →

 ERZSÉBETVÁROS & THE JEWISH QUARTER

TOP SIGHTS
GREAT SYNAGOGUE

As you travel along the Little Ring Rd (this section of it called Károly körút) from Astoria, you can't help but notice a building with a crenulated red-and-yellow glazed brick facade and two enormous Moorish-style towers topped with onion domes on the right. This is the Great Synagogue (Nagy zsinagóga), the largest Jewish house of worship in the world outside New York City. Seating 3000 worshippers, it is sometimes called the Dohány utca Synagogue (Dohány utcai zsinagóga) in reference to its location.

Built in 1859 according to the designs of Viennese architect Ludwig Förster, the copper-domed Neolog (strict conservative) synagogue contains both Romantic-style and Moorish architectural elements. Because some elements of it recall Christian churches – the towers, longitudinal plan with three naves and the central **rose window** with an inscription from the second book of Moses – the synagogue is sometimes referred to as the 'Jewish cathedral'. It was renovated in the 1990s largely with private donations, including a cool US$5 million from fragrance and cosmetics baroness Estée Lauder (1906–2004), who was born Josephine Esther Mentzer in Queens, New York, to Hungarian Jewish immigrants. Inside don't miss some of the decorative fittings, including the carvings on the **Ark of the Covenant** by Frigyes Feszl and the sumptuous **organ**, dating back to 1902. It has been completely rebuilt and concerts are held here in summer.

In an annexe of the synagogue – there's a plaque on the exterior wall noting that Theodore Herzl, the father of modern Zionism, was born at the site in 1860 – is the **Hungarian Jewish Museum** (Magyar Zsidó Múzeum; www.zsidomuzeum .hu), which contains objects related to religious and everyday life. Most of the museum's collection of Judaica came through bequests, gifts and purchases. Interesting items include **3rd-century Jewish headstones** from Roman Pannonia; a vast amount of ritualistic items in silver including a Kiddush cup made for the order of the Óbuda Holy Society in 1749; and a handwritten book of the local Chevra Kadisha (Burial Society) from the late 18th century. The **Holocaust Memorial Room** relates the events of 1944–45, including the infamous mass murder of doctors and patients at a hospital on XII Maros utca south of Moszkva tér (now Széll Kálmán tér) in Buda.

On the synagogue's north side (opposite VII Wesselényi utca 6), the **Holocaust Memorial**, designed by Imre Varga (p75) in 1991, stands over the mass graves of those murdered by the Nazis in 1944–45. On the leaves of the metal 'tree of life' are the family names of some of the hundreds of thousands of victims.

DON'T MISS...

➡ Ark of the Covenant
➡ Rose window
➡ Hungarian Jewish Museum
➡ Holocaust Memorial

PRACTICALITIES

➡ Map p250
➡ www.dohanystreet-synagogue.hu
➡ VII Dohány utca 2-8
➡ adult/child 2400/1650Ft, incl museum 2750/2050Ft
➡ ⊙10am-5.30pm Sun-Thu, to 4pm Fri Apr-Oct, to 3.30pm Sun-Thu, to 2.30pm Fri Nov-Mar
➡ Ⓜ M2 Astoria
➡ 🚌 47, 49

⊙ SIGHTS

⊙ Erzsébetváros

GREAT SYNAGOGUE SYNAGOGUE
See p114.

FERENC LISZT
MUSIC ACADEMY HISTORIC BUILDING
Map p250 (Liszt Zeneakadémia; ☎462 4600; www.zeneakademia.hu; VI Liszt Ferenc tér 8; ⓜM1 Oktogon) A block southeast of Oktogon, what's usually just called the 'music academy' was built in 1907. It attracts students from all over the world and is one of the top venues for concerts. The interior, with large and small concert halls richly embellished with Zsolnay porcelain and frescoes, is worth a look even if you're not attending a performance.

HUNGARIAN ELECTRICAL ENGINEERING
MUSEUM MUSEUM
Map p250 (Magyar Elektrotechnikai Múzeum; www .emuzeum.hu, in Hungarian; VII Kazinczy utca 21; adult/child 50/250Ft; ⓢ10am-5pm Tue-Fri, 9am-4pm Sat; ⓜM2 Astoria) This place doesn't sound like everyone's cup of tea, but the white-coated staff are very enthusiastic and some of the exhibits are unusual enough

THE JEWS OF BUDAPEST

If you travel through parts of Hungary, especially the northeast, you can't help but notice synagogues being used as cultural centres and concert halls, and cemeteries being overtaken by weeds, the broken headstones pitched this way and that. There are no relatives left to tend these graves. Brothers, mothers, husbands, lovers, nephews, granddaughters – all are dead or have gone elsewhere.

It's a somewhat different story in Budapest. Because the fascists emptied the Ghetto of its residents relatively late in the war, tens of thousands of Budapest Jews managed to escape death in German concentration camps. Today Hungary's Jews (not necessarily claiming to be religious) number about 80,000, down from a pre-war population of more than 10 times that amount, with almost 90% living in Budapest.

Jewish contribution to life here, always great, has continued into the 21st century, and the music scene is particularly lively. Several restaurants serve kosher food, even more serve nonkosher Jewish dishes and there are four very active synagogues, including the neoclassical Óbuda Synagogue now being used as a *súl* (prayer house) by the Lubovitch sect.

Jews can trace their presence in Hungary to well before the arrival of the Magyars; indeed, Jewish headstones on exhibit in the Hungarian Jewish Museum date from AD 3rd-century Roman Pannonia. Over the centuries Jews underwent the usual rollercoaster ride of being oppressed, then tolerated and oppressed again so familiar in Europe. They were blamed for the plague and expelled by Louis the Great (Nagy Lajos) in 1360, but then readmitted and prospered under good King Matthias Corvinus and even the Ottoman Turks. With full emancipation after the 1867 Compromise, Jews dominated the burgeoning middle class during Budapest's Golden Age at the end of the 19th century and some were ennobled by the Habsburgs.

After the failure of the Communist Republic of Councils under Béla Kun (himself a Jew) in 1919, Miklós Horthy launched his so-called white terror and Jews again became the scapegoats. Life was no bed of roses for Jews under Horthy between the wars, but they were not deported to Germany. But when Hitler removed Horthy from power and installed the Hungarian pro-Nazi Arrow Cross Party, deportations began. During the summer of 1944, a mere 10 months before the war ended, 60% of Hungarian Jews were sent to Auschwitz and other labour camps where they were murdered or died from abuse.

When Jews die, a prayer called Kaddish is recited for them. This is repeated at Yahrzeit, the first anniversary of the death, and annually after that. Many of those Jews lying in cemeteries in Hungary have no one to say this prayer for them. Your voice can fill a decades-old void. Say Kaddish for those whose relatives cannot.

You can download the prayer from the Judaism 101 (www.jewfaq.org/prayer/kaddish.htm) website.

START VI LISZT FERENC TÉR
FINISH VII DOHÁNY UTCA
DISTANCE 1KM
DURATION ONE TO TWO HOURS

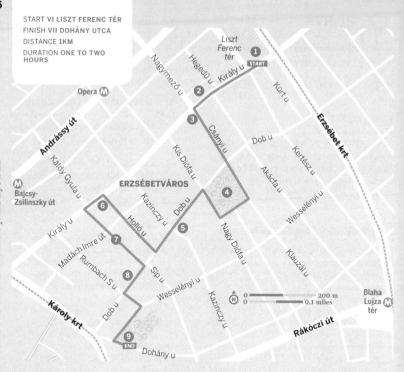

Neighbourhood Walk
Erzsébetváros & the Jewish Quarter

Begin the walk in restaurant- and cafe-packed VI Liszt Ferenc tér, where you'll find the ① **Ferenc Liszt Music Academy** (p115) at the southeastern end. There are always tickets (some very cheap) available to something – perhaps a recital or an early Saturday morning rehearsal.

If you walk southwest along Király utca you'll pass the ② **Church of St Teresa**, built in 1811 and containing a massive neoclassical altar designed by Mihály Pollack in 1822. At Király utca 47 (and directly opposite the large Church of St Teresa) is an interesting ③ **neo-Gothic house** built in 1847 with a protruding window.

Turning into Csányi utca, head southeast over Dob utca to the heart of the old Jewish Quarter, ④ **Klauzál tér**. The square and surrounding streets retain a feeling of pre-war Budapest. A continued Jewish presence is still evident – at a kosher bakery and pizzeria (Kazinczy utca 28), the Fröhlich Cukrászda cake shop and cafe (p123), and a butcher just next to the ⑤ **Orthodox Synagogue** (p117).

Walk up Holló utca and turn left. Enter the gate at Király utca 15 – someone will obligingly buzz you in should it be locked – and at the rear of the courtyard is a 30m-long piece of the original ⑥ **ghetto wall** rebuilt in 2010. Votive lamps and stones stand before it in tribute to victims of the Holocaust. The next turning on the left is the passageway called ⑦ **Gozsdu Udvar**, originally built in 1901 and given a massive facelift over the past five years.

At Dob utca 12 is an unusual antifascist ⑧ **monument to Carl Lutz**, a Swiss consul who, like Raoul Wallenberg (p67), provided Jews with false papers in 1944. It portrays an angel on high sending down a long bolt of cloth to a victim. At the end of the street is the ⑨ **Great Synagogue** (p114).

for a visit. Its collection of 19th-century generators, condensers, motors and (egad) the world's largest supply of electricity-consumption meters is not very inspiring, but the staff will show you how the alarm system of the barbed-wire fence between Hungary and Austria once worked. There's also a display on the nesting platforms that the electric company kindly builds for storks throughout the country so they won't nest on the wires and electrocute themselves.

MIKSA RÓTH MEMORIAL HOUSE MUSEUM
Map p250 (Róth Miksa Emlékház; www.rothmuzeum.hu; VII Nefelejcs utca 26; adult/child 500/250Ft; ☺2-6pm Tue-Sat; Ⓜ M2 Keleti pályaudvar) This fabulous museum exhibits the work of the eponymous art nouveau stained-glass maker (1865–1944) on two floors of the house and workshop where he lived and worked from 1911 until his death. The master's stunning mosaics are less well known. Róth's dark-brown living quarters stand in sharp contrast to the lively, Technicolor creations that emerged from his workshop.

OTHER SYNAGOGUES SYNAGOGUES
Once a half dozen synagogues and prayer houses were in this district, reserved for different sects and ethnic groups (conser-vatives, Orthodox, Poles, Sephardics etc). The **Orthodox Synagogue** (Ortodox zsinagóga, Kazinczy utca Synagogue, Kazinczy utcai zsinagóga; Map p250; VII Kazinczy utca 29-31; admission 800Ft; ☺10am-3.30pm Sun-Thu, to 12.30pm Fri; ☐74), also accessible from Dob utca 35, was built in 1913. The Moorish **Rumbach Sebestyén utca Synagogue** (Rumbach Sebestyén utcai zsinagóga; Map p250; VII Rumbach Sebestyén utca 11; admission 500Ft; ☺10am-5pm Sun-Thu, to 3pm Fri; ☐74), built in 1872 by Austrian Secessionist architect Otto Wagner for the Status Quo Ante (moderate conservative) community, is slowly getting a much-needed facelift.

Andrássy út & Terézváros (East)

ASIAN ART MUSEUMS MUSEUMS
Two fine museums devoted to Asian arts and crafts within an easy walk of one another in the Andrássy út area are branches of the Museum of Applied Arts (p132). The **Ferenc Hopp Museum of East Asian Art** (Hopp Ferenc Kelet-Ázsiai Művészeti Múzeum; Map p250; www.imm.hu/hoppmuzeum; VI Andrássy út 103; adult/child 1000/500Ft; ☺10am-6pm Tue-Sun;

TOP SIGHTS
HUNGARIAN STATE OPERA HOUSE

The small but perfectly formed Hungarian State Opera House (Magyar Állami Operaház) is home to both the state opera company and the Hungarian National Ballet. Rivalled only by the Ferenc Liszt Music Academy (p115) as the city's most important venue for serious cultural performances, it is said to have the third-best acoustics in Europe after Milan's La Scala and the Opéra Garnier in Paris; the latter had apparently inspired the architect Miklós Ybl when he designed the neo-Renaissance building in 1884. The facade is bedecked with statues by opera greats Liszt, Mozart, Verdi and Puccini. Inside prepare to be dazzled by the **main hall**, with its marble columns, gilded vaulted ceilings, murals and chandeliers. The horseshoe-shaped **auditorium** with its (for the time) innovative proscenium arch stage and magnificent ceiling painted by Károly Lotz holds a relatively small number of spectators (1285), but because of the excellent acoustics even those in the 3rd-floor gallery are happy. Hungarians approach music as the French do wine. Performances here are never stuffy and you are as likely to see people in jeans as more formal dress. If you cannot attend an opera, ballet or concert here, join one of the guided tours.

DON'T MISS...
➡ Front facade with statues
➡ Main hall
➡ 3-tonne chandelier
➡ Sweeping main staircase

PRACTICALITIES
➡ Map p250
➡ ☎332 8197
➡ www.opera.hu
➡ VI Andrássy út 22
➡ adult/student 2900/1900Ft
➡ ☺English-language tours 3pm & 4pm
➡ Ⓜ M1 Opera

M1 Bajza utca) is housed in the former villa of its benefactor and namesake. Founded in 1919, the museum has six rooms showing an important collection of Chinese and Japanese ceramics, porcelain, textiles and sculpture, Indonesian *wayang* puppets and Indian statuary, as well as lamaist sculpture and scroll paintings from Tibet. The Ferenc Hopp Museum's temporary exhibits are shown at the **György Ráth Museum** (Ráth György Múzeum; Map p250; www.imm.hu/hoppmuzeum; VI Városligeti fasor 12; adult/child 600/300Ft; ◷10am-6pm Tue-Sun; M1 Bajza utca) in an art nouveau residence a few minutes' walk southwards down Bajza utca. A combined ticket to both costs 1400/700Ft per adult/child.

ISTVÁN ZELNIK SOUTHEAST ASIAN GOLD MUSEUM MUSEUM
Map p250 (Zelnik István Dél-Ázsiai Arany Múzeum; www.thegoldmuseum.eu; VI Andrássy út 110; adult/child 3000/1500Ft; ◷9am-6pm Mon, to 7pm Sun & Tue-Thu, to 9pm Fri & Sat; M1 Bajza utca) As if two Asian museums weren't enough, a career diplomat has renovated and reconstructed the elegant Rausch Villa across the boulevard to house his collection

of some 16,000 glistering masks, statues and religious objects. There's a lovely tropical garden and teahouse here too.

FRANZ LISZT MEMORIAL MUSEUM MUSEUM
Map p250 (Liszt Ferenc Emlékmúzeum; www.lisztmuseum.hu; VI Vörösmarty utca 35; adult/child 900/450Ft; ◷10am-6pm Mon-Fri, 9am-5pm Sat; M1 Vörösmarty utca) This wonderful little museum is housed in the Old Music Academy, where the great composer lived in a 1st-floor apartment for five years until his death in 1886. The four rooms are filled with his pianos (including a tiny glass one), the composer's table, portraits and personal effects. Concerts (included in the entry fee) are usually held here on Saturday at 11am.

POSTAL MUSEUM MUSEUM
Map p250 (Postamúzeum; www.postamuzeum.hu; VI Andrássy út 3; adult/child 750/375Ft; ◷10am-6pm Tue-Sun; M1 Bajcsy-Zsilinszky út) The Postal Museum exhibits the contents of original 19th-century post offices – old uniforms and coaches, those big curved brass horns etc – which probably won't do much for you. But the museum is housed in the seven-room 1st-floor apartment of

---

◉ TOP SIGHTS
HOUSE OF TERROR

The startling museum called the House of Terror (Terror Háza) is housed in what was once the headquarters of the dreaded ÁVH secret police (see p182). The building has a ghastly (and presumably ghostly) history, for it was here that many activists of every political persuasion that was out of fashion before and after WWII were taken for interrogation and torture. The walls were of double thickness to mute the screams.

The museum focuses on the crimes and atrocities committed by both Hungary's fascist and Stalinist regimes in a permanent exhibition called Double Occupation, and visitors are greeted at the entrance by the red communist star and the black 'arrow cross' of the fascists. But the years after WWII leading up to the 1956 Uprising get the lion's share of the exhibition space. The **tank** in the central courtyard is a jarring introduction and the wall outside displaying many of the victims' photos speaks volumes. Even more harrowing are the reconstructed **prison cells** (collectively called 'the gym') and the final **Perpetrators' Gallery**, featuring photographs of the turncoats, spies, torturers and 'cogs in the wheel' from both sides, many of them still alive, who allowed or caused these atrocities to take place. Never again.

DON'T MISS...
➡ Tank in the central courtyard
➡ Reconstructed prison cells
➡ Hall of the 1956 Uprising

PRACTICALITIES
➡ Map p250
➡ www.terrorhaza.hu
➡ VI Andrássy út 60
➡ adult/child 1800/900Ft
➡ ◷10am-6pm Tue-Sun
➡ M1 Vörösmarty utca
➡ 🚊4, 6

START OPERA METRO STATION

FINISH VI HEROES' SQUARE

DISTANCE 2.5KM

DURATION 2½ TO THREE HOURS

Neighbourhood Walk
Andrássy út

The first stop is **①** **Drechsler House** (VI Andrássy út 25) opposite the Opera House and designed by Ödön Lechner (p144) in 1882. It once housed the Hungarian State Ballet Institute. For something even more magical, walk down Dalszínház utca to the southeast to view the **②** **New Theatre** (Új Színház; VI Paulay Ede utca 35), a Secessionist gem that opened as the Parisiana Music Hall in 1909.

The old-world cafe **③** **Művész Kávéház** (p124) is in the next block. The following cross street is **④** **Nagymező utca**, 'the Broadway of Budapest', counting a number of theatres, including the Budapest Operetta (p103) at No 17 and, just opposite, the Thália, lovingly restored in 1997. On the east side of the next block, **⑤** **Fashion Hall** (Divatcsarnok; VI Andrássy út 39), from 1882, was the fanciest emporium in town when it opened as the Grande Parisienne in 1912. It now contains a branch of the Alexandra (p126) bookshop chain.

Andrássy út meets the Nagykörút – Big Ring Rd – at Oktogon. Just beyond it, the former secret police building at Andrássy út 60 now houses the **⑥** **House of Terror** (p118).

Along the next two blocks you will pass some very **⑦** **grand buildings** housing such institutions as the Budapest Puppet Theatre (p125) at No 69; the Hungarian University of Fine Arts, founded in 1871, at No 71; and the headquarters of MÁV, the national railway, at No 73. The next square (more accurately a circus) is **⑧** **Kodály körönd**, one of the most beautiful in the city. Some of the facades of the four neo-Renaissance town houses are at last getting a facelift.

The last stretch of Andrássy út, and the surrounding neighbourhood, are packed with stunning old **⑨** **mansions and embassies** that are among the most desirable addresses in the city. Andrássy út ends at **⑩** **Heroes' Square** (Hősök tere; p141), effectively the entrance to City Park.

a wealthy late-19th-century businessman and is among the best-preserved in the city. Even the communal staircase and hallway are richly decorated with fantastic murals.

EATING

This large area captures a tremendous number of eateries – from silver-service on or just off the Teréz körút and Erzsébet körút sections of the Big Ring Rd to the Jewish *étkezdék* (canteens serving simple Hungarian dishes) of the area, which is still called the Ghetto by some local residents, and backstreet Indian messes. This area is a paradise for self-caterers too.

Erzsébetváros

KŐLEVES
HUNGARIAN €

Map p250 (☑06-20 213 5999; www.koleves.com; Kazinczy utca 35 & Dob utca 26; mains 1640-2970Ft; ☺noon-1am; ☑; ☑74) Always buzzy and lots of fun, the 'Stone Soup' attracts a young crowd with its delicious matzo ball soup (large/small 950/650Ft), plate of tapas (1950Ft), lively decor and reasonable prices. Great vegetarian choices.

PESTI VENDÉGLŐ
HUNGARIAN €

Map p250 (www.pestivendeglo1998.hu, in Hungarian; VI Paulay Ede utca 5; mains 1890-2490Ft; ☑M1/2/3 Deák Ferenc tér) A great choice for someone trying traditional Hungarian specialities for the first time. This very popular upbeat and family-run eatery that looks like a wine cellar offers a lighter take on standard Hungarian favourites, and the staff are welcoming and helpful.

SPINOZA CAFÉ
HUNGARIAN, JEWISH €

Map p250 (☑413 7488; www.spinozacafe.hu; VII Dob utca 15; mains 1750-2450Ft; ☺8am-11pm; ☑; ☑47, 49) This attractive cafe-restaurant has become a favourite both for meals and as a chill-out zone. The venue includes an art gallery and theatre, where *klezmer* (traditional Jewish music) concerts are staged at 7pm on Friday, along with a coffee house and restaurant where there's live piano music nightly. The food is mostly Hungarian/Jewish comfort food, not kosher but no pork and lots of vegetarian choices.

MONTENEGRÓI GURMAN
SOUTH SLAV €

Map p250 (VII Rákóczi út 54; dishes 830-2990Ft; ☺24hr; ☑M2 Blaha Lujza tér; ☑7) When we're famished, broke and it's well past the witch-ing hour, we head for this South Slav eatery and join all the taxi drivers chomping on grills like *csevapcsicsa* (spicy meatballs), *pljeskavica* (spicy meat patties) or *razsncs* (shish kebab) for under 1000Ft.

NAPFÉNYES
VEGETARIAN, CAKES €

Map p250 (www.napfenyes.hu, in Hungarian; VII Rózsa utca 39; mains 1500-1850Ft; ☺noon-10.30pm; ☑; ☑M1 Kodály körönd; ☑73, 76) 'Sunny' is a titch out of the way (though not if you're staying on or near Andrássy út), but the wholesome vegan foods and the speciality cakes are worth the trip. There is an organic shop where you can stock up on both packaged and baked goods, including excellent cakes (280Ft to 370Ft). Set lunches are a bargain at 550Ft to 1300Ft.

TOP CHOICE FLAMINGO
HUNGARIAN, LIVE MUSIC €

Map p250 (☑413 0567; www.flamingorestaurant.hu; VII Dob utca 57; mains 1750-2950Ft, set menu 4000Ft; ☺noon-midnight; ☑4, 6) Anchor tenant at the Fészek Club, meeting place of artists and intellectuals since 1901, this garden restaurant fills what must be the city's most beautiful courtyard (trees, galleries, colourful tile medallions) and entertains diners at night with live music (often *klezmer*) and dance (usually folk). It's a magical evening out. If you pop by during the day have a bagel or sandwich.

CARMEL PINCE
JEWISH, KOSHER €€

Map p250 (☑322 1834; www.carmel.hu; VII Kazinczy utca 31; mains 3800-5500Ft; ☺noon-11pm Sun-Thu, to 4pm Fri; ☑74) With kosher restaurants of any sort at something of a premium in Budapest, the Carmel's metamorphosis from ethnic Jewish to a bona-fide glatt kosher eatery is more than welcome. Try any of its authentic Ashkenazi specialities such as gefilte fish, matzo ball soup and a *cholent* (hearty brisket and bean casserole), which is almost as good as the one Aunt Goldie used to make. There's live *klezmer* (2000Ft) at 7.30pm on Thursday. Pre-paid Shabbat dinner service is available Friday evening and all day Saturday.

M RESTAURANT
HUNGARIAN €€

Map p250 (☑322 3108; http://mrestaurant.blogspot.com, in Hungarian; VII Kertész utca 48; mains 1800-3500Ft; ☺6pm-midnight Mon-Fri, from noon Sat & Sun; ☑4, 6) Having started life a few years back looking a lot more *menza* (drab school canteen) than it does now, M has evolved into a stylish place with an ever-changing menu of Hungarian dishes with a French twist.

KIS PARÁZS
THAI €

Map p250 (VII Kazinczy utca 7; soups 680-1050Ft, wok dishes 1150-1650Ft; ☑7, 74) The sister eatery of Parázs Presszó (p100), with simpler dishes, has become the pre-club chow down venue of choice in central Pest.

ERDÉLYI-MAGYAR ÉTKEZDE
HUNGARIAN, ÉTKEZDE €

Map p250 (www.erdelyimagyar.lapunk.hu; VII Dohány utca 36; daily menu 680Ft; ⊘11am-4pm Mon-Fri; ☑74) This little *étkezde* serves Transylvanian and Hungarian specialities to appreciative diners but, alas, keeps bankers' hours. But if you can do any better than this for the price, let us know.

HANNA
JEWISH, KOSHER €€

Map p250 (☑342 1072; VII Dob utca 35; mains 2200-3800Ft; ⊘8am-10pm Sun-Fri, 11am-2pm Sat; ☑4, 6) Housed upstairs in an old school in the Orthodox Synagogue complex, this eatery is pretty basic, but if you answer to a Higher Authority on matters culinary it is another option for kosher food. On Sabbath, you order and pay for meals in advance, of course. Set three-course menu is 3600Ft.

KÁDÁR
HUNGARIAN, ÉTKEZDE €

Map p250 (X Klauzál tér 9; mains 950-2000Ft; ⊘11.30am-3.30pm Tue-Sat; ☑4, 6) Located in the heart of the Jewish district, Kádár is probably the most popular and authentic *étkezde* you'll find in town and attracts the hungry with its ever-changing menu. Be advised that it usually closes for most of the month of August.

RUMBACH 7
HUNGARIAN €

Map p250 (www.rumbach7.hu, in Hungarian; 2-/3-course lunch 1200/1500Ft; VII Rumbach Sebestyén utca 7; ⊘11am-4pm Mon-Fri; ⓂM1/2/3 Deák Ferenc tér) A fine lunch place, this gastropub (its description, not ours) serves homestyle Hungarian cuisine in contemporary surrounds next to the old synagogue.

CITY MAHARAJA
INDIAN €€

Map p250 (www.maharaja.hu; VII Csengery utca 24; mains 1400-4600Ft; ☑4, 6) This centrally located branch of Óbuda's Maharaja (p80) serves similar subcontinental cuisine.

CORCOVADO BRASIL
BRAZILIAN €€

Map p250 (VI Káldy Gyula utca 5; mains 1490-3690Ft; ⊘noon-10pm Mon-Sat; ⓂM1 Bajcsy-Zsilinszky út) Fancy a fix of *feijoada* (rich bean and meat stew)? The 'Brazil Hunchback' (don't worry – it's the name of the mountain with that statue) can oblige and has music too. Good-value lunch menu for 990Ft.

BANGLA BÜFÉ
BANGLADESHI €

Map p250 (www.banglabufe.com; VII Akácfa utca 40; mains 650-1350Ft; ⊘11am-11pm Sun-Thu, 2.30-11pm Fri; ☑4, 6; ☑74) This place started up by a Bangladeshi expat has as authentic samosas, chicken and lamb *biryani* and dhal as you'll find here. Simple but tasty.

FALAFEL FALODA
VEGETARIAN, MIDDLE EASTERN €

Map p250 (VI Paulay Ede utca 53; sandwiches & salads 480-850Ft; ⊘10am-8pm Mon-Fri, to 6pm Sat; ☑; ☑70, 78) This inexpensive place just south of Budapest's theatre district has Israeli-style nosh. You pay a fixed price to stuff a piece of pita bread or fill a plastic container from a great assortment of salads. It also has a good variety of soups. Loft seating above.

FRICI PAPA KIFŐZDÉJE
HUNGARIAN, ÉTKEZDE €

Map p250 (www.fricipapa.gportal.hu, in Hungarian; VI Király utca 55; mains 570-680Ft; ⊘closed Sun; ☑4, 6) 'Papa Frank's Canteen' is larger and more modern than most *étkezde* in Budapest. Excellent *főzelék* dishes are around 3700Ft. We love the funny old murals of Pest in the days of yore.

FERENC JÓZSEF SÖRÖZŐ
HUNGARIAN €€

Map p250 (☑344 5316; www.etterem.hu/5813; VI Nagymező utca 12; mains 1250-4800Ft; ⊘11am-midnight Mon-Sat, from 1pm Sun; ⓂM1 Opera) The 'Franz Josef Pub' is less of a drinking venue and more one of those very Teutonic pile-it-on-high eateries where you'll leave feeling you'll never eat again. Fun olde-worlde 'almost film set' decor.

TRÓFEA GRILL
INTERNATIONAL, BUFFET €€

Map p250 (www.trofeagrill.hu; VI Király utca 30-32; lunch/dinner Mon-Thu 3499/4999Ft, lunch & dinner Fri-Sun 5499Ft; ⓂM1/2/3 Deák Ferenc tér) The prices at this most central branch of the gobble-fest buffet in Újlipótváros (p109) are the highest of the three, but it's all about location, location, location.

DURAN
SANDWICHES €

Map p250 (www.duran.hu; VI Bajcsy-Zsilinszky út 7; sandwiches 170-300Ft; ⊘8am-7pm Mon-Fri, to 3pm Sat, to noon Sun; ⓂM1/2/3 Deák Ferenc tér) The place to go for bite-sized open-face sandwiches and mini pizzas.

CARIMAMA
KOSHER, PIZZERIA €

Map p250 (www.carimama.hu; pizzas 1700-2200Ft; VI Kazinczy utca 28; ⊙7am-10pm Sun-Thu, to 2pm Fri; 🚊74) It might not be to everyone's taste, but this place will ply you with kosher pizza, baked goods and even breakfast.

HIMALAYA
NEPALESE €

Map p250 (www.maharaja.hu; VII Csengery utca 24; mains 1400-3800Ft; ⊙noon-11pm; 🚊4, 6) You'd look for a month of Sundays for a Nepalese restaurant in most cities, but here's one, a sister to the City Maharaja (p121) Indian restaurant next door, in the heart of Pest serving relatively authentic dishes in a colourful basement eatery. Try the chicken or vegetarian dumplings with chutney, any of the cumin-heavy lamb dishes and the *dhal jhaneko* made with lentils and Nepalese spices.

✖ Andrássy út & Terézváros (East)

TOP CHOICE KLASSZ
HUNGARIAN, WINE €

Map p250 (VI Andrássy út 41; mains 1590-3290Ft; ⊙11.30am-11pm Mon-Sat, to 6pm Sun; Ⓜ️M1 Oktogon) Owned by the local wine society, Klassz is mostly about wine – Hungarian to be precise – and here you can order by the 10cL measure from an ever-changing list of up to four-dozen wines to sip and compare. The food is of a very high standard, with foie gras in its various avatars and native *mangalica* (breed of pig) pork permanent fixtures on the menu, as well as more unusual (and fleeting) dishes like *blanquette de veau* (veal stew) and lamb and vegetable ragout. Reservations are not accepted; just show up and wait.

MENZA
HUNGARIAN €

Map p250 (📞413 1482; www.menza.co.hu; VI Liszt Ferenc tér 2; mains 1990-2390Ft; Ⓜ️M1 Oktogon; 🚊4, 6) This stylish Hungarian restaurant on Budapest's most lively square takes its name from the Hungarian for a drab school canteen – something it is anything but. Book a table if you can; it's always packed with diners who come for its simply but well-prepared Hungarian classics with a modern twist. Weekday two-course set lunches are 990Ft.

CANTINE
FRENCH €€

Map p250 (📞373 0098; www.cantinebudapest .hu; VI Andrássy út 44; mains 1450-3950Ft; ⊙6am-1am Tue-Sun; Ⓜ️M1 Oktogon) Valiant attempt to go *à la française* on Andrássy út doesn't really go much beyond salads and cheese (though oysters make an appearance from time to time). It's small and relaxed and the terrace is a coveted spot on a warm summer's evening.

RING
BURGERS €

Map p250 (www.ringcafe.hu; VI Andrássy út 38; burgers 1390-1990Ft; ⊙9am-4pm & 6pm-midnight Sun-Thu, 10am-1am Fri & Sat; Ⓜ️M1 Oktogon) Don't know how these guys pay the rent, no matter how good the burgers are at this stylish place on affluent Andrássy út. And it's not just a one-trick eatery. Ring also does snacks like hummus and cheese chips, salads and sandwiches.

BARAKA
FRENCH, FUSION €€€

Map p250 (📞4831355; www.barakarestaurant.hu; VI Andrássy út 111; mains 3900-6700Ft; ⊙noon-11pm; Ⓜ️M1 Hősök tere) Long a major presence on V Magyar utca near Astoria in Belváros, Baraka upped the stakes and now calls the black-and-silver ground-floor restaurant of the incomparable Andrássy Hotel (p165) home. It's still French with an Asian twist and still sets the standard for haute cuisine in Budapest. Excellent value two-/three-course lunch menus are 3500/4200Ft.

KARMA
ASIAN, FUSION €€

Map p250 (📞413 6764; www.karmabudapest .com; mains 2850-4700Ft; VI Liszt Ferenc tér 11; ⊙10am-1am; Ⓜ️M1 Oktogon) One of the more interesting choices on Liszt Ferenc tér, Karma serves dishes with Asian touches – chicken with peanut curry rice, shrimp and vegetables fried with sesame oil – and platters of vegetarian tapas (2250Ft). Two courses at lunch are just 1270Ft.

DRINKING & NIGHTLIFE

 Erzsébetváros

TŰZRAKTÉR
BAR

Map p250 (www.tuzrakter.hu, in Hungarian; VI Hegedű utca 3; ⊙noon-2am Sun-Thu, 6pm-5am Fri & Sat; 🚊4, 6) An artist-run space in a 'distressed' location just off Király utca, this independent community with gallery, theatre and bicycle-repair shop turns werewolf by night with DJs, concerts, parties and butch bouncers. Be warned, though: its days may be numbered.

COXX MEN'S BAR   GAY
Map p250 (www.coxx.hu; VII Dohány utca 38; ⊙9pm-4am Sun-Thu, to 5am Fri & Sat; 🚊7) Probably the cruisiest gayme in town, this place with the in-your-face name has 400 sq metres of hunting ground, three bars and some significant play areas in back. Don't bring sunglasses.

📋TOP CHOICE 400   CAFE, BAR
Map p250 (www.400bar.hu; VII Kazinczy utca 52/b; ⊙10am-2am Mon-Fri, from noon Sat & Sun; 🚊74) Just opened and now one of the most popular cafe-bars in Pest, the 'Négyszáz' is a big space, with outside seating in a no-car zone. Come just to relax over a drink, have breakfast (560Ft to 1190Ft, served till noon) or try the daily lunch menu (850Ft).

SZIMPLA   BAR
Map p250 (www.szimpla.hu; VII Kertész utca 48; ⊙10am-2am Mon-Fri, noon-2am Sat, to midnight Sun; 🚊4, 6) A distressed-looking, very un-flashy place, 'Single' remains one of the most popular drinking venues south of VI Liszt Ferenc tér. Cellar bar too.

VITTULA   BAR
Map p250 (www.klubvittula.blogspot.com; VII Kertész utca 4; ⊙6pm-2am Sun-Wed, to 4am Thu-Sat; Ⓜ️M2 Blaha Lujza tér) Great underground (both senses) bar just off the Big Ring Rd, with parties, alternative music and late drinking sessions. Meet zone.

CASTRO BISZTRÓ   CAFE
Map p250 (VII Madách tér 3; ⊙11am-midnight Mon-Thu, 11am-1am Fri, noon-1am Sat, 2pm-midnight Sun; Ⓜ️M1/2/3 Deák Ferenc tér) This eclectic place just off the Little Ring Rd has a mixed clientele, Serbian finger food like *čevapčiči* (spicy meatballs; 940Ft to 1890Ft) and tasty *pljeskavica* (meat patties; 1260Ft), and a chilled vibe.

MOZAIK   TEAHOUSE, CAFE
Map p250 (www.mozaikteahaz.hu, in Hungarian; VI Király utca 18; ⊙9am-10.30pm Mon-Fri, from 1pm Sat & Sun; 🚊4, 6) An eclectic – note the mosaic of a satyr outside and graffiti on the walls – rarity among Budapest teahouses, with non–New Age music and a less-than-

earnest vibe. There are 100 types of tea on offer. Booze now too.

FRÖHLICH CUKRÁSZDA   KOSHER, CAFE
Map p250 (www.frohlich.hu, in Hungarian; VII Dob utca 22; ⊙9am-6pm Mon-Thu, 9am-2pm Fri, 10am-6pm Sun; 🚊74) This kosher cake shop and cafe in the former ghetto, dating back to 1953, makes and sells old Jewish favourites (160Ft to 370Ft) such as *flódni* (a scrumptious three-layer cake with apple, walnut and poppy-seed fillings) as well as holiday sweets: for Purim there is *kindli* (cookies with nuts or poppy seeds) and *hamentaschen* ('pocket' biscuits filled with nuts and poppy seeds or apricot jam) and for Rosh Hashanah, *lekach* (honey and nut pastry). Celebration time is here!

NEW YORK CAFÉ   CAFE
Map p250 (www.boscolohotels.com; VII Erzsébet körút 9-11; ⊙9am-midnight; 🚊4, 6) Considered the most beautiful in the world when it opened in 1894, this Renaissance-style cafe was the scene of many a literary gathering over the years (p194). It has now been extensively renovated but, alas, lacks the warmth and erudite crowd of most traditional cafes, and staff serve sides of attitude with every order. Still, the opulence and the history of the New York will impress and it's a great place for breakfast (1500Ft to 4800Ft) till noon.

DOBLÓ   WINE BAR
Map p250 (www.budapestwine.com; VII Dob utca 20; ⊙5pm-midnight Sun & Tue, to 3am Wed-Sat; 🚊74) Brick-lined and candlelit, Dobló is where you go to taste Hungarian wines, with scores available by the 12.5cL glass for 900Ft to 1350Ft. There's food too, like salads and sandwiches (480Ft to 750Ft) and mixed platters of meat or cheese (2200Ft).

GRANDIÓ   GARDEN CLUB
Map p250 (www.grandiopartyhostel.com; VII Nagy Diófa utca 8; ⊙midnight-2am or 3am; 🚊74) Large *kert* (outdoor garden club) in a courtyard below a party (read noisy) hostel, What sets Grandió apart are the hearty urban weeds that have taken back their share of space and created not a 'garden' but a 'forest club'. Big long bar dispenses great drinks and beer, including Staropramen.

MIKA TIVADAR KERT   GARDEN CLUB
Map p250 (www.mikativadarmulato.hu, in Hungarian; VII Kazinczy utca 47; ⊙4pm-1am Sun-Tue,

ERZSÉBETVÁROS & THE JEWISH QUARTER DRINKING & NIGHTLIFE

to 2am Wed, to 3am Thu-Sat Apr-Sep; 🚇74) In a lot next to a restored building from 1907 that once contained a popular nightclub, one of Budapest's newest *kertek* is also one of the most popular, with concerts, parties and hotdogs.

KŐLEVES KERT
GARDEN CLUB

Map p250 (www.koleves.com; VII Kazinczy utca 37-39; ⊙noon-2am May-Sep; 🚇74) This is a somewhat more subdued – though expanded from the previous year – *kert,* popular with diners from the parent restaurant Kőleves (p120) next door.

ELLÁTÓ KERT
GARDEN CLUB

Map p250 (http://ellatokert.blogspot.com, in Hungarian; VII Kazinczy utca 48; ⊙10am-1am Mon-Thu, to 3am Fri & Sat Apr-Sep; 🚇74) A huge garden club that's mostly under cover, this is where most party people come to meet before they move on (or decide to stay). If the fun and games – ping-pong, billiards, darts and table football – don't keep them, the Mexican food might.

SZIMPLA KERT
GARDEN CLUB, LIVE MUSIC

Map p250 (www.szimpla.hu; VII Kazinczy 14; ⊙noon-3am; 🚇74) One of the capital's first *kertek,* Szimpla has now been winterised – sort of – and opens year-round. Good selection of rock, blues, electronic and funk throughout the week in season, with an open acoustic jam session every Sunday.

BAR LADINO
BAR

Map p250 (http://ladino.hu, in Hungarian; VII Dob utca 53; ⊙11am-midnight; 🚇4, 6) A bistro by day offering breakfast (490Ft to 690Ft) and a set three-course lunch (1190Ft), after nightfall this place is a bar and the wooden tables quickly fill up with imbibers.

MORRISON'S OPERA
CLUB, LIVE MUSIC

Map p250 (VI Révay utca 25; ⊙7pm-4am Mon-Sat; 🅼M1 Opera) The papa of Morrison's 2 (p101), this music pub is smaller and more sedate, with a signature red telephone booth brought all the way from Londontown.

ANKER KLUB
CLUB

Map p250 (http://hu-hu.facebook.com/anker klub, in Hungarian; VI Anker köz 1-2; ⊙10am-1pm Sun-Tue, to 2am Wed & Thu, to 4am Fri & Sat; 🅼M1/2/3 Deák Ferenc tér) Cafe that turns into hipster hangout in the evening, the Anker is spacious and minimalist and about as central as you'll find.

FOGASHÁZ
BAR

Map p250 (www.fogashaz.hu, in Hungarian; VII Akácfa utca 51; ⊙5pm-midnight Sun-Wed, to 4am Thu-Sat; 🚇4, 6) This huge space is one of the latest *romkocsmák* ('ruin bars' not unlike pop-up shops in the West) to open its doors and has nightly concerts and events.

CHAMPS SPORT BAR
BAR

Map p250 (www.champsbuda.hu; VII Dohány utca 20; 🅼M2 Astoria) A more central branch of the popular sports bar in Buda (p61) that was started by a group of Olympic medallists a few years back.

🍺 Andrássy út & Terézváros (East)

ALEXANDRA BOOK CAFÉ
CAFE

Map p250 (www.alexandra.hu; VI Andrássy út 39; dishes 990-1790Ft; ⊙10am-10pm; 🅼M1 Oktogon; 🚇4, 6) The Ceremonial Hall (Díszterem) on the mezzanine floor of the Fashion Hall has been renovated as the Alexandra bookshop's cafe and is positively dripping with gilt, marquetry and restored frescoes by Károly Lotz. There are concerts (2500Ft) usually at 8pm on Monday.

MŰVÉSZ KÁVÉHÁZ
CAFE

Map p250 (www.muveszkavehaz.hu; VI Andrássy út 29; ⊙9am-10pm; 🅼M1 Opera) Almost opposite the Hungarian State Opera House, the 'Artist Coffeehouse' is a more interesting place to people-watch (especially from the shady terrace), though some say its cakes (550Ft to 720Ft) are not what they used to be (though presumably not as far back as 1898 when it opened).

LUKÁCS CUKRÁSZDA
CAFE

Map p250 (www.lukacscukraszda.com; VI Andrássy út 70; ⊙8.30am-8pm Mon-Fri, 9am-8pm Sat, 9.30am-8pm Sun; 🅼M1 Vörösmarty utca) This cafe is dressed up in the finest of decadence – all mirrors and gold – with soft piano music in the background. The selection of cakes (550Ft to 1290Ft) is excellent.

CAFÉ VIAN
CAFE

Map p250 (www.cafevian.com; VI Liszt Ferenc tér 9; ⊙9am-1am; 🅼M1 Oktogon) This comfortable cafe – all done up in warm tones and serving breakfast all day – remains the anchor tenant on the sunny side of the square and the court of Pest's arty aristocracy. Indeed, it displays work for its partner art gallery called **Artitude** (www.artitude.hu).

KÉT SZERECSEN
CAFE

Map p250 (www.ketszerecsen.hu; VI Nagymező utca 14; ⊘8am-1am Mon-Fri, from 9am Sat & Sun; MM1 Opera) Not on VI Liszt Ferenc tér but close enough, the very relaxed 'Two Moors' serves both main meals and decent breakfasts till 11am every morning. Terrace seating is on adjacent Paulay Ede utca.

INCOGNITO BAR CAFÉ
CAFE, BAR

Map p250 (VI Liszt Ferenc tér 3; ⊘2pm-1am; MM1 Oktogon) The 'Unknown' is hardly that. It was the first cafe to open on what everyone now calls 'the tér' almost two decades ago and is still going strong in its own low-key sort of way. Great cocktails from 1050Ft.

 ENTERTAINMENT

FERENC LISZT MUSIC
ACADEMY
CONCERT VENUE

Map p250 (Liszt Zeneakadémia; ☑462 4600, bookings 342 0179; www.zeneakademia.hu; VI Liszt Ferenc tér 8; tickets 500-6000Ft; ⊘box office 2-8pm; MM1 Oktogon) Budapest's most important concert hall was undergoing extensive renovations at the time of research, but should have reopened by the time you read this.

HUNGARIAN STATE OPERA HOUSE
OPERA

Map p250 (Magyar Állami Operaház; ☑info 814 7100, bookings 353 0170; www.opera.hu; VI Andrássy út 22; tickets 500-15,800Ft; ⊘box office 11am-7pm Mon-Sat, 11am-1pm & 4-7pm Sun; MM1 Opera) The gorgeous neo-Renaissance opera house should be visited at least once to admire the incredibly rich decoration inside as much as to view a performance and hear the perfect acoustics.

CENTRAL EUROPE DANCE
THEATRE
DANCE

Map p250 (Közép-Európa Táncszínház; ☑342 7163, 06-30 456 3885; www.cedt.hu; VII Bethlen Gábor tér 3; tickets from 1500Ft; ☐74, 78) This wonderful pan-European dance theatre, Hungary's first when established in 1989, often has cutting-edge contemporary dance performances. Enter from VII István út 4.

LADÓ CAFÉ
LIVE MUSIC, DANCE

Map p250 (www.ladocafe.hu; VII Dohány utca 50; ⊘8am-11.30pm; MM2 Blaha Lujza tér) An unassuming place by day with decent food and excellent service, the Ladó comes into its own at night when it hosts live entertainment – everything from folk music and jazz to opera and tango.

OLD MAN'S MUSIC PUB
LIVE MUSIC

Map p250 (☑322 7645; www.oldmans.hu; VII Akácfa utca 13; ⊘3pm-4am; MM2 Blaha Lujza tér) Jazz and blues, plus swing and Latino and even rap – this fab venue has live music nightly from 8.30pm to 11pm. DJs then take over and dancing continues till dawn.

ÖRÖKMOZGÓ
CINEMA

Map p250 (www.orokmozgo.hu, in Hungarian; VII Erzsébet körút 39; ☐4, 6) Part of the Hungarian Film Institute, this cinema (whose mouthful of a name vaguely translates as 'moving picture') screens an excellent assortment of foreign classic films in their original languages.

BUDAPEST PUPPET THEATRE
THEATRE

Map p250 (Budapest Bábszínház; ☑321 5091, bookings 342 2702; www.budapest-babszinhaz .hu; VI Andrássy út 69; tickets 800-1400Ft; ⊘box office 9am-6pm; MM1 Vörösmarty utca) The city's puppet theatre, which usually doesn't require fluency in Hungarian, presents shows for children at 10am and 3pm.

🔒 SHOPPING

🔒 Erzsébetváros

MASSOLIT
BOOKS

Map p250 (www.massolit.hu; VII Nagy Diófa utca 30; ⊘10am-8pm Mon-Sat; ☐74) Branch of the celebrated bookshop in Kraków, Massolit is now one of Budapest's best, with new and secondhand English-language fiction and nonfiction, including Hungarian history and literature in translation.

TREEHUGGER DAN'S BOOKSTORE
BOOKS

Map p250 (www.treehuggerdans.com; VI Csen-gery utca 48; ⊘10am-7pm Mon-Fri, to 5pm Sat; MM1 Oktogon) This small, rather cramped shop has secondhand English-language books, does trade-ins and serves organic fair-trade coffee. There's also a branch at **Discover Budapest** (Map p250; VI Lázár utca 16; ⊘9.30am-6.30pm Mon-Fri, 10am-4pm Sat & Sun; MM1 Opera).

CONCERTO HANGLEMEZBOLT
MUSIC

Map p250 (www.concertoclassic.com; VII Dob utca 33; ☻noon-7pm Mon-Fri; M M2 Astoria) For classical CDs and vinyl, try the wonderful 'Concerto Record Shop', which is always full of hard-to-find treasures.

ROMANI DESIGN
FASHION, CLOTHING

Map p250 (www.romanidesign.hu; VII Akácfa utca 20; ☻10am-6pm Mon-Fri; 🚋4, 6) At once stylish and theatrical, the Roma-designed ready-to-wear, with its bright colours and extravagant pleating, would literally stop traffic. Designer Erika Varga is a jeweller and many of her pieces in silver and textile bear good-luck motifs: horseshoe, four-leaf clover and lentils (it's a local thing).

TISZA CIPŐ
SHOES

Map p250 (www.tiszacipo.hu; VII Károly körút 1; ☻10am-7pm Mon-Fri, 9am-1pm Sat; M M2 Astoria) 'What goes around comes around', the old saying tells us and that's certainly true of 'Tisza Shoes', which has metamorphosed as a Communist-era producer of forgettable footwear ('since 1971') to trendy trainer manufacturer.

LÁTOMÁS
FASHION, CLOTHING

Map p250 (www.latomas.hu; VII Dohány utca 16-18; ☻11am-7.30pm Mon-Fri, to 4.30pm Sat; 🚋47, 49; 🚎74) One of a trio of shops selling fashionable imported ready-to-wear. The theme of this branch is *'naiva'*. Baby-doll pyjamas, anyone?

M LAMP
HOMEWARES

Map p250 (www.m-lamp.com; VII Dob utca 25; ☻10am-6.30pm Tue-Fri; 🚎74) You can make a lamp out of that?! Lighting from (mostly) found and foraged objects, all shapes and sizes and colours with a preponderance made with designer Mária Fatér's favourite object: the teapot. Buy one and you'll be in good company. Four of the lamps created by the 'queen of recycling' are in the European Parliament in Brussels.

TOP CHOICE BILLERBECK
HOMEWARES

Map p250 (www.billerbeck.hu; VII Dob utca 49; ☻10am-6pm Mon-Fri, 9.30am-2pm Sat; 🚋4, 6) With several branches around town, Billerbeck has a large selection of feather- and goose-down duvets and other bedding sold by helpful staff. Enter from Akácfa utca. There's a **Király utca branch** (Map p250; VII Király utca 3; 🚋47, 49) with the same hours.

PRINTA
CRAFT, CLOTHING

Map p250 (www.printa.hu; VII Rumbach Sebestyén utca 10; ☻11am-7pm Mon-Fri, to 5pm Sat; 🚋47, 49) This wonderful Brazilian-run silkscreen studio, design shop and gallery focuses on local talent: bags, leather goods, prints. And rest assured: the silkscreen process is 100% green and the coffee – best flat white in Budapest! – at their cafe is fair trade.

🏠 Andrássy út & Terézváros (East)

ALEXANDRA
BOOKS, WINE

Map p250 (www.alexandra.hu, in Hungarian; VI Andrássy út 39; ☻10am-10pm M M1 Opera) The shtick at this welcome new addition on Andrássy út is 'books and wine'. The English-language selection in the back of the ground floor of the former is excellent, especially in the art and photo areas, while the choice of wine is 100% Hungarian. Check out the phenomenal Alexandra Book Café (p124) upstairs. There are branches everywhere, including opposite **Nyugati train station** (Map p250; V Nyugati tér 7; ☻10am-10pm Mon-Sat, to 8pm Sun; M Nyugati pályaudvar).

ÍRÓK BOLTJA
BOOKS

Map p250 (www.irokboltja.hu, in Hungarian; VI Andrássy út 45; ☻10am-7pm Mon-Fri, from 11am Sat M M1 Oktogon; 🚋4, 6) For Hungarian authors in translation, including many of those mentioned in the Literature chapter (p193), the 'Writers' Bookshop' is the place to go.

LISZT FERENC ZENEMŰBOLT
MUSIC, BOOKS

Map p250 (www.lisztbolt.hu; VI Andrássy út 45; ☻10am-7pm Mon-Fri, to 1pm Sat; M M1 Oktogon) Next to the Writers' Bookshop, the 'Ferenc Liszt Music Shop' has mostly classical CDs and vinyl as well as sheet music and books of local interest.

Southern Pest

JÓZSEFVÁROS | FERENCVÁROS

Neighbourhood Top Five

1 Taking a trip through the near and distant past by wandering the corridors of the **Hungarian National Museum** (p129), the nation's treasure trove of historical artefacts and its memory for more than a century and a half.

2 Wandering through the **Nagycsarnok** (p136), southern Pest's well-endowed 'Great Market'.

3 Admiring the art and architecture of the art nouveau **Museum of Applied Arts** (p132).

4 Sampling Hungary's signature (and very bitter) aperitif at the **Zwack Unicum Heritage Visitors' Centre** (p132).

5 Paying your respects to the permanent residents of **Kerepesi Cemetery** (p130).

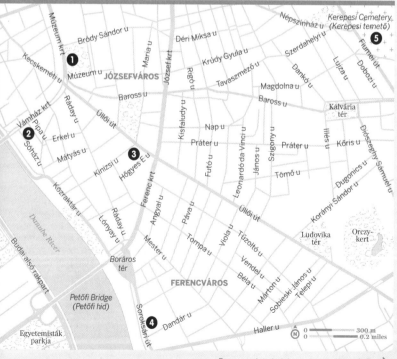

For more detail of this area, see Map p242 ➡

Lonely Planet's
Top Tip

Begin your tour of the traditionally working-class districts of Józsefváros and Ferencváros in VIII Rákóczi tér, the only real square right on the Big Ring Rd and as good a place as any to get a feel for these areas. Rákóczi tér is the site of a busy market hall (*vásárcsarnok*), erected in 1897 and renovated in the early 1990s after a bad fire. It's open daily except Sunday but skip Monday when it's deader than the dodo bird.

Best Places to Eat

➡ Múzeum (p132)
➡ Rosenstein (p133)
➡ Építész Pince (p132)
➡ Fülemüle (p133)

For reviews, see p132 ➡

Best Places to Drink

➡ Café Csiga (p134)
➡ Adonis (p135)
➡ Cökxpôn (p135)

For reviews, see p134 ➡

Best Places to Shop

➡ Nagycsarnok (p136)
➡ Babaház (p137)
➡ Magyar Pálinka Ház (p137)

For reviews, see p136 ➡

Explore: Southern Pest

From Blaha Lujza tér, named after a leading 19th-century stage actress and sheltering one of the liveliest subways in the city (with hustlers, beggars, peasants selling their wares, musicians and, of course, pickpockets), the Big Ring Rd runs through district VIII, also known as Józsefváros (Joseph Town). The western side of Józsefváros transforms itself from a neighbourhood of lovely 19th-century town houses and villas around the Little Ring Rd to a large student quarter. East of the boulevard is the once rough-and-tumble district so poignantly described in the Pressburger brothers' *Homage to the Eighth District,* and where much of the fighting in October 1956 took place (p183). Today it's being developed at breakneck speed.

The neighbourhood south of Üllői út is Ferencváros (Francis Town), home to the city's most popular football team, Ferencvárosi Torna Club (FTC), and many of its tough, green-and-white-clad supporters. There is a tremendous amount of building going on in Ferencváros as well. One highlight of the district is pedestrianised IX Ráday utca, which leads south from V Kálvin tér and is full of cafes, clubs and restaurants where university students entertain themselves these days.

Local Life

➡ **Market** It might attract tourists by droves, but the Nagycsarnok (p136) is always a hive of activity and a great place for one-stop shopping.

➡ **Museum** The Ludwig Museum of Contemporary Art (p131) is cutting edge, but don't expect (or try) to understand everything.

➡ **Classical Music** Some people think the Béla Bartók National Concert Hall at the Palace of Arts (p135) has the best acoustics in Budapest.

Getting There & Away

➡ **Metro** The red M2 line runs along the northern border of Józsefváros while the blue M3 line serves points in Ferencváros. Key stops include Blaha Lujza tér and Keleti Pályaudvar on the M2, and Kálvin tér and Ferenc körút on the M3.

➡ **Tram** Both districts are served by trams 47 and 49, and further east by trams 4 and 6.

HUNGARIAN NATIONAL MUSEUM

The **Hungarian National Museum** (Magyar Nemzeti Múzeum) houses the nation's most important collection of historical relics. Exhibits on the 1st floor trace the history of the Carpathian Basin and its peoples from earliest times to the end of the Avar period in the early 9th century; move upstairs for the ongoing story of the Magyar people and their nation from the conquest of the basin to the present day. On the ground floor and in the basement, lapidaries havebfinds from Roman, medieval and early modern times.

The museum owes its existence to Count Ferenc Széchenyi, who donated his personal collection of more than 20,000 prints, maps, manuscripts, coins and archaeological finds to the state in 1802. The museum moved to the current neoclassical edifice, purpose-built by Mihály Pollack, in 1847. A year later it was the scene of a momentous event (though, as always, not recognised as such at the time). On 15 March a crowd gathered to hear the poet Sándor Petőfi recite 'Nemzeti Dal' (National Song), a prelude to the 1848–49 Revolution (see p178).

Keep an eye open for the 3rd-century **Roman mosaic** from Balácapuszta, near Veszprém; King Stephen's crimson silk **coronation mantle** (robe) stitched by nuns in 1031; a reconstructed **3rd-century Roman villa** from Pannonia; the Treasury Room's Celtic gold and silver **jewellery**; the stunning **baroque library**; **Beethoven's Broadwood piano**; and **memorabilia from socialist times**. There's also a magnificent **funeral crown** dating from the 13th century and found in the ruins of the Dominican church on Margaret Island.

DON'T MISS...

→ coronation mantle
→ Celtic gold and silver jewellery
→ 3rd-century Roman mosaic
→ baroque library
→ socialist memorabilia

PRACTICALITIES

→ Map p242
→ www.mnm.hu, in Hungarian
→ VIII Múzeum körút 14-16
→ adult/child 1100/550Ft
→ ⊙10am-6pm Tue-Sun
→ Ⓜ M3 Kálvin tér
→ 🚌47, 49

⊙ SIGHTS

⊙ Józsefváros

HUNGARIAN NATIONAL MUSEUM
MUSEUM

See p129.

HUNGARIAN NATURAL HISTORY MUSEUM
MUSEUM

Map p242 (Magyar Természettudományi Múzeum; www.nhmus.hu; VIII Ludovika tér 2-6; adult/child 1200/600Ft; ⊙10am-5pm Wed-Mon; MM3 Klinikák) Just one metro stop southeast of the Ferenc körút station, the Natural History Museum has lots of hands-on interactive displays over three floors. The geological park in front of the museum is well designed, the fin-whale skeleton in the entrance lobby is very impressive, and there are interesting exhibits focusing on the biodiversity of coral reefs and the natural resources of the Carpathian Basin. Free admission for under-26s on the first Sunday of the month.

ERVIN SZABÓ CENTRAL LIBRARY
LIBRARY

Map p242 (Fővárosi Szabó Ervin Könyvtár; ☑411 5000; www.fszek.hu; VIII Reviczky utca 1; ⊙10am-8pm Mon-Fri, to 4pm Sat; MM3 Kálvin tér) Southeast of the national museum is the main repository of Budapest's central library system, with access to 800,000 books, 1000 periodicals and 40,000 audiovisual and digital items. Built between 1887 and 1894 and exquisitely renovated in recent years, the public reading room has gypsum ornaments, gold tracery and enormous chandeliers. About 750m further east along Baross utca and across the Big Ring Rd is the old **Telephone Exchange building** (VIII Horváth Mihály tér 18), built in 1910. It has reliefs of classical figures tracing communications through the ages: Mercury, homing pigeons and that newfangled invention, the telephone.

PLANETARIUM
PLANETARIUM

Map p242 (☑263 1811, 265 0725; www.planetarium.hu, in Hungarian; X Népliget; adult/child 1500/1000Ft; ⊙shows 9.30am, 11am, 1pm, 2.30pm & 4pm Tue-Sun, plus 6pm Tue, Thu & Fri; MM3 Népliget) Just over the border from

---

⊙ TOP SIGHTS
KEREPESI CEMETERY

Established in 1847, Kerepesi Cemetery (Kerepesi temető) is Budapest's answer to London's Highgate or Paris' Père Lachaise cemeteries. Some of the 3000 gravestones and mausoleums in this 56-hectare necropolis, which is also called the National Graveyard (Nemzeti Sírkert), are worthy of a pharaoh – especially those of statesmen and national heroes such as Lajos Kossuth, Ferenc Deák and Lajos Batthyány. Other tombs are quite moving (such as those of actress Lujza Blaha and poet Endre Ady). Southeast of the main entrance, plot 21 contains the graves of many who died in the 1956 Uprising. Sitting uncomfortably close by is the huge Workers' Movement Pantheon for party honchos, topped with the words 'I lived for Communism, for the people'. Nearby is the simple grave of János Kádár, who died in 1989 but has not been allowed to rest in peace (see p133). Maps indicating the location of noteworthy graves are available free from the conservation office at the entrance, which is about 500m southeast of Keleti station. About 100m up from the entrance is the **Piety Museum** (Kegyeleti Múzeum; ☑323 5132; admission free; ⊙10am-3pm Mon-Thu, to 1pm Fri), which looks at the way of death through history in Hungary and Hungarian-speaking regions.

DON'T MISS...
➡ Workers' Movement Pantheon
➡ Lajos Kossuth mausoleum
➡ Piety Museum

PRACTICALITIES
➡ Map p242
➡ www.nemzetisirkert.hu, in Hungarian
➡ VIII Fiumei út 16
➡ admission free
➡ ⊙7am-8pm May-Jul, to 7pm Apr & Aug, to 6pm Sep, to 5pm Oct-Feb, to 5.30pm Mar
➡ 🚋24

EAST OF JÓZSEFVÁROS

New Municipal Cemetery

This huge **cemetery** (Új Köztemető; X Kozma utca 6; ☻8am-7pm; 🚋28, 37), easily reached by tram from Blaha Lujza tér, is where Imre Nagy, prime minister during the 1956 Uprising, and 2000 others were buried in unmarked graves (plots 300–301) after executions in the late 1940s and 1950s. The area has been turned into a moving National Pantheon and is about a 30-minute walk from the entrance; follow the signs pointing the way to '300, 301 parcela'. At peak periods you can take a microbus marked 'temető járat' around the cemetery.

Dreher Brewery & Beer Museum

Budapest's – and Hungary's – largest **brewery** (Dreher Sörmúzeum; ☎432 9850; www.dreherrt.hu; X Jászberényi utca 7-11; adult/student 300/150Ft; ☻9am-4pm; 🚋28, 37, 37A) has a museum where you can look at displays of brewing and bottling over the centuries. If you can muster up a group of at 10, you can take a 1½-hour 'Beer Voyage' (adult/student 1300/650Ft), which includes a tour, a film and a tasting; book in advance.

Józsefváros in the sprawling Népliget (People's Park), this large planetarium has star shows as well as 3-D films and cartoons; be sure to check the schedule as it can change without notice. It also houses the hokey but perennially popular Laser Theatre (p135).

☻ Ferencváros

HOLOCAUST MEMORIAL CENTER MUSEUM

Map p242 (Holokauszt Emlékközpont; www.hdke .hu; IX Páva utca 39; adult/child 1400/700Ft; ☻10am-6pm Tue-Sun; ⓂM3 Ferenc körút) This centre, housed in a striking modern building in a working-class neighbourhood, opened in 2004 on the 60th anniversary of the start of the holocaust in Hungary. Both a museum and an educational foundation, the centre's permanent exhibition traces the rise of anti-Semitism in Hungary from 1938 to the mass deportations of Jews to German death camps in 1944–45. In the central courtyard a wonderfully restored synagogue, designed by Leopold Baumhorn and completed in 1924, hosts temporary exhibitions. In the courtyard (admission free) an 8m-high **Memorial Wall of Victims** records the names of Hungarian victims of the Holocaust, while the adjacent glass **Tower of Lost Communities** lists settlements wiped out by the Holocaust.

**LUDWIG MUSEUM OF
CONTEMPORARY ART** GALLERY

Map p242 (Ludwig Kortárs Művészeti Múzeum; www.ludwigmuseum.hu; IX Komor Marcell utca 1; adult/child permanent collection 700/350Ft, incl temporary exhibits 1200/600Ft; ☻10am-8pm Tue-Sun; 🚋2, 24) Housed in the architecturally controversial Palace of Arts (p135) opposite the National Theatre, the Ludwig Museum is Hungary's most important collection of international contemporary art. Works by American, Russian, German and French artists span the past 50 years, while Hungarian, Czech, Slovakian, Romanian, Polish and Slovenian works date from the 1990s onward. The museum also holds frequent and very well-received temporary exhibitions. Note that after 6pm only some of the collection is open to the public.

NATIONAL THEATRE THEATRE

Map p242 (Nemzeti Színház; ☎476 6800; www .nemzetiszinhaz.hu, in Hungarian; IX Bajor Gizi Park 1; 🚋2, 24) Hard by the Danube in southwestern Ferencváros, the National Theatre opened in 2002 to much controversy. The design, by architect Mária Siklós, is supposedly 'Eclectic' to mirror other great Budapest buildings (Parliament, Opera House). But in reality it is a pick-and-mix of classical and folk motifs, porticoes, balconies and columns that just does not work and certainly will date very fast. But then that's what they said about the much-loved Parliament building in 1902. An interesting feature of the theatre is the prow-shaped terrace by the main entrance

TOP SIGHTS
MUSEUM OF APPLIED ARTS

The Museum of Applied Arts (Iparművészeti Múzeum) owns a king's ransom of Hungarian furniture dating from the 18th and 19th centuries, art nouveau and Secessionist artefacts, and objects related to the history of trades and crafts (glassmaking, bookbinding, goldsmithing, leatherwork etc). But only a small part of it forms the 400-piece 'Collectors and Treasures' and the 'Ottoman Carpets' permanent exhibits on the 1st floor. Almost everything else makes up part of one of the two temporary exhibitions on display at any given time. A combined ticket (2500/1250Ft per adult/child) will get you into everything. It's a novel way to rake in the dosh – just make everything a temporary exhibit! Consider visiting the museum's European furniture exhibit at Nagytétény Castle Museum (p68) instead.

The museum building, designed by Ödön Lechner and decorated with Zsolnay ceramic tiles, was completed for the Millenary Exhibition in 1896 but was badly damaged during WWII and again in 1956. It was said to have been inspired by the Victoria & Albert Museum in London. The white-on-white main hall was modelled on the Alhambra in Granada in Spain; check out the beautiful stained-glass skylight.

DON'T MISS...

➡ Moorish main hall
➡ Zsolnay roof tiles
➡ Collection of Herend and other porcelain

PRACTICALITIES

➡ Map p242
➡ www.imm.hu
➡ IX Üllői út 33-37
➡ adult/child 1000/500Ft
➡ ⊙10am-6pm Tue-Sun
➡ Ⓜ M3 Ferenc körút
➡ 🚋4, 6

that appears to be 'sailing' into the Danube. The zigguratlike structure outside, whose ramps lead to nowhere, is particularly odd, though it offers good views of the river and the new maze.

ZWACK UNICUM HERITAGE
VISITORS' CENTRE
MUSEUM

Map p242 (Zwack Unicum Látogató Központ; www.zwackunicum.hu; IX Soroksári út 26; adult/student 1800/1000Ft; ⊙10am-6pm Mon-Fri; 🚋2, 24) Unicum, the thick brown medicinal-tasting bitter aperitif made from 40 herbs, clocks in at 42% alcohol. Supposedly named by Franz Joseph himself, it is bitter as a loser's tears. If you really can't get enough of it, visit this very commercial museum tracing the history of the product since it was first made in 1790 and inviting visitors to buy big at its sample store (mintabolt). Enter from Dandár utca and exit through the gift shop.

🍴 EATING

Rapid development of districts VIII (Józsefváros) and XIX (Ferencváros) have changed the face of the eating scene here, especially in and around IX Ráday utca.

The area west of the Hungarian National Museum, particularly VIII Krúdy Gyula utca in Józsefváros, is another happy hunting ground for restaurants, étkezdék (canteens serving simple Hungarian dishes) and cafes.

🍴 Józsefváros

TOP CHOICE **MÚZEUM**
HUNGARIAN €€€

Map p242 (📞267 0375; www.muzeumkavehaz.hu; VIII Múzeum körút 12; mains 2900-5400Ft; ⊙6pm-midnight Mon-Sat; Ⓜ M3 Kálvin tér; 🚋47, 49) This cafe-restaurant is the place to come if you like to dine in old-world style with a piano softly tinkling in the background. It's still going strong after more than 125 years at the same location near the Hungarian National Museum. The goose-liver parfait (2900Ft) is to die for, the goose leg and cabbage (3600Ft) iconic, and there's a good selection of Hungarian wines.

ÉPÍTÉSZ PINCE
HUNGARIAN €€

Map p242 (📞266 4799; www.epiteszpince.hu, in Hungarian; VIII Ötpacsirta utca 2; mains 1650-3150Ft; ⊙11am-10pm Mon-Thu, to midnight Fri & Sat; Ⓜ M3 Kálvin tér) This basement restaurant behind the Hungarian National Museum is stunningly designed and why wouldn't it be? It's in the neoclassical headquarters of the Magyar Építész Kamara (Chamber of Hungarian Architects). The food is mostly enlightened Hungarian favourites; come here for the decor, the crowd (former artsy dissidents now doing well, thank you very much) and the gorgeous paved courtyard.

TOP CHOICE ROSENSTEIN HUNGARIAN, JEWISH €€€

Map p242 (☏333 3492; www.osenstein.hu; VIII Mosonyi utca 3; mains 3600-6100Ft; ⊙noon-11pm Mon-Sat; ☐24) This is an odd fish: a classy Hungarian place (with Jewish tastes and aromas) and super service in the dark and rather mean streets of district VIII just south of Keleti train station. It is family-run and has been here for years, so expect everyone to know each other. The daily specials (180Ft to 2200Ft) can be excellent value.

FÜLEMÜLE HUNGARIAN, JEWISH €€

Map p242 (☏266 7947; www.fulemule.hu; VIII Kőfaragó utca 5; mains 1800-4900Ft; ⊙noon-10pm Sun-Thu, to 11pm Fri & Sat; Ⓜ︎M2 Blaha Lujza tér; ☐7) This quaint Hungarian restaurant with long wooden tables and old photos on the wall is quite a find in deepest Józsefváros and well worth the search. Dishes mingle Hungarian and international tastes with some old-style Jewish favourites.

AFRICAN BUFFET AFRICAN €

Map p242 (VIII Bérkocsis utca 21; dishes from 500Ft; ⊙11am-11pm Mon-Thu, noon-2am Fri & Sat; ☐4, 6) We love, love, love the food and the warm welcome at this little African oasis just round the corner from the Rákóczi tér

market. It's family-run and the food home-made; try the spicy goat soup and the Zanzibar rice studded with good things.

CSÜLÖK CSÁRDA HUNGARIAN €€

Map p242 (www.oszkarcsulok.hu; VIII Berzsenyi utca 4; mains 1100-1990Ft; ⊙noon-11pm Mon-Fri, 5-11pm Sat; Ⓜ︎M2 Keleti pályaudvar) The rough-and-ready 'Pork Knuckle Inn' serves just that (from 1100Ft) and other country specialities in enormous quantities in a cellar restaurant that you enter through an oversized wine cask. Slide into one of the wooden booths and order a plate to share or the super-saver lunch menu for a mere 650Ft.

STEX HÁZ HUNGARIAN €€

Map p242 (www.stexhaz.hu; VIII József körút 55-57; mains 1890-3290Ft; ⊙8am-4am Mon-Sat, 9am-2am Sun; ☒; Ⓜ︎M3 Ferenc körút) A big, noisy place that's open *almost* round the clock, the Stex is north of the Applied Arts Museum. The menu offers soups, sandwiches, pasta, fish and meat dishes as well as vegetarian choices (1290Ft to 1690Ft). It transforms into a lively bar at night and there's breakfast (310Ft to 1350Ft) too.

MACSKA VEGETARIAN €

Map p242 (VIII Bérkocsis utca 21; dishes 900-1800Ft; ⊙5pm-1am Mon-Thu, 3pm-2am Fri, 5pm-2am Sat; ☒; ☐4, 6) You shall know the 'Cat' by the sign of the feline swinging above the entrance. It's strange that a vegetarian restaurant should take its name from the most vicious and carnivorous of all mammals but the menu here, written in chalk on the beams of this funky loft, is short, with soups, salads and casseroles.

SOUTHERN PEST EATING

SHAKE, RATTLE & ROLL

Hungarians are well honed in matters macabre. Who else could – would – have produced the likes of Béla Lugosi and, for that matter, Zsa Zsa Gabor? And matters can often get pretty bony around here. In 1996, for example, the archbishop of Veszprém near Lake Balaton won almost celebrity status by successfully clasping King St Stephen's revered right hand (p95) with that of his wife, Queen Gizella (borrowed with much advance planning from the Bavarian city of Passau), for the first time in a millennium.

More recently the tales have darkened further. János Kádár, the not-much-missed former Communist leader, had been resting comfortably for some 18 years at Kerepesi Cemetery (p130) when in May 2007 person or persons unknown crept into the graveyard, unceremoniously broke into his coffin and ran off with comrade Kádár's skull and assorted bones, leaving behind a note that read: 'Murderers and traitors may not rest in holy ground 1956–2006'. The remains have yet to be found, though the dogs are on the scent.

✗ Ferencváros

VÖRÖS POSTAKOCSI
HUNGARIAN €€

Map p242 (www.vorospk.com; IX Ráday utca 15; mains 2390-3990Ft; ⊙11.30am-midnight; Ⓜ️M3 Kálvin tér; ⬛15, 115) What was for more than three decades a forgettable eatery serving Hungarian stodge – and overlooked by all but the bravest or most desperate of diners in Ferencváros – has turned into a trendy retro-style Hungarian restaurant with a lively Gypsy band. If you want a take on how modern Hungarians think they used to eat when times were tougher (and less health-conscious), visit the 'Red Postal Coach'.

BORBÍRÓSÁG
HUNGARIAN, WINE €€

Map p242 (☎219 0902; www.borbirosag.com; IX Csarnok tér 5; mains 1690-3950Ft; ⊙noon-11.30pm Mon-Sat; ⬛47, 49) Some people like the idea of the 'Wine Court' where more than 60 Hungarian wines are available by the glass, and the food, especially game, is taken pretty seriously. It's by the Great Market and the large terrace on a quiet square is a delight in the warmer months.

SOUL CAFÉ
INTERNATIONAL €€

Map p242 (www.soulcafe.hu; IX Ráday utca 11-13; mains 1990-4390Ft; ⊙noon-11.30pm; Ⓜ️M3 Kálvin tér) One of the better choices along a street heaving with so-so restaurants and cafes with attitude, the Soul has inventive continental food and decor, and a great terrace on both sides of the street. Three-course daily menu is 980Ft.

TAIWAN
CHINESE €€

Map p242 (www.taiwan-restaurant.hu; IX Gyáli út 3/b; mains 1660-4680Ft; Ⓜ️M3 Nagyvárad tér) In the same building as the Fortuna Hotel in southern district IX, this mammoth (and relatively expensive for Budapest) Chinese restaurant – think airline hangar coloured red – may seem a long way to go for a bit of rice, but it's one of the few places in Budapest that does decent dim sum. The cooks are all Chinese (we peeked).

SHIRAZ
MIDDLE EASTERN €€

Map p242 (www.shirazetterem.hu; IX Ráday utca 21; mains 1850-3850Ft; ⊙noon-midnight; Ⓜ️M3 Kálvin tér; ⬛15, 115) This Persian restaurant is so richly adorned with carpets and brassware that you expect Scheherazade herself to come out to greet you. It lures punters to its terrace seats with hookahs loaded with apple, peach and strawberry tobacco (1490Ft). The food is tasty, with *khoresh* (a kind of stew of meat mixed with Persian herbs) the speciality. Daily lunch menu is 990Ft.

PATA NEGRA
SPANISH €€

Map p242 (www.patanegra.hu; IX Kálvin tér 8; tapas 380-750Ft, plates 850-2200Ft; Ⓜ️M3 Kálvin tér) Centrally located branch of a popular tapas restaurant (p79) in Óbuda.

PINK CADILLAC
ITALIAN €

Map p242 (IX Ráday utca 22; pizzas 1010-1590Ft, pasta 1590-1990Ft; Ⓜ️M3 Kálvin tér; ⬛15, 115) More of an upbeat 1950s diner than a pizzeria, the Pink Cadillac has reigned supreme on IX Ráday utca for more than a decade. If you don't like the surrounds, have your pizza delivered to Paris Texas (p135), the pub next door (not some one-horse town with ambitions in the Lone Star State).

MEZCAL
MEXICAN €

Map p242 (www.mezcal.hu; IX Tompa utca 14; mains 1990-3290Ft; ⊙noon-midnight Mon-Wed, to 1am Thu-Sat, to 10pm Sun; Ⓜ️M3 Ferenc körút) Ferencváros is about the last place you'd expect to find Tex-Mex food, but this bright and upbeat basement cantina serves surprisingly tasty tacos and burritos as well as quesadillas. There's a good selection of tequilas, and the margaritas (1290Ft) are exceptional.

LANZHOU
CHINESE €

Map p242 (☎314 1080; VIII Luther utca 1/b; dishes 990-1490Ft; ⊙noon-11pm; Ⓜ️M2 Keleti pályaudvar) Don't expect miracles at this Chinese place just north of what is now II János Pál pápa tétér (formerly Köztársaság tér). No doubt you'd do better at the Taiwan (p134), but it's here – if and when you need a fix of rice and/or noodles.

🍷 DRINKING & NIGHTLIFE

CAFÉ CSIGA
CAFE

Map p242 (www.cafecsiga.org; VIII Vásár utca 2; ⊙9am-1am Mon-Fri, 11am-1am Sat, noon-midnight Sun; ⬛4, 6) The 'Snail' is a very popular, welcoming place just opposite the Rákóczi tér market. It attracts a mixed, arty crowd especially when there's live music (often

Wednesday evenings). It does food, too, including an excellent set lunch for 900Ft.

CÖKXPÔN
CLUB

Map p242 (www.cokxponambient.hu; IX Soroksári út 8-10; ⊙6pm-midnight Sun-Wed, to 2am Thu, to 4am Fri & Sat; 🚊2, 4, 6) A club, a live-music venue, a cafe, a theatre, a cultural space almost on Boráros tér in Pest – welcome to the world of esoterica. Locals swear Cökxpôn (nope, no idea) offers one of the best underground nights out in Budapest.

ZAPPA CAFFE
CAFE

Map p242 (www.zappacaffe.hu; VIII Mikszáth Kálmán tér 2; ⊙11am-midnight Mon-Wed, to 2am Thu & Fri, noon-2am Sat, noon-midnight Sun; Ⓜ M3 Kálvin tér; 🚊9) An anchor tenant in a car-free square loaded with students, this large cafe (and bar and restaurant) has one of the largest terraces in the area fast becoming known as the Palotanegyed (Palace District). Good music.

DARSHAN UDVAR
BAR

Map p242 (www.darshan.hu, in Hungarian; VIII Krúdy Gyula utca 7; ⊙11am-midnight; 🚊4, 6) This cavernous complex with bar, restaurant and bookshop has decor that combines Eastern flair with what look like Australian Aboriginal motifs. It's an easy escape from the noisy bars of IX Ráday utca, though VIII Krúdy utca has yet to take over as Budapest's next after-hours strip. There is pizza (1250Ft to 1550Ft) and pasta dishes (1290Ft to 1550Ft), as well as more substantial mains (1590Ft to 2990Ft) to accompany the liquid offerings. Occasional concerts, too.

PARIS TEXAS
BAR

Map p242 (www.paristexaskavehaz.hu, in Hungarian; IX Ráday utca 22; ⊙noon-3am; Ⓜ M3 Kálvin tér; 🚊15, 115) One of the original bars on the IX Ráday utca nightlife strip, this place has a coffee-house feel to it with old sepia-tinted photos on the walls and pool tables downstairs. Nurse a cocktail from the huge list and order a pizza from Pink Cadillac (p134) next door.

JELEN
BAR

Map p242 (www.mostjelen.blogspot.com; VIII Blaha Lujza tér 1-2; ⊙4pm-2am Sun & Mon, to 4am Tue-Sat; Ⓜ M2 Blaha Lujza tér) From the guys behind Most! (p99) comes this equally enthusiastic, spacious and bohemian bar open till late. Wanna bop? Climb the stairs to Corvintető.

CORVINTETŐ
GARDEN CLUB

Map p242 (www.corvinteto.com, in Hungarian; VIII Blaha Lujza tér 1-2, 4th fl; ⊙7pm-5am Tue-Sat; Ⓜ M2 Blaha Lujza tér) This 'underground garden above the city' is on the rooftop of the former Corvin department store and has excellent concerts (reggae Tuesday, drum and bass Wednesday). Enter from VIII Somogyi Béla utca and take the goods lift to the top floor.

MORRISON'S KÖZGÁZ
CLUB

Map p242 (www.morrisonskozgaz.hu, in Hungarian; IX Fővám tér 8; ⊙7pm-4am Wed-Sat; 🚊47, 49) Now part of the ever-expanding Morrison's stable, this never-cool club at the Economics University is the pick-up venue of choice for many a student and there's plenty of dance room. Don't hang about if (when) the karaoke kicks in, though.

ADONIS
GAY

Map p242 (www.adonisclub.eu; VIII Baross utca 30; ⊙9pm-late Thu-Sat; 🚊9; 🚊4, 6) Budapest's latest and – from the look of it – largest gay venue seems to be taking the town by storm with its nightly themes (is 'Kindergarten' legal?) and naughtier shows at midnight and 2am.

⭐ ENTERTAINMENT

TOP CHOICE PALACE OF ARTS
CONCERT VENUE, CLASSICAL MUSIC

Map p242 (Művészetek Palotája; ☎555 3301; www.mupa.hu; IX Komor Marcell utca 1; tickets 900-2200Ft; ⊙box office 10am-6pm; 🚊2) The main concert halls at this palatial arts centre by the Danube and just opposite the National Theatre are the 1700-seat **Béla Bartók National Concert Hall** (Bartók Béla Nemzeti Hangversenyterem) and the smaller **Festival Theatre** (Fesztivál Színház) accommodating up to 450 people. Both are purported to have near-perfect acoustics. Students pay 500Ft for a standing-only ticket one hour before all performances.

LASER THEATRE
MUSIC, CINEMA

Map p242 (Lézer Színház; www.lezerszinhaz.hu; X Népliget; adult/child/student 2690/600/2190Ft; ⊙performances 7.30pm Mon-Sat; Ⓜ M3 Népliget) At the Planetarium in Népliget, the Laser Theatre has a mixed bag of video (some 3-D) concerts with laser and canned music featuring the likes of Pink Floyd, Michael Jackson, Madonna, Guns N' Roses, Queen, Mike Oldfield, Jimmy Hendrix and Prodigy. It's all pretty low tech and passé, but fun in a retro kinda way.

TOP CHOICE TRAFÓ HOUSE OF CONTEMPORARY ARTS CONCERT VENUE, DANCE

Map p242 (Trafó Kortárs Művészetek Háza; ☑215 1600; www.trafo.hu; IX Liliom utca 41; tickets 1000-3000Ft; ⓂM3 Ferenc körút) This stage in Ferencváros presents a mixture of music, theatre and especially the cream of the crop of dance, including a good pull of international acts.

TOP CHOICE URÁNIA NATIONAL CINEMA CINEMA

Map p242 (Uránia Nemzeti Filmszínház; www .urania-nf.hu, in Hungarian; VIII Rákóczi út 21; ⒣7) This art-deco/neo-Moorish extravaganza is a tarted-up film palace. It has an excellent cafe on the 1st floor overlooking Rákóczi út.

NATIONAL THEATRE THEATRE

Map p242 (Nemzeti Színház; ☑box office 476 6868; www.nemzetiszinhaz.hu, in Hungarian; IX Bajor Gizi Park 1; tickets 2000-3800Ft; ⓣbox office 10am-6pm Mon-Fri, 2-6pm Sat & Sun; ⒣2, 24) This rather eclectic venue is the place to go if you want to brave a play in Hungarian or just check out the theatre's bizarre and very controversial architecture.

CORVIN FILM PALACE CINEMA

Map p242 (Corvin Filmpalota; www.corvin.hu, in Hungarian; VIII Corvin köz 1; ⓂM3 Ferenc körút) A restored art-deco building, the Corvin sits in the middle of a square flanked by Regency-like houses. Note the two wonderful reliefs outside the main entrance to the cinema and the monument to the *Pesti srácok,* the heroic 'kids from Pest' who fought and died in the neighbourhood during the 1956 Uprising. Heart-wrenching stuff.

ROHAM LIVE MUSIC

Map p242 (www.roham.hu; VIII Vas utca 16; ⓣ10am-midnight Sun-Thu, to 3am Fri & Sat; ⒣4, 6) This pub-cum-concert-venue below the wonderful Casa de la Musica hostel has something for everyone: cafe, bar, gallery – even a magazine. But mostly come for the eclectic nightly concerts at 9pm.

JEDERMANN JAZZ

Map p242 (☑06-30 406 3617; www.jedermann kavezo.blogspot.com, in Hungarian; IX Ráday utca 58; ⓣ8am-1am; ⒣4, 6) This uber-chilled cafe attached to the Goethe Institute at the 'wrong' (some might say right) end of IX Ráday utca is a cafe and a restaurant (excellent Serbian grills) by day and cool jazz venue by night. Gigs start at 9pm most nights but are held less often in summer.

BUDAPEST JAZZ CLUB JAZZ

Map p242 (www.bjc.hu; VIII Múzeum utca 7; ⓂM3 Kálvin tér) A very sophisticated venue – now pretty much the most serious one in town – for traditional, vocal and Latin jazz in the Kossuth Club behind the Hungarian National Museum. Concerts most nights at 9pm, with jam sessions at 10pm or 11pm on Saturday.

NOTHIN' BUT THE BLUES BLUES

Map p242 (www.bluespub.hu, in Hungarian; VIII Krúdy Gyula utca 6; ⓣ11am-midnight Mon-Wed, to 4am Thu-Sat; ⒣47, 49) The oldest blues venue in town, NBB has been wailing for almost two decades now and the Jim Morrison and Blues Brothers posters let you know that. Still, the name is more or less accurate Thursday to Saturday from 7.30pm when there's usually a live strummer.

FLÓRIÁN ALBERT STADIUM FOOTBALL

Map p242 (FTC Stadion Albert Flórián; ☑215 6025; IX Üllői út 129; ⓂM3 Népliget) Though it's not in the premier league at the moment, no other club has dominated Budapest football over the years like Ferencváros Torna Club (FTC), the country's loudest, brashest and most popular team. You either love the Fradi boys in green and white or you hate 'em. Watch them play at Flórián Albert Stadium opposite Népliget station, with space for 18,100 raucous spectators.

🛍 SHOPPING

NAGYCSARNOK MARKET

Map p242 (IX Vámház körút 1-3; ⓣ6am-5pm Mon, 6am-6pm Tue-Fri, 6am-3pm Sat; ⒣47, 49) The 'Great Market' is Budapest's biggest food market, but because it has been attracting tourists ever since it was renovated for the millecentenary in 1996 it now has dozens of stalls on the 1st floor selling Hungarian folk costumes, dolls, painted eggs, embroidered tablecloths, carved hunting knives and so on. Still, gourmets will appreciate the Hungarian and other treats available on the ground floor at a fraction of what they

WORTH A DETOUR

ECSERI PIAC

One of the biggest flea markets in Central Europe, and often just called the *piac* (market), **Ecseri Piac** (www.ecseripiac-budapest.hu, in Hungarian; XIX Nagykőrösi út 156; ⊙6am-4pm Mon-Fri, to 3pm Sat, 8am-1pm Sun; ⊕54, 84E, 89E, 94E) sells everything from antique jewellery and Soviet army watches to Fred Astaire–style top hats. Saturday is said to be the best day to go; dealers get there early to search for those proverbial diamonds in the rust. Take bus 54 from Boráros tér in Pest or, for a quicker journey, the express bus 84E, 89E or 94E from the Határ utca stop on the M3 metro line further afield in Pest and get off at the Fiume utca stop. Follow the crowds over the pedestrian bridge.

would cost in the shops on nearby Váci utca – shrink-wrapped and potted foie gras (3900Ft for 100g), garlands of dried paprika (400Ft to 800Ft), souvenir sacks and tins of paprika powder (790Ft to 1050Ft), and as many kinds of honey (from 800Ft) as you'd care to name.

IGUANA
FASHION, CLOTHING

Map p242 (VIII Krúdy Gyula utca 9; ⊙10am-6pm Mon-Fri, to 2pm Sat; ⊕4, 6) Iguana sells vintage leather, suede and velvet pieces from the 1950s, '60s and '70s, plus its own trousers, skirts and shirts.

CHINESE MARKET
MARKET

Map p242 (VIII Kőbányai út; ⊙6am-6pm; ⊕28) The popular name for what is actually called Józsefvárosi Piac (Józsefváros Market), this is the place to come if you don't feel like doing the laundry and want to replace the wardrobe cheaply. It's chock-a-block with clothing made in China and Vietnam at ultrabargain prices (not to mention cosmetics, cigarettes and alcohol of questionable provenance).

MAGYAR PÁLINKA HÁZ
DRINK

Map p242 (Hungarian Pálinka House; www.magyarpalinkahaza.hu, in Hungarian; VIII Rákóczi út 17; ⊙9am-7pm Mon-Sat; Ⓜ M2 Astoria) This large shop stocks hundreds of varieties of *pálinka*, a kind of eau-de-vie flavoured with a number of fruits and berries. Don't go for anything stronger than 40% as it interferes with the taste of the fruit.

BABAHÁZ
CRAFT

Map p242 (Dollhouse; www.dollhouse.uw.com; IX Ráday utca 14; ⊙11am-7pm Mon-Sat; Ⓜ M3 Kálvin tér; ⊕15, 115) Dolls and their fabulous period outfits are made in-house at this outfit along pedestrianised IX Ráday utca. The owner has a nice line in teddy bears and fabric flowers too.

City Park & Beyond

Neighbourhood Top Five

1 Taking the waters at the 'wedding-cake' **Széchenyi Baths** (p142) in Budapest's sprawling City Park, which boasts some of the hottest thermal water of all the city's spas and arguably its most waterlogged chess players.

2 Enjoying the stunning architecture and the friendly residents of the Elephant House at **Budapest Zoo** (p142).

3 Having a close call with one Great Master after another at the rich **Museum of Fine Arts** (p140).

4 Keeping your cool (and your wits and your change) on the vintage roller-coaster at **Budapest Amusement Park** (p143).

5 Reaching City Park on the toylike **M1 metro** (p139), Continental Europe's first underground train.

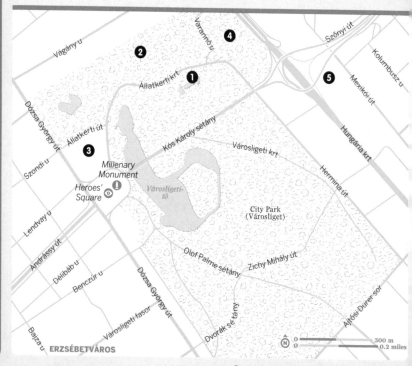

For more detail of this area, see Map p254 →

Explore: City Park & Beyond

Stately Andrássy út ends at Heroes' Square (Hősök tere), which more or less forms the entrance to City Park (Városliget). City Park is Pest's green lung, an open space measuring almost exactly a square kilometre that hosted most of the events during Hungary's 1000th anniversary celebrations in 1896. And while it may not compete with the Buda Hills as an escapist's destination, there are more than enough activities and attractions to keep everyone happy and entertained.

The park area was originally marshland and served for a time as a royal hunting ground. Leopold I (Lipót; r 1658–1705) gave it to the city of Pest, but it was not drained and planted for another half-century. The arrangement you see today dates from the late 19th century when the *angol park* (English park), an idealised view of controlled nature, was all the rage throughout Europe. The park's green spaces contain a large number of both exotic and local trees (largely maple, oak and beech), which attract up to 100 bird species.

Most of the museums, galleries and important statues and monuments lie to the south of XIV Kós Károly sétány, the path that runs east–west just below the top third of the park. Activities and attractions of a less cerebral nature – the Great Capital Circus, Budapest Amusement Park and the Széchenyi Baths – are to the north.

Local Life

⇒ **Eating** Most locals wouldn't consider dining in the evening at pricey Gundel (p144), but come Sunday and the punters arrive in droves for its excellent-value buffet.

⇒ **Architecture** The neighbourhoods south and east of the park are happy hunting grounds for some of the capital's grandest art nouveau buildings (p144).

⇒ **Sport** In winter the City Park Ice-Skating Rink (p142) attracts not just casual skaters but also aficionados of bandy, a sport with its own rules alternatively known as Russian hockey.

Getting There & Away

⇒ **Metro** The M1 metro from Vörösmarty tér and then below Andrássy út to Hősök tere and Széchenyi fürdő.

⇒ **Trolleybus** 70 to/from V Kossuth Lajos tér, 72 to/from V Arany János utca and 79 to/from XIII Jászai Mari tér or VII Baross tér (Eastern Railway Station).

⇒ **Bus** 105 linking points in Buda and V Deák Ferenc tér in Pest with Hősök tere.

Best Buildings

⇒ Palace of Art (p142)
⇒ National Institute for the Blind (p144)
⇒ Vajdahunyad Castle (p143)

For reviews, see p142 ⇒

Best Places to Eat

⇒ Olimpia (p144)
⇒ Gundel (p144)
⇒ Kilenc Sárkány (p145)

For reviews, see p144 ⇒

Best for Spectator Sports

⇒ Hungaroring (p146)
⇒ Ferenc Puskás Stadium (p146)
⇒ Kincsem Park (p146)

For reviews, see p145 ⇒

CITY PARK & BEYOND

TOP SIGHTS
MUSEUM OF FINE ARTS

The Museum of Fine Arts (Szépművészeti Múzeum) houses the city's most outstanding collection of foreign works of art dating from antiquity to the 20th century. The nucleus of the collection dates back to 1870 when the state purchased the private collection of Count Miklós Esterházy. The collection has increased in size over the decades through donations and further acquisitions. It moved into its present home, a neoclassical building on the northern side of Heroes' Square (Hősök tere), in 1906.

The enormous collection is spread over three levels. For the most part, classical and Egyptian artefacts are exhibited on the ground floor. This is also where temporary exhibitions are staged. The bulk of the rest of the works are hung on the 1st floor, though a small section of the top floor is reserved for Dutch paintings dating from about 1600 to 1800.

The Old Masters collection is the most complete, with some 3000 works from the Dutch and Flemish, Spanish, Italian, German, French and British schools between the 13th and 18th centuries. Importantly, the museum owns seven paintings by El Greco, the largest such grouping outside Spain.

Among the most famous of all the works on display is the so-called **Esterházy Madonna**, painted by Raphael, the supreme High Renaissance painter, around 1508. It is unfinished but still manages to achieve the beauty and harmony for which the paragon of classicism is acclaimed. It was among the 700-odd works that formed the original Esterházy collection.

Other sections include 19th- and 20th-century paintings, watercolours, graphics and sculpture, including some important impressionist works. The museum's collection of prints and drawings is among the largest in Europe, counting upwards of 10,000 of the former and 10 times as many of the latter.

Especially fine – and a real crowd-pleaser, especially with children because of a new program that allows them to handle original artefacts and works of art from the period – is the **collection of Egyptian artefacts**, including decorated sarcophagi and mummy portraits. The adjacent Classical section contains Greek, Etruscan and Roman works. The collection of Greek vases and urns ranks among the finest and most complete in Europe.

There's usually a couple of excellent temporary exhibitions going on at any given time; a combined ticket will get you into everything. Free English-language tours of key Old Masters galleries depart at 11am Tuesday to Saturday and at 2pm Tuesday to Friday. Highlights Tours are offered at 1pm on Tuesdays, Wednesdays and Thursdays in summer only.

DON'T MISS...

➡ Black figure amphora by Exekias

➡ Mummy sarcophagus of Dihoriaut

➡ *Esterházy Madonna* by Raphael

➡ *The Penance of St Mary Magdalene* by El Greco

➡ *Nuda Veritas* by Gustav Klimt

PRACTICALITIES

➡ Map p254

➡ www.mfab.hu

➡ XIV Dózsa György út 41 (enter from Hősök tere)

➡ adult/child 1600/800Ft, combined ticket 3400/1700Ft

➡ ⊙10am-6pm Tue-Sun

➡ Ⓜ M1 Hősök tere

➡ 🚍70, 105

HEROES' SQUARE & MILLENARY MONUMENT

Heroes' Square (Hősök tere) is the largest and most symbolic square in Budapest. Flanked by the two important – and luxurious – spaces for art in Pest, the square contains the Millenary Monument (Ezeréves emlékmű), a 36m-high pillar backed by colonnades to the right and left. It was designed in 1896 to mark the 1000th anniversary of the Magyar conquest of the Carpathian Basin.

Seemingly about to take off from the top of the pillar is the Archangel Gabriel, who is offering Vajk – the future King Stephen – the Hungarian crown. At the base of the column is a stone cenotaph called the **Heroes Monument**, dedicated to those 'who gave their lives for the freedom of our people and our national independence'. Surrounding the column are Árpád and six other Magyar chieftains – Előd, Ond, Kond, Tas, Huba and Töhötöm – who occupied the Carpathian Basin in the late 9th century (and even most Hungarians can't name them). The 14 statues in the colonnades are of **rulers and statesmen** (from left): King Stephen, Ladislas I (László), Coloman the Bookish (Könyves Kálmán), Andrew II, Béla IV, Charles Robert (Károly Róbert), Louis the Great (Nagy Lajos), János Hunyadi, Matthias (Mátyás) Corvinus, István Bocskay, Gabriel Bethlen, Imre Thököly, Ferenc II Rákóczi and Lajos Kossuth. The four allegorical figures atop are (from left to right): Work and Prosperity; War; Peace; and Knowledge and Glory.

DON'T MISS...

➡ Archangel Gabriel statue
➡ Magyar chieftains
➡ View down Andrássy út
➡ God of War statue

PRACTICALITIES

➡ Map p254
➡ M1 Hősök tere
➡ 70, 105

⊙ SIGHTS

MUSEUM OF FINE ARTS　　　　GALLERY
See p140.

**HEROES' SQUARE &
MILLENARY MONUMENT**　SQUARE, MONUMENT
See p141.

PALACE OF ART　　　　　　GALLERY
Map p254 (Műcsarnok; ☑460 7000; www
.mucsarnok.hu; XIV Dózsa György út 37; adult/
child 1400/700Ft; ◷10am-6pm Tue, Wed & Fri-
Sun, noon-8pm Thu; ⓂM1 Hősök tere) The Palace
of Art, reminiscent of a Greek temple, is
among the city's largest exhibition spaces
and now focuses on contemporary visual
arts, with some five to six major exhibitions
staged annually. Go for the scrumptious
venue and the excellent museum shop.
Concerts are sometimes staged here as well.

BUDAPEST ZOO　　　　　　ZOO
Map p254 (Budapesti Állatkert; www.zoobuda
pest.com; XIV Állatkerti körút 6-12; adult/child/
family 2100/1500/6100Ft; ◷9am-6.30pm Mon-
Thu, to 7pm Fri-Sun May-Aug, to 5.30pm Mon-Thu,
to 6pm Fri-Sun Apr & Sep, to 5pm Mon-Thu, to
5.30pm Fri-Sun Mar & Oct, to 4pm Nov-Feb; ⓂM1
Széchenyi fürdő; ☐72) This huge zoo, which
opened with 500 animals in 1866, considers
itself a nature reserve and has an excellent
collection of big cats, hippopotamuses,
polar bears and giraffes, and some of the
themed houses (eg Madagascar, wetlands,
nocturnal Australia) are world-class. Away
from our furred and feathered friends,
have a look at the Secessionist animal
houses built in the early part of the 20th
century, such as the **Elephant House** with
pachyderm heads in beetle-green Zsolnay
ceramic, and the **Palm House** with an
aquarium erected by the Eiffel Company of
Paris.

**CITY PARK
ICE-SKATING RINK**　　ICE-SKATING RINK
Map p254 (Városligeti Műjégpálya; ☑364 0013;
www.mujegpalya.hu; XIV Olof Palme sétány 5;
admission weekdays/weekends 800/1200Ft;
◷9am-1pm & 4-8pm Mon-Fri, 10am-2pm &
4-8pm Sat & Sun mid-Nov–Feb; ⓂM1 Hősök

⊙ TOP SIGHTS
SZÉCHENYI BATHS

The gigantic 'wedding cake' of a building in City Park
dates from just before the outbreak of WWI and houses
the Széchenyi Baths (Széchenyi Gyógyfürdő), whose
hot-water spring was discovered while a well was being
drilled in the late 19th century. The water here is the
hottest in the city, reaching the surface at a scalding
76°C. It also stands out for its immensity (it is the largest medicinal bath extant in Europe and counts a dozen
thermal baths and five indoor and outdoor swimming
pools); the bright, clean atmosphere; and the high
temperatures of the water (up to 38°C), which really are
what the wall plaques say they are. It's open to both men
and women at all times in mixed areas, so bathing suits
(available for hire at 1000Ft) must be worn. Use of the
three outdoor thermal pools at the Széchenyi is included in the general admission fee. Because they contain
hot mineral water they are open all year, and it is quite a
sight to watch men and women playing chess on float-
ing boards while snow dusts the treetops in City Park.
The water, high in calcium, magnesium and hydrogen
carbonate, is good for pains in the joints, arthritis, blood
circulation and disorders of the nervous system. Check
to see if the party called Cinetrip (p145) is scheduled
during your visit.

DON'T MISS...
➡ Budapest's hot-
test spa water (up to
38°C)
➡ Chess players in
the outdoor thermal
pools

PRACTICALITIES
➡ Map p254
➡ ☑363 3210
➡ www.budapest
gyogyfurdoi.hu
➡ XIV Állatkerti
körút 11
➡ before/after
5pm with locker
3500/3100Ft, cabin
3750/3300Ft
➡ ◷6am-10pm
➡ ⓂM1 Széchenyi
fürdő

CITY PARK STATUES & MONUMENTS

City Park boasts a number of notable statues and monuments. Americans (and collectors of greenbacks) might be surprised to see a familiar face in the park south of the lake. The **statue of George Washington** (Map p254) on XIV Washington György sétány was funded by Hungarian-Americans and erected in 1906.

The statue of the hooded figure opposite Vajdahunyad Castle is that of **Anonymous** (Map p254), the unknown chronicler at the court of King Béla III who wrote a history of the early Magyars. Note the pen with the shiny tip in his hand; writers (both real and aspirant) stroke it for inspiration.

The **Timewheel** (Időkerék; Map p254) in XIV Felvonulási tér (Procession Sq), on the park's western edge and directly behind the Palace of Art, is the world's largest hourglass, standing 8m high and weighing in at 60 tonnes. The 'sand' (actually glass granules) flows from the upper to lower chamber for one year, finishing exactly at midnight on New Year's Eve, when the wheel is reset to begin its annual flow. Unveiled on 1 May 2004 to commemorate Hungary's entry into the EU, it provocatively stands a short distance from the parade grounds of Dózsa György út, where Communist honchos once stood to watch May Day processions and where the 25m-tall statue of Joseph Stalin was pulled down by demonstrators on the first night of the 1956 Uprising. This spot has now been filled by the **1956 Revolution Monument**, a monolithic assembly of rusting (and controversial) steel columns erected in 2006 to mark the 50th anniversary of the abortive uprising.

tere) In winter Europe's largest outdoor skating rink operates on the western edge of the lake in City Park in the shadow of Vajdahunyad Castle. Skates can be rented. If you want to avoid the crowds, visit on a weekday morning.

BUDAPEST AMUSEMENTPARK
AMUSEMENT PARK

Map p254 (Vidámpark; www.vidampark.hu; XIV Állatkerti körút 14-16; adult/child up to 140cm 4700/3700Ft; ⊘10am-8pm Jun-Aug, 11am-6pm Mon-Fri, 10am-8pm Sat & Sun May & Sep, 11am-6pm Mon-Fri, 10am-6pm Sat & Sun Apr & Oct, 11am-6pm Sat & Sun Mar & Nov; MM1 Széchenyi fürdő; 🚇72) This Luna Park on 2.5 hectares dates back to the mid-19th century. A total 38 rides include the heart-stopping Ikarus Space Needle, a vintage wooden rollercoaster dating from 1922, the Hip-Hop freefall tower, as well as go-karts, dodgem cars, a carousel built in 1906 and a cave railway from 1912. Good old-fashioned fun.

HUNGARIAN AGRICULTURAL MUSEUM
MUSEUM

Map p254 (Magyar Mezőgazdasági Múzeum; www .mezogazdasagimuzeum.hu; XIV Vajdahunyad sétány; adult/child 1000/500Ft; ⊘10am-5pm Tue-Sun Apr-Oct, 10am-4pm Tue-Fri, to 5pm Sat & Sun Nov-Mar; MM1 Hősök tere; 🚇79) This rather esoteric museum is housed in the stunning baroque wing of **Vajdahunyad Castle**. Built

for the 1896 millenary celebrations on the little island in the park's lake, the castle was modelled after a fortress in Transylvania – but with Gothic, Romanesque and baroque wings and additions to reflect architectural styles from all over Hungary. Spread over 5200 sq metres of floor space, it has Europe's largest collection of things agricultural (fruit production, cereals, wool, poultry, pig slaughtering, viticulture etc).

The little church with the cloister opposite the castle is called **Ják Chapel** (Jáki kápolna; ⊘Mass noon Sun) because its intricate portal was copied from the 13th-century Abbey Church in Ják in western Hungary.

TRANSPORTATION MUSEUM
MUSEUM

Map p254 (Közlekedési Múzeum; ☑273 3840; www.km.iif.hu, in Hungarian; XIV Városligeti körút 11; adult/child 1000/500Ft; ⊘10am-5pm Tue-Fri, to 6pm Sat & Sun Apr-Oct, 10am-4pm Tue-Fri, to 5pm Sat & Sun Nov-Mar; 🚇72, 74) The Transportation Museum has one of the most enjoyable collections in Budapest and is a great place for kids. In an old wing and a new wing there are scale models of ancient trains (some of which run), classic late-19th-century automobiles, sailing boats and lots of those old wooden bicycles called 'bone-shakers'. There are a few hands-on exhibits and lots of show-and-tell from the attendants. Outside are pieces

ÖDÖN LECHNER

Hungarian art nouveau, or Secessionism (Szecesszió), owes its greatest debt to Ödön Lechner (1845–1914). Lechner created a true national style, using motifs from Hungarian folk art in the decoration of his buildings as well as incorporating architectural elements from Eastern cultures. As a result, his style has become iconic for Budapest.

Lechner studied architecture at Budapest's József Trade School, precursor to the University of Technology and Economics (BME) in Buda, and later at the Schinkel Academy of Architecture in Berlin. At the start of his career, Lechner worked in the prevailing styles and there were few immediate signs that he would leave such an indelible mark on his city and his epoch. The firm he formed in 1869 received a steady flow of commissions in Pest during the boom years of the 1870s, but like everyone else, he worked in the popular and all-too-common historicist and neoclassical styles.

Between 1875 and 1878 Lechner worked in France under the architect Clément Parent on the renovation and redesign of chateaux. At this time he was also influenced by the emerging style of art nouveau. After his return to Budapest Lechner began to move away from historicism to more modern ideas and trends. A turning point in his career was his commission for Thonet House on Váci utca, his innovative steel structure that he covered with glazed ceramics from the Zsolnay factory in Pécs. ('Birds have eyes too,' he explained when asked about the expense.) More ambitious commissions followed, including the Museum of Applied Arts and the Institute of Geology. But not all was right in the world of Hungarian art nouveau. Lechner's Royal Postal Savings Bank building, now often seen as the architect's tour de force, was not well received when completed in 1901 and Lechner never really worked independently on a commission of that magnitude again.

from the original Danube bridges that were retrieved after the bombings of WWII, and a cafe in an old MÁV coach.

ART NOUVEAU BUILDINGS
ARCHITECTURE, HISTORIC BUILDINGS

Two of the most extravagant art nouveau/Secessionist buildings in Budapest are within easy walking distance of City Park. To the southeast is Sándor Baumgarten's **National Institute for the Blind** (Map p254; XIV Ajtósi Dürer sor 39) dating from 1904 and to the south the **Institute of Geology** (Map p254; XIV Stefánia út 14), designed by Ödön Lechner (p144) in 1899 and probably his best-preserved work. Check out the three figures bent under the weight of a globe atop the stunning blue Zsolnay-tiled roof.

✖ EATING

City Park itself offers some wonderful options for dining alfresco in the warmer months. A bit farther afield there's no end to the choice of eateries – be it very traditional Hungarian or even hard-to-find ethnic.

BAGOLYVÁR
HUNGARIAN €€

Map p254 (☑468 3110; www.bagolyvar.com; XIV Állatkerti út 2; mains 1490-4480Ft; ☉noon-11pm; Ⓜ︎M1 Hősök tere) With reworked Hungarian classics that make it a winner, the 'Owl's Castle' attracts the Budapest cognoscenti, who leave its sister restaurant, Gundel, next door, to the expense-account brigade. It's staffed entirely by women – in the kitchen, at table, front of house. There's a bargain-basement three-course set menu with wine for 2800Ft.

TOP CHOICE OLIMPIA
HUNGARIAN €€

Map p254 (☑321 2805; www.alparutca.hu, in Hungarian; VII Alpár utca 5; set lunch 1500-2050Ft, dinner 5700-8300Ft; ☉noon-3pm Mon-Fri, 7-10pm Mon-Sat; ☐79) Traditional Hungarian with a twist is on offer at this brilliant newcomer that offers a table d'hôte set-lunch menu of one to three courses and a dinner menu of up to seven. Book ahead.

GUNDEL
HUNGARIAN €€€

Map p254 (☑486 4040; www.gundel.hu; XIV Állatkerti út 2; mains 5590-9890Ft; ☉noon-2.30pm & 6.30pm-midnight Mon-Sat, 11.30am-2pm Sun; Ⓜ︎M1 Hősök tere) Gundel, next to the zoo and directly behind the Museum of Fine Arts, is the city's fanciest (and most famous) restaurant, with a tradition dating back to 1894. Indeed, apparently it still feeds the Habsburgs (or what's left of them) when they're in town. But we've always found Gundel to be vastly overpriced, offering little value for money. Except, that is, for Sunday brunch (adult/child 6400/3200Ft), a multicourse themed gobble-fest of cold and warm dishes and desserts that changes every week. Recommended.

ROBINSON
INTERNATIONAL €€€

Map p254 (☏422 0222; www.robinsonrestaurant.hu; XIV Városligeti tó; mains 3660-6500Ft; ☺noon-5pm & 6-11pm; ⛰M1 Hősök tere) Located within the leafy park, Robinson is the place to secure a table on the lakeside terrace on a warm summer's evening. Starters include sliced goose liver with fresh vegetables (3200Ft) and smoked salmon with celery (2900Ft), and mains feature grilled *fogas* (Balaton pike-perch; 4200Ft) and classic steaks (4400Ft to 6490Ft). It's pricey but, as ever, it's all about location, location, location. Kid's menu is just 1600Ft.

HAN KUK GUAN
KOREAN €€€

Map p254 (XIV Ilka utca 22; starters 2800-3600Ft, grills 3000-6800Ft; ☺noon-10pm Mon-Sat; ⛰75, 77) No one is going to be able to tell you what a Korean joint is doing way out in district XIV southeast of City Park, but what difference does it make? It's about as authentic as you'll find. If you can afford it, try one of the barbecues. Otherwise stick to things like the *pajon* (green onion pancakes) served with seafood or any of the rice and noodle dishes (2600Ft to 3200Ft).

KILENC SÁRKÁNY
CHINESE €

Map p254 (www.kinaietterem.hu/etterem/kilenc-sarkany; VII Dózsa György út 56; mains 1200-3600Ft; ⛰79) We asked friends at the Chinese Embassy where they go for their fix of pork dumplings and fried rice, and the unanimous verdict was Nine Dragons at the southwestern end of City Park. Bearing the same name as Kowloon, it's not surprising the restaurant also does that Cantonese favourite, dim sum.

DRINKING & NIGHTLIFE

DÜRER KERT
GARDEN CLUB

Map p254 (www.durerkert.com, in Hungarian; XIV Ajtósi Dürer sor 19-21; ☺5pm-5am; ⛰74, 75) A very relaxed open space and club on the southern edge of City Park, Dürer Kert boasts some of the best DJs on the 'garden' circuit. Concerts, too, from indie to jazz.

CINETRIP
CLUB

(www.cinetrip.hu; admission from 7000Ft; ☺10pm-3.30am Sat; ⛰M1 Széchenyi fürdő) Once a regular feature at the Rudas Baths, this extraordinary event has shifted to the Széchenyi Baths (p142) and you just can't miss it if one is taking place during your visit. It combines partying and dancing with music, video, acrobatics and bathing and is just short of being an all-out orgy. Woohoo! Check schedules online.

PÁNTLIKA
BAR

Map p254 (www.pantlika.hu; XIV Városligeti körút; ☺noon-midnight; ⛰72, 74) For a real retro bar in City Park housed in a Communist-era kiosk dating back to the 1970s with a bizarre flyaway roof, this DJ bar and cafe is very Bambi (p61) and has a great terrace. Food – soups, stews and hamburgers from around 850Ft – emerges from a tiny kitchen, and the selection of *pálinka* (fruit brandy) is astonishing. It's opposite XIV Hermina út 47.

⭐ ENTERTAINMENT

GREAT CAPITAL CIRCUS
CIRCUS

Map p254 (Fővárosi Nagycirkusz; ☏344 6008; www.fnc.hu; XIV Állatkerti körút 7; adult 2400-3100Ft, child 2000-2500Ft; ⛰M1 Széchenyi fürdő; ⛰72) Europe's only permanent big top has everything one would expect from a circus, including acrobats, daredevils on horseback and ice shows in season. Performances are usually at 3pm Wednesday to Sunday, with additional shows at 11am and 7pm on Saturday and at 11am Sunday, but call ahead or check the website.

LÁSZLÓ PAPP BUDAPESTSPORTARÉNA
CONCERT VENUE

Map p254 (☏422 2682; www.budapestarena.hu; XIV Stefánia út 2; ☺ticket office 9am-6pm Mon-Fri; ⛰M2 Puskás Ferenc Stadion) This

WORTH A DETOUR

HUNGARORING

Reintroduced in 1986 after a break of half a century, the Formula 1 Hungarian Grand Prix, Hungary's prime sporting event, is part of the World Championship Series that takes place at the **Hungaroring** (☏28-444 444; www.hungaroring.hu) in Mogyoród, 24km northeast of Budapest, in August. Practice is on the Friday, the qualifying warm-up on Saturday and the race begins after morning practice at 2pm on Sunday. The only seats with views of the starting grid are Super Gold ones and cost €450 for the weekend; cheaper are Gold (€270 to €299), which are near the pit lane, and Silver (€199 to €270) tickets. Standing room costs €99 for the weekend, €90 for Sunday.

purpose-built 15,000-seat arena named after a local boxing great is where big local and international acts (eg George Michael, Britney Spears, Rihanna) perform.

PETŐFI CSARNOK   CONCERT VENUE
Map p254 (☏363 3730; www.petoficsarnok.hu; XIV Zichy Mihály út 14; ⊙ticket office 2.30-7pm Mon-Fri; ⓂM1 Széchenyi fürdő; ☐72, 74) In the southeast corner of City Park is Budapest's main youth leisure centre with an outside stage for up to 6000 spectators and the indoor Nagyterem (Great Hall) with space for up to 2500 people.

FERENC PUSKÁS STADIUM   FOOTBALL
Map p254 (Stadion Puskás Ferenc; ☏471 4100; XIV Istvánmezei út 1-3; ⓂM2 Puskás Ferenc Stadion) Hungary's national football team plays at the erstwhile 'People's Stadium', accommodating almost 70,000 fans. But don't expect any miracles (p40).

KINCSEM PARK   HORSE RACING
(☏433 0521; www.kincsempark.com, in Hungarian; X Albertirsai út 2; ⓂM2 Pillangó utca) Kincsem Park, named after a 19th-century horse called 'My Treasure', is the place to go for both *ügető* (trotting) and *galopp* (flat racing). Schedules can change, but in general three trotting meetings of 10 or 11 races take place from 2pm to 9pm on Saturday year-round and flat racing from 2pm on Sunday between April and late November. The biggest event of the year is Ügetőszilveszter, a vastly popular extraordinary trotting meeting that attracts all ages on the afternoon of New Year's Eve. It's about 2.5km southeast of City Park close to Ferenc Puskás Stadium.

🛍 SHOPPING

CITY PARK FLEA MARKET   MARKET
Map p254 (Városligeti Bolhapiac; www.bolhapiac .com; XIV Zichy Mihály út; ⊙7am-2pm Sat & Sun; ☐1; ☐72, 74) If you don't have the time for Ecseri Piac (p137), the next best thing is this Hungarian boot (garage) sale held next to the Petőfi Csarnok. There's everything from old records and draperies to candles and honey on offer. Sunday is the better day.

Day Trips from Budapest

Szentendre p148
A town on the scenic Danube Bend that has changed little since the 18th century, Szentendre is well worth the easy trip from Budapest for its museums, galleries, architecture and shops.

Gödöllő p149
Hungary's most beautifully restored aristocratic residence, Gödöllő Royal Palace, is within easy striking distance of the capital and a veritable tour through Hungarian history.

Eger p150
Provincial Hungary's prettiest city contains an embarrassment of museums and important architecture, a castle that saved the nation and a valley devoted to bacchanalia.

Balatonfüred p153
Arguably the most stylish of all the settlements along Lake Balaton, Balatonfüred was once the preserve of the ill and infirm, but now attracts both fun- and sun-seekers in equal measure.

Szentendre

Explore

Szentendre, Hungarian for 'St Andrew', is the gateway to the Danube Bend, the S-shaped curve in Hungary's mightiest river that begins just below Esztergom and twists for 20km before reaching Budapest. As an art colony turned lucrative tourist centre, Szentendre strikes many as a little too cute and the town can get pretty crowded in high season. Still, the many art museums, galleries and Orthodox churches (built largely by Serbians fleeing unrest in the 18th century), which give the town its unique Balkan feel, make the easy trip worthwhile.

The Best...

➡ **Sight** Hungarian Open-Air Ethnological Museum (p149)

➡ **Place to Eat** Erm's (p149)

➡ **Place to Drink** Adria (p149)

Top Tip

Szentendre is best avoided on weekends in summer when hordes of tourists descend and between November and mid-March when much of the town shuts down on weekdays.

Getting There & Away

Boat From May to September, a Mahart ferry plies the Danube to/from Vigadó tér (Map p238) in Pest and Batthyány tér (Map p230) in Buda, departing at 10.30am daily except Monday and arriving in Szentendre at noon (one-way/return 1590/2385Ft, 1½ hours). The return boat leaves at 5pm and takes one hour. The service reduces to weekends only in April and October.

Bus Buses from Pest's Újpest-Városkapu train station, which is on the M3 blue metro line, run to Szentendre at least once an hour (365Ft, 25 minutes).

HÉV Trains depart from Batthyány tér (Map p230) in Buda (640Ft, 40 minutes) every 10 to 20 minutes throughout the day. Note that a yellow city bus/metro ticket is good only as far as the Békásmegyer stop on the way; you'll have

to pay 320Ft extra to get to Szentendre. Also, many HÉV trains run only as far as Békásmegyer, where you must cross the platform to board the train for Szentendre. The last train returns to Budapest just after 11pm.

Need to Know

➡ **Area Code** ☑26

➡ **Location** 21km north of Budapest

➡ **Tourist Office** (☑317 965; www .szentendreprogram.hu; Bercsényi utca 4; ☉9am-5.30pm Mon-Fri, 10am-4pm Sat & Sun Jun-Aug, 9am-4.30pm Mon-Fri, 10am-4pm Sat & Sun Apr-May & Sep-Oct, 9am-4.30pm Mon-Fri, 10am-2pm Sat & Sun Nov-Mar)

◉ SIGHTS

FŐ TÉR   SQUARE

The colourful heart of Szentendre is surrounded by 18th- and 19th-century burghers' houses and contains the **Memorial Cross** (1763), an iron cross decorated with icons on a marble base. To the northeast is the Serbian Orthodox **Blagoveštenska Church** (admission 300Ft; ☉10am-5pm Tue-Sun), built in 1754. With fine baroque and rococo elements, it hardly looks 'eastern' from the outside, but the ornate iconostasis and elaborate 18th-century furnishings inside give the game away.

MARGIT KOVÁCS CERAMIC
COLLECTION   MUSEUM

(Kovács Margit Kerámiagyüjtemény; www.mu seum.hu; Vastagh György utca 1; adult/child 1000/500Ft; ☉10am-6pm) If you descend Görög utca and turn right, you'll reach this museum dedicated to the work of Szentendre's most famous artist. Kovács (1902–77) was a ceramicist who combined Hungarian folk, religious and modern themes to create elongated, Gothic-like figures. Much of it is very powerful indeed.

BELGRADE CATHEDRAL   CHURCH

(Belgrád Székesegyház; Alkotmány utca; adult/ child incl art collection 600/300Ft; ☉10am-6pm Tue-Sun May-Sep, 10am-4pm Tue-Sun Oct-Dec, 10am-4pm Fri-Sun Jan-Apr) The seat of the Serbian Orthodox bishop in Hungary built in 1764 rises from within a walled courtyard to the north of Fő tér. One of the cathedral's outbuildings contains the excellent **Serbian**

Ecclesiastical Art Collection (Szerb Egyházművészeti Gyűjtemény; Pátriárka utca 5), a treasure trove of icons, vestments and gold church plate.

ART MILL
GALLERY
(Művészetmalom; www.szentendreprogram.hu/mmalom; Bogdányi utca 32; adult/child 1000/500Ft; ☻10am-6pm) This enormous gallery spread over three floors of an old mill exhibits both local and national artists and underscores Szentendre's renewed commitment to become once again a centre for serious art.

HUNGARIAN OPEN-AIR ETHNOLOGICAL MUSEUM
OPEN-AIR MUSEUM
(Magyar Szabadtéri Néprajzi Múzeum; www.skanzen.hu; Sztaravodai út; adult/student 1400/700Ft; ☻9am-5pm Tue-Sun Apr-Oct, 10am-4pm Sat & Sun Nov-early Dec) Just 5km northwest of the centre (and accessible by bus 7 from the main bus station) is Hungary's most ambitious *skanzen* (open-air folk museum displaying village architecture), with farmhouses, churches, bell towers, mills and so on set up in seven regional divisions. There's a direct **skanzen bus** (☎06-70 367 6237; adult/child return 600/400Ft) departing from along the Duna korzó at 9.30am, 11am, noon, 2pm and 3.30pm Wednesday to Sunday May to September.

✖ EATING & DRINKING

ERM'S
HUNGARIAN €€
(www.erms.hu, in Hungarian; Kossuth Lajos utca 22; mains 1760-3990Ft) Subtitled 'Csülök & Jazz', retro-style Erm's, with simple wooden tables and walls festooned with early 20th-century memorabilia, is where to go for Hungarian-style *csülök* (pork knuckle) in all its guises and live music at the weekend.

PROMENADE
INTERNATIONAL €€
(www.promenade-szentendre.hu; Futó utca 4; mains 2600-3950Ft; ☻11am-11pm Tue-Sun) Vaulted ceilings, whitewashed walls and a wonderful terrace overlooking the Danube are all highlights at Promenade, one of Szentendre's best restaurants serving 'enlightened' Hungarian and international grilled dishes.

PALAPA
MEXICAN €€
(www.palapa.hu, in Hungarian; Dumtsa Jenő utca 14/a; mains 1580-3950Ft; ☻5pm-midnight Mon-Fri, from noon Sat & Sun) The Mexican food – from tacos to fajitas – at this colourful restaurant with live music at the weekend makes it the perfect place for a change from Hungarian fare.

GÖRÖG KANCSÓ
GREEK €€
(www.gorogkancsoetterem.hu, in Hungarian; Duna korzó 9; mains 1990-3590Ft) Should you crave a fix of taramasalata and moussaka, the 'Greek Jug' can accommodate. and boasts the prettiest (and greenest) terrace in town.

ADRIA
CAFE
(Kossuth Lajos utca 4; ☻noon-10pm) This funky little spot by the canal has a cosy interior bedecked in bright colours and a tree-shaded terrace. Expect soulful music served alongside your coffee or tea and cake.

Gödöllő

Explore
The main draw at Gödöllő (roughly pronounced 'good-duh-luh' and easily accessible on the HÉV suburban train) is the Royal Palace, which rivalled aristocratic residences throughout the Habsburg empire when it was completed in the 1760s and is the largest baroque manor house in Hungary. But Gödöllő does not live by its palace alone. The town itself, full of lovely baroque buildings and monuments and home to the erstwhile (and seminal) Gödöllő Artists' Colony (1901–20) and a couple of important music festivals each year, is also worth seeing.

The Best...
➡ **Sight** Gödöllő Royal Palace (p150)
➡ **Place to Eat** Kastélykert (p150)

Top Tip
The only way to visit the unique **Baroque Theatre** (adult/student 1200/600Ft) in the palace's southern wing is by prebooked guided tour. A combined ticket offering entry to the museum, theatre and the

DAY TRIPS FROM BUDAPEST GÖDÖLLŐ

18th-century **Royal Hill Pavilion** in the park costs 3300/1650Ft.

Getting There & Away

Bus Buses from Puskás Ferenc Stadion bus station (Map p254) in Pest serve Gödöllő (550Ft, 40 minutes) about once an hour throughout the day. The last bus back is around 5.30pm on weekdays and about 7.30pm on Saturday and Sunday.

HÉV Trains from Örs vezér tere, at the terminus of the M2 metro in Pest, leave for Gödöllő (685Ft, 45 minutes) every 20 minutes to an hour throughout the day. Get off at Szabadság tér, the third to last stop. The last train for Budapest leaves from here at 10.45pm.

Need to Know
➡ **Area Code** ⌕26
➡ **Location** 28km northeast of Budapest
➡ **Tourist Office** (⌕415 402; www.gkrte .hu; ⊙10am-6pm Apr-Oct, to 5pm Tue-Sun Nov-Mar) Just inside the palace's main entrance.

 ## SIGHTS

GÖDÖLLŐ ROYAL PALACE   PALACE
(Gödöllői Királyi Kastély; www.kiralyikastely. hu; Szabadság tér 1; adult/child 1800/900Ft; ⊙10am-6pm Apr-Oct, 10am-5pm Tue-Sun Nov-Mar) This palace was designed in 1741 by Antal Mayerhoffer for Count Antal Grassalkovich (1694–1771), confidante of Empress Maria Theresa. After the formation of the Dual Monarchy more than two centuries later, it was enlarged as a summer retreat for Emperor Franz Joseph and soon became the favoured residence of his consort, the much-loved Habsburg empress and Hungarian queen, Elizabeth (1837–98), affectionately known as Sissi (see p67). Between the two world wars, the regent, Admiral Miklós Horthy, also used it as a summer residence, but after the Communists came to power part of the mansion was used as barracks for Soviet and Hungarian troops and as an old people's home. The rest was left to decay.

Partial renovation of the mansion began in the 1990s, and today 26 rooms are open to the public as the **Palace Museum** on the ground and 1st floors. They have

been restored to the period when the imperial couple were in residence, and Franz Joseph's suites (done up in manly maroon) and Sissi's lavender-coloured private apartments on the 1st floor are impressive. Check out the **Ceremonial Hall**, all gold tracery, stucco and chandeliers, where chamber-music concerts are held throughout the year but especially in October during the Liszt and International Harp Festivals. Also see the **Queen's Reception Room**, with a Romantic-style oil painting of Sissi patriotically repairing the coronation robe of King Stephen with needle and thread; and the **Grassalkovich Era Exhibition**, which offers a look at the palace during its first century.

 ## EATING

KASTÉLYKERT   HUNGARIAN €€
(www.kastelykertetterem.hu, in Hungarian; Szabadság út 4; mains 1890-3150Ft) The 'Castle Garden', situated in a lovely old baroque house opposite the palace, is a central choice for buffet lunch (1800Ft, weekdays only) or an evening meal.

SZÉLKAKAS   HUNGARIAN €€
(www.szelkakasetterem.hu, in Hungarian; Bajcsy-Zsilinszky utca 27; mains 1600-2650Ft) The 'Weathervane' is a pleasant eatery with covered garden in a neighbourhood of 18th- and 19th-century farmhouses about 500m north of the Szabadság tér HÉV station.

PIZZA PALAZZO   PIZZERIA €
(www.pizzapalazzo.hu, in Hungarian; Szabadság tér 2; pizza & pasta 970-1450Ft) This popular pizzeria with more substantial pasta dishes is conveniently attached to the Szabadság tér HÉV station.

Eger

Explore
Everyone loves Eger and it's immediately apparent why. Lavished with beautifully preserved baroque architecture, Eger is a jewellery box of a town with loads to see and do. Explore the bloody history of Turkish occupation and defeat at the hilltop

castle, climb an original minaret or hear an organ performance at the colossal basilica. Then spend time traipsing from cellar to cellar in the Valley of the Beautiful Women, tasting the celebrated Eger Bull's Blood (Egri Bikavér) and other local wines from the cask, and the following morning take the cure in a renovated Turkish bath. Eger could easily become a 'days trip'.

The Best...

➡ **Sight** Valley of the Beautiful Women (p152)

➡ **Place to Eat** Senator Ház (p153)

Top Tip

Even though Eger Castle is closed to the public on Monday you can still visit the castle grounds, Heroes' Hall and casemates at a reduced price of 1100/550Ft per adult/child.

Getting There & Away

Bus Buses link Eger with Puskás Ferenc Stadion bus station (Map p254) in Pest (2480Ft, two hours) hourly.

Train There are eight direct trains a day to and from Keleti train station (Map p242) in Pest (2160Ft, 2½ hours).

Need to Know

➡ **Area Code** 📞 36

➡ **Location** 130km northeast of Budapest

➡ **Tourist Office** (📞 517 715; www.eger. hu, in Hungarian; Bajcsy-Zsilinszky utca 9; ⏰ 9am-6pm Mon-Fri, to 1pm Sat & Sun mid-Jun–mid-Sep, to 5pm Mon-Fri, to 1pm Sat mid-Sep–mid-Jun)

 # SIGHTS

EGER CASTLE
CASTLE

(Egri Vár; www.egrivar.hu; Vár köz 1; adult/child castle & grounds 1400/700Ft, grounds only 700/350Ft; ⏰ exhibits 9am-5pm Tue-Sun Apr-Oct, 10am-4pm Tue-Sun Nov-Mar, grounds 8am-8pm daily May-Aug, 8am-7pm Apr & Sep, 8am-6pm Mar & Oct, 8am-5pm Nov-Feb) The castle, accessible via cobblestone lane from Dózsa György tér, was erected in the 13th century after the Mongol invasion. Models and drawings in the **István Dobó Museum** housed in the former Bishop's Palace (1470) painlessly explain the history of the castle. On the ground floor a statue of Dobó takes pride of place in **Heroes' Hall**. The 19th-century building on the northwestern side of the courtyard houses the **Eger Art Gallery**, with several works by Mihály Munkácsy. The terrace of the renovated **Dobó Bastion** (1552) offers stunning views of the town. Beneath the castle are **casemates** hewn from solid rock, which you may tour with a Hungarian-speaking guide included in the price (English-language guide 800Ft extra).

EGER CATHEDRAL
CHURCH

(Egri Főszékesegyház; Pyrker János tér 1; ⏰ 7.30am-6pm Mon-Sat, from 1pm Sun) A highlight of the town's amazing architecture, this neoclassical monolith was designed by József Hild in 1836 and is surprisingly light and airy inside. There are half-hour **organ concerts** (admission 800Ft; ⏰ 11.30am Mon-Sat, 12.45pm Sun) daily from mid-May to mid-October. Recommended.

LYCEUM
HISTORIC BUILDING

(Líceum; 📞 520 400; Eszterházy tér 1; ⏰ 9.30am-3.30pm Tue-Sun mid-Mar–mid-Oct, 9.30am-1pm Sat & Sun mid-Oct–mid-Mar) Directly opposite

THE SIEGE OF EGER

The story of the Turkish attempt to take Eger Castle is the stuff of legend. Under the command of István Dobó, a mixed bag of 2000 soldiers held out against more than 100,000 Turks for a month in 1552. As every Hungarian kid in short trousers can tell you, the women of Eger played a crucial role in the battle, pouring boiling oil and pitch on the invaders from the ramparts.

Also significant was Eger's wine – if we are to believe the tale. Apparently Dobó sustained his soldiers with the ruby-red local vintage. When they fought on with increased vigour – and stained beards – rumours began to circulate among the Turks that the defenders were gaining strength by drinking the blood of bulls. Egri Bikavér (Eger Bull's Blood) was born.

Géza Gárdonyi's *Eclipse of the Crescent Moon* (1901), which describes the siege in thrilling detail, can be found in English translation in many Budapest bookshops.

SLEEPING IN EGER

Senator Ház (☎320 466; www.senatorhaz.hu; Dobó István tér 11; s/d €60/80; P ⊖ ❄ @ 🛜) 'Senator House' has 11 warm and cosy rooms on the upper two floors of a delightful 18th-century inn on Eger's main square. Its ground floor is shared between a quality restaurant and a reception area stuffed with antiques and curios.

Dobó Vendégház (☎421 407; www.dobovendeghaz.hu; Dobó utca 19; s/d €35/52; P ⊖ 🛜🐾) Tucked away along one of the old town's pedestrian streets just below the castle, this guesthouse is a boon for sightseers. The seven rooms are spick and span and some have little balconies. Check out the museum-quality Zsolnay porcelain collection in the breakfast room.

Agria Retur Panzió (☎416 650; http://agria.returvendeghaz.hu; Knézich Károly utca 18; s/d 3800/6400Ft; P ⊖ 🛜🐾) You couldn't find sweeter hosts than the daughter and mother who own this *panzió* (pension) near the Minaret. Walking up three flights you enter a cheery communal kitchen/eating area central to four rooms. Out back is a huge garden with tables and barbecue at your disposal.

the cathedral is this sprawling Zopf-style building dating from 1765. It was under massive renovation when we last visited (call for updates and entrance fees) but contains a 20,000-volume **library** on the 1st floor of the south wing with hundreds of priceless manuscripts and codices. The *trompe l'œil* **ceiling fresco** (1778) depicts the Counter-Reformation's Council of Trent (1545–63) and a lightning bolt setting heretical manuscripts ablaze. The **Observatory** on the 6th floor of the east wing contains 18th-century astronomical equipment; climb three more floors up to the observation deck to try out the camera obscura, a kind of periscope designed in 1779 to spy on the town and to entertain townspeople.

DOBÓ ISTVÁN TÉR   SQUARE
On the southern side of Eger's main square below the castle stands the **Minorite church** (Minorita templom; Dobó István tér 4; ☺9am-5pm Tue-Sun), built in 1771 and one of the most beautiful baroque buildings in the world. Statues of István Dobó and his comrades-in-arms routing the Turks fill the square in front of the church. Just north of and visible from the square is the 40m-tall **minaret** (Knézich Károly utca; admission 200Ft; ☺10am-6pm Apr-Oct), which can be climbed via 97 narrow spiral steps.

COUNTY HALL   HISTORIC BUILDING
(Megyeháza; Kossuth Lajos utca 9) To the south of the square is Kossuth Lajos utca, a tree-lined street with dozens of architectural gems including this delightful building whose main entrance is crowned by a wrought-iron representation of Faith, Hope and Charity by Henrik Fazola, a Rhinelander who settled in Eger in the mid-18th century. Walk down the passageway and you'll see more of his magnificent work two baroque wrought-iron gates.

VALLEY OF THE BEAUTIFUL WOMEN   WINE CELLARS
(Szépasszony-völgy) Don't miss visiting the wine cellars of this evocatively named valley just over a kilometre southwest of the centre. This is the place to sample Bull's Blood – one of very few reds produced in Eger – or any of the whites: Leányka, Olaszrizling and sweet Muscatel. The choice of wine cellars can be a bit daunting, so walk around and have a look yourself (hint: we like Nos 40, 43 and 46 on the south side of the green). Be careful, though: those 1dL glasses (around 100Ft) go down easily and quickly. The taxi fare back to the centre of Eger costs between 700Ft and 1000Ft.

TURKISH BATH   THERMAL BATHS
(Török Fürdő; ☎510 552; www.egertermal.hu; in Hungarian; 3-4 Furdő utca; 2½hr session adult/child 1900/1500Ft; ☺4.30-9pm Mon & Tue, 3-9pm Wed-Fri, 9am-9pm Sat & Sun) After a hard day's drinking over in the valley, nothing beats a soak and a steam at this historic spa, which has at its centre a bath dating to 1617. A multimillion-forint addition that opened in 2009 has added five pools, saunas, steam rooms and a hamam. Various kinds of massage and treatments are also available.

EATING & DRINKING

TOP CHOICE SENATOR HÁZ
HUNGARIAN €€

(www.senatorhaz.hu; Dobó István tér 11; mains 1500-3500Ft) Places in the antique-filled dining room of this charming hotel are coveted, but the ones outdoors are the hot seats of Eger's main square. Try the cream of garlic soup served with Camembert (650Ft), the smoked local trout (1500Ft) and the *borjúpaprikás* (veal stew; 2000Ft).

PALACSINTAVÁR
CREPERIE €

(www.palacsintavar.hu, in Hungarian; Dobó István utca 9; mains 1290-1820Ft) Pop art and postcards line the walls and groovy music fills the rest of the space in this eclectic eatery. Savoury *palacsinták* – 'pancakes' for want of a better word – are served with an abundance of fresh vegetables and there's a large choice of sweet ones too.

SZANTOFER
HUNGARIAN €€

(www.szantofer.hu, in Hungarian; Bródy utca 3; mains 1700-2200Ft) The best choice in town for hearty, homestyle Hungarian fare, Szantofer oozes a rustic atmosphere. Two-course weekday lunches are a snip at 850Ft.

MARJÁN CUKRÁSZDA
CAFE

(Kossuth Lajos utca 28; ⊙9am-10pm Jun-Sep, 9am-7pm Oct-May) Linger over coffee and sweets on the big terrace south of Dózsa György tér and directly below the castle.

LA ISLA
BAR

(www.laislabarandgrill.hu, in Hungarian; Foglár György utca 2; ⊙10am-midnight Sun-Thu, 10am-2am Fri & Sat) As much a Latin cocktail bar as a cafe, this is a fine place to kick back in.

Balatonfüred

Explore

Balatonfüred is the oldest and most fashionable resort on Lake Balaton, Hungary's 'inland sea' 100km or so southwest of Budapest. In its glory days in the 19th century the wealthy and famous built large villas along its tree-lined streets, and their architectural legacy can still be seen today. More recently, the lake frontage received a massive makeover and it now sports the most stylish marina on Balaton. The town is also known for its thermal water, but it's reserved for patients at the town's world-famous heart hospital. You'll have to content yourself with swimming in the lake.

The Best...

➡ **Sight** Kisfaludy Strand (p155)
➡ **Place to Eat** Balaton (p155)
➡ **Place to Drink** Karolina (p155)

Top Tip

If you're staying the night in Balatonfüred, ask your hotel about the free Füred Card, which offers between 5% and 25% discount on various sights, activities and restaurants around town.

WORTH A DETOUR

TIHANY

While in Balatonfüred, don't miss the opportunity to visit Tihany, a small peninsula 14km to the southwest and the place with the greatest historical significance on Lake Balaton. Activity here is centred on the tiny settlement of the same name, which is home to the celebrated **Benedictine Abbey Church** (Bencés Ápátsági Templom; http://tihany.osb.hu, in Hungarian; András tér 1; adult/child 800/400Ft; ⊙9am-6pm May-Sep, 10am-5pm Oct & mid-Mar–Apr, 10am-4.30pm Nov–mid-Mar), filled with fantastic altars, pulpits and screens carved in the mid-18th century by an Austrian lay brother: all are baroque-rococo masterpieces in their own right. The church attracts a lot of tourists, but juxtaposing this claustrophobic vibe is the peninsula itself – a nature reserve of hills and marshy meadows – which has an isolated, almost wild feel to it. **Hiking** is one of Tihany's main attractions; there's a good map outlining the trails near the front of the church. Buses bound for Tihany depart Balatonfüred's bus and train station (305Ft, 30 minutes) at least hourly, with the last returning just after 10pm.

SLEEPING IN BALATONFÜRED

Blaha Lujza Hotel (☑581 210; www.hotelblaha.hu; Blaha Lujza utca 4; s/d from €38/56; P🅿⊖🛜) This small hotel is one of the loveliest places to stay in Balatonfüred. Its 20 rooms are a little compact but very comfy. This was the summer home of the much-loved 19th-century actress-singer Lujza Blaha from 1893 to 1916.

Anna Grand Hotel (☑581 200; www.annagrandhotel.eu; Gyógy tér 1; s/d €120/140; P⊖🛜🏊) In a former life the Anna Grand was the town's sanatorium, but it has now metamorphosed into a wowee-zowee hotel with 101 rooms. Choose ones with either period antiques or modern furnishings, and views of the hotel's peaceful inner courtyard or tree-shaded Gyógy tér. There's a very sophisticated wellness centre with a swimming pool, and a bowling alley.

Hotel Park (☑788 477; www.hotelpark.hu; Jókai Mór utca 24; s/d €52/82; P⊖🛜🏊) A massive villa away from the lake is the site of this old-world hotel, where you'll find some two-dozen huge rooms (some with balcony). The private garden with swimming pool is a plus.

Getting There & Away

Bus Six direct buses link Népliget station (Map p242) in Pest (2480Ft, 2½ hours) with Balatonfüred every day. Otherwise, change in Veszprém.

Train Seven daily trains not requiring a change connect Déli train station (Map p230) in Buda with Balatonfüred. Lots more go via Székesfehérvár.

Need to Know

➤ **Area Code** ☑87
➤ **Location** 130km southwest of Budapest
➤ **Tourist Office** (☑580 480; www.balatonfured.hu; Blaha Lujza utca 5; ⊙9am-7pm Mon-Fri, to 6pm Sat, to 1pm Sun Jul & Aug, to 5pm Mon-Fri, to 1pm Sat May, Jun & Sep, to 4pm Mon-Fri Oct-Apr)

👁 SIGHTS

GYÓGY TÉR   SQUARE

Leafy 'Cure Sq' is the heart of the Balatonfüred spa. In the centre, the **Kossuth Pump House** (1853) dispenses slightly sulphuric, but drinkable, thermal water. This is as close as you'll get to the hot spring; the mineral baths are reserved for patients of the **State Hospital of Cardiology** (Országos Szívkórház; Gyógy tér 2) on the eastern side of the square. On the northern side is the **Balaton Pantheon**, with memorial plaques from those who took the cure at the hospital, while on the western side is the late baroque **Horváth House** (Gyógy tér 3), the site of the first Anna Ball – Balatonfüred's red-letter annual event – in 1825. It's now held at the Anna Grand Hotel (p154) every year on 26 July.

MÓR JÓKAI MEMORIAL MUSEUM   MUSEUM

(Jókai Mór Emlékmúzeum; www.furedkult.hu; Honvéd utca 1; adult/child 700/350Ft; ⊙10am-6pm Tue-Sun May-Sep) Housed in the prolific writer's summer villa, this recently renovated museum is filled with period furniture and family memorabilia. In his study here, Jókai churned out many of his 200 novels under the stern gaze of his wife, the actress Róza Laborfalvi. A member of parliament for 30 years, he was only able to write – so the explanatory notes tell us – in 'purple ink on minister's paper'.

ROUND CHURCH   CHURCH

(Kerektemplom; Blaha Lujza utca 1; ⊙Mass 11am Sun) Opposite the museum is this tiny neoclassical church completed in 1846. *The Crucifixion* (1891) by János Vaszary (1867–1939) sits above the altar on the western wall and is the most notable thing inside. The basement gallery hosts occasional art exhibitions.

VASZARY VILLA   GALLERY

(www.vaszaryvilla.hu, in Hungarian; Honvéd utca 2-4; adult/child 1700/850Ft; ⊙noon-8pm Fri & Sat, 10am-6pm Sun & Tue-Thu May-Sep, 10am-6pm Thu-Sun Oct-Mar) This beautifully restored villa (1892), once the residence of the Vaszarys, exhibits some works of the best-known family member, the painter János Vaszary, as well as a wonderful collection of arts and crafts from the 18th century.

ESZTERHÁZY & KISFALUDY STRANDS
BEACHES

Balatonfüred's most accessible grassy beaches, measuring about a kilometre in length, are **Eszterházy Strand** (www.balatonfuredistrandok.hu; Tagore sétány; adult/child 810/490Ft; ☺8.30am-7pm mid-Jun–mid-Aug, 9am-6pm mid-May–mid-Jun & mid-Aug–mid-Sep), with a water park right in town, and the more attractive **Kisfaludy Strand** (www.balatonfuredistrandok.hu; Aranyhíd sétány; adult/child 550/350Ft; ☺8am-7pm mid-Jun–mid-Aug, 8am-6pm mid-May–mid-Jun & mid-Aug–mid-Sep) further east.

 EATING & DRINKING

BALATON
HUNGARIAN €€

(www.balatonetterem.hu, in Hungarian; Kisfaludy utca 5; mains 1790-4600Ft) This leafy oasis amid all the hubbub is set back from the lake in the shaded park area and has a huge terrace. It serves generous portions and has an extensive selection of fish dishes.

ALCATRAZ
PIZZERIA €

(www.alcatrazpizzeria.eu, in Hungarian; Blaha Lujza utca 9; mains 550-1450Ft) Just short of Gyógy tér, this eatery with a jail theme serves mostly (but not only) pizza from 990Ft. Try the not-often-seen *lepények* (pies stuffed with meat or cheese; 990Ft to 1190Ft).

KAROLINA
CAFE

(www.karolina.hu, in Hungarian; Zákonyi Ferenc sétány 4) Karolina is a sophisticated cafe-bar that does an excellent job serving fresh coffee, aromatic teas and quality local wines. The terrace looking out to the new marina couldn't be more laid-back.

KEDVES
CAFE

(Blaha Lujza utca 7; ☺8am-8pm) Join fans of Lujza Blaha and take coffee and cake at the cafe where the famous actress used to while away the hours. It's also appealing for its location, just slightly away from the madd(en)ing crowds.

Sleeping

Accommodation in Budapest runs the gamut from hostels in converted flats and private rooms in far-flung housing estates to luxury guesthouses in the Buda Hills and five-star properties charging upwards of €300 a night. It's difficult to generalise, but accommodation in the Buda neighbourhoods is more limited than on the other side of the Danube River in Pest.

Hotels

Hotels – *szállók* or *szállodák* in Hungarian – can be anything from the rapidly disappearing rundown socialist-era hovels to luxurious five-star palaces.

A cheap hotel is generally more expensive than a private room, but may be the answer if you are only staying one night or arrive too late to get a room through an agency. Two-star hotels usually have rooms with a private bathroom; bathrooms are almost always in the hall in one-star places. Three- and four-star hotels can be excellent value compared with those in Western European cities.

Because of the changing value of the forint, many midrange and top-end hotels quote their rates in euros.

Serviced Apartments

Budapest is chock-a-block with serviced apartments and apartment hotels. Apartments all have private bathrooms and usually kitchens – at the very least. Some are positively luxurious while others are bare-bones.

Guesthouses

Budapest has scores of *panziók* (pensions) and *vendégházak* (guesthouses), but many are in the outskirts of Pest or the Buda Hills and not very convenient unless you have your own (motorised) transport. They're popular with Germans and Austrians who like the homey atmosphere and (usually) better breakfasts. Pensions can cost as much as a moderate hotel, although there are some worthwhile exceptions.

Hostels

Ifjúsági szállók (youth hostels) are open year-round, with the number of options increasing substantially during the university summer holidays (mid-June or July to late August) when private outfits rent vacant dormitories and turn them into hostels.

You don't need to belong to Hostelling International or an associated organisation to stay at any of Budapest's hostels, but membership will sometimes get you a 10% discount or an extra night's accommodation. For information, check out the **Hungarian Youth Hostel Association** (MISZSZ; www .miszsz.hu).

Private Rooms

Fizetővendég szolgálat (paying-guest service) in Budapest is a great deal and still relatively cheap, but with the advent of stylish and affordable guesthouses it's not as widespread as it was a decade or so ago.

Private rooms generally cost 6000Ft to 7500Ft for a single, 7000Ft to 8500Ft for a double and 9000Ft to 13,000Ft for a small apartment. To get a room in the centre of town you may have to try several agencies. Individuals on the streets outside the main train stations may offer you a private room, but prices are usually higher and there is no quality control.

Tourinform does not arrange private accommodation, but will send you to a travel agency such as **To-Ma** (☑353 0819; www.to matour.hu; V Október 6 utca 22; ⊙9am-5pm; Ⓜ M3 Arany János utca). Among the best agencies for private rooms: Ibusz (p210) and Vista (p210).

SLEEPING

Lonely Planet's Top Choices

Four Seasons Gresham Palace Hotel (p162) The city's most luxurious hotel, risen phoenixlike from a derelict art nouveau palace.

Gerlóczy Rooms deLux (p161) Tastefully designed, homey accommodation above a popular cafe-restaurant in a quiet central square.

Zara Continental Hotel (p164) Stunning spa hotel recreated from an old-time city bath, with a rooftop swimming pool and panoramic garden.

Bródy House (p165) Old and new meeting and greeting in what was once the residence of Hungary's prime minister.

Best by Budget

€
Spinoza Apartments (p164)
Medosz Hotel (p163)
Hotel Császár (p160)
Maria & István (p166)

€€
Beatrix Panzió Hotel (p160)
Soho Hotel (p164)
Hotel Sissi (p167)
Hotel Victoria (p159)

€€€
Andrássy Hotel (p165)
Art'otel Budapest (p159)
Kempinski Hotel Corvinus (p160)
Residence Izabella (p165)

Best Gay Stays
Connection Guest House (p164)
Kapital Inn (p165)
KM Saga Guest Residence (p166)

Best Boutique Hotels
Buda Castle Fashion Hotel (p159)
Zara Boutique Hotel (p161)
Soho Hotel (p164)
La Prima Fashion Hotel (p162)

Best for Spas
Corinthia Hotel Budapest (p164)
Danubius Hotel Gellért (p159)
Danubius Grand Hotel Margitsziget (p163)
Hotel Parlament (p162)

Best Luxury Historic Hotels
Hotel Palazzo Zichy (p166)
Hilton Budapest (p159)
Corinthia Hotel Budapest (p164)
Danubius Hotel Gellért (p159)

Best Budget Hotels with History
Hotel Kálvin House (p166)
Hotel Kulturinnov (p159)
Citadella Hotel (p160)
Hotel Császár (p160)

Best Cool Hostels
Maverick Hostel (p161)
Big Fish Hostel (p164)
Back Pack Guesthouse (p160)
Green Bridge Hostel (p161)

Best Hotels with a Garden
Hotel Papillon (p160)
Beatrix Panzió Hotel (p160)
Kisgellért Vendégház (p159)
Hotel Anna (p166)

NEED TO KNOW

Price Ranges
In our Sleeping reviews the following price indicators represent the cost per night of a standard double room in high season.

€   under 15,000Ft (€55)

€€   15,000Ft to 33,500Ft (€55 to €125)

€€€ over 33,500Ft (€125)

Extra Costs

➡ Travel agencies generally charge a small fee for booking a private room or other accommodation, and there's usually a surcharge if you stay for fewer than three nights (at least on the first night).

➡ Budapest levies a 3% local tourist tax on those aged 18 to 70.

➡ Some top-end hotels in Budapest do not include the whopping 18% VAT in their listed rack rates; make sure you read the bottom line.

Seasons
The low season for hotels runs roughly from mid-October or November to March (not including the Christmas and New Year holidays). The high season is the rest of the year (a lengthy seven months or so) when prices can increase substantially.

Breakfast
The rate quoted for hostel and hotel accommodation usually includes breakfast, but check.

Where to Stay

Neighbourhood	For	Against
Castle District	In the thick of historic Buda with million-dollar views of the Danube and city	Not particularly good value for money; relatively limited entertainment
Gellért Hill & Tabán	Great views of the city and river; greenery; quietude	Away from it all in a negative sense, though transport links are good
Óbuda & Buda Hills	Excellent choice if you're looking for the countryside in the city	Terrible choice if you're not looking for the countryside in the city
Belváros	Close to just about everything, especially eating and drinking options and entertainment	Noisy day and night; more expensive than other parts of the city
Parliament & Around	Very central to things that matter; lots of important sights	Not always a great selection of places to eat and things to do after dark
Margaret Island & Northern Pest	Excellent mix of built-up areas and parkland	Not much by way of sights; transport gaps (unless you count trolleybuses)
Erzsébetváros & the Jewish Quarter	Entertainment central – the district for the party animal in you	In-your-face; touristy; can be noisy at night
Southern Pest	Full of 'real' neighbourhoods with far fewer tourists than other districts	Red-light districts and dodgy bars – the only area in the city where you should keep your eyes open at all times
City Park & Beyond	Budapest's biggest park, with lots and lots of things to see and do	Very far away from real life, despite relatively good transport links

🛏 Castle District

HILTON BUDAPEST
HOTEL €€€

Map p230 (☎889 6600; www.budapest.hilton
.com; I Hess András tér 1-3; r €130-240; ☐16A,
116; P ⊖ ✴ 🐾 🛜) Perched above the Danube on
Castle Hill, the Hilton was built carefully
in and around a 14th-century church and
baroque college (though it still has its
uber-preservationist detractors). It has
322 somewhat sombre rooms, with dark
carpeting and low lighting but fantastic
views. Guests pay for wi-fi.

BUDA CASTLE FASHION
HOTEL
BOUTIQUE HOTEL €€€

Map p230 (☎2247900; www.budacastlehotelbuda
pest.com; I Úri utca 39; s €95-134, d €110-149;
☐6A, 116; ⊖ ✴ 🛜) The Mellow Mood Group's
flagship top-end hotel is housed in a 15th-
century town house, but apart from a bit
of vaulted brick ceiling in the lobby you'd
never know that once you've entered. The
25 rooms and suites, done up in warm
shades of brown, tan and beige, look on to a
cobbled street or face a relaxing courtyard
planted with grass and trees.

HOTEL KULTURINNOV
HOTEL €€

Map p230 (☎224 8102; www.mka.hu; I Szentháromság tér 6, 1st fl; s/d €64/80; ☐16A, 116;
🛜🐾) A 16-room hotel in the former Finance
Ministry, this neo-Gothic structure dating
back to 1904 can't be beat for location and
price in the Castle District. The guestrooms,
though clean and with private bathrooms,
are not as nice as the public areas seem to
promise. No lift.

BURG HOTEL
HOTEL €€

Map p230 (☎212 0269; www.burghotelbudapest
.com; I Szentháromság tér 7-8; s €59-105, d €69-
115, ste €99-145; ☐16A, 116; ⊖ ✴ 🛜🐾) This
small hotel with all the mod cons has 26
refurbished rooms that look fresher but are
not much more than just ordinary. But, as
they say, location is everything. It's just opposite Matthias Church.

ART'OTEL BUDAPEST
HOTEL €€€

Map p230 (☎487 9487; www.artotels.com; I Bem
rakpart 16-19; s/d/ste €198/218/298, with Danube view €218/238/318; ☐86; 🚋19; P ⊖ ✴ 🛜🐾)
The Art'otel is a minimalist establishment
that would not look out of place in London
or New York. But what makes this 165-room
place unique is that it cobbles together a
seven-storey modern building (views of the
castle and the Danube) and an 18th-century
baroque building, linking them with a leafy
courtyard-atrium. We love the gaming
theme throughout.

HOTEL VICTORIA
HOTEL €€

Map p230 (☎457 8080; www.victoria.hu; I Bem
rakpart 11; s €79-102, d €86-107; ☐86; 🚋19;
P ⊖ ✴ @ 🛜🐾) This rather elegant hotel has
27 comfortable and spacious rooms with
million-dollar views of Parliament and
the Danube. Despite its small size it gets
special mention for its friendly service and
facilities, including the recently renovated
rooms of the 19th-century Jenő Hubay
Music Hall (p62), attached to the hotel,
which now serves as a small concert venue
and theatre.

BÜRO PANZIÓ
GUESTHOUSE €

Map p230 (☎212 2929; www.buropanzio.hu; II
Dékán utca 3, 1st fl; s €34-40, d €43-60; Ⓜ M2
Széll Kálmán tér; P ⊖ ✴ 🛜🐾) Just a block
off the northern side of Széll Kálmán
tér (formerly Moszkva tér), this pension
looks simple from the outside but has 10
comfortable, though small, rooms. Decor
is the basic 'just off the assembly line' look.

🛏 Gellért Hill & Tabán

DANUBIUS HOTEL GELLÉRT
HOTEL €€€

Map p236 (☎889 5500; www.danubiusgroup
.com/gellert; XI Szent Gellért tér 1; s €67-110,
d €134-216, ste €232-268; ☐18, 19, 47, 49;
P ⊖ ✴ @ 🛜🐾) Buda's *grande dame* is a
234-room four-star hotel with loads of
character. Completed in 1918, the hotel
contains examples of the late art nouveau,
notably the thermal spa with its enormous
arched glass entrance hall and Zsolnay
ceramic fountains in the bathing pools.
Use of the thermal baths is free for guests,
but overall the Gellért's other facilities are
forgettable. Prices depend on which way
your room faces and what sort of bathroom
it has.

KISGELLÉRT VENDÉGHÁZ
GUESTHOUSE €

(☎279 0346; www.kisgellert.hu; XI Otthon utca
14; s 5000-7000Ft, d 7000-9500Ft; ☐8, 112;
🚋61; P ⊖ @) This cute little guesthouse
with 10 rooms is named after the 'Little
Gellért' hill to the west of the more famous
larger one and sits dreamily in 'At Home St'.
Away from the action but leafy and quiet.

CITADELLA HOTEL
HOTEL, HOSTEL €

Map p236 (☎466 5794; www.citadella.hu; XI Citadella sétány; dm 2560Ft, r 11,500-12,500Ft; ☐27) This hotel in the fortress atop Gellért Hill is pretty threadbare, though the dozen guestrooms are extra large, retain some of their original features and have their own shower or bath (toilets are on the circular corridor). The two dorm rooms have six and 12 beds and shared facilities.

CHARLES HOTEL & APARTMENTS
SERVICED APARTMENTS €€

off Map p236 (☎212 9169; www.charleshotel.hu; I Hegyalja út 23; studios €45-80, apt €75-155; ☐8, 112, 178; P🚭@🛜❄) On the Buda side and somewhat off the beaten track (a train line runs right past it), the Charles has 70 'studios' (larger-than-average rooms) with tiny kitchens and weary-looking furniture as well as two-room apartments.

HOTEL ORION
HOTEL €€

Map p236 (☎356 8583; www.bestwestern-ce .com/orion; I Döbrentei utca 13; d €42-99, ste €120; ☐18, 19; 🚭❄🛜❄) Hidden away in the Tabán district, the Orion is a cosy place with a relaxed atmosphere and within easy walking distance of the Castle District. The 30 rooms are bright and of a good size, and there's a small sauna for guest use.

BACK PACK GUESTHOUSE
HOSTEL €

(☎385 8946; www.backpackbudapest.hu; XI Takács Menyhért utca 33; bed in yurt 3000Ft, dm 3800-4500Ft, d 11,000Ft; ☐7, 173; P🚭@🛜) We've always loved this laid-back hostel – Budapest's first! – located in a colourfully painted suburban 'villa' in south Buda. It's relatively small, with just 50 beds, but the fun (and sleeping bodies in high season) spills out into a lovely landscaped garden, with hammocks, a yurt and a Thai-style lounging platform. The upbeat attitude of friendly, much-travelled owner-manager Attila seems to permeate the place, and the welcome is always warm.

🛏 Óbuda & Buda Hills

HOTEL PAPILLON
HOTEL €€

Map p234 (☎212 4750; www.hotelpapillon.hu; II Rózsahegy utca 3/b; s €31-46, d €41-60, apt from €72; ☐4, 6; P🚭@🛜❄) One of Buda's best-kept accommodation secrets, this small 20-room hotel in Rózsadomb (Rose Hill) has a delightful back garden with a small swimming pool, and some rooms have balconies. There are also four apartments available in the same building, one boasting a lovely roof terrace.

HOTEL CSÁSZÁR
HOTEL €

Map p234 (☎336 2640; www.csaszarhotel.hu; II Frankel Leó utca 35; s €39-49, d €39-53, ste €39-105; ☐86; ☐17; 🚭❄🛜❄) The huge yellow building in which the 'Emperor' is located was built in the 1850s as a convent, which might explain the size of the 45 cell-like rooms. Request one of the superior rooms, which are larger and look onto the nearby outdoor Olympic-size pools of the huge Császár-Komjádi swimming complex.

BEATRIX PANZIÓ HOTEL
GUESTHOUSE, HOTEL €€

Map p233 (☎275 0550; www.beatrixhotel.hu; II Széher út 3; s €45-55, d €50-60, apt €50-80; ☐29; ☐18, 61; P🚭@🛜❄) On the way up to the Buda Hills, but still easily accessible by frequent public transport, this is an attractive award-winning pension with 18 rooms and four apartments. Surrounding the property is a lovely garden with a fish pond, sun terraces and a grill; a barbecue might even be organised during your stay.

HOTEL NORMAFA
GUESTHOUSE, HOTEL €€

Map p233 (☎395 6505; www.normafahotel.com; XII Eötvös út 52; s €50-80, d €55-90, ste €65-110; ☐90, 90A; P🚭🛜❄) This 62-room guesthouse-cum-hotel sits atop Sváb-hegy on the edge of the Buda Hills protected nature area. It has a gorgeous swimming pool, a fitness room and sauna, and a highly praised restaurant. If something should tempt you away from all of this, the Normafa stop of the Cog Railway (p74) is across the way.

🛏 Belváros

KEMPINSKI HOTEL CORVINUS
HOTEL €€€

Map p238 (☎429 3777; www.kempinski-buda pest.com; V Erzsébet tér 7-8; r €250-350, ste from €525; Ⓜ M1/2/3 Deák Ferenc tér; P🚭❄@ 🛜❄) Essentially for business travellers on hefty expense accounts, the Kempinski offers European service, American efficiency, Hungarian charm and fusion Japanese food at the all-star Nobu (p87). The hotel's public areas and 366 guestrooms and suites remain among the classiest in town, even with the advent of so many five-star and boutique hotels. There's a lovely spa on the 2nd floor.

GERLÓCZY ROOMS DELUX

TOP CHOICE

HISTORIC HOTEL €€

Map p238 (📞501 4000; www.gerloczy.hu; V Gerlóczy utca 1; r €90; ⓂM1/2/3 Deák Ferenc tér; ❄✳@✿) A favourite new place to stay – we hesitate calling this tastefully appointed hostelry a 'guesthouse' – above a popular cafe and restaurant, it has 15 individually designed and well-proportioned rooms in muted shades of grey, green and red. The attention to detail is phenomenal (we love the frogs and dragonflies etched into the glass shower doors) and the features left over from the 1890s building's previous incarnation – winding wrought-iron staircase, domed stained-glass skylight – give weight to the place. Two rooms have balconies overlooking what must be the prettiest square in Budapest.

MAVERICK HOSTEL

HOSTEL €

Map p238 (📞267 3166; www.maverickhostel. com; V Ferenciek tere 2; dm €9-14, d €38-52; ⓂM3 Ferenciek tere; ❄@✿✲) If this is the way of the future for Budapest hotels, we're coming along for the ride. With some 19 movie-themed rooms, a more-than-comfortable common room and an up-to-date kitchen over three floors in a splendid old building, the Maverick is practically a cut-price mid-range hotel in the very heart of town. Only two rooms share a bathroom and the three dorms count between five and 10 beds (no bunks).

ZARA BOUTIQUE HOTEL

BOUTIQUE HOTEL €€

Map p238 (📞577 0700; www.zarahotels.com; V Só utca 6; s €95-150, d €100-165; 🚌47, 49; ❄✳✿✲) This boutique hotel with 74 small-ish but recently renovated rooms on seven floors is cobbled together from two buildings linked by an open-air corridor. Make sure you ask for a room facing Só utca (eg No 37) as half of the rooms look down onto an uninspiring courtyard. And if you're impressed with this Zara, wait till you see her sister, the Zara Continental Hotel (p164).

HOTEL ART

HOTEL €€

Map p238 (📞266 2166; www.hotelart.hu; V Királyi Pál utca 12; s €61-101, d €69-107; ⓂM3 Kálvin tér; 🅿❄✳✿✲) This Best Western property has art-deco touches (including a pink facade) in the public areas, a small fitness centre and sauna, and 32 upgraded guestrooms, including four apartments with separate sitting and sleeping areas.

GINKGO HOSTEL

HOSTEL €

Map p238 (📞266 6107; www.ginkgo.hu; V Szép utca 5; dm/d €14/40; ⓂM3 Ferenciek tere; ❄@✿) This very green (as in colour) hostel with between 20 and 30 beds (depending on the season) in seven big rooms is one of the best hostels in town and the font-of-all-knowledge managers keep it so clean you could eat off the floor. There are books to share, bikes to rent (1500Ft for 24 hours) and a positively enormous double giving on to quiet Reáltanoda utca.

MILLENNIUM COURT MARRIOTT EXECUTIVE APARTMENTS

SERVICED APARTMENTS €€€

Map p238 (📞235 1800; www.marriott.com/buder; V Pesti Barnabás utca 4; s €75-145, d €125-165; ⓂM3 Ferenciek tere; 🅿❄✳@✿) This rather flash place to stay in Pest has 108 serviced studio apartments measuring about 60 sq metres, one-bedroom apartments of 32 to 64 sq metres, and two-bedroom apartments of 57 to 87 sq metres. Stays of eight nights and more earn big discounts. Guests get to use facilities of the Budapest Marriott Hotel, a block to the northwest.

HOTEL ERZSÉBET

HOTEL €€

Map p238 (📞889 3700; www.danubiusgroup .com/erzsebet; V Károlyi Mihály utca 11-15; s €72-102, d €84-114; ⓂM2 Ferenciek tere; ❄✳@✲) One of Budapest's first independent hotels, the Erzsébet is in a very good location in the centre of the university district and within easy walking distance of the pubs and bars of Ráday utca. The 123 guestrooms – mostly twins and spread over eight floors – are small and dark, with generic hotel furniture but comfortable enough. Guests pay for wi-fi.

LEO PANZIÓ

GUESTHOUSE €€

Map p238 (📞266 9041; www.leopanzio.hu; V Kossuth Lajos utca 2/a, 2nd fl; s €49-79, d €76-99; ⓂM3 Ferenciek tere; ❄✳✿) This place with a lion (thus 'leo') theme would be a 'find' just on the strength of its central location, but when you factor in the low cost, it becomes the king of the jungle. A dozen of its 14 immaculate rooms look down on busy Kossuth Lajos utca, but they all have double-glazing and are quiet. Two rooms face a rather dark internal courtyard.

GREEN BRIDGE HOSTEL

HOSTEL €

Map p238 (📞266 6922; www.greenbridgehostel .com; V Molnár utca 22-24; dm €14-18, d €36; ⓂM3 Kálvin tér; ❄@✿) Few hostels truly stand out in terms of comfort, location and reception, but Green Bridge has it all – and in spades. There are doubles, triples and dorms with a maximum four beds in the seven rooms, with bunks nowhere to be seen. It's in a beautiful 19th-century building on a quiet street just one block in from the Danube.

COSMO FASHION HOTEL
BOUTIQUE HOTEL €€

Map p238 (☎799 0077; www.cosmohotel.hu; V Váci utca 77; r €80-120; ☐47, 49; P❂@☏) 'Fashion hotels' are all the rage in Budapest these days and a radical facelift has turned a rather ordinary Mellow Mood hostelry on southern Váci utca (enter from Havas utca 6) into just that. The 36 guestrooms are of a good size and stylish, with a lavender-and-black colour scheme and quirky geometric-patterned carpet. We're not keen about the cramped lobby but the attached Cosmo Rézangyal Bistro offers guests a 10% discount. Even more central is blue-and-chocolate sister hotel **La Prima Fashion Hotel** (Map p238; ☎799 0088; www .laprimahotel.hu; V Pesti Barnabás utca 6; ⓂM3 Ferenciek tere; P❂@☏), with 80 rooms, similar rates and an attached Italian restaurant.

RED BUS HOSTEL
HOSTEL €

Map p238 (☎266 0136; www.redbusbudapest.hu; V Semmelweiss utca 14, 1st fl; dm 3500-4000Ft, s 8500-9000Ft, d 9000-10,000Ft; ⓂM2 Astoria; ❂@☏) One of the very first independent hostels for travellers in Pest, Red Bus is a central and well-managed place, with four large and airy rooms with four to five beds, as well as five private rooms for up to three people. It's quiet with a lot of rules – a full 16 are listed in reception – so don't expect to party here. No lift.

🛏 Parliament & Around

🔝 FOUR SEASONS GRESHAM PALACE HOTEL
HOTEL €€€

Map p244 (☎268 6000; www.fourseasons.com/ budapest; V Széchenyi István tér 5-6; s €290-570, d €310-590, ste from €1100; ⓂM1 Vörösmarty tér; ☐16; P❂✳@☏⚘♨) This magnificent 179-room hotel was created out of the long-derelict art nouveau Gresham Palace (1906) and a lot of blood, sweat and tears. No expense was spared to piece back together the palace's Zsolnay tiles, mosaics and celebrated wrought-iron Peacock Gates leading north and south from the enormous

lobby, and the hotel is truly worthy of its name. The spa on the 5th floor, with a smallish infinity lap pool and iced towels at the ready, is among the most beautiful in the city.

HOTEL PARLAMENT
HOTEL €€

Map p244 (☎374 6000; www.parlament-hotel.hu; V Kálmán Imre utca 19; r €90-160; ⓂM2 Kossuth Lajos tér; P❂✳@☏) This minimalist delight in Lipótváros has 65 standard rooms done up in blacks, greys and reds. The nonallergenic white pine floors (there's carpet just in the hallways) are a plus, as is the self-service bar off the lobby, the dedicated ironing room, the adorable wellness centre with its own private dressing room, and the free tea and coffee at 5pm daily. Test your knowledge on the unique 'design wall' in the lobby with photographs and the names of famous Magyars etched in the glass.

GARIBALDI GUESTHOUSE & APARTMENTS
GUESTHOUSE, HOSTEL €

Map p244 (☎302 3456, 06-30 951 8763; www .garibaldiguesthouse.hu; V Garibaldi utca 5, 5th fl; dm €10-16, s €28-36, d €44-68; ⓂM2 Kossuth Lajos tér; @☏) This welcoming hostel-cum-guesthouse has five rooms with shared bathroom and kitchen in a flat just around the corner from Parliament. In the same building, the gregarious owner has at least a half-dozen apartments available on four floors; one large one has a balcony overlooking Garibaldi utca. There's hostel accommodation, too, in four rooms with five to six beds.

CENTRAL BACKPACK KING
HOSTEL €

Map p244 (☎06-30 200 7184; www.centralbpk .hu; V Október 6 utca 15, 1st fl; dm €15-19, d €54-58; ⓂM1/2/3 Deák Ferenc tér; ☐15, 115; ❂@☏) This upbeat place in the heart of the Inner Town has rooms with between seven and nine dorm beds on one floor and doubles, triples and quads on another. There's a small but scrupulously clean kitchen, a large, bright common room, and views across Október 6 utca to the lovely 1910 apartment block at No 16-18, where your humble author usually stays when in town.

COTTON HOUSE
HOTEL €€

Map p244 (☎354 2600; www.cottonhouse.hu; VI Jókai utca 26; r €55-99; ☐4, 6; ❂✳@☏) This 22-room place has a jazz/speakeasy theme that gets a bit tired after a while (though the old radios and vintage telephones do actually work). Prices vary widely depending on the season and rooms have either a shower, tub or jacuzzi.

MEDOSZ HOTEL   HOTEL €€
Map p244 (☑374 3000; www.medoszhotel.hu; VI Jókai tér 9; s €49-59, d €59-69, ste €89-100; Ⓜ M1 Oktogon; Ⓟ😊🛜📶) One of the most central cheap hotels in Pest, the Medosz is just opposite the restaurants and bars of Liszt Ferenc tér. Two-thirds of the 68 rooms have recently been refitted and boast parquet floors, double-glazing and small but up-to-the-minute bathrooms. The best rooms (eg 704) are in the main block, not in the labyrinthine wings.

🏠 HOME-MADE HOSTEL   HOSTEL €
Map p244 (☑302 2103; www.homemadehostel. com; VI Teréz körút 22, 1st fl; dm €8-17, d €40-58; Ⓜ M1 Oktogon; 😊@📶) This homey, extremely welcoming hostel with 20 beds in four rooms is truly unique, with recycled tables hanging upside down from the ceiling and old valises under the beds serving as lockers. The whole idea was to use forgotten objects from old Budapest homes in a new way. There's a warmth to this place that will make you want to stay forever, and the old-style kitchen is museum-quality.

BUDAPEST ART HOSTEL   HOSTEL €
Map p244 (☑302 3739; www.arthostel.hu; VI Podmaniczky utca 19; dm €10-14, d €38-42; Ⓜ M3 Nyugati pályaudvar; 😊@📶) Among the most chilled and tastefully decorated of Budapest's hostels, the Art Hostel is small, with just two dorms (four to six beds), a room for two and another with loft sleeping for three. The kitchen is especially well equipped and Nyugati metro station is in sight.

🛏 Margaret Island & Northern Pest

NH BUDAPEST   HOTEL €€
Map p248 (☑814 0000; www.nh-hotels.com; XIII Vígszínház utca 3; r €74-130; �̥4, 6; Ⓟ😊❄@📶🏊) There are 160 rooms spread out over this eight-floor purpose-built hotel, and two or three rooms on each floor have a balcony. We especially like the hotel's location behind the Comedy Theatre, the minimalist but welcoming and very bright atrium lobby, and the flash fitness centre on the 8th floor.

BOAT HOTEL FORTUNA   HOTEL, HOSTEL €€
Map p248 (☑288 8100; www.fortunahajo.hu; XIII Szent István Park, Pesti alsó rakpart; r with bathroom €40-70, with washbasin €24-55; 🚌76; 😊❄@📶🏊) Sleeping on a one-time river ferry anchored in the Danube may not be everyone's idea of a good time, but it's a unique experience. This 'boatel' has 42 single and double air-conditioned rooms with shower and toilet at water level. Below deck, an additional 14 rooms with one, two or three beds and washbasin are not unlike old-fashioned hostel accommodation.

AVENTURA HOSTEL   HOSTEL €
Map p248 (☑239 0782; www.aventurahostel .com; XIII Visegrádi utca 12, 1st fl; dm €12-21, d €36-56, apt €50-66; Ⓜ M3 Nyugati pályaudvar; 🚌4, 6; 😊@📶) This has got to be the most chilled hostel in Budapest. Run by two affable ladies, it has four themed rooms (India, Japan, Africa and – our favourite – Space) and is slightly away from the action in Újlipótváros but easily accessible by public transport. We love the colours and fabrics, the in-house massage, and the dorms with loft sleeping for five to eight.

PETER'S APARTMENTS   SERVICED APARTMENTS €
Map p248 (☑06-30 520 0400; www.peters.hu; XIII Victor Hugó utca 25-27; s/d from €40/45; Ⓜ M3 Lehel tér; 🚌15, 76, 115; ❄@📶) This budget place in Pest offers 15 studio apartments of approximately 20 sq metres with kitchenettes in a basic but clean building at some rock-bottom prices. The more expensive units have air-con and balconies; all have TV. Prices are negotiable, especially during the low season (November to mid-March) and at weekends.

DANUBIUS GRAND HOTEL MARGITSZIGET   HOTEL €€€
Map p248 (☑889 4700; www.danubiushotels .com; XIII Margitsziget; s €86-126, d €116-156, ste €186-226; 🚌26; Ⓟ😊❄🛜🏊) Constructed in the late 19th century, this comfortable (but not grand) and tranquil hotel has 164 rooms that boast all the mod cons. It's connected to the Danubius Thermal Hotel Margitsziget via a heated underground corridor, and the cost of taking the waters is included in the hotel rate. Guests pay for wi-fi.

🛏 Erzsébetváros & the Jewish Quarter

TOP CHOICE ZARA CONTINENTAL HOTEL
HOTEL €€€

Map p250 (📞815 1000; www.continental hotelbudapest.com; VII Dohány utca 42-44; r €90-145, ste from €175; MM2 Blaha Lujza tér; 🏠4, 6; 🛏73; P✤❄@🛜🏊🐾) At long last someone has taken the decrepit Hungária Fürdő (Hungária Bath), given it the kiss of life and brought it into the 21st century. It's a humdinger of a hotel, with 272 large and beautifully furnished rooms (though shades of brown, the Zara signature colour, predominate) and a huge atrium lobby retaining some of the original 19th-century building's features. But best of all are the wellness centre on the top floor and the panoramic garden with swimming pool. This is Budapest from a different vantage point and you'll want a look-in too.

CORINTHIA HOTEL BUDAPEST
HOTEL €€€

Map p250 (📞479 4000; www.corinthia.hu; VII Erzsébet körút 43-49; r €210-450, ste from €550; P✤❄@🛜🏊🐾) Decades in the remaking, the one-time Royal Hotel on the Big Ring Rd is now a very grand 440-room five-star hotel. Its lobby – a double atrium with massive marble staircase – is among the most impressive in the capital, while the restored Royal Spa dating back to 1886 is now as modern as tomorrow with a 15m-long pool and a dozen massage and treatment rooms.

SOHO HOTEL
BOUTIQUE HOTEL €€

Map p250 (📞872 8292; www.sohohotel.hu; VII Dohány utca 64; s €79-125, d €89-135, ste €169-199; MM2 Blaha Lujza tér; 🏠4, 6; P✤❄@🐾) This delightfully stylish boutique hotel with 68 rooms and six suites stands opposite the New York Palace, and we know which one feels more like the Big Apple. We adore the lobby bar in eye-popping reds, blues and lime greens, nonallergenic rooms with bamboo matting on the walls and parquet floors, and the music/film theme throughout (check out the portraits of Bono, George Michael and – sigh – Marilyn).

SPINOZA APARTMENTS
SERVICED APARTMENTS €

Map p250 (📞06-30 491 7069; www.spinoza.hu; VII Dob utca 15; studios €30-40, 2-/3-room apt from €60/80; 🏠47, 49) These four apartments, which rose above a bakery when the building went up in 1903 but now sit contentedly above the Spinoza Café (p120) and its wonderful little theatre, offer some of the best value for money in central Pest. There's a three-room apartment sleeping up to eight on the 1st floor and apartments with one and two rooms on the 2nd, but no lift. All have modern kitchens.

TOP CHOICE CONNECTION GUEST HOUSE
HOTEL €

Map p250 (📞267 7104; www.connectionguest house.com; VII Király utca 41, 1st fl; s €30-45, d €45-60; MM1 Opera; ❄@🛜🐾) It's all change at this very central gay guesthouse above a leafy courtyard that was recently stripped naked, scrubbed clean and then dressed to the nines. Pretty girl. It looks better than ever and attracts a young crowd due to its proximity to all the queer nightlife venues. Two of the nine rooms share a bathroom off the hallway and face partially pedestrianised Király utca.

HOTEL BAROSS
HOTEL €€

Map p250 (📞461 3010; www.barosshotel.hu; VII Baross tér 15; s €60-82, d €74-98; MM2 Keleti pályaudvar; ❄@🛜🐾) Another Mellow Mood property, the Baross is a comfortable, 51-room caravanserai conveniently located directly opposite Keleti train station. The very blue inner courtyard is a delight, and reception, which is on the 5th floor, is clean and bright, with a dramatic central staircase.

10 BEDS
HOSTEL €

Map p250 (📞06-20 933 5965; adrianzador@hot mail.com; VII Erzsébet körút 15, 3rd fl; dm 3000Ft; 🏠4, 6) It's misnamed – the place really has 14 beds in three rooms. But that's about the only thing wrong with this laid-back hostel with great kitchen, free use of a washing machine and your own set of keys. Ask nicely and you might get a key to the lift too.

BIG FISH HOSTEL
HOTEL €

Map p250 (📞06-70 302 2432; www.bigfishbuda pest.hu; VII Kertész utca 20; dm €12-18; r & apt per person €10-30; MM2 Blaha Lujza tér; 🏠4, 6; ❄@🛜) If you like your music, you'll want to stay in this not-so-small pond where visiting bands lay their weary heads and the sound-engineer owner is a nightlife encyclopedia. There are four rooms – two dorms with eight to 10 beds, and two private rooms for two or three people – plus a separate apartment. Excellent kitchen too.

MARCO POLO HOSTEL   HOSTEL €

Map p250 (☎413 2555; www.marcopolohostel
.com; VII Nyár utca 6; dm 3000-4500Ft; s 9000-
14,000Ft, d 12,000-17,200Ft; Ⓜ M2 Blaha Lujza
tér; ☖@☎) The Mellow Mood Group's very
central flagship hostel is a swish, powder-
blue, 47-room place with TVs in all the
rooms (except the dorms) and a lovely
courtyard. Even the five spotless dorms
are 'private', with the dozen beds separated
by lockers and curtains. The basement bar
rages 24 hours a day.

CARMEN MINI HOTEL   GUESTHOUSE €

Map p250 (☎352 0798; carmen@t-online.hu;
VII Károly körút 5/b, 2nd fl; s €40-50, d €45-60;
Ⓜ M1/2/3 Deák Ferenc tér; ☖@☎☀) With nine
rooms, the Carmen Mini Hotel is about the
nearest you'll find to a rock-bottom B&B in
central Pest. It's very close to Deák Ferenc
tér and convenient to all forms of transport,
but, frankly, it's none too salubrious. Expect
no frills, lots of spills – and you won't be
disappointed.

ANDRÁSSY HOTEL   HOTEL €€€

Map p250 (☎462 2100; www.andrassyhotel.com;
VI Andrássy út 111; r €100-235, ste from €245;
Ⓜ M1 Bajza utca; Ⓟ☖✳@☎☀) This stunning five-star hotel just off leafy Andrássy
út (enter from Munkácsy Mihály utca 5-7)
has 68 tastefully decorated rooms (almost
half of which have balconies) in a heritage-
listed building. The use of etched glass and
mirrors as well as wrought iron in many
is inspired. The ground-floor restaurant,
Baraka (p122), receives consistently good
reviews.

RESIDENCE IZABELLA   SERVICED APARTMENTS €€€

Map p250 (☎475 5900; www.residence-izabella
.com; VI Izabella utca 61; apt 1-bedroom €159-
179, 2-bedroom €249-269; Ⓜ M1 Vörösmarty
utca; ☐73, 76; Ⓟ☖✳@☎☀) This fabulous
conversion of a 19th-century Eclectic building has 38 apartments measuring between
45 and 97 sq metres just off swanky
Andrássy út. The apartments surround
a delightful and very tranquil central
courtyard garden and the decor mixes
materials such as wood, terracotta and
basketry to great effect.

RADIO INN   GUESTHOUSE €€

Map p250 (☎342 8347; www.radioinn.hu; VI
Benczúr utca 19; s/d €48/70, apt from €80; Ⓜ M1
Bajza utca; ☖@☎) Just off leafy Andrássy út,
this place is a real find, with 23 large one-

bedroom apartments with bathroom and
kitchen, 10 with two bedrooms, and two
with three bedrooms measuring between
44 and 60 sq metres, all spread over five
floors. The garden courtyard is a delight;
try to get a room with a small balcony.

HOTEL BENCZÚR   HOTEL €€

Map p250 (☎479 5662; www.hotelbenczur.hu; VI
Benczúr utca 35; s €46-74, d €60-86; Ⓜ M1 Bajza
utca; Ⓟ☖✳@☎☀) This somewhat faded
place done up in creams and oranges has
161 serviceable rooms over seven floors,
of which about 65 have been renovated in
recent years. Some of these look down on
a leafy garden. It's got a great location: the
hotel is just minutes away from Andrássy
út, Heroes' Square and City Park.

KAPITAL INN   B&B €€

Map p250 (☎06-30 931 1023; www.kapitalinn
.com; VI Aradi utca 30, 4 fl; r €79-125; Ⓜ M1
Vörösmarty utca; ☐4, 6; ☖✳@☎☀) This gay-
owned and -operated B&B with four rooms
offers quite luxurious accommodation up
under the stars; the 56-sq-metre terrace
has to be seen to be believed. Guests get
to use a little office with its own laptop,
the breakfast room and bar has a fridge
stocked with goodies that can be raided
at any time, and the entrance to the 1893
building is a stucco masterpiece. Alas,
there's no lift and the cheaper pair of rooms
share a bathroom.

UNITY HOSTEL   HOSTEL €

Map p250 (☎413 7377; www.unityhostel.com; VI
Király utca 60, 3rd fl; dm €12-16, s/d from €29/36;
☐4, 6; ☖@☎☀) This hostel's location in
the heart of party town would be draw
enough, but add to that a roof terrace
with breathtaking views of the Ferenc
Liszt Music Academy, ceiling fans to cool
you down and a resident bearded collie to
grab your attention and you have a winner.
There are 24 beds in five rooms over two
levels.

🛏 Southern Pest

TOP CHOICE ▶ **BRÓDY HOUSE**   HISTORIC HOTEL €€

Map p242 (☎266 1211; www.brodyhouse.com;
VIII Bródy Sándor utca 10; r €55-100; Ⓜ M3 Kálvin
tér; ☐47, 49; ☖✳@☎) Offering retro chic
at its hippest, this erstwhile residence of
the prime minister when parliament sat
next door at No 8 (as seen on the back of

the 20,000Ft note) has been refurbished but not altered substantially, with antique furnishings and modern art blending seamlessly in its eight guestrooms dedicated to local artists. The public rooms are light, breezy and enormous; one even has a piano. The only drawback is the lack of a lift.

HOTEL PALAZZO ZICHY HISTORIC HOTEL €€

Map p242 (☑235 4000; www.hotel-palazzo-zichy .hu; VIII Lőrinc pap tér 2; r €90-180, ste €120-210; Ⓜ️M3 Ferenc körút; 🛏4, 6; P➘✳@🛜🛁) No doubt members of the aristocratic Zichy family would be pleased to see their one-time residence (dating from the end of the 19th century) spruced up and put to such good use. The 'palace' is now a fabulous hotel looking out onto a lovely quiet square. The 80 up-to-the-minute guestrooms are beautifully designed and comfortable, with wooden floors, red glass-topped desks and enormous shower heads. The fitness room and sauna are in the cellar crypt, and the atrium breakfast room was once a central courtyard.

CASA DE LA MUSICA HOSTEL €

Map p242 (☑06-70 373 7330; www.casadelamu sicahostel.com; VIII Vas utca 16; dm €9-12, s/d €20/26; 🛏4, 6; ➘@🛜🛁) This very cool place above a Latin American cultural centre and the ever-popular Roham (p136) music pub has 86 beds on two levels, including dorm rooms with four to 12 beds (one with 10 beds is for women only) and seven twins and doubles. There's a great kitchen and common room, the psychedelic-socialist murals throughout are eye-catching, and music is never far away. And there's even a pool in the courtyard. It's small and plastic but full of water. It's a pool, trust us.

HOTEL ANNA HOTEL €

Map p242 (☑327 2000; www.annahotel.hu; VIII Gyulai Pál utca 14; s/d/ste €39/45/82; Ⓜ️M2 Blaha Lujza tér; 🛏7, 78; ➘@) Run by the same people who own Fülemüle (p133) across the street, Anna has 42 fairly basic rooms but feels twice that size as they are strewn over three floors of two 18th-century buildings surrounding an enormous courtyard and garden. The rooms are quieter than the grave, the location is great and the prices can't be beat.

ATLAS CITY HOTEL HOTEL €€

Map p242 (☑299 0256; www.atlashotel.hu; VIII Népszínház utca 39-41; s €45-55, d €55-65; 🛏28, 37; P➘✳@🛜🛁) This enormous place spread over eight floors in less-than-salubrious district VIII has 136 standard (though comfortable) and renovated singles, doubles, triples and quads as well as 36 superior doubles, four of them with jacuzzis. It is said that you'll always find a room at the Atlas, which may (or may not) be a good recommendation.

HOTEL KÁLVIN HOUSE HOSTEL €€

Map p242 (☑216 4365; www.kalvinhouse.hu; IX Gönczy Pál utca 6; s €40-70, d €50-90, ste €70-100; Ⓜ️M3 Kálvin tér; 🛏47, 49; ➘@🛜🛁) If you've ever wondered what it's like to live in one of those big old apartment blocks along Budapest's ring roads, then stay at Kálvin House, with 36 rooms over four floors next to the Nagycsarnok (Great Market). Rooms have original wooden floors, enormously high ceilings (check out the one in room 109) and vintage furniture dating to the early 20th century. The rooms facing the inner courtyard are cooler in summer.

TOP CHOICE KM SAGA GUEST RESIDENCE GUESTHOUSE €€

Map p242 (☑217 1934; www.km-saga.hu; IX Lónyay utca 17, 3rd fl; s €25-63, d €28-80; Ⓜ️M3 Kálvin tér; 🛏15, 115; 🛏47, 49; ✳@🛜) This unique place has five themed rooms, an eclectic mix of 19th-century furnishings, and hospitable, multilingual Hungarian-American owner Shandor. It's essentially a gay B&B, but everyone is welcome. Two rooms share a bathroom.

MARIA & ISTVÁN B&B €

Map p242 (☑216 0768, 06-20 931 2223; www .mariaistvan.hu; IX Ferenc körút 39, 4th fl; s €20-22, d €32-34, apt for 2/3/4 from €40/54/68; Ⓜ️M3 Ferenc körút; 🛏4, 6; P➘) This Italian-Hungarian couple must be doing something right; they've been welcoming guests to their bright and spotless flat for decades and no one has a bad word to say about it. Choose between two twin rooms here (use of kitchen included) or a flat just two metro stops away. It's like staying with friends.

HOTEL SISSI HOTEL €€

Map p242 (215 0082; www.hotelsissi-budapest
.com; IX Angyal utca 33; s €60-100, d €70-120,
ste €100-140; M3 Ferenc körút; P❄@⦿)
Named in honour of Elizabeth, the Habsburg empress, Hungarian queen and
consort of Franz Joseph much beloved by
Hungarians, the Hotel Sissi is decorated in
a minimalist-cum-elegant sort of style, and
the 44 guestrooms spread over six floors are
of a good size. Some rooms look onto a back
garden.

CORVIN HOTEL HOTEL €€

Map p242 (218 6566; www.corvinhotelbuda
pest.hu; IX Angyal utca 31; s €50-85, d €60-99, apt
€80-129; M3 Ferenc körút; P❄@⦿) Hard
by the Danube, this purpose-built hotel in
up-and-coming Ferencváros has 47 very
comfortable rooms with all the mod cons
and secure parking in a covered garage.
The bright and airy breakfast room is a
bonus.

HOTEL THOMAS HOTEL €€

Map p242 (218 5505; www.hotelthomas.eu; IX
Liliom utca 44; s €40-55, d €55-75; M3 Ferenc
körút; P❄@⦿) A brightly coloured
place, the Thomas has 43 rooms that are a
real bargain for its central location. Some
rooms have balconies looking onto an inner
courtyard. The goofy-looking kid in the
logo is the owner as a young 'un.

FORTUNA HOTEL HOTEL, HOSTEL €

Map p242 (215 0660; www.fortunahotel.hu;
IX Gyáli út 3/b; dm/s/d €15/35/40; M3
Nagyvárad tér; 24; P❄@⦿) With 30
rooms (including dorms with four or five
beds) this place is not in the best part of
Budapest, but it's quiet and superclean and
the huge Taiwan (p134) restaurant is at your
feet. Reception (and all the guestrooms, for
that matter) are on the 2nd floor but there's
a lift.

KINIZSI HOSTEL HOSTEL €

Map p242 (787 4321, 06-20 776 2264; www
.hostels.hu; IX Kinizsi utca 2-6; dm/s/d
€12/25/30; ☼Jul & Aug; M3 Ferenc körút; ⦿)
This nothing-special summer-only hostel in
Pest managed by the Mellow Mood Group
has basic rooms with two to five beds (total
124 beds) in a modern, six-storey student
residence close to the Danube and the IX
Ráday utca nightlife strip.

City Park & Beyond

DOMINIK PANZIÓ GUESTHOUSE €

Map p254 (460 9428; www.dominikpanzio.hu;
XIV Cházár András utca 3; s/d €26/35; 7, 173;
P@⦿) Just off Thököly út, beside a large
church, Dominik Panzió is on a leafy street
lined with 19th-century villas and just two
stops northeast of Keleti train station by
bus. The 36 rooms are simple but clean and
come with shared bathroom. There is a five-
person apartment available (from €70).

HOTEL GÓLIÁT HOTEL €

off Map p254 (350 1456; www.gerandhotels.hu;
XIII Kerekes utca 12-20; s/d 6300/7600Ft; 32;
14; P❄@) This very basic but spot-
lessly clean hotel in Angyalföld northeast
of the Belváros and the Lehel market has
135 basic rooms with between one and four
beds. There are washbasins in the rooms,
and showers and toilets in the corridor.

HOTEL FLANDRIA HOTEL €

off Map p254 (350 3181; www.hotelflan
dria.hu; XIII Szegedi út 27; s/d with washbasin
7100/7800Ft, with shower 10,200/12,400Ft; 4;
32; P⦿) The Flandria is a classic example
of a former workers' hostel that has metamorphosed into a budget hotel. Don't expect anything within a couple of light years
of luxury, but the 125 guestrooms, which
have from one to four beds, TV and refriger-
ator, are clean, serviceable and very cheap.

Understand Budapest

Budapest Today

There was a moment in 2010 when the Hungarian economy rebounded with a boost from exports, and observers thought just maybe Budapesters might stop whingeing. But people here 'take their pleasure sadly', a bizarre arrangement there's even a phrase for, and it was pointed out that unemployment remains high (more than 10%), the city is still torn apart by Metro 4 construction and mass protests at every public holiday, and everyone holds a mortgage in Swiss francs, which now cost a fortune in forint to repay.

Best on Film

Moszkva tér (Moscow Square; 2001) Comic tale of Buda teenage boys in 1989 oblivious to the events taking place around them.

Ein Lied von Liebe und Tod (Gloomy Sunday; 1999) German romantic drama set in a Budapest restaurant just before the Nazi invasion.

Children of Glory (Szabadság, Szerelem; 2006) The 1956 Uprising in Budapest through the eyes of a player on the Olympic water polo team.

Zimmer Feri (1998) Set on Lake Balaton; a young practical joker takes on a bunch of loud German tourists.

Best in Print

Prague (Arthur Phillips; 2002) Young expat American who wants to live in more bohemian Prague focuses on life in Budapest just after the changes in 1989.

Under the Frog (Tibor Fischer; 2001) Amusing account of two members of Hungary's elite national basketball team in Budapest from WWII to 1956.

The Paul Street Boys (Ferenc Molnár; 1906) Satirical turn-of-the-century novel about boys growing up in the tough Józsefváros district.

The Invisible Bridge (Julie Orringer; 2010) Epic saga of a Hungarian-Jewish family during WWII.

Change of Guard Part I

The big news from Budapest: after two decades and five terms of office for SZDSZ (Alliance of Free Democrats) liberal Gábor Demszky, the electorate voted in a new mayor in 2010, only its second since the end of communism in 1989. He's István Tarlós, Fidesz (Federation of Young Democrats) chairman and FOV – 'friend of Viktor' (Orbán, head of the Fidesz-led coalition government that won national elections the same year and brought him back as prime minister after eight years in opposition). As his final act, Demszky made the Dalai Lama – he of the 'you-only-live-twice' school – an honorary citizen of Budapest. Oh dear. There goes any business with China for a while.

Change of Guard Part II

Orbán has moved quickly to lay his scent. He has changed the constitution – Hungary is no longer 'the republic of'. He has tried to get criminal charges brought against his predecessor, Ferenc Gyurcsány. He has passed a controversial media law and been read the riot act for that in public by MEP Daniel Cohn-Bendit known as 'Danny the Red' for his revolutionary activities in Paris in 1968 – as Hungary took control of the EU presidency at the start of 2011. To add to his misery, the right-wing nationalist Jobbik party ('Jobbik' is a kind of pun on the word 'right') garnered over 16% of the vote in the national elections and its uniformed militia wing, Magyar Gárda (Hungarian Guard), has been accused of bullying and intimidating Roma people in villages of the northeast. And those rumours about Orbán's Roma ancestry just won't go away. Oh double dear.

Name-Change Game

Tarlós too has been leaving his mark. While there is no cash to get Demszky-style legacy projects like Lágymányosi – ooops, Rákóczi – Bridge up and running, he's begun playing the name-change game. It's been nothing like the one played after April 1989, when names were changed – some 400 in fact – with a determination that some people felt was almost obsessive. But the more than two dozen involved this time around are highly visible. Ferihegy International Airport is now Ferenc Liszt International Airport; II Moszkva tér (Moscow Square; including the metro stop) becomes Széll Kálmán tér; V Roosevelt tér is Széchenyi István tér; VIII Köztársaság tér (Republic Sq) is now known as János Pál pápa tér (Pope John Paul II Sq); Lágymányosi Bridge becomes Rákóczi Bridge; and a nameless little park on the Buda side of Margaret Bridge has become Elvis Presley tér. We are not making this up. Apparently the King dedicated a spiritual song called 'Peace in the Valley' he sang on national TV in the US in January 1957 to the people of Hungary and asked viewers to send money for the refugees in Austria. Who said Magyars don't have elephantine memories?

Smoke-Free at Last

And in a move that shocked even those who supported the legislation, Hungary outlawed indoor smoking in all public places, including restaurants, bars and clubs, from the start of 2012 (though there was a three-month grace period to the start of April). Offenders now face a fine of 30,000Ft. Who would have thought it possible in this nation of butt fiends?

Moving Forward

Despite what some locals might suggest, Budapest is moving along just fine, thank you. The clubs – especially the outdoor 'garden clubs' – heave throughout the week, there's often a queue at the Gellért and Rudas Baths, and you won't get a table at the Ruszwurm on Castle Hill in a month of Sundays. Another restaurant in Belváros has been awarded a Michelin star, and the city looks great, with newly pedestrianised streets planted with lime trees and nonpolluting lighting installed. A long, long time ago, the man they call 'the greatest Hungarian', István Széchenyi, wrote: 'Many people think that Hungary was. I like to believe that she will be!' Wake up, *magyar barátokom* (my Hungarian friends), and smell the coffee. You've arrived.

if Budapest were 100 people

92 would be Magyar (Hungarian)
3 would be Roma
5 would be other

belief systems
(% of population)

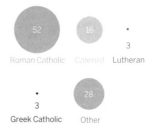

52 Roman Catholic
16 Calvinist
3 Lutheran
3 Greek Catholic
28 Other

population per sq km

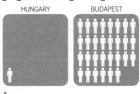

HUNGARY   BUDAPEST

≈ 110 people

History

Strictly speaking, the story of Budapest begins only in 1873 when hilly, residential Buda and historic Óbuda on the western bank of the Danube River merged with flat, industrial Pest on the eastern side to form what at first was called Pest-Buda. But like everything here, it's not that simple; a lot more had taken place before the late 19th century.

EARLY INHABITANTS

The Carpathian Basin, in which Hungary lies, has been populated for at least half a million years. But the earliest evidence of human settlement around Budapest is the remains of a Neanderthal hunting camp in a gorge on the Érd plateau to the southwest dating back 50,000 years. The first *permanent* settlement in this area – on the Buda side near the Danube – dates from between 4600 and 3900 BC. Remains from that culture include bone utensils, fishing nets and even a primitive loom, and have been unearthed as far north as Békásmegyer and south at Nagytétény.

In about 2000 BC fierce Indo-European tribes from the Balkan Peninsula reached as far as the Carpathian Basin in horse-drawn carts, bringing bows and arrows and copper tools. After the introduction of more durable bronze, forts were built and a military elite developed.

Over the next millennium, invaders from the west (Illyrians and Thracians) and the east (Scythians) brought iron, but that metal was not in common use until the Celts arrived in the early 3rd century BC. They also introduced glass and crafted some of the fine gold and silver jewellery at the Hungarian National Museum (p129; Room 5, 1st floor).

THE ROMAN CONQUEST

In about 35 BC the Romans conquered the area west and south of the Danube River. By AD 10 they had established Pannonia province, which was later divided into Upper (Superior) and Lower (Inferior). The Romans brought writing, viticulture, stone architecture and Christianity. At the end of the 1st century AD the Romans established Aquincum (p73), a key military garrison and trading settlement along the Danube in

TIMELINE	4600–3900 BC	AD 106	Late 430s
	The first permanent settlement is established on the Buda side of the Danube; remains uncovered in the area include bone utensils, fishing nets and a primitive loom.	Roman Aquincum in today's Óbuda becomes the administrative seat of the province of Pannonia Inferior and a fully fledged colony less than a century later.	Aquincum offers little protection to the civilian population when Huns burn the colony to the ground, forcing the Romans and other settlers to flee.

today's Óbuda that would become the administrative seat of Pannonia Inferior in AD 106. A fortress, whose remains are still visible, was built at Contra Aquincum (p85) in what is now V Március 15 tér in Pest.

THE GREAT MIGRATIONS

The first of the so-called Great Migrations of nomadic peoples from Asia reached the eastern outposts of the Roman Empire in Dacia (now Romania) early in the 3rd century AD. Within two centuries the Romans were forced by the Huns, whose short-lived empire was established by Attila, to flee Aquincum.

After the death of Attila in 453, other Germanic tribes occupied the region for the next century and a half until the Avars, a powerful Turkic people, gained control of the Carpathian Basin in the late 6th century and established their main base at the northern end of Csepel Island. They in turn were subdued by Charlemagne in the early 8th century, and the area around Budapest and the Danube Bend was incorporated into the Frankish empire.

THE MAGYARS

The origin of the Magyars – as the Hungarians call themselves – is a complicated subject, not helped by the similarity (in English and some other languages) of the words 'Hun' and 'Hungary', which are *not* related. The Magyars belong to the Finno-Ugric group of peoples, who inhabited the forests somewhere between the middle Volga River and the Ural Mountains in western Siberia as early as 4000 BC.

By about 2000 BC, population growth forced the Finnish-Estonian branch to move west, ultimately reaching the Baltic Sea. The Ugrians moved from the southeastern slopes of the Urals into the region's valleys, and switched from hunting and fishing to farming and raising livestock, especially horses. Their equestrian skills proved useful half a millennium later when drought forced them north onto the steppes.

On the grasslands, the Ugrians turned to nomadic herding. After 500 BC, a group moved west to Bashkiria area in Central Asia. Here, living among Persians and Bulgars, they began referring to themselves as Magyars (from the Finno-Ugric words *mon,* to speak and *er,* man).

After several centuries, another group split away and moved south to the Don River under the control of the Turkic Khazars. Here they lived under a tribal alliance called *onogur* ('10 peoples'), thought to be the origin of the word 'Hungary'. The Magyars' last migration before the so-called conquest *(honfoglalás)* of the Carpathian Basin brought

The mystery surrounding the origins of the Magyars have led to some unusual theories. When asked whether he believed extraterrestrial beings existed, Italian-American Nobel Prize–winning physicist Enrico Fermi (1901–54) replied: 'Of course they do (and) they are already here among us. They are called Hungarians.'

If you'd like to learn more about the nomadic Magyars, their history, civilisation and/or art, go to http://ancientmagyarworld.tripod.com, which also offers a number of useful and interesting links.

Early 8th century	896–98	955	1000
Charlemagne subdues the Avars, a powerful Turkic people who occupied the Carpathian Basin since the late 6th century; the Budapest area is incorporated into the Frankish empire.	Nomadic Magyar tribes set up camp in the Carpathian Basin, with five of the seven original tribes settling in the area that is now Budapest.	Hungarian raids outside the Carpathian Basin as far as Germany, Italy and Spain are stopped for good by German king Otto I at the battle of Augsburg.	Stephen (István in Hungarian) is crowned 'Christian King' of Hungary on Christmas Day with a crown sent from Rome by Pope Sylvester II.

them to what modern Hungarians call the Etelköz, the region between the Dnieper and lower Danube rivers and north of the Black Sea.

THE CONQUEST OF THE CARPATHIAN BASIN

The Magyars were exceedingly skilled at riding and shooting and a common Christian prayer during medieval times was 'Save us, O Lord, from the arrows of the Hungarians.'

In about 895 and under attack seven Magyar tribes in the Etelköz settlements struck out for the Carpathian Basin under the leadership of Árpád, the chief military commander *(gyula)*. They probably crossed the Verecke Pass in today's Ukraine sometime between 896 and 898.

The two principal leaders of the tribes made their bases in Buda-pest. Árpád established his seat on Csepel while his brother Kurszán, the chief *táltos* (shaman), based himself in Óbuda. On Kurszán's death, Árpád took all power for himself and moved his seat to Óbuda; at this time Buda and Pest were no more than small villages.

The Magyars had met almost no resistance in the Carpathian Basin. Being highly skilled at riding and shooting, they plundered and pillaged in all directions, taking slaves and amassing booty. Their raids took them as far as Germany, Italy and Spain, but in 955 they were stopped in their tracks by the German king Otto I at the battle of Augsburg.

The ancient Magyars were strong believers in magic and celestial intervention, and the shaman *(táltos)* enjoyed an elevated position in their society. Certain animals were totemic, and none was more sacred than the *turul,* a hawklike bird that supposedly begat the ancestors of Árpád, the nation's first military leader.

This and subsequent defeats forced them to form an alliance with the Holy Roman Empire. In 973 Prince Géza, Árpád's great-grandson, asked the Emperor Otto II to send Catholic missionaries to Hungary. Géza was baptised in his capital city, Esztergom, 46km upriver from Budapest, as was his son Vajk, who took the Christian name Stephen (István in Hungarian). When Géza died, Stephen ruled as prince, but on Christmas Day in the year 1000 he was crowned 'Christian King' Stephen I.

KING STEPHEN I

Stephen set about consolidating royal authority by expropriating the land of the clan chieftains and establishing a system of counties *(megyék)* protected by castles *(várak)*. Shrewdly, he transferred much land to loyal (mostly German) knights, and the crown began minting coins.

The king sought the support of the Church and, to hasten the conversion of the populace, ordered one in every 10 villages to build a church. He also established 10 episcopates. By the time of Stephen's death in 1038, Hungary was a nascent Christian nation, increasingly westward-looking and multiethnic.

1083

King Stephen is canonised as St Stephen by Pope Victor III in Rome, and 20 August is declared his feast day.

1220

The Gothic style of architecture extends into Hungary from northern France, superseding the heavier Romanesque style.

MARTIN MOOS / LONELY PLANET IMAGES ©

Statue of St Stephen on Castle Hill

THE HOUSE OF ÁRPÁD

The next two and a half centuries – the lifespan of the Árpád dynasty – would test the new kingdom to the limit. The period was marked by dynastic intrigues and relentless struggles among pretenders to the throne, which weakened the young nation's defences against its more powerful neighbours.

Tension rose outside the borders when the Byzantine emperor made a grab for Hungary's provinces in Dalmatia and Croatia, which it had acquired by the early 12th century and, together with Slovakia and Transylvania, were deemed the 'crown lands of St Stephen'. He was stopped by Béla III (r 1172–96), who had a permanent residence built at Esztergom but was headquartered at Óbuda. Béla's son Andrew II (András; r 1205–35), however, weakened the crown when he gave in to local barons' demands for more land in order to fund his crusades. This led to the Golden Bull, a kind of Magna Carta signed in 1222, which limited some of the king's powers in favour of the nobility, recognised the 'Hungarian nation' and allowed for a diet, or assembly, of nobles to meet regularly in Pest.

Weakened by the charter, his successor Béla IV (r 1235–70) feared Mongol expansion but realised he could not count on local help and brought in Germans and Slovaks. But his efforts were in vain. In March 1241 the Mongols, who had raced through the country, attacked the city from every direction. By January 1242 Pest and Óbuda had been burned to the ground and some 100,000 people killed.

To rebuild the royal capital, Béla again encouraged Germans and Turkic Cuman (Hungarian: Kun) tribes displaced by the Mongols in the east to settle here. He also ordered those still living in Pest and Óbuda to relocate to Castle Hill and build a fortified town. Béla proclaimed Buda a municipality by royal charter in 1244 and bestowed civic rights on the citizens of Pest in 1255.

But Béla had been forced to appease the lesser nobility with large tracts of land and more independence; by the time of his death in 1270, anarchy reigned. The Árpád line died out in 1301 with the death of Andrew III, who left no heir.

> Because legal judgments in Hungary had always been handed down 'in the name of St Stephen's Crown', it was considered a living symbol and during its decades in the USA after WWII before it was returned in 1978 the crown was deemed to have been 'kidnapped'.

> In 1046 a Venice-born bishop named Gerard (Gellért), who had been brought to Hungary by King Stephen himself, was hurled to his death from a Buda hilltop in a spiked barrel by pagan Magyars resisting conversion. Gellért Hill now bears the bishop's name.

MEDIEVAL BUDAPEST

The struggle for the Hungarian throne after the death of Andrew III involved several European dynasties, with the crown first going to Charles Robert (Károly Róbert) of the French House of Anjou in 1307.

In the following century an alliance between Poland and Hungary gave the former the Hungarian crown. When Vladislav I (Úlászló),

1222	1241–42	1301	1458–90
King Andrew II signs the Golden Bull, according the nobility increased rights and powers; it is renewed nine years later in 1231.	Mongols sweep across Hungary, killing some 100,000 people in Pest and Óbuda alone and reducing the national population by up to a half.	The line of the House of Árpád ends with the death of Andrew III, who leaves no male heir; a period of great turmoil follows.	Medieval Hungary enjoys a golden age under the enlightened reign of King Matthias Corvinus and Queen Beatrix, daughter of the king of Naples.

son of the Polish Jagiellonian king, was killed fighting the Ottoman Turks at Varna (in today's Bulgaria) in 1444, János Hunyadi was made regent. A Transylvanian general born of a Wallachian (Romanian) father, János Hunyadi began his career at the court of Sigismund. His victory over the Turks at Belgrade (Hungarian: Nándorfehérvár) in 1456 checked the Ottoman advance into Hungary for 70 years and assured the coronation of his son Matthias (Mátyás), the greatest ruler of medieval Hungary.

Historical Reads

Budapest: A Cultural & Literary History (Bob Debt)

Budapest 1900: A Historical Portrait of a City and Its Culture (John Lukacs)

Battle for Budapest: 100 Days in WWII (Krisztián Ungváry)

Twelve Days: The Story of the 1956 Revolution (Victor Sebestyen)

A Good Comrade: János Kádár, Communism & Hungary (Roger Gough)

Through his military exploits Matthias (r 1458–90), nicknamed 'the Raven' (Corvinus) from his coat of arms, made Hungary one of central Europe's leading powers. Equally important, under his rule Buda enjoyed a golden age and for the first time became the true focus of the nation. His wife, Queen Beatrix, the daughter of the king of Naples, brought artisans from Italy who completely rebuilt, extended and fortified the Royal Palace (p50) in the Renaissance style. The Corvina Library of more than 2000 codices and incunabula was second only to the library in the Vatican.

But while Matthias busied himself with centralising power for the crown in the capital, he ignored the growing Turkish threat. Under his successor Vladislav II (Úlászló; r 1490–1516) what had begun as a crusade in 1514 turned into an uprising against the landlords by peasants who rallied near Pest under their leader, György Dózsa.

The revolt was repressed by Transylvanian leader John Szapolyai (Zápolyai János) and some 70,000 peasants were tortured and executed, as was Dózsa himself. The retrograde Tripartitum Law that followed codified the rights and privileges of the barons and nobles, and reduced the peasants to perpetual serfdom. By the time Louis II (Lajos) took the throne in 1516 at the tender age of nine, he couldn't rely on either side.

THE BATTLE OF MOHÁCS

The defeat of Louis' ragtag army by the Ottoman Turks at Mohács in 1526 is a watershed in Hungarian history. On the battlefield near this small town in Southern Transdanubia, some 195km south of Budapest, a relatively prosperous and independent Hungary died, sending the nation into a tailspin of partition and foreign domination that would last for centuries.

It would be unfair to put all the blame on the weak and indecisive teenager King Louis. Bickering among the nobility and the brutal crackdown of the Dózsa uprising had severely weakened Hungary's military power, and there was virtually nothing left in the royal cof-

1514	1526	1541	1566
The peasant uprising is crushed; 70,000 people are executed, including leader György Dózsa, who dies on a red-hot iron throne wearing a scalding crown.	Hungary is soundly defeated by the Ottomans at the Battle of Mohács and young King Louis is killed; the ensuing Turkish occupation lasts more than a century and a half.	Buda Castle falls to the Ottomans; Hungary is partitioned and shared by three separate groups: Turks, the Habsburgs and the Transylvanian princes.	Miklós Zrínyi and his 2500 soldiers make their heroic sally at Szigetvár Castle in southern Hungary; Sultan Suleiman I dies in battle.

fers. By 1526 Ottoman sultan Suleiman the Magnificent (r 1520–66) had taken much of the Balkans, including Belgrade, and was poised to march on Buda and Vienna with a force of up to 90,000 men.

Unwilling to wait for reinforcements from Transylvania under the command of his rival John Szapolyai, Louis rushed from Buda with a motley army of just over 25,000 men to battle the Turks and was soundly thrashed. Among the estimated 18,000 dead was the king himself – crushed by his horse while trying to retreat across a stream.

The Turks then turned north, sacking and burning Buda before retreating. Szapolyai, who had sat out the battle in the castle at Tokaj with forces of up to 13,000 men, was crowned king three months later.

TURKISH OCCUPATION

After the Turks had returned and occupied Buda in 1541, Hungary was divided into three parts. The central section, with Buda as the provincial seat, went to the Ottomans while parts of Transdanubia and what is now Slovakia were governed by the Austrian House of Habsburg, assisted by the Hungarian nobility based at Bratislava (Hungarian: Pozsony). The principality of Transylvania prospered as a vassal state of the Ottoman Empire. This division of the country would remain in place for almost a century and a half.

Turkish power began to wane in the 17th century, especially after the Turkish attempt to take Vienna was soundly defeated. Buda was liberated in 1686 and an imperial army under Eugene of Savoy wiped out the last Turkish army in Hungary at the Battle of Zenta (now Senta in Serbia) 11 years later.

THE HABSBURGS

The expulsion of the Turks did not result in a free and independent Hungary. Buda and the rest of the country were under military occupation, and the policies of the Catholic Habsburgs' Counter-Reformation and heavy taxation further alienated the nobility. In 1703, Transylvanian prince Ferenc Rákóczi II raised an army of Hungarian mercenaries *(kuruc)* against the Habsburgs. The war dragged on for eight years, but superior imperial forces and lack of funds forced the *kuruc* to negotiate a separate peace with Vienna behind Rákóczi's back. The 1703–11 War of Independence had failed, but Rákóczi was the first leader to unite Hungarians against the Habsburgs.

Hungary was now a mere province of the Habsburg empire. With the ascension of Maria Theresa to the throne in 1740, the Hungarian

A Hungarian expression recalls the Turkish occupation: *Hátravan még a feketeleves* ('Still to come is the black soup'), suggesting something painful or difficult is on the cards. After a meal the Turks would serve their Hungarian guests an unknown beverage – coffee – which meant it was time to talk about taxes.

1686	1699	1703–11	1795
Austrian and Hungarian forces backed by the Polish army liberate Buda from the Turks, though little of the castle is left standing.	Austria, Poland, Venice and Russia sign peace treaty with the Turks; Austria receives large accessions of territory in Hungary and Transylvania.	Ferenc Rákóczi II fights and loses a war of independence against the Habsburgs; he is given asylum in Thrace by the Turkish Sultan Ahmet III.	Seven pro-republican Jacobites, including the group's leader Ignác Martonovics, are beheaded at Vérmező in Buda for plotting against the Habsburg throne.

nobility pledged their 'lives and blood' to her at the diet in Bratislava in exchange for concessions. Thus began the period of enlightened absolutism that would continue under her son, Joseph II, who ruled for a decade from 1780.

Under the reigns of both Maria Theresa and Joseph, Hungary took great steps forward economically, culturally and politically – in 1784 Joseph ordered the government to move from Bratislava to Buda, the nation's new administrative centre.

But Joseph's attempts to modernise society by dissolving the all-powerful (and corrupt) monastic orders, abolishing serfdom and replacing 'neutral' (but archaic) Latin with German as the official language of state administration were opposed by the Hungarian nobility, and the king rescinded some of the reforms on his deathbed.

Dissenting voices could still be heard, and the ideals of the French Revolution of 1789 began to take root in certain intellectual circles in Budapest. In 1795 seven republican Jacobites were beheaded at Vérmező (Blood Meadow; Map p230), near today's Déli train station in Buda, for plotting against the crown.

By 1800 Pest, with a population of about 30,000, was the nation's most important commercial centre while Buda, with 24,000 people, remained a royal garrison town. But 90% of the national population worked the land, and it was primarily through agriculture that modernisation would come to Hungary.

Liberalism and social reform found their greatest supporters among certain members of the aristocracy in Pest, including Count István Széchenyi (1791–1860), a true Renaissance man, who advocated the abolition of serfdom and returned much of his own land to the peasantry, proposed the first permanent link between Buda and Pest (Chain Bridge) and oversaw the regulation of the Danube as much for commerce and irrigation as for safety.

But a more radical faction, dominated by Lajos Kossuth (1802–94), demanded more immediate action. It was this dynamic lawyer and journalist who would lead Hungary to its greatest ever confrontation with the Habsburgs.

> Joseph II, who ruled as Habsburg emperor from 1780 to 1790, was nicknamed the 'hatted king' because he was never actually crowned within the borders of Hungary.

THE 1848–49 WAR OF INDEPENDENCE

The Habsburg empire began to weaken as Hungarian nationalism increased early in the 19th century and certain reforms (eg a law allowing serfs alternative means of discharging their feudal obligations of service, and increased Hungarian representation in the Council of State in Vienna) were introduced.

1825	1848–49	1867	1873
So-called Reform Era in full swing; Pest becomes cultural and economic centre of the country; first National Theatre is built along with first Hungarian National Museum.	During the War of Independence, Sándor Petőfi dies fighting, Lajos Batthyány and 13 of his generals are executed for their roles, and leader Kossuth goes into exile.	The Act of Compromise creates Dual Monarchy of Austria (the empire), based in Vienna, and Hungary (the kingdom), with its seat at Budapest.	Hilly residential Buda and historic Óbuda on the western bank of the Danube merge with flat industrial Pest on the eastern side to form what is at first called Pest-Buda.

But the reforms carried out were too limited and far too late. On 3 March 1848, Kossuth, who had been imprisoned by the Habsburgs at I Táncsics Mihály utca 9 on Castle Hill for three years (1837–40; see p57), made a fiery speech in Parliament demanding an end to feudalism. On 15 March a group calling itself the Youth of March led by the poet Sándor Petőfi, who read out his poem 'Nemzeti Dal' (National Song) on the steps of the Hungarian National Museum, took to the streets of Pest with hastily printed copies of their Twelve Points to press for radical reforms and even revolution.

Habsburg patience began to wear thin and in September 1848 its forces launched an attack on Hungary. The Hungarians hastily formed a national defence commission and moved the government seat to Debrecen in the east, where Kossuth was elected leader. In April 1849 the Parliament declared Hungary's full independence.

New Habsburg emperor Franz Joseph (r 1848–1916) quickly took action. He sought the assistance of Russian tsar Nicholas I, who obliged with 200,000 troops. Weak and vastly outnumbered, the rebel troops were defeated by August 1849. Martial law was declared and a series of brutal reprisals and executions ensued. Kossuth went into exile. Habsburg troops then went around the country systematically blowing up castles and fortifications lest they be used by resurgent rebels.

THE DUAL MONARCHY

Hungary was again merged into the Habsburg empire as a vanquished province and 'neo-absolutism' was the order of the day. Passive resistance among Hungarians and disastrous military defeats for the Habsburgs by the French in 1859 and the Prussians in 1866 pushed Franz Joseph to the negotiating table under the leadership of liberal reformer Ferenc Deák.

The result was the Compromise of 1867, which fundamentally restructured the Habsburg monarchy and created the Dual Monarchy of Austria (the empire) and Hungary (the kingdom) ruled by Emperor/King Franz Joseph. It was a federated state of two parliaments and two capitals – Vienna and Budapest (the result of the union of Buda, Pest and Óbuda in 1873).

This 'Age of Dualism' would carry on until 1918 and spark an economic, cultural and intellectual rebirth in Budapest. Trade and industry boomed, factories were established, and the composers Franz (Ferenc) Liszt and Ferenc Erkel were making beautiful music. The middle class – dominated by Germans and Jews in Pest – burgeoned, and the capital entered into a frenzy of building. Much of what you see

For all his many accomplishments, Count István Széchenyi's contemporary and fellow reformer, Lajos Kossuth, called him 'the greatest Hungarian'. For many of his fellow countrymen, this dynamic but troubled visionary retains that accolade today.

1896	1900	1918	1920
Millennium of the Magyar conquest of the Carpathian Basin is marked by a major exhibition in City Park that attracts four million people over six months.	The population of Budapest has increased to 750,00 by the turn of the century, up from 280,000 just 50 years before.	Austria-Hungary loses WWI in November and the political system collapses; Hungary declares itself a republic under the leadership of Count Mihály Károlyi.	Treaty of Trianon carves up much of Central Europe, reducing Hungary by almost two-thirds and enlarging the ethnic Hungarian populations in Romania, Yugoslavia and Czechoslovakia.

in Budapest today – from the grand boulevards and their Eclectic-style apartment blocks to the Parliament building, State Opera House and Palace of Art – was built at this time.

But all was not well in the kingdom. The working class, based almost entirely in Budapest, had almost no rights and the situation in the countryside was almost as dire as it had been in the Middle Ages. Despite a new law enacted in 1868 to protect their rights, minorities under Hungarian control (Czechs, Slovaks, Croats and Romanians) were under increased pressure to 'Magyarise' and many viewed their new rulers as oppressors.

WWI & THE REPUBLIC OF COUNCILS

On 28 July 1914 Austria-Hungary declared war on Serbia and entered WWI allied with the German empire. The result of this action was disastrous, with widespread destruction and hundreds of thousands killed on the Russian and Italian fronts. At the armistice in 1918, the fate of the Dual Monarchy – and Hungary as a multinational kingdom – was decided and the terms spelled out by the Treaty of Trianon (p181) less than two years later.

The minister of culture in Béla Kun's short-lived Republic of Councils was one Béla Lugosi, who fled to Vienna in 1919 and eventually made his way to Hollywood where he achieved fame as the lead in several Dracula films.

A new republic was set up in Budapest five days after the armistice was signed, but it would not last long. Rampant inflation, mass unemployment, the occupation and dismemberment of Hungary by the Allies and the victory of the Bolshevik Revolution in Russia all combined to radicalise much of the Budapest working class.

In March 1919 a group of Hungarian Communists led by a former Transylvanian journalist called Béla Kun seized power. The so-called Republic of Councils (Tanácsköztársaság) set out to nationalise industry and private property and build a fairer society, but Kun's failure to regain the 'lost territories' brought mass opposition and the government unleashed a reign of 'red terror' around the country.

In August, Romanian troops occupied the capital, and Kun fled to Vienna. The Romanians left Budapest in November, just ahead of Admiral Miklós Horthy, mounted on a white steed and leading 25,000 Hungarian troops into the capital.

THE HORTHY YEARS & WWII

In March 1920, by secret ballot, Parliament chose a kingdom as the form of state and – lacking a king – elected as its regent Admiral Horthy, who would remain in that position until the penultimate year of WWII.

1931	1939	1941	1944
Strongman Miklós Horthy declares martial law in the face of economic unrest; suspected Communists are rounded up, imprisoned and, in some cases, executed.	Nazi Germany invades Poland; Britain and France declare war on Germany two days later but Hungary remains neutral for the time being.	Hungary joins the Axis led by Germany and Italy against the Allies in WWII, largely in order to recover territories lost under the terms of the Treaty of Trianon.	Germany invades and occupies Hungary; most Hungarian Jews, who had largely been able to avoid persecution under Horthy, are deported to Nazi concentration camps.

Horthy embarked on a 'white terror' – every bit as brutal as Béla Kun's red one – that attacked Jews, social democrats and communists for their roles in supporting the Republic of Councils. As the regime was consolidated, it showed itself to be extremely rightist and conservative, advocating the status quo and 'traditional values'. Very few reforms were enacted; the lot of the working class and the peasantry actually worsened.

Everyone agreed that the return of the territories lost through the Treaty of Trianon was essential for national development. Hungary obviously could not count on the victors – France, Britain and the US to help recoup its land; instead, it would have to seek help from the fascist governments of Germany and Italy.

Hungary's move to the right intensified throughout the 1930s, though it remained silent when WWII broke out in September 1939. Horthy hoped an alliance would not mean actually having to enter the war but joined the German- and Italian-led Axis in June 1941. The war was just as disastrous for Hungary as the 1914–18 one had been and Horthy began secret discussions with the Allies.

When Hitler caught wind of this in March 1944 he sent in his army. Ferenc Szálasi, the leader of the pro-Nazi Arrow Cross Party, was installed as prime minister and Horthy deported to Germany.

The Arrow Cross Party moved quickly to quash any opposition, and thousands of the country's liberal politicians and labour leaders were arrested. At the same time, its puppet government introduced anti-Jewish legislation similar to that in Germany, and Jews, who

Hungary under Admiral Horthy confused US President Franklin D Roosevelt. After being briefed by an aide on the country's government and leadership, he reportedly said: 'Let me see if I understand you right. Hungary is a kingdom without a king run by a regent who's an admiral without a navy?'

THE DESPISED TREATY OF TRIANON

In June 1920, scarcely a year and a half after the treaty ending WWI was signed, the victorious Allies drew up a postwar settlement under the Treaty of Trianon at Versailles, near Paris, that enlarged some countries, truncated others and created several 'successor states'. As one of the defeated enemy nations and with large numbers of minorities clamouring for independence within its borders, Hungary stood to lose more than most. And it did. It was reduced to 40% of its historical size and, while now a largely uniform, homogeneous state, for millions of ethnic Hungarians in Romania, Yugoslavia and Czechoslovakia, they were in the minority for the first time.

'Trianon' became the singularly most hated word in Hungary, and 'Nem, Nem, Soha!' (No, No, Never!) the rallying cry during the interwar years. Many of the problems the diktatum created remained in place for decades, and it has coloured Hungary's relations with its neighbours for upwards of a century.

1945	1946	1949	1956
Budapest is liberated by the Soviet army in April, a month before full victory in Europe, with three-quarters of its buildings and all of its bridges in ruins.	Hungary experiences the world's worst hyperinflation, with notes of up to 10,000 trillion pengő issued; Liberty Bridge, the first of the spans over the Danube to be rebuilt, reopens.	The Communists, in complete control, form the 'People's Republic of Hungary'; Stalinist show trials of 'Titoists' and other 'enemies of the people' begin in Budapest.	Budapest is in flames after October riots; Hungary briefly withdraws from the Warsaw Pact as neutral; the status quo is restored and János Kádár is installed as leader.

lived in fear but were still alive under Horthy, were rounded up into ghettos by Hungarian pro-Nazis. During the summer of 1944, just 10 months before the war ended, approximately 450,000 Hungarian Jewish men, women and children – almost 60% of Hungarian Jewry – were deported to Auschwitz and other labour camps in just over eight weeks, where they either starved to death, succumbed to disease or were brutally murdered. Many of the Jews who did survive owed their lives to heroic men like Raoul Wallenberg (p67), a Budapest-based Swedish diplomat, and the Swiss consul, Carl Lutz.

Budapest now became an international battleground for the first time since the Turkish occupation, and bombs began falling everywhere. By Christmas 1944 the Soviet army had surrounded Budapest. When the Germans and Hungarian Nazis rejected a settlement, the siege of the capital began. By the time the German war machine had surrendered in April 1945, three-quarters of the city's homes, historical buildings and churches had been severely damaged or destroyed. Some 20,000 Hungarian soldiers and 25,000 civilians of Budapest had been killed. And as they retreated the vindictive Germans blew up Buda Castle and knocked out every bridge spanning the Danube.

> In 1948, Joseph Cardinal Mindszenty, primate of Hungary, was arrested by the communists, tortured and sentenced to life imprisonment for treason. Released during the 1956 Uprising, Mindszenty took refuge in the US embassy on Szabadság tér when the communists returned to power and remained there until 1971.

THE PEOPLE'S REPUBLIC

When free parliamentary elections were held in November 1945, the Independent Smallholders' Party received 57% of the vote. But Soviet political officers, backed by the occupying army, forced three other parties – the Communists, Social Democrats and National Peasants – into a coalition.

Within a couple of years the Communists were ready to take complete control. After a disputed election in 1947 they declared their candidate, Mátyás Rákosi, the winner. The following year the Social Democrats merged with the Communists to form the Hungarian Workers' Party.

In 1948 Rákosi, a big fan of Stalin, began a process of nationalisation and unrealistically fast industrialisation at the expense of agriculture. Peasants were forced into collective farms and a network of spies and informers exposed 'class enemies' such as Cardinal József Mindszenty (p97) to the secret police – the ÁVO (ÁVH after 1949) – who interrogated them at their headquarters at VI Andrássy út 60 (now the House of Terror; p118) in Pest and sent them to trial at the then Military Court of Justice (p58) in Buda. Some were executed; many more were sent into internal exile or condemned to labour camps.

Bitter feuding within the party began, and purges and Stalinist show trials became the order of the day. László Rajk, the Communist

1957	1958	1968	1978
Rock-and-roll legend Elvis Presley performs a spiritual song called 'Peace in the Valley' on US TV to express his 'preoccupation with Hungary's plight' after the Uprising.	Imre Nagy and others are executed by the Communist regime for their role in the uprising and buried in unmarked graves in Budapest's New Municipal Cemetery.	Plans for a liberalised economy are introduced in an attempt to overcome the inefficiencies of central planning, but are rejected as too extreme by conservatives.	The Crown of St Stephen is returned to Hungary from the USA, where it had been held at Fort Knox in Kentucky since the end of WWII.

minister of the interior (which also controlled the secret police), was arrested and later executed for 'Titoism'; his successor János Kádár was jailed and tortured. In August 1949 the nation was proclaimed the 'People's Republic of Hungary'. In the years that followed – among the darkest and bleakest in Budapest's history – apartment blocks, small businesses and retail outlets were expropriated by the state.

After the death of Stalin in 1953 and Khrushchev's denunciation of him three years later, Rákosi's tenure was up and the terror began to abate. Under pressure from within the party, Rajk was posthumously rehabilitated and former Minister of Agriculture Imre Nagy, who had been expelled from the party a year earlier for suggesting reforms, was readmitted. By October 1956 during Rajk's reburial, murmured calls for a real reform of the system – 'socialism with a human face' – were already being heard.

THE 1956 UPRISING

The nation's greatest tragedy – an event that for a while shook the world, rocked international Communism and pitted Hungarian against Hungarian – began in Budapest on 23 October 1956 when some 50,000 university students assembled at II Bem József tér in Buda, shouting anti-Soviet slogans and demanding that Nagy be named prime minister. That night a crowd pulled down and sawed into pieces the colossal statue of Stalin on Dózsa György út on the edge of City Park (Városliget; Map p254) and shots were fired by ÁVH agents on another group gathering outside the headquarters of Hungarian Radio (Magyar Rádió) at VIII Bródy Sándor utca 5-7 in Pest. Budapest was in revolution.

Next day Nagy formed a government while János Kádár was named president of the Central Committee of the Hungarian Workers' Party. Over the next few days the government offered an amnesty to those involved in the violence, promised to abolish the ÁVH and announced that Hungary would leave the Warsaw Pact and declare its neutrality.

At this, Soviet tanks and troops crossed into Hungary and within 72 hours attacked Budapest and other centres. Kádár had slipped away from Budapest to join the Russian invaders; he was installed as leader.

Fierce street fighting continued for several days, encouraged by Radio Free Europe broadcasts and disingenuous promises of support from the West, which was embroiled in the Suez Canal crisis at the time. When the fighting was over, 2,500 people were dead. Then the reprisals began. An estimated 20,000 people were arrested and 2000 – including Imre Nagy and his associates – were executed.

The award-winning website of the Institute for the History of the 1956 Hungarian Revolution (www.rev.hu) will walk you through the build-up, outbreak and aftermath of Hungary's greatest modern tragedy through photographs, essays and timelines.

HISTORY THE 1956 UPRISING

WEBSITE

1988

János Kádár is forced to retire in May after more than three decades in power; he dies and is buried in Budapest's Kerepesi Cemetery the following year.

1989

Communist monopoly on power is relinquished and the national borders are opened; Imre Nagy is reburied in Budapest; The Republic of Hungary is declared.

RICHARD I'ANSON / LONELY PLANET IMAGES ©

Communist-era statue at Memento Park (p68)

KÁDÁR BONES

Another 250,000 refugees fled to Austria. The government lost what little credibility it ever had and the city many of its most competent and talented citizens. You can still see the bullet holes and shrapnel damage on the exterior walls of many buildings in Pest.

HUNGARY UNDER KÁDÁR

After the revolt, the ruling party was reorganised as the Hungarian Socialist Workers' Party, and Kádár, now both party president and premier, launched a program to liberalise the social and economic structure based on compromise. He introduced greater consumerism and market socialism and by the mid-1970s Hungary was light years ahead of any other Soviet-bloc country in its standard of living, freedom of movement and opportunities to (softly) criticise the government. The 'Hungarian model' attracted Western attention and investment.

Things soured in the 1980s. The Kádár system of 'goulash socialism' was incapable of dealing with 'unsocialist' problems: unemployment, soaring inflation and the largest per-capita foreign debt in Eastern Europe. Worse, Kádár and the 'old guard' refused to hear talk about party reforms. In June 1987 Károly Grósz took over as premier, and less than a year later Kádár was booted out of the party and forced to retire.

In 2007 the grave of the late Communist leader János Kádár in the New Municipal Cemetery was broken into and his skull and assorted bones removed. The only clue was a note that read: 'Murderers and traitors may not rest in holy ground 1956–2006'. The remains have yet to be recovered.

THE END OF AN ERA

A group of reformers, eg Imre Pozsgay, Miklós Németh and Gyula Horn, took control. Party conservatives at first put a lid on any real change by demanding a retreat from political liberalisation in exchange for their support of the new regime's economic policies.

But the tide had turned. Throughout 1988's summer and autumn, new political parties formed and old ones revived. In January 1989 Pozsgay, second-guessing what was to come as Mikhail Gorbachev launched sweeping reforms in the Soviet Union, announced that the events of 1956 had been a 'popular insurrection' and not the 'counter-revolution' that the regime had always dubbed it. In June 1989 250,000 people attended ceremonies marking the reburial of Imre Nagy and other victims of 1956 in Budapest's New Municipal Cemetery (p131).

In July 1989, again at Pozsgay's instigation, Hungary began to demolish the electrified wire fence separating it from Austria. The move released a wave of East Germans holidaying in Hungary into the West and the opening attracted thousands more. The collapse of the Communist regimes around the region was now unstoppable.

1990	1991	1994	1995
The centrist MDF wins the first free elections in 43 years in April; Árpád Göncz is chosen the republic's first president in August.	Last Soviet troops leave Hungary in June, two weeks ahead of schedule; Parliament passes the first act dealing with the return of property seized under Communist rule since 1949.	Socialists win a decisive victory in the general election and form a government under Gyula Horn for the first time since the changes of 1989.	Árpád Göncz of the SZDSZ, arguably the most popular politician in Hungary, is elected for a second (and, by law, final) five-year term as president of the republic.

THE REPUBLIC OF HUNGARY REBORN

At its party congress in February 1989, the ruling Hungarian Socialist Workers' Party changed its name to the Hungarian Socialist Party (MSZP) and later in the year agreed to surrender its monopoly on power, paving the way for free elections in the spring of 1990. On 23 October 1989, the 33rd anniversary of the 1956 Uprising, the nation once again became the Republic of Hungary.

The 1990 election was won by the centrist Hungarian Democratic Forum (MDF), which advocated a gradual transition to capitalism and was led by a softly spoken former museum curator, József Antall. The social-democratic Alliance of Free Democrats (SZDSZ), which had called for much faster change, came in a distant second with 18% of the vote. As Gorbachev looked on, Hungary changed political systems as if it were clothing and the last Soviet troops left Hungarian soil in June 1991. Street names in Budapest such as Lenin körút and Marx tér ended up on the rubbish tip of history, and monuments to 'glorious workers' and 'esteemed leaders' were packed off to a socialist-realist theme park called Memento Park (p68).

In coalition with two smaller parties, the MDF governed Hungary soundly during its difficult transition to a full market economy. But despite initial successes in curbing inflation and lowering interest rates, economic problems slowed development; the government's laissez-faire policies did not help. In a poll taken in mid-1993, 76% of respondents were 'very disappointed' with the way things had worked out.

Perhaps not surprisingly, in the May 1994 elections the MSZP, led by Gyula Horn, won an absolute majority in Parliament. This in no way implied a return to the past, and Horn was quick to point out that his party had initiated the whole reform process in the first place.

THE ROAD TO EUROPE

After its dire showing in the 1994 elections, the Federation of Young Democrats (Fidesz) – which until 1993 had limited membership to those under 35 to emphasise a past untainted by communism, privilege and corruption – moved to the right and added the extension 'MPP' (Hungarian Civic Party) to its name to attract the support of the burgeoning middle class. In 1998 it campaigned for integration with Europe; Fidesz-MPP won the vote by forming a coalition with the MDF and the agrarian conservative FKgP. The party's youthful leader, Viktor Orbán, was named prime minister. Hungary became a fully fledged NATO member the following year.

1999

Hungary becomes a fully fledged member of NATO, along with the Czech Republic and Poland; NATO aircraft heading for Kosovo begin using Hungarian airfields.

MARTIN MOOS / LONELY PLANET IMAGES ©

2002

Budapest, in particular the banks of the Danube, the Castle District and Andrássy út, is included in Unesco's list of World Heritage Sites.

Crown of St Stephen (p93)

Despite the astonishing economic growth and other gains made under the coalition government, the electorate grew increasingly hostile to Fidesz-MPP's – and Orbán's – strongly nationalistic rhetoric and perceived arrogance. In April 2002 the largest turnout of voters in Hungarian history unseated the government in a closely fought election and returned the MSZP, allied with the SZDSZ, to power under Prime Minister Péter Medgyessy, a free-market advocate who had served as finance minister in the Horn government. Hungary was admitted into the EU in May 2004, but three months later Medgyessy resigned when it was revealed he had served as a counterintelligence officer in the late 1970s and early 1980s while working in the finance ministry. Sports Minister Ferenc Gyurcsány became prime minister.

> The extreme right-wing nationalist party Jobbik Magyarországért Mozgalom (Movement for a Better Hungary) won just under 17% of the vote nationwide in 2010 and currently holds 26 seats in parliament.

AT HOME AT LAST

Reappointed prime minister in April 2006 after the electorate gave his coalition 55% of 386 parliamentary seats, Gyurcsány immediately began austerity measures to tackle Hungary's budget deficit, which had reached a staggering 10% of GDP. But in September, just as these unpopular steps were being put into place, an audiotape recorded shortly after the election at a closed-door meeting of the prime minister's cabinet had Gyurcsány confessing that the party had 'lied morning, evening and night' about the state of the economy since coming to power and now had to make amends. Gyurcsány refused to resign, and public outrage led to a series of demonstrations near the Parliament building in Budapest, culminating in widespread rioting that marred the 50th anniversary of the 1956 Uprising.

Since then, demonstrations – sometimes violent – have become a regular feature on Budapest, especially during national holidays. The radical right-wing nationalist party Jobbik Magyarországért Mozgalom (Movement for a Better Hungary), better known as just Jobbik, and its uniformed militia arm, Magyar Gárda (Hungarian Guard), have been at the centre of many of these demonstrations and riots.

Gyurcsány led a feeble minority government until general elections in 2010 when Fidesz-MPP won a majority of 52% in the first round of voting and joined forces with the Christian Democratic People's Party (KDNP) to rule with a two-thirds or 263 of 386 seats majority.

Hungary's most recent appearance on the world stage came in the first half of 2011 when it assumed presidency of the EU Council. A new constitution that went into effect at the start of 2012 contains an extended preamble (the so-called National Creed) that declares the period from March 1944 (Nazi occupation of Hungary) to May 1990 (first free election since 1945) to be legally nonexistent.

2004	2006	2008	2011
Hungary is admitted to the EU along with nine other new member-nations, including neighbouring states Slovakia and Slovenia, with Romania following three years later.	Socialist Ferenc Gyurcsány is re-elected as prime minister; antigovernment riots rock Budapest during the 50th anniversary celebrations of the 1956 Uprising.	Government loses key referendum on health-care reform; SZDSZ quits coalition, leaving the socialists to form a minority government; Hungary is particularly hard hit by the world economic crisis.	In its most high-profile role on the European stage to date Hungary assumes presidency of the EU council; a number of key streets and squares are renamed.

Architecture

Budapest's architectural waltz through history begins with the Romans at Aquincum, moves up to Castle Hill's medieval streets, over to the ruins of Margaret Island and into the many splendid baroque churches on either side of the Danube. Neoclassicism chips in with the Basilica of St Stephen and the Hungarian National Museum. But the capital really hits its stride with its art nouveau buildings: such gems as the Royal Post Savings Bank and Museum of Applied Arts.

ROMAN

The Romans established Aquincum (p73), a key military garrison and civilian settlement, in today's Óbuda, and you can still see the remains of paved streets as well as the outlines of houses and shops, large public baths, a market, an early Christian church and a temple dedicated to the god Mithra. Nearby are two amphitheatres – one for the military and one for civilians – and a villa with astonishing 3rd-century floor mosaics of Hercules. The ruins of a fortress called Contra Aquincum (p85) can still be seen in what is now V Március 15 tér in front of the Inner Town Parish Church in Pest's Belváros.

The amphitheatre in Óbuda built in the 2nd century for the Roman garrisons could seat up to 15,000 spectators and was larger than the Colosseum in Rome.

MEDIEVAL

You won't find as much Romanesque and Gothic architecture in Budapest as you will in, say, Prague – the Mongols, Turks and Habsburgs destroyed most of it – but the Royal Palace (p50) incorporates many Gothic features, and the *sedilia* (niches with seats) at the entrances to many of the houses in the Castle District, most notably on I Úri utca and I Országház utca, are pure Gothic. The chapels in Pest's Inner Town Parish Church (p85) have some fine Gothic and Renaissance tabernacles, and you can't miss the Renaissance stonework – along with the Gothic wooden sculptures and panel paintings and late-Gothic triptychs – at the Hungarian National Gallery (p50). There's a heap of ruins dating back to the 12th and 13th centuries on Margaret Island, including the remains of a Franciscan church and monastery and a Dominican convent.

TURKISH

The Turks did little building in Buda (or Budan as they called it) apart from several bathhouses still extant, including the Király and Rudas Baths, dervish monasteries and tombs and city walls and bastions. For the most part they used existing civic buildings for administration and converted churches such as the Inner Town Parish Church into mosques.

During their occupation, the Turks converted Matthias Church on Castle Hill into the Büyük Cami (Great Mosque), and the heart of the Royal Palace became a gunpowder store and magazine.

BAROQUE

Baroque architecture abounds in Budapest; you'll see excellent examples of it everywhere. The Church of St Anne (p56) on I Batthyány tér in Buda and the Óbuda Parish Church (p77) on III Flórián tér are fine examples of ecclesiastical baroque, while the Citadella (p65) on Gellért Hill in Buda and the municipal council office (Map p238) on V Városház utca in Pest are baroque in its civic or secular form. The Royal Palace (p50), largely reconstructed in the mid-18th century, contains baroque elements. One of the best examples of baroque outdoor sculpture in Budapest is the statue of the Holy Trinity (p57) in I Szentháromság tér in Castle Hill.

NEOCLASSICISM

The so-called Age of Reform beginning in the 1820s brought with it neoclassicism in the arts (including architecture), a style that was rigorous, majestic and sober at the same time. The Hungarian National Museum (p129), purpose-built in 1847, is a textbook example of this style. Other examples are Adam Clark's Chain Bridge (p54), the Basilica of St Stephen (p95) and the delightful Lutheran church (p85) in V Deák Ferenc tér, which was designed by Mihály Pollack, the great planner of neoclassical Pest. Equally influential was Miklós Ybl who designed the neo-Renaissance Hungarian State Opera House (p117) and worked on the Basilica of St Stephen.

ART NOUVEAU & SECESSIONISM

Art nouveau architecture and its Viennese variant, Secessionism, abound here, and examples can be seen throughout the city; it is Budapest's signature style. Its sinuous curves, flowing, asymmetrical forms, colourful tiles and other decorative elements stand out like beacons in a sea of refined and elegant baroque and mannered, geometric neoclassical buildings. It will have you gasping in surprise.

The Beginning & the End

Art nouveau was both an architectural style and an art form that flourished in Europe and the USA from 1890 to around 1910 (or even the outbreak of WWI in 1914). It began in Britain as the Arts and Crafts Movement founded by William Morris (1834–96), which stressed the importance of manual processes and attempted to create a new organic style in direct opposition to the imitative banalities spawned by the Industrial Revolution.

The yellow ochre that became the standard colour for all Habsburg administrative buildings and many churches in the late 18th century and is ubiquitous throughout Budapest and the rest of Hungary is called 'Maria Theresa yellow'.

The style soon spread to Europe, where it took on distinctly local and/or national characteristics. In Vienna a group of artists called the Secessionists lent its name to the more geometric local style of art nouveau architecture: Sezessionstil (Hungarian: Szecesszió). In Budapest, the use of traditional facades with allegorical and historical figures and scenes, folk motifs and Zsolnay ceramics and other local materials led to an eclectic style. Though working within an art nouveau/Secessionist framework, this style emerged as something that was uniquely Hungarian.

But fashion and styles changed as whimsically and rapidly at the start of the 20th century as they do today, and by the end of the first decade art nouveau and its variants were considered limited, passé, even tacky. Fortunately for the good citizens of Budapest and us, the economic and political torpor of the interwar period and the 40-year 'big sleep' after WWII left many art nouveau/Secessionist buildings beaten but standing – a lot more, in fact, than remain in such important art nouveau centres as Paris, Brussels and Vienna.

Budapest Makes Its Mark

The first Hungarian architect to look to art nouveau for inspiration was Frigyes Spiegel, who covered traditional facades with exotic and allegorical figures and scenes. At the northern end of VI Izabella utca at No 94 is the restored Lindenbaum apartment block (Map p244), the first in the city to use art nouveau ornamentation, including suns, stars, peacocks, flowers, snakes, foxes and long-tressed nudes.

The master of the style, however, was Ödön Lechner (p144) and his most ambitious work in Budapest is the Museum of Applied Arts (p132). Purpose-built as a museum and completed in time for the millenary exhibition in 1896, it was faced and roofed in a variety of colourful Zsolnay ceramic tiles, and its turrets, domes and ornamental figures lend it an 'Eastern' or 'Mogul' feel. His crowning glory (though not seen as such at the time), however, is the sumptuous Royal Postal Savings Bank (p96) at V Hold utca 4, a Secessionist extravaganza of floral mosaics, folk motifs and ceramic figures just off Szabadság tér in Lipótváros and dating from 1901.

The Ferenc Liszt Music Academy (p115), completed in 1907, is not so interesting for its exterior as for its decorative elements inside. There's a dazzling art nouveau mosaic called *Art Is the Source of Life* by Aladár Kőrösfői Kriesch, a leader of the seminal Gödöllő Artists' Colony (p149), on the 1st-floor landing and some fine stained glass by master craftsman Miksa Róth, whose home and workshop in central Pest is now a museum (p117). In the music academy take a look at the grid of laurel leaves below the ceiling of the main concert hall, which mimics the ironwork dome of the Secession Building (1897–1908) in Vienna, and the large reflecting sapphire-blue Zsolnay ball finials on the stair balusters.

The Danubius Hotel Gellért (p159), designed by Ármin Hegedűs, Artúr Sebestyén and Izidor Sterk in 1909 and completed in 1918, contains examples of late art nouveau, notably the thermal spa with its enormous arched glass entrance hall and Zsolnay ceramic fountains in the bathing pools. The architects were clearly influenced by Lechner but added other elements, including baroque ones.

Very noteworthy indeed is the arcade near V Ferenciek tere called Párizsi Udvar (p84) built in 1909 by Henrik Schmahl. The design contains a myriad influences – from Moorish Islamic and Venetian Gothic architecture to elements of Lechner's own eclectic style.

In 2008 the Hungarian government submitted five of Ödön Lechner's works, including the Museum of Applied Arts, the Royal Postal Savings Bank and the Institute of Geology, for inclusion in Unesco's World Heritage List.

ÖDÖN LECHNER

In Pursuit of the Finest

One of the joys of exploring the 'Queen of the Danube' is that you'll find elements of art nouveau and Secessionism in the oddest places. A street with a unified image is a rarity in Budapest; keep your eyes open and you'll spot bits and pieces everywhere and at all times. The following are our favourites:

Bedő House (p96; V Honvéd utca 3) Emil Vidor, 1903

Budapest Zoo's Elephant House (p142; XIV Állatkerti körút 6-12) Kornél Neuschloss-Knüsli, 1912

City Park Calvinist Church (Map p250; VII Városligeti fasor 7) Aladár Arkay, 1913

Egger Villa (Map p250; VII Városligeti fasor 24) Emil Vidor, 1902

Institute of Geology (p144; XIV Stefánia út 14) Ödön Lechner, 1899

Léderer Mansion (Map p250; VI Bajza utca 42) Zoltán Bálint & Lajos Jámbor, 1902

National Institute for the Blind (p144; XIV Ajtósi Dürer sor 39) Sándor Baumgarten, 1904

Philanthia (p84; V Váci utca 9) Kálmán Albert Körössy, 1906

Primary school (Map p250; VII Dob utca 85) Ármin Hegedűs, 1906

Schmidl tomb (p131; New Municipal Cemetery, X Kozma utca 6) Ödön Lechner & Béla Lajta, 1903

Sonnenberg Mansion (Map p250; VI Munkácsy Mihály utca 23) Albert Körössy, 1903

Thonet House (p84; V Váci utca 11/a) Ödön Lechner, 1890

Török Bank House (Map p238; V Szervita tér 3) Henrik Böhm & Ármin Hegedűs, 1906

Vidor Villa (Map p250; VII Városligeti fasor 33) Emil Vidor, 1905

WEKERLE ESTATE

This leafy residential estate in Kispest, a successful experiment in social housing dating back to the early 20th century, is well worth a visit for its unique architecture. Designed by an eclectic group of 15 architects including Károly Kós (1883–1977), who used structural details and motifs from his native Transylvania both here and at the Budapest Zoo, the estate was built to house 20,000 railway workers and employees. Construction began in 1908 under Prime Minister Sándor Wekerle and was halted during WWI only to resume at a slower and more curtailed pace later on. Wekerle was completed in 1926.

From a central square (now called XIX Kós Károly tér), tree-lined streets fan out to family houses and apartment blocks. Many sport attractive Transylvanian-style gables, wooden balconies and pitched roofs and are arranged around their own lush gardens. As Wekerle was meant to provide for all the needs of a community and not just residential units, schools, shops, churches and even a police station were built where streets intersected and formed triangular squares.

Today Wekerle still feels like a small self-contained village within a city and is a highly desirable place to live. To reach it, take the M3 metro to Határ út and walk due south along XIX Pannónia út for about a kilometre. Buses 99, 194 and 199 also serve Wekerle.

MODERNISM

Modernism did not reach Budapest until the decade before WWII, but a number of earlier buildings give hints as to what was coming. A wonderful example of early Modernism is Béla Lajta's Rózsavölgyi House (Map p238; V Szervita tér 5). You would probably never guess it, but this apartment block was built in 1912.

Bauhaus was a dominant architectural style in Budapest between 1930 and just after the war. Large residential buildings were built in this style particularly along Pozsonyi út (Map p248) in Újlipótváros and in the Városmajor district of Buda, where you'll see the stunning Városmajor Church (Map p230; XII Csaba utca 5) designed by Bertalan Árkay and completed in 1937.

Ödön Lechner has been nicknamed 'the Hungarian Gaudí' because, like the great Catalan master, he took an existing style and put his own spin on it, creating something new and unique for his time and place.

CONTEMPORARY

Postwar modern architecture in Budapest is almost completely forgettable – with the one notable exception of Imre Makovecz, who has developed his own 'organic' style using unusual materials like tree trunks and turf, and whose work can be seen at the Makovec office building (Map p242) at VIII Szentkirályi utca 18 and the spectacular funerary chapel with its reverse vaulted ceiling at the Farkasréti Cemetery (Map p233) in district XII. The National Theatre (p131), designed by Mária Siklós in 2002 in the 'Eclectic' style to mirror other great Budapest buildings of that style, is nothing short of a disaster.

Music

Hungary's contribution to music – especially the classical variety, called *komolyzene* ('serious music') in Hungarian – belies the size of the country and its population; its operas are world class. Of particular note and interest is Hungarian folk music, which has enjoyed something of a renaissance over the past few decades thanks to the *táncház* ('dance house') phenomena.

CLASSICAL MUSIC

One person stands head and shoulders above the rest: Franz (Ferenc) Liszt (1811–86). He established the sublime Ferenc Liszt Music Academy (p115), still the performance space of choice in Budapest, and lived in an apartment on VI Vörösmarty utca from 1881 until his death, which is now the Franz Liszt Memorial Museum (p118). Liszt liked to describe himself as 'part Gypsy', and some of his works, notably the 20 *Hungarian Rhapsodies*, do echo the traditional music of the Roma people.

Béla Bartók (1881–1945) and Zoltán Kodály (1882–1967) were both long-term residents of Budapest; Bartók lived at II Csalán út 29 in the Buda Hills (the house is now a museum; p78) while Kodály had an apartment at VI Kodály körönd 1 along Andrássy út. They made the first systematic study of Hungarian folk music together, travelling and recording throughout the Magyar linguistic regions in 1906. Both integrated some of their findings into their own compositions – Bartók in *Bluebeard's Castle,* for example, and Kodály in his *Peacock Variations*.

The most prestigious orchestras are the Budapest-based Hungarian National Philharmonic Orchestra and the Budapest Festival Orchestra, which has been voted by the London-based music magazine *Gramophone* as one of the world's top 10 symphonies.

OPERA & OPERETTA

Ferenc Erkel (1810–93), who taught at the Ferenc Liszt Music Academy from 1879 to 1886 and was the State Opera House's first musical director, is considered the father of Hungarian opera. Two of his works – the stirringly nationalistic *Bánk Bán,* based on József Katona's play of that name, and *László Hunyadi* – are standards at the State Opera House despite the dated political content of some of the librettos.

Imre Kálmán (1882–1953) is Hungary's most celebrated composer of operettas. *The Gypsy Princess* and *Countess Marica* are two of his most popular works and standard fare at the Budapest Operetta on Nagymező utca. Hungarian by birth but settling in Vienna in his late 20s, Franz (Ferenc) Lehár is also famous for his operettas, the most successful of which was *The Merry Widow*. It opened at the Magyar Színház (Hungarian Theatre, now the National Theatre) in November 1906 and ran for more than 100 performances.

FOLK MUSIC

Hungarian vs Gypsy Folk Music

It is important to distinguish between Hungarian folk music and so-called Gypsy music. Gypsy music as it is known and heard in Hungarian restaurants from Budapest to Boston is urban schmaltz and based on rousing recruitment tunes called *verbunkos,* played during the Rákóczi

Ferenc Liszt was born in the Hungarian village of Doborján (now Raiding in Austria) to a Hungarian father and an Austrian mother but never learned to speak Hungarian fluently.

TÁNCHÁZ

independence wars. For a century the international acclaim afforded the *verbunkos* eclipsed all other forms of traditional Hungarian folk music. At least two fiddles, a bass and a cymbalom (a curious stringed instrument played with sticks) are de rigueur in 'Gypsy' music. You can hear this saccharine music at hotel restaurants throughout Budapest or get hold of a recording by Sándor Déki Lakatos, the sixth band leader from the famous Lakatos dynasty.

Roma Folk Music

To confuse matters, real Roma – as opposed to Gypsy – music traditionally does not use instruments but is sung a cappella, though a technique called oral-bassing which vocally imitates the sound of instruments is often used. Some modern Roma music groups – Kalyi Jag (Black Fire), Romano Drom (Gypsy Road) and Romani Rota (Gypsy Wheels) – have added guitars, percussion and electronics to create a whole new sound. Gyula Babos' Project Romani has used elements of avant-garde jazz.

Instruments & Táncház

Hungarian folk musicians play violins, zithers, hurdy-gurdies, pipes, bagpipes and lutes on a five-tone diatonic scale; this makes it quite different from the Italian and German music that dominated the rest of Europe and not to everyone's taste (at least at first). Attending a *táncház* (literally 'dance house'; really folk-music workshops) is an excellent way to hear the music and even to learn to dance. It's all good fun and they're easy to find in Budapest, where the dance-house revival began.

For a complete and up-to-date listing of times, dates and places of *táncház* meetings and performances in Budapest, check out www.tanchaz.hu.

Hungarian Folk Musicians

Watch out for Muzsikás, Márta Sebestyén, Ghymes (a Hungarian folk band from Slovakia) and the Hungarian group Vujicsics, which mixes elements of South Slav music. Anyone playing the haunting music of the Csángó, an ethnic group of Hungarians living in eastern Transylvania and Moldavia, is a good bet. Another folk musician with eclectic tastes is the Paris-trained Beáta Pálya, who combines such sounds as traditional Bulgarian and Indian music with Hungarian folk.

Klezmer Music

In Anthony Minghella's film *The English Patient* (1996), when László Almásy (Ralph Fiennes) plays a Hungarian folk song on the phonograph for Katharine Clifton (Kristin Scott Thomas), it is Márta Sebestyén singing 'Szerelem, Szerelem' (Love, Love).

Traditional Yiddish music is not as well known as the Gypsy and Roma varieties but is of similar origin, having once been closely associated with central European folk music. Until WWI, *klezmer* dance bands were led by the violin and cymbalom, but the influence of Yiddish theatre and the first wax recordings inspired the inclusion of the clarinet. *Klezmer* music is currently going through something of a renaissance in Budapest and there are several bands performing, most at venues in the Jewish Quarter of Erzsébetváros.

POP MUSIC

Pop music is as popular here as anywhere and covers the full range – from punk (Auróra) and hip-hop (Bëlga) to electronic (Ferenc Vaspöeri) and bubblegum (just tune into any AM station to hear that style of music). In fact, Budapest hosts one of Europe's biggest annual pop events, the Sziget Music Festival (www.sziget.hu) in mid-August on Budapest's Óbuda (Hajógyári) Island north of Margaret Island. It boasts more than 1000 performances over a week and attracts an audience of more than 400,000 people.

Literature

No one could have put it better than the poet Gyula Illyés (1902–83), who wrote: 'The Hungarian language is at one and the same time our softest cradle and our most solid coffin.' The difficulty and subtlety of the Magyar tongue has excluded most outsiders from Hungarian literature, and though it would be wonderful to be able to read much of what is discussed here in the original, most people will have to make do with what they can find in English. Most of the works mentioned here are available in translation at the bookshops listed on p43.

TURKISH OCCUPATION

Hungarian literature really only came into its own after the Battle of Mohács in 1526 and the century and a half of Turkish occupation. The most important poets of the period were Bálint Balassi (1554–94) and Miklós Zrínyi (1620–64). Balassi's poetry shows medieval influences and his work is divided among love poems, swashbuckling odes and religious poems. Zrínyi's most significant work, the epic *Peril of Sziget* (1651), is written in a fashion similar to the Iliad and describes the heroic 1566 Battle of Szigetvár in Southern Transdanubia, in which his great-grandfather famously died while defending the castle there.

Hungarian Literature Online (www.hlo.hu) leaves no page unturned in the world of Hungarian books, addressing everyone from writers and editors to translators and publishers, with a useful list of links as well.

BORN OF STRUGGLE

Sándor Petőfi (1823–49), who led the Youth of March through the streets of Pest in 1848, is Hungary's most celebrated and widely read poet, and a line from his work 'Nemzeti Dal' (National Song) became the rallying cry for the 1848–49 War of Independence, in which the young poet fought and died. A deeply philosophical play called *The Tragedy of Man* by his colleague, Imre Madách (1823–64), published a decade after Hungary's defeat in the War of Independence, is still considered to be the country's greatest classical drama. Madách did not participate in the war due to illness but was imprisoned in Pest for assisting Lajos Kossuth's secretary in 1852.

GET-READY READING

Tony Láng, doyen of Budapest booksellers and owner of Bestsellers (p103), recommends any of the following five books as reading in preparation for your visit to Budapest.

➡ **Budapest 1900: A Historical Portrait of a City and Its Culture** (John Lukacs; 1994) Still a classic, this illustrated social history is indispensable for understanding Budapest today.

➡ **Castles Burning: A Child's Life in War** (Magda Dénes; 1998) Gripping but never sentimental, very detailed story of how a nine-year-old survived the Nazi occupation of Budapest.

➡ **The Will to Survive: A History of Hungary** (Bryan Cartledge; 2011) The best all-round general history of Hungary by a former British diplomat.

➡ **Ballad of the Whiskey Robber** (Julian Rubinstein; 2005) Almost unbelievable true story of one Attila Ambrus, who took up bankrobbing when not playing professional ice hockey – a portrait of what was the 'Wild East' of Budapest in the early 1990s.

➡ **Twelve Days: The Story of the 1956 Hungarian Revolution** (Victor Sebestyen; 2007) Meticulously researched and comprehensive day-by-day account of the 12 days between the outbreak of the popular revolt and its brutal suppression by the Soviets.

HISTORICAL ROMANTICISM & POPULISM

Hungary's defeat by the Habsburgs in 1849 led many writers to look to Historical Romanticism – a rose-coloured view of the past – for comfort and inspiration: winners, heroes and knights in shining armour became popular subjects. Petőfi's comrade-in-arms, János Arany (1817–82), whose name is synonymous with impeccable Hungarian and who edited two Pest literary journals in the 1860s, wrote epic poetry (including the *Toldi Trilogy*) and ballads.

Another friend of Petőfi, the prolific novelist Mór Jókai (1825–1904), who divided his time between his villa in Buda and his summer retreat at Balatonfüred on Lake Balaton, wrote of heroism and honesty in such wonderful works as *The Man with the Golden Touch* and *Black Diamonds*. This 'Hungarian Dickens' still enjoys widespread popularity. Another perennial favourite, Kálmán Mikszáth (1847–1910) wrote satirical tales such as *St Peter's Umbrella* in which he poked fun at the declining gentry and *The Good Palóc People*. (The Palóc are a distinct Slovakian-influenced Hungarian group living in the fertile hills and valleys of northern Hungary.)

Zsigmond Móricz (1879–1942), one of the cofounders of the influential literary magazine *Nyugat* (West) in 1908, was a very different type of writer. His works, in the tradition of the French naturalist Émile Zola (1840–1902), examined the harsh reality of peasant life in late 19th-century Hungary. His contemporary, Mihály Babits (1883–1941), poet and the editor of *Nyugat*, made the rejuvenation of Hungarian literature his lifelong work.

> The former US president Theodore Roosevelt (1858–1919) enjoyed *St Peter's Umbrella* by Kálmán Mikszáth so much that he insisted on meeting the ageing novelist during a European tour in 1910.

MY CAFE, MY CASTLE

Budapest cafes of the 19th century were a lot more than just places to drink coffee that was 'black like the devil, hot like hell and sweet like a kiss', as they used to say here. They embodied the progressive liberal ideal that people of all classes could mingle under one roof, and acted as an incubator for Magyar culture. Combining the neighbourliness of a local pub, the bonhomie of a gentlemen's club and the intellectual activity of an open university, coffee houses were places to relax, gamble, work, network, do business and debate. As the writer Dezső Kosztolányi put it in his essay *Budapest, City of Cafés: 'Az én kávéházam, az én váram'* (My cafe is my castle).

Different cafes catered to different groups. Actors preferred the Pannónia, artists the Café Japán and businessmen the Orczy, while cartoonists frequented the Lánchíd and stockbrokers the Lloyd. But the two most important cafes in terms of the city's cultural life were the New York and the Central.

The New York Café (p123), which opened in 1894 and quickly became the city's most celebrated literary cafe, hosted virtually every Hungarian writer of note at one time or another – from Kosztolányi and Endre Ady to Gyula Krúdy and Ferenc Molnár. Molnár, playwright-in-residence at the Comedy Theatre, famously threw the key to the New York into the Danube the night the cafe opened so that it would never close. And that's just what it did, remaining open round the clock 365 days a year for decades. The Central Kávéház (p87) attracted the same literati as well as the playwright Sándor Bródy and novelist Kálmán Mikszáth. Two literary journals – *Nyugat* (West) and *A Hét* (The Week) – were edited here. The gallery where the work was done is now the Central's restaurant section.

But all good things must come to an end, and the depression of the 1930s, the disruption of WWII and the dreary days of Communism conspired against grand old cafes in favour of the cheap (and seldom cheerful) *eszpresszó* (coffee shop). By 1989 and the return of the Republic of Hungary only about a dozen remained.

Nowadays, though, you're more likely to find young Budapesters drinking a beer or a glass of wine at one of the new modern cafes. It's true – the cafe is very much alive in Budapest. It's just reinvented itself, that's all.

20TH CENTURY

Two important names of this period are the poet and short-story writer Dezső Kosztolányi (1885–1936), who met his lifelong friend Babits at university in Pest, and the novelist Gyula Krúdy (1878–1933), whose *Adventures of Sinbad* experiments with time and space. His *Sunflower* is considered one of the most original novels in the Hungarian language.

A pair of 20th-century poets are unsurpassed in Hungarian letters. Endre Ady (1877–1919), who is sometimes described as the successor to Petőfi, was a reformer who ruthlessly attacked the complacency and materialism of Hungary at that time, provoking a storm of protest from right-wing nationalists. He died in his flat on V Veres Pálné utca in Pest at the age of 42. The work of the socialist poet Attila József (1905–1937), who was raised in the slums of Ferencváros, expressed the alienation felt by individuals in the modern age; his poem *By the Danube* is brilliant, even in translation.

Very popular worldwide is the work of the late Sándor Márai (1900–89), whose crisp, spare style has single-handedly encouraged worldwide interest in Hungarian literature.

The novelist Gyula Krúdy, who lived in Óbuda in the early part of the 20th century, enjoyed the bone marrow on toast as served at Kéhli (p79) so much that he included a description of it in his *Adventures of Sinbad*.

HUNGARIAN LITERATURE TODAY

Among Hungary's most important contemporary writers are Imre Kertész (1929–), György Konrád (1933–), Péter Nádas (1942–) and Péter Esterházy (1950–). Konrád's *A Feast in the Garden* (1985) is an almost autobiographical account of the fate of the Jewish community in a small eastern Hungarian town. *A Book of Memoirs* by Nádas concerns the decline of Communism in the style of Thomas Mann. In *The End of a Family Story*, Nádas uses a child narrator as a filter for the adult experience of 1950s Communist Hungary. Esterházy's *Celestial Harmonies* (2000) is a partly autobiographical novel that paints a favourable portrait of the protagonist's father. His subsequent *Revised Edition* (2002) is based on documents revealing his father to have been a government informer during the Communist regime. Oh-oh.

Novelist and Auschwitz survivor Kertész won the Nobel Prize for Literature in 2002, the first time a Hungarian has gained that distinction. Among his novels available in English are *Fatelessness* (1975), *A Detective Story* (1977), *Fiasco* (1988), *Kaddish for an Unborn Child* (1990) and *Liquidation* (2003). Hungary's foremost female contemporary writer, the widely read Magda Szabó, died in 2007 at age 90. Her best known works are *Katalin Street* (1969), *Abigail* (1970) and *The Door* (1987), a compelling story of a woman writer and the symbiotic relationship she has with her peasant housekeeper.

Folk Art

Hungary has one of the richest folk traditions in Europe and, quite apart from its music, this is where the country has often walked across the world stage in art. Many Budapesti probably wouldn't want to hear that, considering folk art a bit déclassé and its elevation the work of the former communist regime, but it's true. It would be foolish – if not impossible – to ignore folk art when discussing fine art. The two have been inextricably linked for several centuries and have greatly influenced one another. The music of Béla Bartók and the ceramic sculptures of Margit Kovács are deeply rooted in traditional culture.

BUYING & SEEING

The best place in Budapest to view work by the finest folk artists in Hungary is the sprawling Ethnography Museum (p96), opposite the Parliament building with thousands of displays in more than a dozen rooms. To see many of these objects in situ and 'at work' visit the Hungarian Open-Air Ethnological Museum (p149), in Szentendre, which is an easy day trip from Budapest. You'll see a lot of 'folk art' for sale in the capital but a sign announcing a shop to be a *népművészeti bolt* (folk-art shop) is not enough. More often than not they're filled with mass-produced kitsch. To separate the wheat from the chaff (and the China-made), see the Best for Hungarica list on p43.

ORIGINS

From the beginning of the 18th century, as segments of the Hungarian peasantry became more prosperous, ordinary people tried to make their world more beautiful by painting and decorating objects and clothing. It's important to remember two things when looking at folk art. First, with very few exceptions, only practical objects used daily were decorated. Second, this was not 'court art' or the work of artisans making Chinese cloisonné or Fabergé eggs. It was the work of ordinary people trying to express the simple world around them in a new and different way. Some of it is excellent and occasionally you will spot the work of a genius who probably never ventured beyond his or her village or farm.

Outside museums most folk art produced and used in daily life in Hungary is largely moribund though the ethnic Hungarian regions of Transylvania in Romania are a different story. Through isolation or a refusal to let go for economic or aesthetic reasons, however, pockets remain throughout the country.

WEAVING & NEEDLEWORK

The main centre of cottage weaving has always been the Sárköz region near Szekszárd in Southern Transdanubia – its distinctive black and red fabric is copied everywhere. Simpler homespun material can be found in the Northeast, especially around the Tiszahát.

Three groups of people stand out for their embroidery, the acme of Hungarian folk art: the Palóc of the Northern Uplands, especially around the village of Hollókő; the Matyó from Mezőkövesd, who stitch

PICTURE BOOK

Hungarian Folk Art by Tamás Hofer and Edit Fél is an oversized *picture book* that offers a good introduction, but the real gem is *Hungarian Ethnography and Folklore* by Iván Balassa and Gyula Ortutay, an 800-page opus that leaves no question unanswered. It's out of print but available used online.

predominantly in reds, blues and blacks; and the women of Kalocsa on the southern part of the Great Plain, who produce the most colourful work. Each style has its own merits but to our minds no one works a needle like a Matyó seamstress. Also impressive are the woollen waterproof coats called *szűr*, once worn by herders on the Great Plain, which were masterfully embroidered by men using thick, furry yarn.

POTTERY

Folk pottery is world-class here and no Hungarian kitchen is complete without a couple of pairs of matched plates or shallow bowls hanging on the walls. The centre of this industry is in the Great Plain towns of Hódmezővásárhely, Karcag and Tiszafüred, though fine examples also come from Transdanubia, especially the Őrség region. There are jugs, pitchers, plates, bowls and cups, but the rarest and most attractive are the *irókázás fazékok* (inscribed pots) – usually celebrating a wedding day or in the form of animals or the form of people, such as the *Miskai kancsó* (Miska jugs), not unlike Toby jugs in England – from the Tisza River region. Nádudvar near Hajdúszoboszló on the Great Plain specialises in black pottery – striking items and far superior to the greyish stuff produced at Mohács in Southern Transdanubia.

Though a commercial website, www.folk-art-hungary.com is an excellent introduction and primer to embroidery and other textile folk art by artisans in Kalocsa, Mezőkövesd and Hollókő.

WOODCARVING & FURNITURE

Objects carved from wood or bone – mangling boards, honey-cake moulds, mirror cases, tobacco holders, salt cellars – were usually the work of herders or farmers idle in winter. The shepherds and swineherds of Somogy County south of Lake Balaton and the cowherds of the Hortobágy excelled at this work, and their illustrations of celebrations and local 'Robin Hood' outlaws – including the paprika-tempered Patkós István (Horseshoe Steve) – are always fun to look at.

Most people made and decorated their own furniture in the old days, especially cupboards for the *tiszta szoba* (parlour) and *tulipán ládák* (trousseau chests with tulips painted on them). Among the finest traditional furniture in Hungary are the tables and chairs made of golden spotted poplar from the Gemenc Forest near Szekszárd in Southern Transdanubia. The oaken chests decorated with geometrical shapes from the nearby Ormánság region are superior to the run-of-the-mill tulip chests.

PAINTING

One art form that ventures into the realm of fine art is ceiling and wall folk painting. Among the best examples of the former can be found in churches, especially in the Northeast (eg at Tákos), the Northern Uplands (Füzér) and the Ormánság (Drávaiványi) of Southern Transdanubia. The women of Kalocsa also specialise in colourful wall painting, some of them so overdone as to be garish. Easter-egg painting remains popular throughout the country. Eschew the multicoloured kitsch ones in favour of the ones in just one or two colours.

Survival Guide

Transport

GETTING TO BUDAPEST

Budapest is accessible by just about any form of transport you care to name. Arrival by air is the most common way, but you can also reach Budapest from dozens of European cities by bus and from points as far away as London (via Munich and Paris), Stockholm (via Hamburg and Copenhagen), Moscow, Rome and Istanbul (via Belgrade). You can even get to Budapest by hydrofoil on the Danube from Vienna and Bratislava.

And then, of course, there's road travel – by car, motorbike and bicycle.

Border formalities with three of Hungary's EU neighbours – Austria, Slovenia and Slovakia – are virtually nonexistent. However, as a member state that forms part of the EU's external frontier, Hungary must implement the strict Schengen border rules so expect a somewhat closer inspection of your documents when travelling to/from Croatia, Ukraine, Serbia and Romania, which though a member of the EU has not yet been allowed to join the Schengen area.

Everyone needs a valid passport or, for many EU citizens, a national identification card to enter Hungary. For more on visas, see p211.

Flights, tours and rail tickets can be booked online at lonelyplanet.com/bookings.

Air

Budapest can be reached directly from destinations around the world but its most important gateways are in continental Europe, served mostly by what Hungarians call the *fapados* (wooden bench) airlines – the super-discount carriers such as **EasyJet** (www.easyjet.com), **Germanwings** (www.germanwings.com) and **Wizzair** (www.wizzair.com).

The national carrier, **Malév Hungarian Airlines** (✆06-40 212 121, from abroad +36-1 802 1111; www.malev.com) flies to Budapest from North America, the Middle East and more than 50 cities in continental Europe and the British Isles.

The central **Malév Air Tours** (✆769 0717; www.airtours.hu, in Hungarian; V Petőfi Sándor utca 10; ◷9am-6pm Mon-Fri, to 1pm Sat; Ⓜ M3 Ferenciek tere) issues tickets. Malév also has ticket-issuing desks at the airport.

There are no scheduled flights within Hungary.

Airport

Budapest's **Ferenc Liszt International Airport** (✆296 9696, flight info 296 7000; www.bud.hu), what everyone still calls Ferihegy, has two modern terminals side by side 24km southeast of the city centre and an older one about 5km to the west.

Malév and airlines flying to/from countries with the Schengen border use Terminal 2A. Other international flights use Terminal 2B, which is next door and within easy walking distance. The discount European carriers use Terminal 1.

Malév has ticket-sales counters in **Terminal 2A** (◷5am-11pm) and **Terminal 2B** (◷6am-8.30pm). At both terminals you'll also find currency-exchange desks operated by **Interchange** (◷5am-midnight) and ATMs. In Terminal A there are half a dozen car-rental desks and a **left-luggage office** (◷24hr).

Bus

All international buses and domestic ones to/from western Hungary arrive at and depart from **Népliget bus station** (Map p242; ✆219 8030; IX Üllői út 131; Ⓜ M3 Népliget) in Pest. The **international ticket office** (✆219 8020; ◷6am-6pm Mon-Fri, to 4pm Sat & Sun) is upstairs. **Eurolines** (✆382 0888; www.eurolines.hu) is represented here, as is its Hungarian associate, **Volánbusz** (✆219 800; www.volanbusz.hu). There's a **left-luggage office** (per piece per day 300Ft; ◷6am-9pm) downstairs.

Stadion bus station (Map p254; ✆220 6227; XIV Hungária körút 48-52; Ⓜ M2 Puskás Ferenc Stadion) generally serves cities and towns in eastern Hungary. The **ticket office** (◷6am-6pm Mon-Fri, to 5pm Sat & Sun) and the **left-luggage office** (per piece per day 300Ft; ◷6am-7pm) are on the ground floor.

CLIMATE CHANGE & TRAVEL

Every form of transport that relies on carbon-based fuel generates CO_2, the main cause of human-induced climate change. Modern travel is dependent on aeroplanes, which might use less fuel per kilometre per person than most cars but travel much greater distances. The altitude at which aircraft emit gases (including CO_2) and particles also contributes to their climate change impact. Many websites offer 'carbon calculators' that allow people to estimate the carbon emissions generated by their journey and, for those who wish to do so, to offset the impact of the greenhouse gases emitted with contributions to portfolios of climate-friendly initiatives throughout the world. Lonely Planet offsets the carbon footprint of all staff and author travel.

Train

Magyar Államvasutak (☑06-40 494 949, from abroad +36-1 444 4499; www.mav.hu), which translates as Hungarian State Railways and is universally known as MÁV, links up with the European rail network in all directions and its trains run as far as London (via Munich and Paris), Stockholm (via Hamburg and Copenhagen), Moscow, Rome and Istanbul (via Belgrade). Internally MÁV operates reliable and relatively comfortable train services on just over 7600km of track.

Budapest has three main train stations:

Keleti pályaudvar (Eastern train station; Map p254; VIII Kerepesi út 2-6; ⓂM3 Keleti pályaudvar) Most international trains; domestic traffic to/from the north and northeast.

Nyugati pályaudvar (Western train station; Map p244; VI Teréz körút 55-57; ⓂM3 Nyugati pályaudvar) Some international destinations (eg Romania); trains for the Danube Bend and Great Plain.

Déli pályaudvar (Southern train station; Map p230; I Krisztina körút 37; ⓂM2 Déli pályaudvar) Some destinations in the south, eg Osijek in Croatia and Sarajevo in Bosnia.

The train stations all have amenities, including small/large left-luggage lockers costing 400/600Ft per 24-hour day. You'll also find post offices and grocery stores that are open late. All three stations are on metro lines and night buses serve them when the metro is closed.

Avoid the queues at the train stations by buying your tickets in advance at the **MÁV-Start passenger service centre** (☑512 7921; www.mav-start.hu; V József Attila utca 16; ⓒ9am-6pm Mon-Fri; ⓂM1/2/3 Deák Ferenc tér).

Car & Motorcycle

In Hungary you drive on the right. Speed limits are consistent across the country and strictly enforced: 50km/h in built-up areas; 90km/h on secondary and tertiary roads; 110km/h on most highways/dual carriageways; and 130km/h on motorways. Exceeding the limit will earn a fine of between 10,000Ft and 45,000Ft.

The use of seat belts in the front (and in the back – if fitted – outside built-up areas) is compulsory. Motorcyclists must wear helmets, a law strictly enforced. Another law taken very seriously is the one requiring all drivers to use their headlights throughout the day outside built-up areas. Motorcycles must illuminate headlights at all times, everywhere. Using a mobile phone while driving is prohibited.

There is a 100% ban on drinking alcohol before driving, which is very strictly enforced (see p208).

All cars must bear a motorway pass or *matrica* (vignette) to access Hungary's motorways. Passes, which cost 1650Ft for four days, 2750Ft for 10 days and 4500Ft for a month, are available at petrol stations, post offices and some motorway entrances and border crossings. A Hungarian rental car will already have one.

Motorists anywhere in Hungary can call the **Hungarian Automobile Club** (Magyar Autóklub; ☑188) for roadside assistance.

Boat

A hydrofoil service on the Danube River between Budapest and Vienna (5½ to 6½ hours) is run by **Mahart PassNave** (☑484 4013; www.mahart.info; V Belgrád rakpart; ⓒ8am-6pm Mon-Fri, from 9.15am Sat & Sun) and operates from late April to early October; passengers can board or disembark at Bratislava with advance notice. Boats leave from Budapest at 9am daily in August, but on Tuesday, Thursday and Saturday only during the rest of the period of operation. From Vienna they go at 9am daily in August and Wednesday, Friday and Sunday only otherwise. Adult one-way/return fares for Vienna are €89/109 and for Bratislava €79/99. Students with ISIC cards receive 25% discount, and children between two and 14 years of age travel for half price. Taking a bicycle costs €20 one-way.

In Budapest, hydrofoils arrive at and depart from the **International Ferry Pier**

GETTING INTO TOWN FROM THE AIRPORTS

Reaching the centre of Budapest from the airports is straightforward and inexpensive, thanks to a raft of public-transport options.

Fő Taxi (☎06 222 2222; www.fotaxi.hu) has the monopoly on picking up taxi passengers at the airport. Fares to most locations in Pest are 5100Ft, and in Buda 5300Ft to 5700Ft. Of course you can take any taxi to the airport and several companies have a flat, discounted fare on offer. **City Taxi** (☎211 1111; www.citytaxi.hu), for example, charges 4800Ft from points in Pest and 5300Ft from Buda.

The **Airport Shuttle Minibusz** (☎296 8555; www.airportshuttle.hu) ferries passengers from all three terminals directly to their hotel, hostel or residence (one-way/return 2990/4990Ft). Tickets are available at a clearly marked desk in the arrivals halls though you may have to wait while the van fills up. You need to book your journey back to the airport at least 12 hours in advance, but remember that, with a number of pick-ups en route, this can be a nerve-wracking way to go should you be running late.

The confusingly named **Weekend Bus** (☎262 6262; www.weekendbus.hu; 1400Ft) runs buses daily from all three terminals to central Erzsébet tér (opposite Le Meridien Budapest) and Széchenyi István tér (near the Four Seasons Gresham Palace Hotel) from 5am to midnight. The first and last pick-ups from town are an hour earlier.

The cheapest (and most time-consuming) way to get into the city centre from Terminal 2 is to take **city bus 200E** (320Ft, on the bus 400Ft) – look for the stop on the footpath between terminals 2A and 2B – which terminates at the Kőbánya-Kispest metro station. From there take the M3 metro into the city centre. The total cost is 640Ft to 720Ft. Bus 93 runs from Terminal 1 to the same metro station.

Trains link Terminal 1 (only) with Nyugati station. They run between one and six times an hour from 4am to 11pm and cost 365Ft. The journey takes just 20 minutes.

(Nemzetközi hajóállomás; Map p238; ☎06-30 332 4431; V Belgrád rakpart), which is between Elizabeth and Liberty Bridges on the Pest side. In Vienna, the boats dock at the Reichsbrücke pier near Mexikoplatz.

GETTING AROUND BUDAPEST

Budapest is a very easy city to negotiate – the Danube clearly defines east and west and Pest and Buda. There is a safe, efficient and inexpensive public transport system that is rapidly being upgraded and will never have you waiting more than five or 10 minutes for any conveyance. Five types of vehicle are in general use: metro trains on three (soon to be four) city lines, green HÉV trains on four suburban lines, blue buses, yellow trams and red trolleybuses. But you can also do it yourself by bicycle, car or motorbike.

Bicycle

More and more cyclists can be seen on the streets of Budapest, taking advantage of the city's growing network of dedicated bike paths. Some of the main roads might be a bit too busy for enjoyable cycling, but the side streets are fine and there are some areas (eg City Park, Margaret Island) where cycling is positively ideal. You can hire bicycles from the following:

Bike Base (Map p244; ☎06-70 625 8501; www.bikebase.hu; VI Podmaniczky utca 19; per 6hr/same day/24hr 1600/2000/2400Ft; ⏰9am-7pm; ⒨M3 Nyugati pályaudvar)

Budapest Bike (Map p250; ☎06-30 944 5533; www.budapestbike.hu; VII Wesselényi utca 13; per 6/24hr 2000/3000Ft; ⏰9am-6pm; ⒨M2 Astoria; ⒯4, 6; ⒝74)

Discover Budapest (Map p250; ☎269 3843; www.discoverbudapest.com; VI Lázár utca 16; per hr/same day 500/1500Ft; ⏰9.30am-8pm May-Oct, to 6pm Mon-Fri, 10am-4pm Sat & Sun Nov-Mar, 9.30am-7pm Apr; ⒨M1 Opera)

Gödör Bike Rental (Map p238; ☎06-70 506 6345; www.godorklub.hu; V Erzsébet tér; per 4/8/12/24hr 2300/3200/3600/4100Ft; ⏰8am-8pm May-Oct; ⒨M1/2/3 Deák Ferenc tér)

For places to rent bikes on Margaret Island, see p106.

Bus

An extensive system of buses running on some 240 routes day and night serves greater Budapest. On certain bus lines the same bus may have an 'E' after the number, meaning it is express and makes limited stops.

Buses run from around 4.15am to between 9pm and 11.30pm, depending on the line. From 11.30pm to just after 4am a network of 35 night buses (always with three digits and beginning with '9') operates every 15 to 60 minutes, again depending on the route. For information on fares and passes, see the boxed text, p205.

Following are bus routes (shown with blue lines on most Budapest maps) that you might find useful:

7 Cuts across a large swath of central Pest from XIV Bosnyák tér and down VII Rákóczi út before crossing Elizabeth Bridge to southern Buda. The 7E makes limited stops on the same route.

15 Takes in most of the Inner Town from IX Boráros tér to XIII Lehel tér north of Nyugati train station.

86 Runs the length of Buda from XI Kosztolányi Dezső tér to Óbuda.

105 Goes from V Deák Ferenc tér to XII Apor Vilmos tér in central Buda.

Metro & HÉV

Budapest has three underground metro lines that converge at Deák Ferenc tér only: the little yellow (or Millennium) line designated M1 that runs from Vörösmarty tér to Mexikói út in Pest; the red M2 line from Déli train station in Buda to Örs vezér tere in Pest; and the blue M3 line from Újpest-Központ to Kőbánya-Kispest in Pest. The city's long-awaited M4 metro line is currently under construction and will run from Kelenföldi train station in southern Buda to XIV Bosnyák tér in northeastern Pest. The first section, between Kelenföldi and Keleti train stations, covering 7.5km and 10 stations (two of them transfers to lines M2 and M3), is due to open in 2014.

All three metro lines run from about 4am and begin their last journey at around 11.15pm. See the boxed text,

p205, for information about fares and passes.

The HÉV suburban train line, which runs on four lines (north from Batthyány tér in Buda via Óbuda and Aquincum to Szentendre, south to both Csepel and Ráckeve, and east to Gödöllő), is almost like an additional above-ground metro line.

Taxi

Taxis in Budapest are cheap by European standards, but be careful when hailing one on the street. Avoid at all costs 'taxis' with no name on the door and only a removable taxi light on the roof. Never get into a taxi that does not have a yellow licence plate and an identification badge displayed on the dashboard (as required by law), the logo of one of the reputable taxi firms on the outside of the side doors and a table of fares clearly visible on the right-side back door.

In any case, Budapest residents – both Hungarian and foreign – rarely flag down taxis in the street. They almost always ring for them; fares are actually cheaper if you book over the phone.

Not all taxi meters are set at the same rates, but there are price ceilings under which taxi companies are free to manoeuvre. From 6am to 10pm the highest legal fee at flag fall is 300Ft, the per-kilometre charge is 240Ft and the waiting fee 60Ft. The per-kilometre charge rises to 300Ft after 10pm.

Reputable taxi firms:

City (☎211 1111; www.city taxi.hu)

Fő (☎222 2222; www.fo taxi.hu)

Rádió (☎377 7777; www .radiotaxi.hu)

Taxi 4 (☎444 4444; www .taxi4.hu)

Tram

BKV currently runs 30 tram lines. Trams are often faster and generally more pleasant for sightseeing than buses.

Important tram lines (always marked with a red line on a Budapest map):

2 & 2A Scenic tram that travels along the Pest side of the Danube from V Jászai Mari tér to IX Boráros tér and beyond.

4 & 6 Extremely useful trams that start at XI Fehérvári út and XI Móricz Zsigmond körtér in south Buda, respectively, and follow the entire length of the Big Ring Rd in Pest before terminating at II Széll Kálmán tér in Buda. Tram 6 now runs every 10 to 15 minutes round-the-clock.

18 Runs from southern Buda along XI Bartók Béla út through the Tabán to II Széll Kálmán tér before carrying on into the Buda Hills.

19 Covers part of the same route as 18, but then runs along the Buda side of the Danube to I Batthyány tér.

47 & 49 Link V Deák Ferenc tér in Pest with points in southern Buda via the Little Ring Rd.

61 Connects XI Móricz Zsigmond körtér with Déli train station and II Széll Kálmán tér in Buda.

Trolleybus

Trolleybuses on 15 lines only go along cross streets in central Pest and so, in general, are of little use to most visitors, with the sole exception of the ones to, from and around City Park (70, 72 and 74) and down to Puskás Ferenc Stadion (75 and 77). A broken red line on a map indicates a trolleybus route.

Car & Motorcycle

Driving in Budapest can be a nightmare: ongoing roadworks reduce traffic to a snail's pace; there are more serious accidents than fender-benders; and parking spots are near impossible to find in some neighbourhoods. The public transport system is good and cheap. Use it.

For information on traffic and road conditions in the capital, ring **Főinform** (☑317 1173; ☉6am-9pm Mon-Fri, 7am-7pm Sat & Sun).

Hire

All the international car-rental firms have offices in Budapest, but don't expect many bargains. A Suzuki Swift from **Avis** (☑318 4240; www.avis.hu; V Arany János utca 26; ☉7am-6pm Mon-Fri, 8am-2pm Sat & Sun; Ⓜ3 Arany János utca), for example, costs €58/370 per day/week, with unlimited kilometres, collision damage waiver (CDW) and theft protection (TP) insurance. The same car and insurance with 750km costs just €65 for a weekend.

Parking

Parking costs between 120Ft and 430Ft per hour on the street (more on Castle Hill), generally between 8am and 6pm Monday to Friday and 8am and noon Saturday. There are 24-hour covered car parks charging from 490Ft to 750Ft per hour (4000Ft to 6500Ft overnight) below the Millennium Center at V Pesti Barnabás utca 4 (Map p238), at V Szervita tér 8 (Map p238) and at V Aranykéz utca 4–6 (Map p238) in the Inner Town, as well as at VII Nyár utca 20 (Map p250).

Illegally parked cars are usually clamped or booted.

Boat

Between late April and late August passenger ferries run by **BKV** (Budapest Transport Company; ☑258 4636; www.bkv.hu) depart from IX Boráros tér (Map p242) just north of Petőfi Bridge

between five and seven times daily and head for III Pünkösdfürdő in Óbuda, a 2¼-hour trip with 13 stops along the way. Tickets (adult/child 900/450Ft from end to end or between 250/150Ft and 600/300Ft for intermediate stops) are sold on board. The ferry stop closest to the Castle District is I Batthyány tér (Map p230), and V Petőfi tér is not far from the pier just west of Vörösmarty tér (Map p238). Transporting a bicycle costs 700Ft.

TOURS

If you can't be bothered making your own way around Budapest or don't have the time, a guided tour can be a great way to learn the lie of the land.

Boat Tours

Several companies offer cruises on the Danube that include taped commentary in a multitude of languages and a free drink.

Mahart PassNave (☑484 4013; www.mahart.info.hu; V Belgrád rakpart; adult/child 2900/1490Ft; ☉10am-10pm May-late Sep, 11am-8pm late Sep-Oct & Apr; ⓠ2) One-hour trip between Margaret and Rákóczi bridges departs hourly.

Legenda (☑266 4190; www.legenda.hu; V Vigadó tér, pier 7; day cruise 1/2hr 2900/3900Ft, night cruise 4900Ft; ☉Mar-Oct; ⓠ2) Similar deal in 30 different languages has between four and eight daily departures.

River Ride (☑332 255; www.riverride.com; V Széchenyi István tér 7-8; adult/child 7500/5000Ft; ☉Mar-Oct; ⓠ2) Amphibious bus takes you on a weird two-hour heart-stopping tour of Budapest by road and river; live commentary.

Bus Tours

Increasingly popular are hop-on, hop-off bus tours that allow you to get off and on as you please for a selected time.

Program Centrum (☑317 7767; www.programcentrum.hu; V Erzsébet tér 9-10; tours 5000Ft; ☉10am-6pm Mar-Oct; Ⓜ1/2/3 Deák Ferenc tér) Valid on two bus routes (one taped in 23 languages, one live commentary in English and German) and a one-hour river cruise for 24 hours.

City Tour Budapest (☑374 7070; www.citytour.hu; VI Andrássy út 2; tours 4500Ft; ☉10am-7.30pm Mar-Oct; Ⓜ1/2/3 Deák Ferenc tér) Similar but cheaper deal in 16 languages.

If you prefer to stay seated, **Cityrama** (☑302 4382; www.cityrama.hu; V Báthory utca 22; adult/child 6500/3000Ft; ☉10am & 2.30pm Mar-Oct; Ⓜ3 Arany János utca) offers three-hour city tours, including several photo-op stops, with live commentary in five languages.

Cycling Tours

All of the bike-hire companies listed on p202 offer tours for around 5000Ft per person, but itineraries really depend on the whim of the group leader.

Yellow Zebra Bikes (www.yellowzebrabikes.com) Based at Discover Budapest (p202), Yellow Zebra runs cycling tours (adult/student 5500/5000Ft) of the city that take in Heroes' Square, City Park, inner Pest and Castle Hill in around 3½ hours. Tours, which include the bike, depart from in front of the Lutheran church in V Deák Ferenc tér (Map p238) at 11am daily from April to October, with an additional departure at 4pm in July and August. In November and March they depart

PUBLIC TRANSPORT FARES & PASSES

Budapest's public transport system is operated by **BKV** (Budapest Transport Company; ☑258 4636; www.bkv.hu). Anyone planning to travel extensively by public transport should invest in the invaluable *Budapesti Közlekedési Térképe* (Budapest Public Transport Map; 650Ft). You might also try the Route Planner on the BKV website.

To ride the metro, trams, trolleybuses, buses and the HÉV as far as the city limits, you must have a valid ticket, which you can buy at kiosks, newsstands, metro entrances, machines and, in some cases, on the bus for an extra charge. Children aged under six and EU seniors over 65 travel free. Bicycles can only be transported on the HÉV.

The basic fare for all forms of transport is 320Ft (2800Ft for a block of 10), allowing you to travel as far as you like on the same metro, bus, trolleybus or tram line without changing/transferring. A 'transfer ticket' allowing unlimited stations with one change within one hour costs 490Ft. On the metro exclusively, the base fare drops to 260Ft if you are just going three stops within 30 minutes. Tickets bought on the bus and all night buses cost 400Ft.

You must always travel in one continuous direction on any ticket; return trips are forbidden. Tickets have to be validated in machines at metro entrances and aboard other vehicles – inspectors will fine you for not doing so.

Life will most likely be simpler if you buy a travel pass. Passes are valid on all trams, buses, trolleybuses, HÉV (within the city limits) and metro lines, and you don't have to worry about validating your ticket each time you board. The most central places to buy them are ticket offices at the Deák Ferenc tér metro station (Map p238), the Nyugati pályaudvar metro station (Map p250) and the Déli pályaudvar metro station (Map p230), all open from 6am to 8pm daily.

A 24-hour travel card is poor value at 1550Ft, but the 72-hour one for 3850Ft and the seven-day pass for 4600Ft are worthwhile for most people. You'll need a photo for the fortnightly/monthly passes (6500/9800Ft).

Travelling 'black' (ie without a valid ticket or pass) is risky; with what seems like constant surveillance (especially in the metro), there's an excellent chance you'll get caught. The on-the-spot fine is 6000Ft, which doubles if you pay it at the **BKV office** (☑461 6800; VII Akácfa utca 22; ⊙6am-8pm Mon-Fri, 8am-1.45pm Sat; ⓜM2 Blaha Lujza tér) up to 30 days later, and 24,500Ft after that.

If you've left something on any form of public transport, contact the **BKV lost & found office** (☑461 6688; VII Akácfa utca 18; ⊙8am-5pm Mon-Fri; ⓜM2 Blaha Lujza tér).

TRANSPORT TOURS

---

at 11am on Friday, Saturday and Sunday only.

Walking Tours

Free Budapest Tours
(☑06-20 534 5819; www.free budapesttours.hu) Innovative and professional walking tours organised by an outfit whose name is as descriptive as it is, err, pedestrian; the guides work for tips only so dig deep into your pockets. The 1½-hour tour of Pest leaves from V Deák Ferenc tér (Map p238) daily at 10.30am and the 2½-hour tour of Buda from the front of Gerbeaud in V Vörösmarty tér (Map p238) daily at 2pm.

See the website for details on private tours.

Absolute Walking Tours
(www.absolutetours.com) A three-hour guided promenade through City Park, central Pest and Castle Hill (adult/student 4500/4000Ft) run by the people behind Yellow Zebra Bikes. Tours depart at 10.30am year-round, with an extra one at 2.30pm on Monday, Wednesday and Friday in July and August, from the steps of the Lutheran church in V Deák Ferenc tér (Map p238). It also has specialist tours, including the popular 3½-hour Hammer & Sickle Tour (adult/student 6200/5200Ft) of Budapest's communist past.

Hungária Koncert (☑317 1377; www.ticket.info.hu) Focusing on Budapest's Jewish heritage, a 1½- to two-hour tour leaves at 10am Monday to Friday, again at 2pm Monday to Thursday and at 11am Sunday year-round. The tour includes a visit to the Great Synagogue, the Jewish Museum and the Holocaust Cemetery for 3900Ft. The Grand Tour (an hour longer) adds the Orthodox Synagogue, a ghetto walking tour and a kosher snack, for 9400/8900Ft per adult/student. Tickets are available from locations throughout the city, including the **Duna Palota** (Map p244; V Zrínyi utca 5) entertainment centre.

Directory A–Z

Business Hours

The opening hours of any business are usually posted on the front door; *nyitva* means 'open', *zárva* is 'closed'.

In summer, some shops close early on Friday and shut down altogether for at least part of August.

In this guide, reviews only include business hours if they differ from the following standard hours:

Banks	7.45am-5pm or 6pm Mon, to 4pm or 5pm Tue-Thu, to 4pm Fri
Bars	11am-midnight Sun-Thu, to 1am or 2am Fri & Sat
Post offices	main offices: 7am or 8am-7pm or 8pm Mon-Fri, to noon or 2pm Sat; branches: 7am or 8am-4pm Mon-Fri
Restaurants	10am or 11am-11pm or midnight
Shops	9am or 10am-6pm Mon-Fri, 9am or 10am-1pm Sat, some to 8pm Thu
Supermarkets	6am or 7am-6pm or 7pm Mon-Fri, 7.30am-3pm Sat, some 7am-noon Sun

Customs Regulations

There is no longer duty-free shopping within the EU, of which Hungary is a member. You cannot, for example, buy tax-free goods in, say, Slovakia or Austria and take them to Hungary. However, you can still enter an EU country with duty-free items from countries outside the EU.

Allowances on duty-free goods purchased at airports or on ferries originating outside the EU are as follows: 200 cigarettes or 50 cigars or 250g loose tobacco; 4L still wine; 1L spirits. In addition you must declare the import/export of any amount of cash, cheques, securities etc exceeding the sum of €10,000.

When leaving Hungary, you are not supposed to take out valuable antiques without a special permit, which should be available from the place of purchase. For details, see p43.

Discount Cards

Budapest Card (www.buda pestinfo.hu; per 24/48/72hr 5500/6900/8300Ft) Free admission to selected museums and other sights in and around the city; unlimited travel on all forms of public transport; two free guided tours; and discounts for organised tours, car rental, thermal baths and selected shops and restaurants. Available online and at Tourinform offices.

European Youth Card (Euro<26 card; www.euro26.org; 1yr 1900Ft) Wide range of discounts for under-26s.

International Student Identity Card (ISIC; www.isic .org; 1yr 2480Ft) Discounts on some transport and cheap admission to museums and other sights for full-time students.

International Teacher Identity Card (ITIC; www.isic .org; 1yr 2480Ft) Similar benefits to ISIC for full-time teachers.

International Youth Travel Card (IYTC; www.isic.org; 1yr 2480Ft) Similar benefits to ISIC for nonstudents under 26.

Electricity

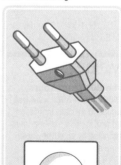

230v/50hz

PRACTICALITIES

➡ **Newspapers & Magazines** Budapest has two English-language newspapers: *Budapest Times* (www.budapesttimes.hu; 750Ft), a weekly with straightforward news, opinion pieces and reviews appearing on Friday, and the *Budapest Business Journal* (www.bbj.hu; 1250Ft), an almost archival publication of financial news and business, appearing every other Friday. The monthly *Diplomacy & Trade* (www.dteurope.com; 840Ft) offers a glimpse into the expat community. The erudite *Hungarian Quarterly* (www.hungarianquarterly.com; 1500Ft) is a valuable source of current Hungarian thinking in translation, as is the bimonthly *Hungarian Review* (www.hungarianreview.com; 1280Ft).

➡ **Radio** Magyar Radio (www.radio.hu) runs three main stations: MR1-Kossuth (107.8FM; news, talkback and jazz), MR2-Petőfi (94.8FM; popular music) and MR3-Bartók (105.3FM; classical music).

➡ **TV & Video** Like Australia and most of Europe, Hungary uses PAL, which is incompatible with the North American and Japanese NTSC system or the SECAM system used in France.

➡ **Smoking** From January 2012, smoking is illegal in all indoor public places including restaurants and bars.

➡ **Weights & Measures** Hungary uses the metric system.

Emergency

Any crime must be reported at the police station of the district you are in; if possible, bring along a Hungarian speaker.

Ambulance (☑104)

Belváros-Lipótváros police station (☑373 1000; V Szalay utca 11; Ⓜ M2 Kossuth Lajos tér) In the centre of Pest.

Crime hotline (☑438 8080; ⊗8am-8pm) English spoken.

Emergency (☑112) English spoken.

Fire (☑105)

Police (☑107)

Roadside assistance (☑188; ⊗24hr)

Gay & Lesbian Travellers

Budapest offers just a reasonable gay scene for its size. Most gay people are discreet in public places and displays of affection are rare. Lesbian social life remains very much underground, with a lot of parties private. Attitudes are changing but society generally remains conservative on this issue. The biggest news is that Budapest successfully bid to host the 2012 EuroGames, Europe's largest gay, lesbian and gay-friendly sporting event.

Top gay and lesbian venues are listed on p38, and gay-friendly accommodation on p157.

Useful resources:

Budapest Gay Guide (www.budapest.gayguide.net) Recommendations and insider advice.

Company (www.company media.hu) Free monthly magazine with up-to-date info on venues, events, parties and so on, available at gay venues throughout Budapest.

Gay Budapest (www.buda pest-gay.com) Recommendations and insider advice.

Háttér Gay & Lesbian Association (☑329 3380, 06-80 505 605; www.hatter.hu, in Hungarian; ⊗6-11pm) Advice and help line.

Labrisz Lesbian Association (www.labrisz .hu) Info on the city's lesbian scene.

Internet Access

Almost without exception wireless (wi-fi) access is available at hostels and hotels, though some of the latter charge for the service. More and more cafes and bars offer wi-fi, usually free to paying customers.

Most hostels and some hotels have at least one computer terminal available to guests either free or a nominal sum. If you can't log on where you're staying there's probably an internet cafe nearby, but they open and close at a rapid rate. Among the better equipped are the following:

Chatman Internet (VII Dohány utca 30; per 30/60min 80/100Ft; ⊗8am-11pm Mon-Fri, from 10am Sat & Sun; Ⓜ M2 Astoria; ☒74) Small, very friendly cafe just north of Rákóczi út.

Electric Café (VII Dohány utca 37; per 30/60min 100/200Ft; ⊗9am-midnight; Ⓜ M2 Blaha Lujza tér) Large place popular with travellers.

Haifa Internet Kavézó (VI Király utca 18; per 1hr 180Ft;

⊘24hr; MM1/2/3 Deák Ferenc tér) Very central.

Narancs (VII Akácfa utca 5; per 30/60min 100/150Ft; ⊘9am-2am Mon-Sat, from 10am Sun; MM2 Blaha Lujza tér) Très charming French-run neighbourhood internet cafe.

Vist@netcafe (XIII Váci út 6; 1st 15min 150Ft, per subsequent 30min 250Ft; ⊘24hr; MM3 Nyugati pályaudvar)

Tourinform (p210) offers internet access for 150Ft per 15 minutes.

Legal Matters

Penalties for possession, use or trafficking in illegal drugs in Hungary are severe, and convicted offenders can expect long jail sentences and heavy fines.

There's zero tolerance – a 100% ban – on alcohol when driving. Police conduct routine roadside checks with breathalysers and if you're found to have even 0.001% of alcohol in the blood, you risk having your licence confiscated. If the level is over 0.5% there's a fine up to 100,000Ft and a driving ban of up to a year. In the event of an accident, the drinking party is automatically regarded as guilty.

Medical Services

Foreigners are entitled to first-aid and ambulance services only when they have suffered an accident; follow-up treatment and medicine must be paid for. Treatment at a public outpatient clinic (rendelő intézet) costs little, but a consultation in a doctor's surgery (orvosi rendelő) costs from around 6000Ft (home visits 8000Ft to 10,000Ft).

Clinics

Consultations and treatment are very expensive in private clinics catering to foreigners.

Dental work is usually of a high standard and cheap by European standards.

FirstMed Centers (☎224 9090; www.firstmedcenters.com; I Hattyú utca 14, 5th fl; ⊘8am-8pm Mon-Fri, to 2pm Sat, urgent care 24hr; MM2 Széll Kálmán tér) Modern private medical clinic with very expensive round-the-clock emergency treatment (basic consultation 18,100/36,000Ft for under 10/20 minutes).

SOS Dent (☎269 6010, 06 30 383 3333; www.sosdent.hu, in Hungarian; VI Király utca 14; ⊘24hr; MM1/2/3 Deák Ferenc tér) Free dental consultations, with extractions 7000Ft to 9000Ft, fillings 7000Ft to 11,000Ft and crowns from 40,000Ft.

Pharmacies

Each of Budapest's 23 districts has a rotating all-night pharmacy; a sign on the door of any pharmacy will help you locate the nearest 24-hour place. Conveniently located pharmacies:

Csillag Gyógyszertár (☎314 3695; VIII Rákóczi út 39; ⊘7.30am-9pm Mon-Fri, to 2pm Sat; MM2 Blaha Lujza tér)

Déli Gyógyszertár (☎355 4691; XII Alkotás utca 1/b; ⊘7am-8pm Mon-Fri, to 2pm Sat; MM2 Déli pályaudvar)

Teréz Gyógyszertár (☎311 4439; VI Teréz körút 41; ⊘8am-8pm Mon-Fri, to 2pm Sat; MM3 Nyugati pályaudvar)

Money

Hungary's currency is the forint (Ft). Notes come in six denominations: 500Ft, 1000Ft, 2000Ft, 5000Ft, 10,000Ft and 20,000Ft and there are coins of 5Ft, 10Ft, 20Ft, 50Ft, 100Ft and 200Ft.

Prices in shops and restaurants are always quoted in forint, but many hotels and guesthouses and

even MÁV (the national rail company) state their prices in euros.

ATMs

Automated teller machines (ATMs) are everywhere in Budapest, including in the train and bus stations and at the airport terminals. Be warned that many of the ATMS at branches of Országos Takarékpénztár (OTP), the national savings bank, dispense difficult-to-break 20,000Ft notes.

Changing Money

Avoid moneychangers (especially those on V Váci utca) in favour of banks if possible. The following banks offer good rates and service and are centrally located. Arrive about an hour before closing time to ensure the bureau de change desk is still open.

K&H (V Deák Ferenc utca 1; ⊘8am-5pm Mon, to 4pm Tue-Thu, to 3pm Fri; MM1 Vörösmarty tér) Just west of the main shopping drag.

OTP (V Deák Ferenc utca 7-9; ⊘7.45am-6pm Mon, to 5pm Tue-Thu, to 4pm Fri; MM1 Vörösmarty tér) The national savings bank offers among the best exchange rates for cash and travellers cheques.

Credit Cards

Credit cards are widely accepted. Use them at restaurants, shops, hotels, car-rental firms, travel agencies and petrol stations, but don't assume they are accepted at supermarkets or train and bus stations.

Many banks give cash advances on major credit cards, but they involve both fees (about US$10) and interest so ask your credit-card issuer for details.

Tipping

Hungarians are very tip-conscious and nearly everyone in Budapest will routinely hand gratuities to waiters, hairdressers and taxi drivers; doctors and dentists accept 'gratitude money'; even petrol-station attendants and thermal-spa attendants who walk you to your changing cabin, expect a little something. If you aren't impressed with the service, leave little or nothing at all.

The way you tip in restaurants in Hungary is unusual. You never leave the money on the table – that is considered both stupid and rude – but tell the waiter how much you're paying in total. If the bill is, say, 2700Ft, you're paying with a 5000Ft note and you think the waiter deserves a gratuity of around 10%, first ask if service is included (some Budapest restaurants now add it to the bill automatically). If it isn't, tell the waiter you're paying 3000Ft or that you want 2000Ft back.

Travellers Cheques

You can change travellers cheques at most banks and post offices but shops never accept them as payment. *Bureaux de change* generally don't take a commission, but exchange rates can vary; private agencies are always the most expensive. OTP has branches throughout the city and offers among the best rates, and Ibusz (p210) is a good bet (though banks and travel agencies usually take a commission of 1% to 2%).

Post

The **Hungarian Postal Service** (Magyar Posta; www .posta.hu) has improved greatly in recent years, but the post offices themselves are usually fairly crowded and service can be slow. To beat the crowds, ask at kiosks, newsagents or stationery shops if they sell stamps (*bélyeg*).

Hungarian addresses start with the name of the recipient, followed on the next line by the postal code and city or town and then the street name and number. The Hungarian postal code consists of four digits. The first indicates the city or town ('1' is Budapest), the second and third the district (*kerület*) and the last the neighbourhood.

Conveniently located post offices:

Main post office (Map p244; V Bajcsy-Zsilinszky út 16; ☉8am-8pm Mon-Fri, to 2pm Sat; MM1/2/3 Deák Ferenc tér) Where you pick up poste restante.

Nyugati train station branch (Map p244; VI Teréz körút 51-53; ☉7am-8pm Mon-Fri, 8am-6pm Sat; MM3 Nyugati pályaudvar) Just south of the station.

Keleti train station branch (Map p242; VIII Baross tér 11 & Kerepesi út 2-6; ☉7am-9pm Mon-Fri, 8am-2pm Sat; MM2 Keleti pályaudvar) Most easily reached from platform 6.

Public Holidays

New Year's Day 1 January
National Day 15 March
Easter Sunday & Monday March/April
Labour Day 1 May
Whit Sunday & Monday (Pentecost) May/June
St Stephen's Day 20 August
1956 Remembrance Day/ Republic Day 23 October
All Saints' Day 1 November
Christmas holidays 25 & 26 December

Taxes & Refunds

ÁFA, a value-added tax of between 5% and 25%, covers the purchase of all new goods in Hungary. It's usually included in the quoted price but not always, so it pays to check. Visitors are not exempt, but non-EU residents can claim refunds for total purchases of at least 50,000Ft on one receipt as long as they take the goods out of the country (and the EU) within 90 days.

The ÁFA receipts (available from where you make the purchases) should be stamped by customs at the border, and the claim has to be made within 183 days of exporting the goods. You can collect your refund minus commission – from the VAT refund desk at Terminals 1 and 2 at Ferenc Liszt International Airport in Budapest or at branches of the Ibusz chain of travel agencies at some nine border crossings. You can also have it sent to you by bank cheque or deposited into your credit-card account.

Telephone

You can make domestic and international calls from public telephones, with both coins and phonecards. Telephone boxes with a black and white arrow and red target, and the word *Visszahívható* on the door, display a telephone number so you can be phoned back.

All localities in Hungary have a two-digit area code, except for Budapest, which has just a '1'. To make a local call, pick up the receiver and listen for the neutral and continuous dial tone, then dial the phone number (seven digits in Budapest, six elsewhere).

For an intercity landline call within Hungary and whenever you are calling a mobile phone, dial ☎06 and wait for the second, more melodious, tone. Then dial the area code and phone number. Cheaper or toll-free blue and green numbers start with the digits ☎06-40 and ☎06-80 respectively.

The procedure for making an international call is the

same as for a local call, except that you dial ☎00, wait for the second dial tone, then dial the country code, the area code and the number.

The country code for Hungary is ☎36.

The following are useful numbers (with English spoken). For emergency numbers, see p206.

Information Plus (☎197) Any enquiry.

Domestic enquiries (☎198)

International enquiries (☎199)

Mobile Phones

You must always dial ☎06 when ringing mobile phones, which have specific area codes depending on the telecom company:

Telenor (☎06-20; www.telenor.hu)

T-Mobile (☎06-30; www.t-mobile.hu)

Vodafone (☎06-70; www.vodafone.hu)

Consider buying a rechargeable SIM chip, which will reduce the cost of making local calls. Vodafone, for example, sells prepaid vouchers for 1680Ft, with 500Ft worth of credit. Top-up cards cost from 2000Ft to 12,000Ft.

The following are centrally located offices of mobile-phone providers:

Telenor (II Mammut I, 2nd fl, Lövőház utca 2-6; ⊗9am-8pm Mon-Sat, to 6pm Sun; Ⓜ M2 Széll Kálmán tér)

T-Mobile (V Petőfi Sándor utca 12; ⊗9am-7pm Mon-Fri, 10am-1pm Sat; Ⓜ M3 Ferenciek tere)

Vodafone (West End City Centre, VI Váci út 1-3, Ybl Miklós sétány, 1st fl; ⊗10am-9pm Mon-Sat, to 6pm Sun; Ⓜ M3 Nyugati pályaudvar)

Phonecards

Standard phonecards issued by Magyar Telekom and available from post offices, newsagents, hotels and petrol stations come in values of 1000Ft, 2000Ft and 5000Ft. But discount phonecards and phonecards with codes offer much better rates (it can cost as little as 9Ft per minute to the US, Australia and New Zealand) and are available at newsstands everywhere. Try the following:

Barangoló (www.telekom.hu)

NeoPhone (www.neophone.hu)

No Limits (www.nolimits.hu)

Tik Tak Talk (www.tiktaktalk.hu)

Time

Budapest lies in the Central European time zone. Winter time is GMT plus one hour and in summer it is GMT plus two hours. Clocks are advanced at 2am on the last Sunday in March and set back at 2am on the last Sunday in October.

The following times do not take daylight-saving times into account.

CITY	NOON IN BUDAPEST
Auckland	11pm
Bucharest	1pm
London	11am
Moscow	2pm
New York	6am
Paris	noon
San Francisco	3am
Sydney	9pm
Tokyo	8pm

Like some other European languages, Hungarian tells the time by making reference to the next hour – not the one before as we do in English. Thus 7.30 is 'half eight' (*fél nyolc óra*) and the 24-hour system is often used in giving the times of movies, concerts and so on. So a film

at 7.30pm could appear on a listing as 'f8', 'f20', '½8' or '½20'. A quarter to the hour has a ¾ in front (thus '¾48' means 7.45) while quarter past the hour is ¼ of the next hour (eg '¼49' means 8.15).

Tourist Information

Run by the Hungarian National Tourist Office, **Tourinform** (☎438 8080; www.tourinform.hu) has three branches in central Budapest and info desks in the arrivals sections of Ferenc Liszt International Airport's Terminals 1, 2A and 2B.

Main branch (Map p238; V Sütő utca 2; ⊗8am-8pm; Ⓜ M1/2/3 Deák Ferenc tér) Best single source of information about Budapest.

Castle Hill branch (Map p230; I Szentháromság tér 6; ⊗9am-7pm May-Oct, 10am-6pm Nov-Apr; 🚌16, 16A, 116) Small and often very busy in summer.

Oktogon branch (Map p250; VI Liszt Ferenc tér 11; ⊗noon-8pm May-Oct, 10am-6pm Nov-Apr; Ⓜ M1 Oktogon) Least busy branch.

Travel Agencies

If your query is about private accommodation, flights or international train travel, or you need to change money, you could turn to a commercial travel agency.

Ibusz (☎501 4910; www.ibusz.hu; V József Attila utca 20; ⊗9am-6pm Mon-Fri, to 1pm Sat; Ⓜ M1 Bajcsy-Zsilinszky út) The best agency for booking private rooms but also books other types of accommodation, changes money and sells transport tickets.

Vista (☎429 9999; www.vista.hu, in Hungarian; VI Andrássy út 1; Ⓜ M1 Bajcsy-Zsilinszky út; ⊗9.30am-6pm Mon-Fri, 10am-2.30pm Sat)

Excellent for all your travel needs, both outbound (air tickets, package tours etc) and incoming (room bookings, organised tours, study etc).

Wasteels (☑210 2802, 343 3492; www.wasteels.hu; VIII Kerepesi út 2-6; ☺8am-8pm Mon-Fri, to 6pm Sat; Ⓜ M2 Keleti pályaudvar) Next to platform 9 at Keleti train station; sells Billet International de Jeunesse (BIJ) discounted train tickets to those 26 years and under.

Travellers with Disabilities

Budapest has taken great strides in recent years in making public areas and facilities more accessible to the disabled. Wheelchair ramps, toilets fitted for the disabled and inward-opening doors, though not as common as in Western Europe, do exist and audible traffic signals for the blind are becoming commonplace as are Braille plates in public lifts. For more information and advice, contact the following:

Hungarian Federation of Disabled Persons' Associations (MEOSZ;

☑388 2387; www.meoszinfo .hu; III San Marco utca 76)

Visas

Check current visa requirements at a Hungarian consulate, Hungarian National Tourist Office (HNTO) or Malév Hungarian Airlines office, or on the website of the **Hungarian Foreign Ministry** (www.mfa .gov.hu) as requirements often change without notice.

Citizens of all European countries as well as Australia, Canada, Israel, Japan, New Zealand and the US do not require visas to visit Hungary for stays of up to 90 days. Nationals of South Africa (among others) still require visas.

Visas are issued at Hungarian consulates or missions, most international highway border crossings, Ferenc Liszt International Airport and the International Ferry Pier in Budapest. They are rarely issued on international buses and never on trains. Be sure to retain the separate entry and exit forms issued with the visa that is stamped in your passport.

Short-stay visas (€60), which are the best for tourists as they allow stays

of up to 90 days, are issued at Hungarian consulates or missions in the applicants' country of residence. They are only extended in emergencies (eg medical ones) and this must be done at the central police station 15 days before the original one expires.

Women Travellers

Hungarian men can be sexist in their thinking, but women in Budapest do not suffer any particular form of harassment (though domestic violence and rape get relatively little media coverage here). Most men – even drunks – are effusively polite with women. Women may not be made to feel especially welcome when eating or drinking alone, but it's really no different from most other countries in Europe.

If you need assistance or information ring either of the following:

Women for Women Against Violence (NANE; ☑267 4900; www.nane.hu)
Women's Line (Nővonal; ☑06-80 505 303; ☺6-10pm)

Language

Hungarian (*magyar* mo·dyor) belongs to the Finno-Ugric language family and has more than 14.5 million speakers worldwide. Though distantly related to Finnish, it has no significant similarities to any other language in the world. And while it's very different from English in both vocabulary and structure, it's surprisingly easy to pronounce. If you follow the coloured pronunciation guides that accompany each phrase in this chapter and read them as if they were English, you'll be understood.

A horizontal line over a vowel in written Hungarian (eg *ā*) indicates the vowel is pronounced as a long sound. Double consonants (eg *tt*) are drawn out a little longer than in English.

Note that aw is pronounced as in 'law', eu as in 'nurse', ew as 'ee' with rounded lips, and zh as the 's' in 'pleasure'. Also, r is rolled in Hungarian and the apostrophe (') indicates a slight y sound.

In our pronunciation guides, the syllables are separated by a dot (eg *kawn*·tsert) so you can easily isolate each unit of sound. Accent marks in written Hungarian don't influence word stress which always falls on the first syllable of the word. We've indicated stress with italics.

BASICS

Hungarian has separate polite and informal forms of the personal pronoun 'you', as well as the corresponding verbs forms. The polite *Ön* eun form is generally used with strangers, new acquaintances, older people, officials and service personnel. The informal *te* te form is used with relatives, friends, colleagues, children ar sometimes foreigners. The form appropriate for the context is used throughout this chapter. For phrases where either form might be appropriate we've given both, indicated by th abbreviations 'pol' and 'inf'.

Hello.	Szervusz. (sg)	*ser*·vus
	Szervusztok. (pl)	*ser*·vus·tawk
Goodbye.	Viszlát.	*vis*·lat
Excuse me.	Elnézést kérek.	*el*·ney·zeysht *key*·rek
Sorry.	Sajnálom.	*shoy*·na·lawm
Please.	Kérem. (pol)	*key*·rem
	Kérlek. (inf)	*keyr*·lek
Thank you.	Köszönöm.	*keu*·seu·neum
You're welcome.	Szívesen.	*see*·ve·shen
Yes.	Igen.	*i*·gen
No.	Nem.	nem

How are you?
Hogy van/vagy? (pol/inf) hawj von/voj

Fine. And you?
Jól. És Ön/te? (pol/inf) yāwl aysh eun/te

What's your name?
Mi a neve/neved? (pol/inf) mi o *ne*·ve/*ne*·ved

My name is ...
A nevem ... o *ne*·vem ...

Do you speak English?
Beszél/Beszélsz angolul? (pol/inf) be·seyl/be·seyls *on*·gaw·lul

I don't understand.
Nem értem. nem *eyr*·tem

ACCOMMODATION

campsite	kemping	*kem*·ping
guesthouse	panzió	*pon*·zi·āw
hotel	szálloda	*sal*·law·do
youth hostel	ifjúsági szálló	*if*·yū·sha·gi *sal*·lāw

WANT MORE?

For in-depth language information and handy phrases, check out Lonely Planet's *Hungarian phrasebook*. You'll find it at **shop.lonelyplanet.com**, or you can buy Lonely Planet's iPhone phrasebooks at the Apple App Store.

Do you have a ... room?	Van Önnek kiadó egy ... szobája?	von eun·nek ki·o·dāw ed' ... saw·ba·yo
single	egyágyas	ej·a·dyosh
double	duplaágyas	dup·lo·a·dyosh

How much is it per ...?	Mennyibe kerül egy ...?	men'·nyi·be ke·rewl ej ...
night	éjszakára	ey·so·ka·ro
person	főre	fēū·re

air-con	légkondicionálás	layg·kawn·di·tsi·aw·naa·laash
bathroom	fürdőszoba	fewr·dēū·saw·bo
laundry	mosoda	maw·shaw·do
window	ablak	ob·lok

DIRECTIONS

Where's (the market)?
Hol van (a piac)? hawl von (o pi·ots)

What's the address?
Mi a cím? mi o tseem

Could you please write it down?
Leírná, kérem. le·eer·naa kay·rem

How do I get there?
Hogyan jutok oda? haw·dyon yu·tawk aw·do

How far is it?
Milyen messze van? mi·yen mes·se von

Can you show me (on the map)?
Meg tudja mutatni nekem (a térképen)? meg tud·yo mu·tot·ni ne·kem (o tayr·kay·pen)

Turn ...	Forduljon ...	fawr·dul·yawn ...
at the corner	be a saroknál	be o sho·rawk·naal
at the traffic lights	be a közlekedési lámpánál	be o keuz·le·ke·day·shi laam·paa·naal
left	balra	bol·ro
right	jobbra	yawbb·ro

Signs	
Bejárat	Entrance
Kijárat	Exit
Nyitva	Open
Zárva	Closed
Információ	Information
Tilos	Prohibited
Mosdó	Toilets
Férfiak	Men
Nők	Women

It's ...	... van.	... von
behind ...	... mögött	... meu·geutt
in front of ...	... előtt	... e·lēūtt
near ...	... közelében	... keu·ze·lay·ben
next to ...	... mellett	... mel·lett
on the corner	a sarkon	o shor·kawn
opposite ...	...val szemben	...vol sem·ben
straight ahead	egyenesen előttünk	e·dye·ne·shen e·lēūt·tewnk

EATING & DRINKING

I'd like to reserve a table for ...	Szeretnék asztalt foglalni ...	se·ret·nayk os·tolt fawg·lol·ni ...
(eight) o'clock	(nyolc) órára	(nyawlts) āw·raa·ro
(two) people	(két) főre	(kayt) fēū·re

I'd like the menu, please.
Az étlapot szeretném. oz eyt·lo·pawt se·ret·neym

What would you recommend?
Mit ajánlana? mit o·yan·lo·no

What's in that dish?
Mit tartalmaz ez a fogás? mit tor·tol·moz ez o faw·gaash

Do you have vegetarian food?
Vannak Önöknél vegetáriánus ételek? von·nok eu·neuk·neyl ve·ge·ta·ri·a·nush ey·te·lek

I don't eat ...	Én nem eszem ...	ayn nem e·sem ...
eggs	tojást	taw·yaasht
fish	halat	ho·lot
pork	disznóhúst	dis·nāw·hüsht
poultry	szárnyast	saar·nyosht

I'll have ...	... kérek.	... key·rek

Cheers! (to one person)
Egészségedre! e·geys·shey·ged·re

Cheers! (to more than one person)
Egészségetekre! e·geys·shey·ge·tek·re

That was delicious.
Ez nagyon finom volt. ez no·dyawn fi·nawm vawlt

I'd like the bill, please.
A számlát szeretném. o sam·lat se·ret·neym

Key Words

bottle	üveg	ew·veg
bowl	tál	taal
breakfast	reggeli	reg·ge·li

cafe	kávézó	kaa·vay·zāw
cold	hideg	hi·deg
cup	csésze	chey·se
dinner	vacsora	vo·chaw·ro
dish	edény	e·dayn'
drink	ital	i·tol
food	ennivaló	en·ni·vo·lāw
fork	villa	vil·lo
glass	pohár	paw·har
hot (warm)	forró	fawr·rāw
knife	kés	kaysh
lunch	ebéd	e·beyd
menu	étlap	ayt·lop
plate	tányér	taa·nyayr
restaurant	étterem	ayt·te·rem
serviette	szalvéta	sol·vay·to
spoon	kanál	ko·naal
with	-val/-vel	·vol/·vel
without	nélkül	nayl·kewl

Meat & Fish

beef	marhahús	mor·ho·hūsh
chicken	csirkehús	chir·ke·hūsh
duck	kacsa	ko·cho
fish	hal	hol
lamb	bárány	baa·raan'
meat	hús	hūsh
oyster	osztriga	awst·ri·go
pork	disznóhús	dis·nāw·hūsh
prawn	garnélarák	gor·nay·lo·raak
salmon	lazac	lo·zots
tuna	tonhal	tawn·hol
turkey	pulyka	pu·y·ko
veal	borjúhús	bawr·yū·hūsh

Fruit & Vegetables

apple	alma	ol·mo
bean	bab	bob
cabbage	káposzta	kaa·paws·to
capsicum	paprika	pop·ri·ko
carrot	répa	ray·po
cauliflower	karfiol	kor·fi·awl
cucumber	uborka	u·bawr·ko
fruit	gyümölcs	dyew·meulch
grapes	szőlő	sēū·lēū
legume	hüvelyes	hew·ve·yesh

KEY PATTERNS

To get by in Hungarian, mix and match these simple patterns with words of your choice:

Where's (a market)?
Hol van (egy piac)?   hawl von (ej pi·ots)

Where can I (buy a padlock)?
Hol tudok   hawl tu·dawk
(venni egy lakatot)? (ven·ni ej lo·ko·tawt)

I'm looking for (a hotel).
(Szállodát) keresek. (saal·law·daat) ke·re·shek

Do you have (a map)?
Van (térképük)?   von (tayr·kay·pewk)

Is there (a toilet)?
Van (vécé)?   von (vay·tsay)

I'd like (the menu).
(Az étlapot)   (oz ayt·lo·pawt)
szeretném.   se·ret·naym

I'd like to (buy a phonecard).
Szeretnék   se·ret·nayk
(telefonkártyát   (te·le·fawn·kaar·tyaat
venni).   ven·ni)

Could you please (write it down)?
(Leírná), kérem.   (le·eer·naa) kay·rem

Do I have to (pay)?
Kell érte (fizetni)? kell ayr·te (fi·zet·ni)

I need (assistance).
(Segítségre)   (she·geet·shayg·re)
van szükségem.   von sewk·shay·gem

lemon	citrom	tsit·rawm
lentil	lencse	len·che
mushroom	gomba	gawm·bo
nut	dió	di·āw
onion	hagyma	hoj·mo
orange	narancs	no·ronch
pea	borsó	bawr·shāw
peach	őszibarack	ēū·si·bo·rotsk
pear	körte	keur·te
pineapple	ananász	o·no·naas
plum	szilva	sil·vo
potato	krumpli	krump·li
spinach	spenót	shpe·nāwt
tomato	paradicsom	po·ro·di·chawm
vegetable	zöldség	zeuld·shayg

Other

bread	kenyér	ke·nyayr
cheese	sajt	shoyt
egg	tojás	taw·yaash

honey	méz	mayz
ice	jég	yayg
ice cream	fagylalt	foj·lolt
noodles	metélt	me·taylt
oil	olaj	aw·lo·y
pasta	tészta	tays·to
pepper (black)	bors	bawrsh
rice	rizs	rizh
salad	saláta	sho·laa·to
salt	só	shāw
soup	leves	le·vesh
sugar	cukor	tsu·kawr
vinegar	ecet	e·tset

Drinks

beer	sör	sheur
coffee	kávé	ka·vey
juice	gyümölcslé	dyew·meulch·lay
milk	tej	te·y
mineral water	ásványvíz	aash·vaan'·veez
orange juice	narancslé	no·ronch·lay
red wine	vörösbor	veu·reush·bawr
soft drink	üdítőital	ew·dee·tēū·i·tal
sparkling wine	habzóbor	hob·zāw·bawr
tea	tea	te·o
water	víz	veez
white wine	fehérbor	fe·hayr·bawr
wine	bor	bawr

EMERGENCIES

Help!
Segítség! — she·geet·sheyg

Go away!
Menjen innen! — men·yen in·nen

Call a doctor!
Hívjon orvost! — heev·yawn awr·vawsht

Call the police!
Hívja a rendőrséget! — heev·yo o rend·ēūr·shey·get

There's been an accident.
Baleset történt. — bo·le·shet teur·taynt

Question Words

What?	Mi?	mi
When?	Mikor?	mi·kawr
Where?	Hol?	hawl
Which?	Melyik?	me·yik
Who?	Ki?	ki
Why?	Miért?	mi·ayrt

I'm lost.
Eltévedtem. — el·tey·ved·tem

Where are the toilets?
Hol a vécé? — hawl o vey·tsey

Can I use your phone?
Használhatom a telefonját? — hos·naal·ho·tawm o te·le·fawn·yaat

I'm ill.
Rosszul vagyok. — raws·sul vo·dyawk

It hurts here.
Itt fáj. — itt faa·y

I'm allergic to (antibiotics).
Allergiás vagyok (az antibiotikumokra). — ol·ler·gi·aash vo·dyawk (oz on·ti·bi·aw·ti·ku·mawk·ro)

SHOPPING & SERVICES

I'd like to buy (an adaptor plug).
Szeretnék venni (egy adapter dugót). — se·ret·nayk ven·ni (ej o·dop·ter du·gāwt)

I'm just looking.
Csak nézegetek. — chok nay·ze·ge·tek

Can I look at it?
Megnézhetem? — meg·nayz·he·tem

How much is it?
Mennyibe kerül? — men'·nyi·be ke·rewl

That's too expensive.
Ez túl drága. — ez tül dra·go

Do you have something cheaper?
Van valami olcsóbb? — von vo·lo·mi awl·chāwbb

There's a mistake in the bill.
Valami nem stimmel a számlával. — vo·lo·mi nem shtim·mel o saam·laa·vol

bank	bank	bonk
credit card	hitelkártya	hi·tel·kaar·tyo
internet cafe	Internet kávézó	in·ter·net kaa·vay·zāw
market	piac	pi·ots
mobile phone	mobil telefon	maw·bil te·le·fawn
post office	posta-hivatal	pawsh·to·hi·vo·tol
tourist office	turista-iroda	tu·rish·to·i·raw·do

TIME & DATES

What time is it?
Hány óra? — haan' āw·ra

It's (one) o'clock.
(Egy) óra van. — (ej) āw·ra von

It's (10) o'clock.
(Tíz) óra van. — (teez) āw·ra von

Half past (10).
Fél (tizenegy). — fayl (ti·zen·ej)

morning	reggel	reg·gel
afternoon	délután	dayl·u·taan
evening	este	esh·te
yesterday	tegnap	teg·nop
today	ma	mo
tomorrow	holnap	hawl·nop
Monday	hétfő	hayt·fēū
Tuesday	kedd	kedd
Wednesday	szerda	ser·do
Thursday	csütörtök	chew·teur·teuk
Friday	péntek	payn·tek
Saturday	szombat	sawm·bot
Sunday	vasárnap	vo·shaar·nop
January	január	yo·nu·aar
February	február	feb·ru·aar
March	március	maar·tsi·ush
April	április	aap·ri·lish
May	május	maa·yush
June	június	yū·ni·ush
July	július	yū·li·ush
August	augusztus	o·u·gus·tush
September	szeptember	sep·tem·ber
October	október	awk·tāw·ber
November	november	naw·vem·ber
December	december	de·tsem·ber

Numbers

1	egy	·ej
2	kettő	ket·tēū
3	három	ha·rawm
4	négy	neyj
5	öt	eut
6	hat	hot
7	hét	heyt
8	nyolc	nyawlts
9	kilenc	ki·lents
10	tíz	teez
20	húsz	hūs
30	harminc	hor·mints
40	negyven	nej·ven
50	ötven	eut·ven
60	hatvan	hot·von
70	hetven	het·ven
80	nyolcvan	nyawlts·von
90	kilencven	ki·lents·ven
100	száz	saaz
1000	ezer	e·zer

bike path	bicikliút	bi·tsik·li·ūt
bus stop	buszmegálló	bus·meg·aal·lāw
platform	peron	pe·rawn
taxi stand	taxiállomás	tok·si·aal·law·maash
ticket office	jegypénztár	yej·paynz·taar
timetable	menetrend	me·net·rend
train station	vasútállomás	vo·shūt·aal·law·maash

What's the next stop?
Mi a következő
megálló?
mi o keu·vet·ke·zēū
meg·aal·lāw

Please tell me when we get to (...).
Kérem, szóljon,
amikor (...)be
érünk.
kay·rem sāwl·yawn
o·mi·kawr (...)·be
ay·rewnk

Please take me to (this address).
Kérem, vigyen el
(erre a címre).
kay·rem vi·dyen el
(er·re o tseem·re)

I'd like to get off here.
Le szeretnék
szállni itt.
le se·ret·nayk
saall·ni itt

I'd like my bicycle repaired.
Szeretném
megjavíttatni
a biciklimet.
se·ret·naym
meg·yo·veet·tot·ni
o bi·tsik·li·met

TRANSPORT

When's the ... (bus)?	Mikor megy ... (busz)?	mi·kawr mej ... (bus)
first	az első	oz el·shēū
last	az utolsó	oz u·tawl·shāw
next	a következő	o keu·vet·ke·zēū

Which ... goes to (the parliament)?	Melyik ... megy (a Parlament)hez?	me·yik ... mej (o por·lo·ment)·hez
bus	busz	bus
metro line	metró	met·rāw
tram	villamos	vil·lo·mawsh
trolleybus	troli	traw·li

One ... ticket to (Eger), please.	Egy ... jegy (Eger)be.	ej ... yej (e·ger)·be
one-way	csak oda	chok aw·do
return	oda-vissza	aw·do·vis·so

GLOSSARY

ÁFA – value-added tax (VAT)

alagút – tunnel

ÁVO – Rákosi's hated secret police in the early years of communism; later renamed ÁVH

bélyeg – stamps

BKV – Budapest Közlekedési Vallálat (Budapest Transport Company)

bolhapiac – flea market

borozó – wine bar; any place serving wine

Bp – abbreviation for Budapest

búcsú – farewell; also a church patronal festival

büfé – snack bar

centrum – town or city centre

cukrászda – cake shop or patisserie

Eclectic – an art/architectural style popular in Hungary in the Romantic period, drawing from indigenous and foreign sources

eszpresszó – coffee shop, often also selling alcoholic drinks and snacks; strong, black coffee; same as *presszó*

étkezde – canteen that serves simple dishes

étterem – restaurant

fapados – wooden bench; budget (in reference to airlines)

fasor – boulevard, avenue

forint (Ft) – Hungary's monetary unit

főkapitányság – main police station

gyógyfürdő – thermal bath, spa

gyógyszertár – pharmacy

gyűjtemény – collection

hajóállomás – ferry pier, landing

ház – house

hegy – hill, mountain

HÉV – Helyiérdekű Vasút (suburban commuter train)

híd – bridge

HNTO – Hungarian National Tourism Office

ifjúsági szálló – youth hostel

kastély – manor house or mansion (see *vár*)

kávéház – coffee house

képtár – picture gallery

kertek – literally 'gardens', but in Budapest any outdoor spot that has been converted into an entertainment zone

kerület – city district

kincstár – treasury

Kiskörút – 'Little Ring Road'

kocsma – pub or saloon

könyvtár – library

korsó – 0.4L glass

körút – ring road

korzó – embankment, promenade

köz – alley, mews, lane

központ – centre

krt – *körút* (ring road)

labdarúgás – football

lángos – deep-fried dough with various toppings, usually cheese and sour cream

lépcső – stairs, steps

Mahart – Hungarian passenger ferry company

Malév – Hungary's national airline

MÁV – Magyar Államvasutak (Hungarian State Railways)

megyék – counties

Nagykörút – 'Big Ring Road'

nyitva – open

nyitvatartás – opening hours

önkiszolgáló – self-service

OTP – Országos Takarékpenztár (National Savings Bank)

pálinka – fruit brandy

palota – palace

pályaudvar – train or railway station

panzió – pension, guest house

patyolat – laundry

pénztár – cashier

piac – market

pince – wine cellar

pohár – 0.3L glass

presszó – aka *eszpresszó* (coffee shop; strong, black coffee)

pu – abbreviation for *pályaudvar* (train station)

puttony – the number of 'butts' of sweet *aszú* essence added to base wines in making Tokaj wine

rakpart – quay, embankment

rendőrkapitányság – police station

rendőrség – police

romkocsma – 'ruin bar', temporary bars/entertainment zones set up in disused building or site

Secessionism – art/architectural style similar to art nouveau

sedile (pl **sedilia**) – medieval stone niche with seats

sétány – walkwawy, promenade

skanzen – open-air museum displaying village architecture

söröző – beer bar or pub

szálló or **szálloda** – hotel

székesegyház – cathedral

sziget – island

színház – theatre

táncház – folk music and dance workshop

templom – church

tér – town or market square

tere – genitive form of *tér* as in Hősök tere (Square of the Heroes)

tó – lake

turul – eaglelike totem of the ancient Magyars and now a national symbol

u – abbreviation for *utca* (street)

udvar – court

út – road

utca – street

utcája – genitive form of *utca* as in Ferencesek utcája (Street of the Franciscans)

útja – genitive form of *út* as in Mártíroká útja (Street of the Martyrs)

vár – castle

város – city

városház or **városháza** – town hall

vásárcsarnok – market hall

vendéglő – a type of restaurant

zárva – closed

Behind the Scenes

SEND US YOUR FEEDBACK

We love to hear from travellers – your comments keep us on our toes and help make our books better. Our well-travelled team reads every word on what you loved or loathed about this book. Although we cannot reply individually to postal submissions, we always guarantee that your feedback goes straight to the appropriate authors, in time for the next edition. Each person who sends us information is thanked in the next edition – and the most useful submissions are rewarded with a free book.

Visit **lonelyplanet.com/contact** to submit your updates and suggestions or to ask for help. Our award-winning website also features inspirational travel stories, news and discussions.

Note: We may edit, reproduce and incorporate your comments in Lonely Planet products such as guidebooks, websites and digital products, so let us know if you don't want your comments reproduced or your name acknowledged. For a copy of our privacy policy visit lonelyplanet.com/privacy.

OUR READERS

Many thanks to the travellers who used the last edition and wrote to us with helpful hints, useful advice and interesting anecdotes:

Janos Deli, Helene Eichholz, Moorthamers Gino, Linda Grimmer, Mike Harthan, Anders Jeppsson, Niko Nieminen, Clive Probert, Danielle Retera, Mario Salgado, Caroline Savoie, Jane Steinberg, Mihály Tóth, Miguel Urdanoz, Jack Verouden, Indiya Whitehead.

ACKNOWLEDGMENTS

Cover photograph: Fishermen's Bastion at dawn / Rellini Maurizio/LPI.

Many of the images in this guide are available for licensing from Lonely Planet Images: www.lonelyplanetimages.com.

AUTHOR THANKS
Steve Fallon

I'd like to thank friends Bea Szirti, Ildikó Nagy Moran and Judit Maróthy for helpful suggestions and assistance on the ground.

Péter Lengyel showed me the correct wine roads, and Regina Bruckner, Adrian Zador and Erik D'Amato provided useful insights into what's on in Budapest after dark. Special thanks to János Botond Csepregi and Ágnes Pap for guiding me in Wekerle. It was great hanging out again with old mate Judy Finn and the angelic Téglássy trio.

I'd like to dedicate this book to my partner Michael Rothschild, with love and gratitude.

THIS BOOK

This 5th edition of *Budapest* was written and updated by Steve Fallon, as were the previous four editions. This guidebook was commissioned in Lonely Planet's London office, and produced by the following:

Commissioning Editor Dora Whitaker

Coordinating Editors Jackey Coyle, Gabrielle Stefanos

Coordinating Cartographer Hunor Csutoros

Coordinating Layout Designer Sandra Helou

Managing Editors Kirsten Rawlings, Tasmin Waby McNaughtan

Senior Editor Susan Paterson

Managing Cartographers David Connolly, Mandy Sierp

Managing Layout Designer Chris Girdler

Assisting Editors Alice Baker, Charles Rawlings-Way

Assisting Cartographer Ildikó Bogdanovits

Cover Research Naomi Parker

Internal Image Research Aude Vauconsant

Language Content Branislava Vladisavljevic

Thanks to Stefanie di Trocchio, Janine Eberle, Ryan Evans, Liz Heynes, Laura Jane, David Kemp, Trent Paton, Piers Pickard, Averil Robertson, Lachlan Ross, Michael Ruff, Julie Sheridan, Laura Stansfeld, John Taufa, Gerard Walker, Clifton Wilkinson

See also separate subindexes for:

✖️ **EATING P224**

🍷 **DRINKING & NIGHTLIFE P225**

☆ **ENTERTAINMENT P226**

🔒 **SHOPPING P226**

🛏️ **SLEEPING P226**

Index

✕ EATING

W

🍷 DRINKING & NIGHTLIFE

⭐ ENTERTAINMENT

Sights p000
Map Pages **p000**
Photo Pages **p000**

227

INDEX SLEEPING

Budapest Maps

Map Legend

Sights
- Beach
- Buddhist
- Castle
- Christian
- Hindu
- Islamic
- Jewish
- Monument
- Museum/Gallery
- Ruin
- Winery/Vineyard
- Zoo
- Other Sight

Eating
- Eating

Drinking & Nightlife
- Drinking & Nightlife
- Cafe

Entertainment
- Entertainment

Shopping
- Shopping

Sleeping
- Sleeping
- Camping

Sports & Activities
- Diving/Snorkelling
- Canoeing/Kayaking
- Skiing
- Surfing
- Swimming/Pool
- Walking
- Windsurfing
- Other Sports & Activities

Information
- Post Office
- Tourist Information

Transport
- Airport
- Border Crossing
- Bus
- Cable Car/ Funicular
- Cycling
- Ferry
- Metro
- Monorail
- Parking
- S-Bahn
- Taxi
- Train/Railway
- Tram
- Tube Station
- U-Bahn
- Other Transport

Routes
- Tollway
- Freeway
- Primary
- Secondary
- Tertiary
- Lane
- Unsealed Road
- Plaza/Mall
- Steps
- Tunnel
- Pedestrian Overpass
- Walking Tour
- Walking Tour Detour
- Path

Boundaries
- International
- State/Province
- Disputed
- Regional/Suburb
- Marine Park
- Cliff
- Wall

Geographic
- Hut/Shelter
- Lighthouse
- Lookout
- Mountain/Volcano
- Oasis
- Park
- Pass
- Picnic Area
- Waterfall

Hydrography
- River/Creek
- Intermittent River
- Swamp/Mangrove
- Reef
- Canal
- Water
- Dry/Salt/ Intermittent Lake
- Glacier

Areas
- Beach/Desert
- Cemetery (Christian)
- Cemetery (Other)
- Park/Forest
- Sportsground
- Sight (Building)
- Top Sight (Building)

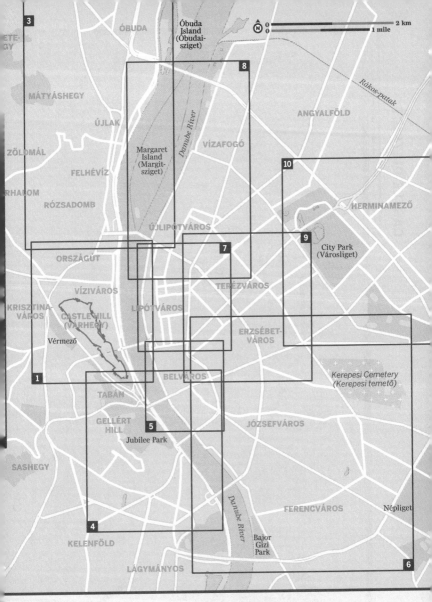

Óbuda Island (Óbudai-sziget)

ÓBUDA

3

ETE-GY

MÁTYÁSHEGY

ÚJLAK

ZÖLÖMÁL

FELHÉVÍZ

RHALOM

RÓZSADOMB

Margit Island (Margit-sziget)

Danube River

VÍZAFOGÓ

ÚJLIPÓTVÁROS

ANGYALFÖLD

8

Rákos-patak

10

HERMINAMEZŐ

9

City Park (Városliget)

ORSZÁGÚT

7

VÍZIVÁROS

TERÉZVÁROS

KRISZTINA-VÁROS

CASTLE HILL (VÁRHEGY)

Vérmező

LIPÓTVÁROS

ERZSÉBET-VÁROS

1

TABÁN

BELVÁROS

Kerepesi Cemetery (Kerepesi temető)

GELLÉRT HILL

5

Jubilee Park

JÓZSEFVÁROS

SASHEGY

4

KELENFÖLD

Danube River

FERENCVÁROS

Népliget

6

Bajor Gizi Park

LÁGYMÁNYOS

0   2 km
0   1 mile

CASTLE DISTRICT

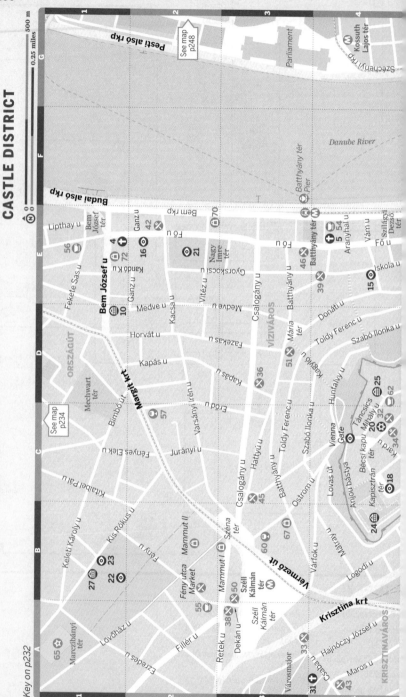

See map p248

See map p234

Key on p232

0 0.25 miles
0 500 m

Pesti alsó rkp

Pesti alsó rkp

Budai alsó rkp

Parliament

Kossuth
Lajos tér

Széchenyi rkp

Danube River

Batthyány tér
Pier

Batthyány tér

Lipthay u
Bem
József
tér

Ganz u 42

Fő u

Bem rkp 70

Nagy
Imre
tér

Gyorskocsi u

Csalogány u

Batthyány u

Aranyhal u

Vám u

Szilágyi
Dezső
tér

Fő u

5 54

Fekete Sas u

56

4
72

16

21

Kandó K u

Ganz u

Medve u

Kacsa u

Vitéz u

Medve u

Csalogány u

Mária
tér

VÍZIVÁROS

46

39

Iskola u

15

Bem József u

10

Horvát u

Fazekas u

Szabó Ilonka u

Donáti u

Toldy Ferenc u

Szabó Ilonka u

ORSZÁGÚT

Mechwart
tér

Birkmbó út

Margit krt

Kapás u

Varsányi Irén u

Erőd u

Kapás u

57

Csalogány u

Hattyú u

36

51

Táncsics
Mihály u

Hunfalvy u

25

62

Fényes Elek u

Jurányi u

Batthyány u

Toldy Ferenc u

Szabó Ilonka u

Vienna
Gate

20 32

34

Kitaibel Pál u

45

Ostrom u

Lovas út

Bécsi kapu
tér

Kard u

18

Keleti Károly u

Kis Rókus u

Fény u

Mammut II

Széna
tér

Csalogány u

60

67

Várfok u

Anjou bástya

Kapisztrán
tér

24

27

22 23

Fény utca
Market

Mammut I

Szél
Kálmán
tér

Vérmező út

Máty u

Logodi u

Lövőház u

55

Fillér u

Retek u

Dekán u

38

50

Széll
Kálmán
tér

33

Krisztina krt

Hajnóczy József u

KRISZTINAVÁROS

Marczibányi
tér

65

Erdödy u

Városmajor

Csaba u

31

43

Maros u

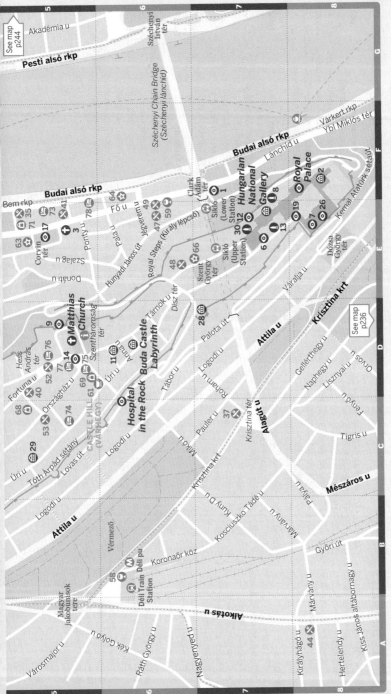

See map p244

Akadémia u

Pesti alsó rkp

Pesti alsó rkp

Széchenyi István tér

Széchenyi Chain Bridge (Széchenyi lánchíd)

Budai alsó rkp

Várkert rkp

Ybl Miklós tér

Budai alsó rkp

Lánchíd u

Budai alsó rkp

Bem rkp

Fő u

Clark Ádám tér

Hungarian National Gallery

Royal Palace

Corvin tér

Ponty u

Pala u

Jégverem u

Siklő (Lower Station)

Kemál Atatürk sétaút

Szalag u

Hunyadi János u

Royal Steps (Király lépcső)

Szent György tér

Siklő (Upper Station)

Váralja u

Dózsa György tér

Donáti u

Matthias Church

Szentháromság tér

Tárnok u

Dísz tér

Anna u

Palota út

Krisztina krt

See map p236

Hess András tér

Úri u

Buda Castle Labyrinth

Tábor u

Logodi u

Attila u

Gellérthegy u

Orvos u

Fortuna u

Országház u

Hospital in the Rock

Roham u

Naphegy u

Lisznyai u

Fenyő u

CASTLE HILL (VÁRHEGY)

Pauler u

Krisztina tér

Tigris u

Úri u

Tóth Árpád sétány

Lovas út

Logodi u

Mikó u

Krisztina krt

Alagút u

Attila u

Logodi u

Vérmező

Koronaőr köz

Kuny D u

Kosciuszko Tádé u

Mándiy u

Pálya u

Mészáros u

Győri út

Magyar Jakobinusok tere

Déli Train Déli pu Station

Alkotás u

Márvány u

Királyhágó u

Hertelendy u

Kiss János altábornagy u

Városmajor u

Kék Golyó u

Ráth György u

Nagyenyed u

CASTLE DISTRICT

CASTLE DISTRICT Map on p230

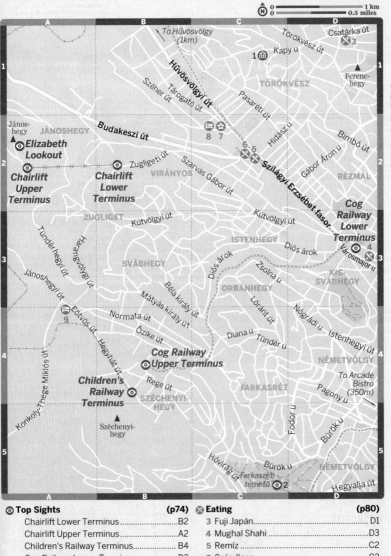

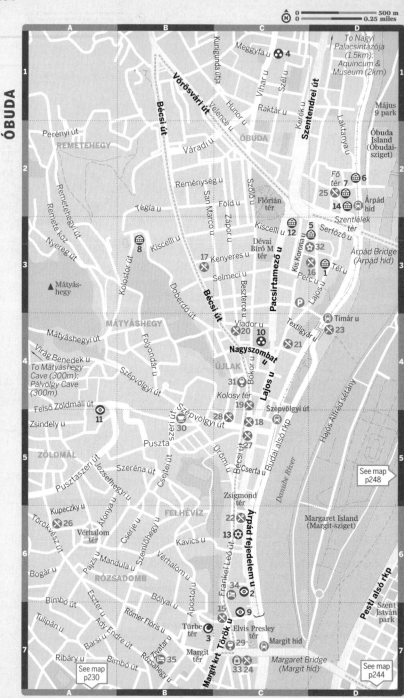

See map p248

See map p230

See map p244

ÓBUDA

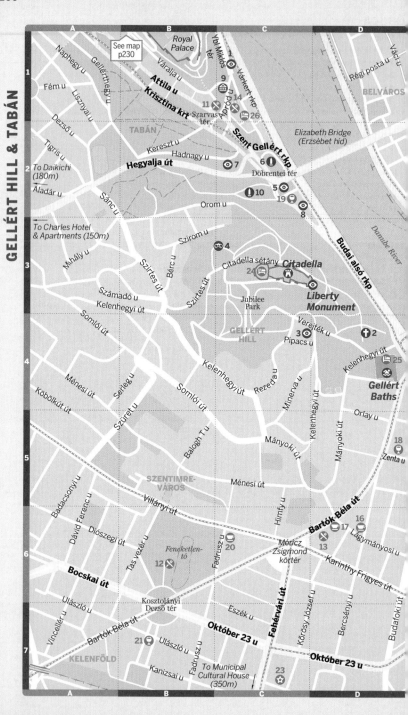

◎ **Top Sights** (p65)
Citadella..C3
Gellért Baths.....................................D4
Liberty Monument............................D3

◎ **Sights** (p66)
1944 Bunker Waxworks....................(see 24)
1 Castle Garden Palace.....................C1
2 Cave Chapel....................................D4
3 Former Swedish Embassy.............C4
4 Lookout...C3
5 Pump Room....................................C2
6 Queen Elizabeth Statue................C2
7 Rácz Baths.....................................C2
8 Rudas Baths...................................C2
9 Semmelweis Museum of Medical History..C1
10 St Gellért Monument....................C2

✕ **Eating** (p67)
11 Aranyszarvas................................B1
12 Hemingway...................................B6
13 Marcello.......................................D6
14 Tabáni Terasz...............................C1

🍷 **Drinking & Nightlife** (p69)
15 A38 Hajó.......................................F6
16 Café Ponyvaragény......................D6
17 Hadik Kávéház & Szatyor Bár......D6
18 Kisrabló Pub.................................D5
19 Romkert.......................................C2
20 Shambala Café.............................C6
21 Tranzit Art Café............................B7
22 Zöld Pardon..................................F6

🎭 **Entertainment** (p70)
23 MU Színház...................................C7

🛏 **Sleeping** (p159)
24 Citadella Hotel.............................C3
25 Danubius Hotel Gellért.................D4
26 Hotel Orion...................................C1

BELVÁROS

Key on p240

200 m
0.1 miles
See map p244
See map p250
Széchenyi István tér
Eötvös tér
József Attila u
Nádor u
Hild tér
Sas u
Bajcsy-Zsilinszky út
József nádor tér
Október 6 u
Erzsébet tér
Király u
Gozsdu Udvar
Holló u
Kazinczy u
Dob u
Madách Imre út
ERZSÉBETVÁROS
Asboth u
Rumbach Sebestyén u
Síp u
Wesselényi u
Apáczai Csere János u
Belgrád rkp
Dorottya u
Harmincad u
Deák Ferenc tér
Sütő u
Vörösmarty tér
Deák Ferenc u
Károly krt
Tourinform (Main Office)
Vigadó u
Bécsi u
Fehér Hajó u
Bárczy I u
Gerlóczy u
Vigadó tér
Váci u
Kristóf tér
Vigadó tér Pier
Szervita tér
Municipal Council Office
Türr István u
Városház u
Vitkovics M u
Semmelweiss u
Dohány u
Aranykéz u
Pest County Hall
Duna korzó
Petőfi Sándor u
BELVÁROS
Vármegye u
Rákóczi út
Régi posta u
Váci utca
Pilvax köz
Párizsi u
Haris köz
Astoria
Galamb u
Magyar u
Kossuth Lajos u
Petőfi tér

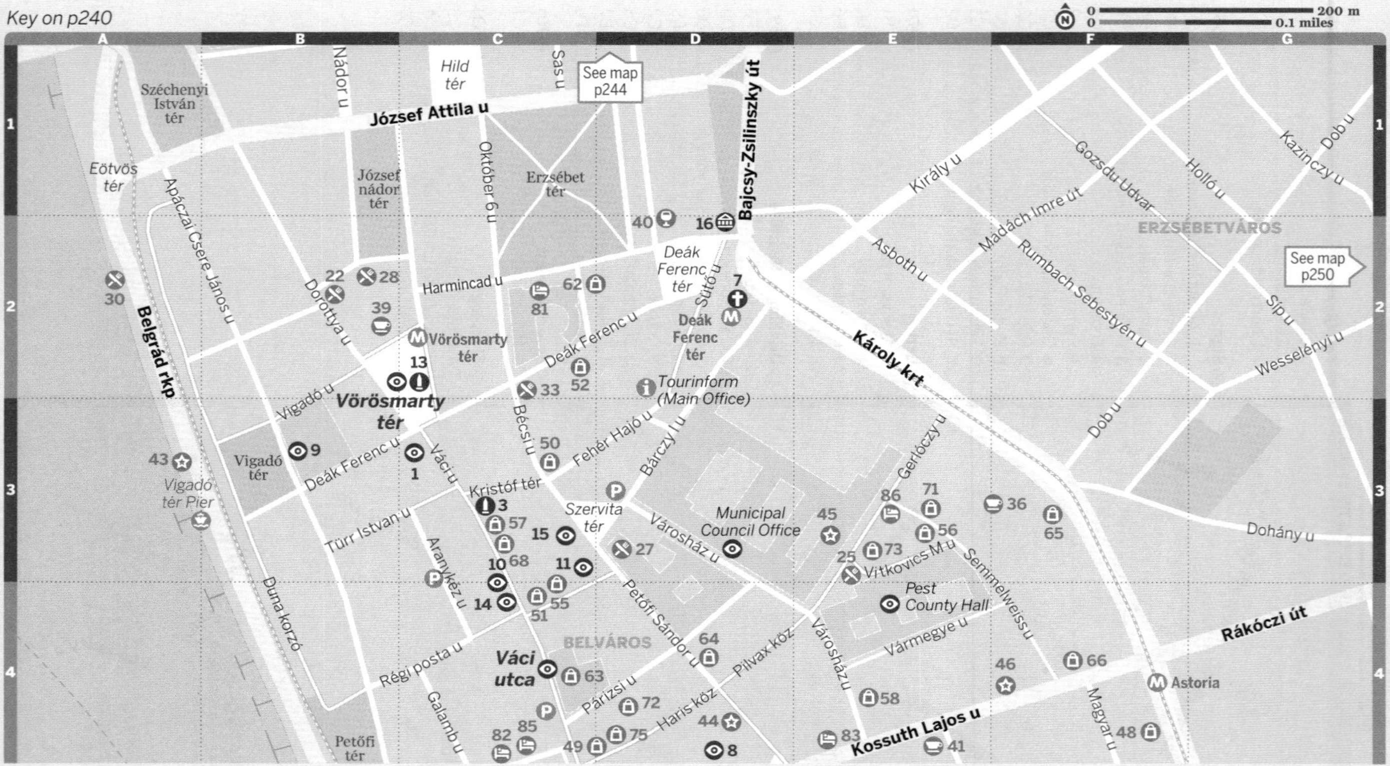

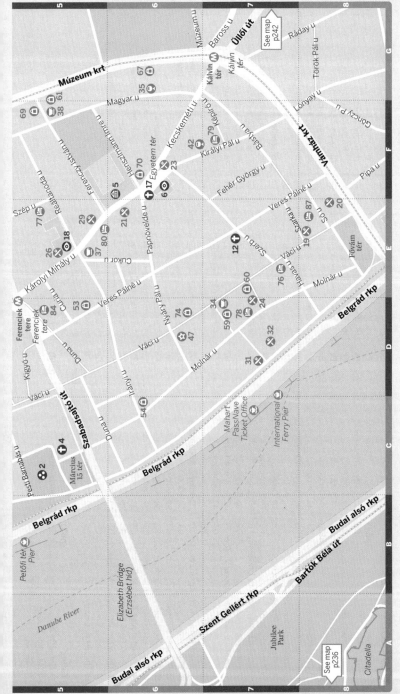

BELVÁROS

BELVÁROS *Map on p238*

Key on p241

N
500 m
0.25 miles

See map p254

See map p250

See map p244

See map p238

Andrássy út

Opera Ⓜ

Dózsa György út

Ferenc Puskás Stadium

Asztalos Sándor u

Kőbányai út

Verseny u

Keleti Train Station

Kerepesi út

Kerepesi Cemetery

Salgótarjáni u

Józsefvárosi pu

47

Törköly út

Rottenbiller u

Péterfy Sándor u

Garay u

Garay tér

Keleti pu Ⓜ

Baross tér

Mosonyi u

22

12

Fiumei út

Dobozi u

Baross u

Csobánc u

Sárkány u

Izabella u

Almássy tér

Dohány u

Rózsák tere

Alsóerdősor u

Szövetség u

Rákóczi út

Légszesz u

Berzsenyi u

II. János Pál pápa tér

15

Luther u

51

Népszínház u

Bérkócsis u

Aurora u

Teleki László tér

Mátyás tér

Dankó u

Magdolna u

JÓZSEFVÁROS

Luiza u

Karácsony Sándor u

Szerdahelyi u

Bauer Sándor u

Kun u

Alföldi u

Baross u

Kálvária tér

Losonci tér

Köris u

Hárfa u

Kürt u

Kertész u

Nyár u

Erzsébet krt

Barcsay u

Kertész u

Blaha Lujza tér Ⓜ

Blaha Lujza tér

31

Somogyi B u

Gutenberg tér

Rökk Szilárd u

Bacsó u

16

29

Vig u

Bezerédi u

Tolnai Lajos u

21

Vig u

Krúdy Gy u

Német u

Rigó u

Horváth Mihály tér

Nap u

Futó u

Vajdahunyad u

Kisfaludy u

Práter u

Szigony u

Práter u

9

József krt

25

37

Rákóczi út

Gyulai Pál u

Stáhly u

53

14

43

Horánszky u

Vas u

5

45

Szentkirályi u

Museum of Applied Arts

Ferenc krt

Markusovszky tér

41

35

13

28

32

48

55

Üllői út

20

34

Kinizsi u

27

23

59

Puskin u

Bródy Sándor u

52

49

Múzeum u

36

40

19

Török Pál u

46

24

54

11

Kálvin tér Ⓜ

Lónyay u

Imre u

Kazinczy u

Síp u

Dohány u

18

Múzeum krt

Hungarian National Museum

Magyar u

Astoria Ⓜ

Bástya u

Váci krt

50

Szerb u

Sóház u

33

Fővám tér Ⓜ

Fővám tér

Károlyi M u

Károly krt

Madách Imre út

Paulay Ede u

Király u

Dob u

Klauzál tér

Wesselényi u

Kazinczy u

ERZSÉBETVÁROS

Mária u

Ⓜ Kálvin tér

Revicky u

Ⓜ

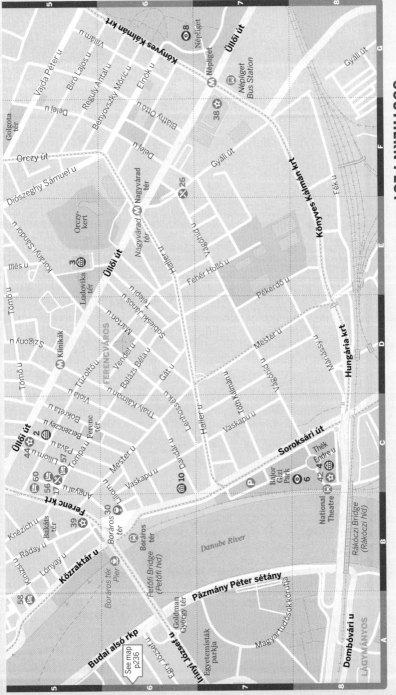

SOUTHERN PEST

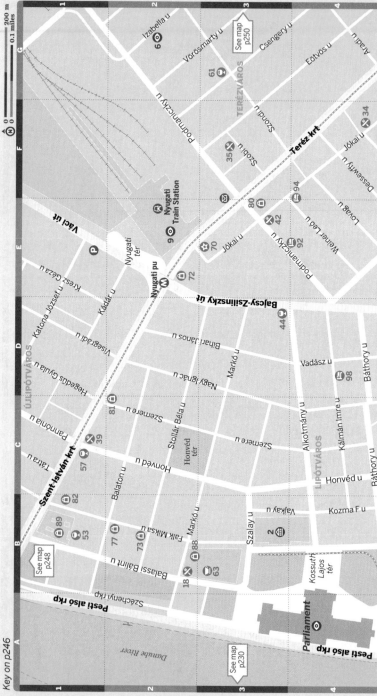

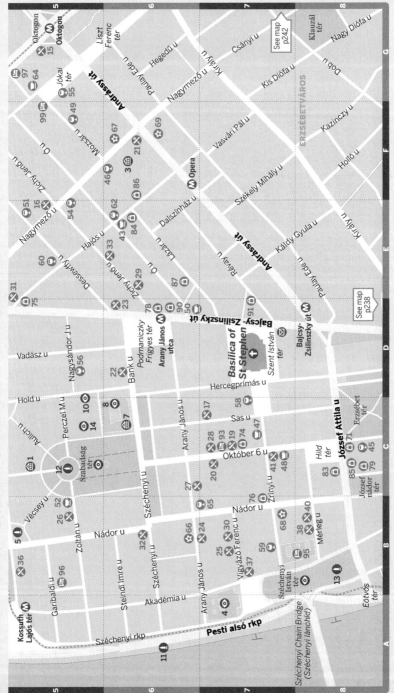

See map p242

See map p238

Oktogon

Oktogon

Liszt Ferenc tér

Andrássy út

Jókai tér

Nagymező u

Király u

Csányi u

Kis Diófa u

Klauzál tér

Nagy Diófa u

Dob u

ERZSÉBETVÁROS

Kazinczy u

Holló u

Király u

Opera

Vasvári Pál u

Székely Mihály u

Dalszínház u

Lázár u

Révay u

Andrássy út

Kaldy Gyula u

Paulay Ede u

Bajcsy-Zsilinszky út

Basilica of St Stephen

Szent István tér

Bajcsy-Zsilinszky út

Bajcsy-Zsilinszky tér

Podmaniczky Frigyes tér

Arany János utca

Bank u

Hercegprímás u

Vadász u

Nagysándor J u

Hold u

Perczel M u

Aulich u

Szabadság tér

Arany János u

Sas u

József Attila u

Erzsébet tér

Hild tér

Október 6 u

Zrínyi u

Nádor u

József nádor tér

Vécsey u

Zoltán u

Nádor u

Garibaldi u

Steindl Imre u

Széchenyi u

Akadémia u

Arany János u

Vigyázó Ferenc u

Mérleg u

Széchenyi István tér

Kossuth Lajos tér

Széchenyi rkp

Pesti alsó rkp

Széchenyi Chain Bridge (Széchenyi lánchíd)

Eötvös tér

Hegedű u

Paulay Ede u

Mozsár u

Ó u

Zichy Jenő u

Dessewffy u

Nagymező u

Hajós u

Zichy Jenő u

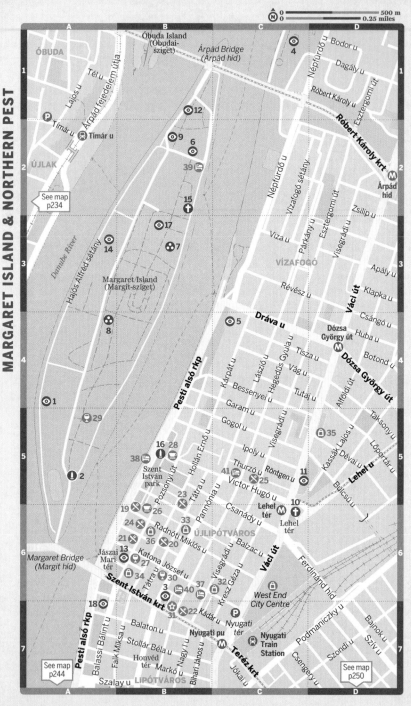

0 500 m
0 0.25 miles

ÓBUDA

Óbuda Island
(Óbudai-
sziget)

Árpád Bridge
(Árpád híd)

Róbert Károly u

Esztergomi út

Bodor u

Dagály u

Néptürdő u

Róbert Károly krt

ÚJLAK

Tél u

Lajos u

Árpád fejedelem útja

Tímár u

Tímár u

See map
p234

Danube River

Hajós Alfréd sétány

Margaret Island
(Margit-sziget)

VÍZAFOGÓ

Néptürdő u

Vízafogó sétány

Esztergomi út

Párkány u

Visegrádi u

Viza u

Zsilip u

Apály u

Révész u

Csángó u

Klapka u

Váci út

Dráva u

Dózsa
György út

Dózsa György út

Huba u

Botond u

Tisza u

Hegedüs Gyula u

Vág u

Tutaj u

Taksony u

Lőportár u

Lehel u

Kassák Lajos u

Dévai u

Alföldi út

Bulcsú u

Kárpát u

László u

Bessenyei u

Garam u

Gogol u

Ipoly u

Visegrádi u

Pesti alsó rkp

Holán Ernő u

Thurzó u

Röntgen u

Szent
István
park

Pozsonyi út

Tátra u

Victor Hugó u

Pannónia u

Csanády u

Lehel
tér

Lehel
tér

ÚJLIPÓTVÁROS

Radnóti Miklós u

Balzac u

Katona József u

Ferdinánd híd

Margaret Bridge
(Margit híd)

Jászai
Mari
tér

Tátra u

Szent István krt

Visegrádi u

Kresz Géza u

Váci út

West End
City Centre

Podmaniczky u

Bajnok u

Szív u

Szondi u

Csengery u

Balaton u

Nagy u

Kádár u

Nyugati
tér

Nyugati
Train
Station

Balassi Bálint u

Falk Miksa u

Stollár Béla u

Honvéd
tér

Markó u

Bihari János u

Jókai u

Nyugati pu

Teréz krt

See map
p244

Pesti alsó rkp

LIPÓTVÁROS

Szalay u

See map
p250

MARGARET ISLAND & NORTHERN PEST

ERZSÉBETVÁROS & THE JEWISH QUARTER

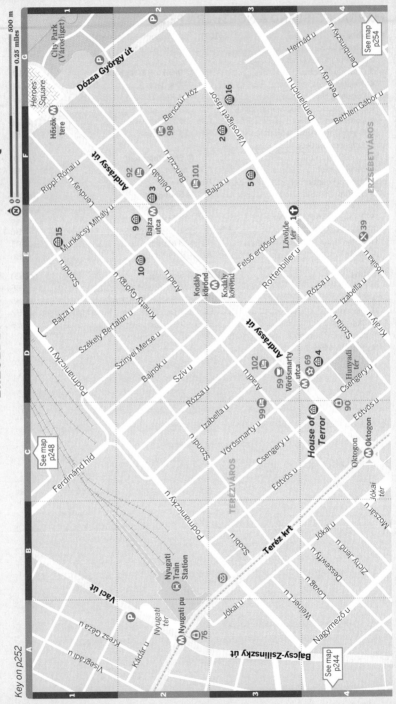

Key on p252

0 0.25 miles
0 500 m

See map p252
See map p248
See map p244
See map p254

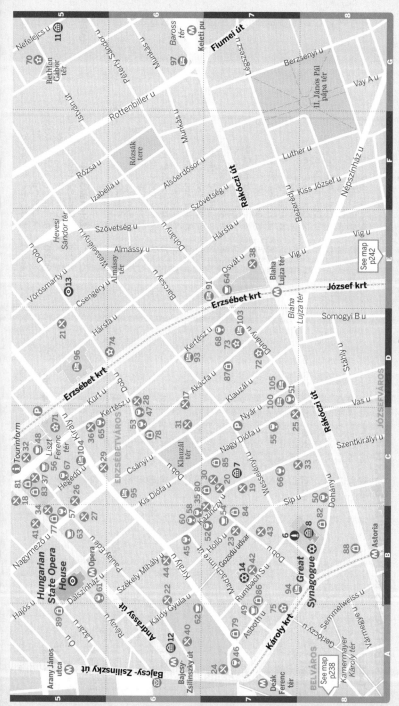

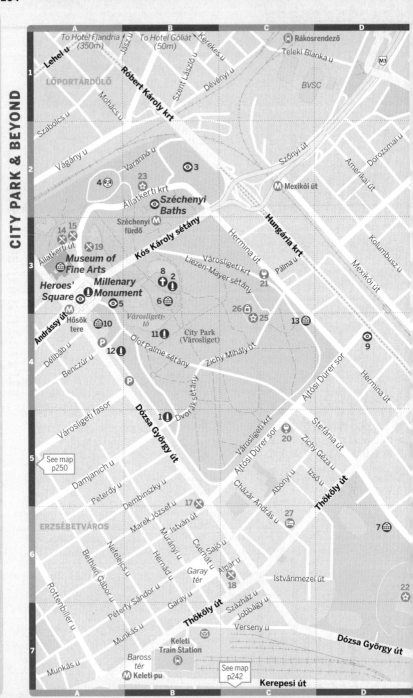

To Hotel Flandria (350m)

To Hotel Góliát (50m)

Lehel u

LŐPORTÁRDŰLŐ

Róbert Károly krt

Szabolcs u

Mohács u

Vágány u

Varannó u

Szent László u

Kerekes u

Dévényi u

Rákosrendező

Teleki Blanka u

BVSC

M3

Dorozsmai u

Szőnyi út

Amerikai út

Mexikói út

Kolumbusz u

Mexikói út

23

4

3

Állatkerti krt

Széchenyi Baths

Széchenyi fürdő

14 15

Állatkerti út

19

Museum of Fine Arts

Heroes' Square

Millenary Monument

5

Kós Károly sétány

Hermina út

Hungária krt

Városligeti krt

Liezen-Mayer sétány

Pálma u

21

8

2

6

Andrássy út

Hősök tere

10

12

Délibáb u

Benczúr u

Dvořák sétány

Városligeti fasor

Dózsa György út

Olor Palme sétány

11

City Park (Városliget)

Városliget-tó

26

25

13

9

Zichy Mihály út

Ajtósi Dürer sor

Hermina út

Stefánia út

Zichy Géza u

Izsó u

Thököly út

See map p250

Damjanich u

Peterdy u

Dembinszky u

ERZSÉBETVÁROS

Marek József u

Murányi u

Hernád u

István út

Csáki út

Sajó u

Abonyi u

Cházár András u

20

27

7

Bethlen Gábor u

Nefelejcs u

Garay tér

Alpár u

18

Istvánmezei út

22

Rottenbiller u

Péterfy Sándor u

Garay u

Thököly út

Százház u

Jobbágy u

Verseny u

Munkás u

Keleti Train Station

Baross tér

Keleti pu

See map p242

Dózsa György út

Kerepesi út

CITY PARK & BEYOND

Map labels:
0 500 m
0 0.25 miles

Ungvár u
Dorozsmai u
Lőcsei u
Fürész u
Czobor u
Ilosvai Selymes u
Gervay u
Nagy Lajos király útja
Erzsébet királyné út
Uzsoki u
Róna út
Gyarmat u
HERMINAMEZŐ
Korong u
Amerikai út
Laky Adolf u
Bácskai u
Gyarmat u
Thököly út
Torontál u
Amerikai út
Kolumbusz u
Zugló Train Station
Újvidék tér
Szugló u
Gizella út
Hungária krt
Semsey Andor u
Mexikói út
Emilia u
Egressy út
Ilka u
16
Egressy út
Szobránc u
Stefánia út
24
Stadion Bus Station
Puskás Ferenc Stadion
E F

Our Story

A beat-up old car, a few dollars in the pocket and a sense of adventure. In 1972 that's all Tony and Maureen Wheeler needed for the trip of a lifetime – across Europe and Asia overland to Australia. It took several months, and at the end – broke but inspired – they sat at their kitchen table writing and stapling together their first travel guide, *Across Asia on the Cheap*. Within a week they'd sold 1500 copies. Lonely Planet was born.

Today, Lonely Planet has offices in Melbourne, London and Oakland, with more than 600 staff and writers. We share Tony's belief that 'a great guidebook should do three things: inform, educate and amuse'.

Our Writer

Steve Fallon

Steve, who has written every edition of *Budapest*, first visited the Hungarian capital in the early 1980s by chance – he'd stopped off on his way to Poland (then under martial law) to buy bananas for his friends and their children. It was a brief visit but he immediately fell in love with thermal baths, Tokaj wine and *bableves* (bean soup). Not able to survive on the occasional fleeting fix, he moved to Budapest in 1992 so he could enjoy all three in abundance and *magyarul* (in Hungarian). Now based in London, Steve returns to Hungary regularly for all these things and more: *pálinka* (brandy), art nouveau, the haunting voice of Márta Sebestyén and the best nightlife in Central Europe.

Published by Lonely Planet Publications Pty Ltd
ABN 36 005 607 983
5th edition – February 2012
ISBN 978 1 74179 690 2
© Lonely Planet 2012   Photographs © as indicated 2012
10 9 8 7 6 5 4 3 2
Printed in China